The Treatise on Law

Notre Dame Studies
in Law and Contemporary Issues

Volume Four

Volume One
Nazis in Skokie:
Freedom, Community, and the First Amendment
Donald Alexander Downs

Volume Two
Public Virtue:
Law and the Social Character of Religion
Christopher F. Mooney, S.J.

Volume Three
Boundaries Dimly Perceived:
Law, Religion, Education, and the Common Good
Christopher F. Mooney, S.J.

The University of Notre Dame Press gratefully acknowledges
the generous support of The Honorable James J. Clynes, Jr.,
of Ithaca, New York, in the publication of titles in this series.

Saint Thomas Aquinas
The Treatise on Law

[BEING *SUMMA THEOLOGIAE,* I–II, QQ. 90 THROUGH 97]

Edited
with Introduction, Latin Text,
Translation, and Commentary
by

R. J. HENLE, S.J.

UNIVERSITY OF NOTRE DAME PRESS
NOTRE DAME   LONDON

Library of Congress Cataloging-in-Publication Data

Thomas Aquinas, Saint, 1225?–1274.
   [Summa theologica. Prima secundae. Quaestio 90-97. English &
Latin]
   Saint Thomas Aquinas, the Treatise on law : [being Summa
theologiae, I-II; QQ. 90 through 97] / edited with introduction,
latin text, translation, and commentary by R.J. Henle.
   p. cm. — (Notre Dame studies in law and contemporary issues
; v. 4)
   English and Latin.
   ISBN 0-268-01880-4
   1. Law—Philosophy. 2. Christianity and law. 3. Natural law.
I. Henle, R. J. (Robert John), 1909– . II. Title. III. Title:
Treatise on law. IV. Series.
K230.T54S8513   1993
340'.1—dc20   92-56861
                                                    CIP

∞The paper used in this publication meets the minimum requirements
of the American National Standard for Information Sciences—Permanence of Paper
for Printed Library Materials, ANSI Z39.48-1984.

CONTENTS

NOTES ON STYLE   *xii*
PREFACE   *xiii*
INTRODUCTION   *xv*

PART A:
BACKGROUND FOR ST. THOMAS'S
TREATISE ON LAW

CHAPTER I: INTRODUCTION TO ST. THOMAS

	Para	Page
Section 1: St. Thomas Aquinas		
a. His Life	001	*3*
b. St. Thomas's Work	005	*4*
c. His Writings	010	*5*
Section 2: St. Thomas and Jurisprudence	012	*5*
a. Teaching Materials in Jurisprudence	014	*6*
b. In Scholarship	016	*6*
c. In Court Decisions	017	*7*
Section 3: On Reading St. Thomas	024	*8*
Section 4: The Structure of the Summa Theologiae	039	*11*
a. The Style of the *Summa*	039	*11*
b. The Structure of the *Summa*	044	*12*
c. The Style of Reference	049	*13*
d. The Composition of the *Summa*	050	*13*
Section 5: Scholasticism	053	*14*
a. Introduction	053	*14*
1. Methodology	058	*15*
a. The Method of Distinguishing	059	*15*
2. The Use of *Auctoritates*	064	*16*
3. The Disputation Method	065	*16*
Section 6: St. Thomas's Approach to the Study of Law	067	*17*

CHAPTER II:
THE NATURE OF DEFINITION AND
THE ART OF DEFINING   074   20

Section 1: Introduction   074   20

Section 2: The Nature of Definition   082   21

Section 3: Types of Definition   085   22
     a. The Logical Mode of Defining   086   22
     b. The Descriptive Mode of Defining   095   23
     c. The Explanatory Mode of Defining   097   24
     d. The Constructural Mode of Defining   098   24
     e. Definition by Instances   101   25
     f. Partial Definitions   103   25

Section 4: The Ambiguity of Words   108   26
     a. Equivocal, Univocal and Analogous Terms   109   27
         i. Equivocal Terms   109   27
         ii. Univocal Terms   117   28
         iii. Analogous Terms   122   28

Section 5: The Central Case   139   31

*Section 6: A Further Note on the Ambiguity
     of Words*   147   33

*Section 7: On Analyzing and Evaluating a
     Definition of "Law"*   152   34
     a. Introduction   152   34
     b. What Is the Author Defining?   154   34
     c. What Methodology Does the Author Use?   156   35
     d. What Are the Substantive Positions and
         Principles of the Author?   163   36

CHAPTER III:
GENERAL DOCTRINAL BACKGROUND
FOR THE *TREATISE*   170   38

Section 1: Introduction   170   38
     Preliminary Clarification of Key Terms   172   38

i. Positive Law	172	*38*
ii. Positivism	173	*39*
iii. Natural Law	174	*39*
iv. Positive Morality	176	*39*
v. Moral Relativism	177	*40*

Section 2: The Doctrine of the Four Causes 178 *40*
a. Introduction 178 *40*
b. The Four Causes 183 *41*
   1. The Material Cause 184 *41*
   2. The Efficient Cause 191 *42*
   3. The Final Cause 194 *42*
   4. The Formal Cause 199 *43*

Section 3: St. Thomas's World View 213 *45*
a. Introduction 213 *45*
b. The Theological Outline 215 *46*
c. The Metaphysical Outline 221 *47*

Section 4: "Nature" and "Essence" 232 *48*

Section 5: Human Nature 266 *54*
a. Introduction 266 *54*
b. Thomism vs. Materialism 267 *54*
c. Intelligence, Will, and Free Choice 269 *55*
d. The Soul 271 *55*
e. Thomistic Doctrine and Religion 276 *56*
f. Man's Orientation to the Good 277 *56*

Section 6: The Nature of Human Acts 278 *57*

Section 7: "Rule and Measure" 284 *59*

Section 8: Habit 291 *60*
a. Introduction 291 *60*
b. An Important Meaning of "Habit" in
   Thomistic Philosophy 292 *60*

*Section 9: The Speculative Intellect, the Practical
      Intellect, and Right Reason* 298 *62*
a. Introduction 298 *62*
b. The Speculative Intellect 301 *62*
c. The Practical Intellect 304 *63*

d. Right Reason   310   *64*

Section 10: Voluntarism vs. Practical
          Reasonableness   313   *65*

Section 11: The Virtues   322   *66*
  a. Introduction   322   *66*
  b. The Virtues in General   325   *67*
  c. The Theological Virtues   329   *67*
  d. The Intellectual Virtues   332   *68*
  e. The Moral Virtues   336   *69*
      1. Temperance   339   *69*
      2. Fortitude   344   *70*
      3. Justice   349   *70*
          i. Introduction   349   *70*
          ii. Justice in General   350   *70*
          iii. Commutative Justice   356   *72*
          iv. Distributive Justice   358   *72*
          v. Contributive Justice   359   *72*
          vi. Social Justice   360   *73*
          vii. Right Relationship   361   *73*
      4. Prudence   362   *73*
  f. Final Note on the Virtues   375   *75*

Section 12: Happiness: The Last End of Man   379   *76*

Section 13: The Common Good   393   *79*

Section 14: Obligation   405   *81*
  a. The Questions about Obligation   406   *82*
  b. The Thomistic View of Obligation   408   *82*
  c. Moral Obligation and Positive (Human) Law   413   *83*

Section 15: A Synopsis of St. Thomas's
          Doctrine of Natural Law   421   *85*
  a. Introduction   421   *85*
      i. Prenote   421   *85*
  b. The Principles and Precepts of the Natural
     Law (The Formal Cause)   432   *86*
  c. The Common Good of the Natural Law
     (The Final Cause)   440   *87*
  d. The Material Cause of Natural Law   444   *88*

e. The Efficient Cause of Natural Law   446   *89*
f. Promulgation of the Natural Law   448   *89*
g. The Exemplar Cause of Natural Law   458   *91*
h. Natural Law and Positive Law   464   *92*
i. Natural Law and Natural Rights   469   *93*

CHAPTER IV:
ST. THOMAS'S SOURCES AND
HIS USE OF THEM   474   *94*

Section 1: The Use of Auctoritates   474   *94*
a. Introduction   474   *94*
b. The Function of *Auctoritates* in
   Argumentation   484   *96*
c. A Non-Evidential Use of *Auctoritates*   492   *97*
d. St. Thomas's Technique in Dealing with
   Auctoritates Presented in the Objections   499   *99*
e. The Use of *Auctoritates* in the On the
   Contrary   505   *101*
f. A Concluding Comment   516   *102*

Section 2: The Auctores *Quoted in the* Treatise 518   *103*
A. The Major Sources   524   *103*
   A1: The Bible   524   *103*
   A2: Aristotle   532   *106*
   A3: St. Augustine, Bishop of Hippo   537   *107*
   A4: St. Isidore of Seville   540   *107*
B. The Secondary Sources   541   *108*
   B1: St. Basil the Great   541   *108*
   B2: Anicius Manlius Severinus Boethius   543   *108*
   B3: Julius Caesar   545   *108*
   B4: Marcus Tullius Cicero   547   *109*
   B5: Damascene   549   *109*
   B6: The Decretals   550   *109*
   B7: The Glosses   551   *109*
   B8: Gratian   553   *110*
   B9: St. Hilary of Poitiers   555   *110*
   B10: The "Jurist"   556   *110*

B11: Peter Lombard   563   *111*
B12: Pope Urban II   564   *112*

PART B:
ST. THOMAS AQUINAS: THE TREATISE ON LAW
[BEING SUMMA THEOLOGIAE, I-II, QQ. 90
THROUGH 97]
With Latin Text, English Translation,
Introduction, and Commentary

Introduction   *115*
De Lege   *117*
          QUESTION 90: DE ESSENTIA LEGIS   *118*
Article 1   *118*
Article 2   *127*
Article 3   *135*
Article 4   *140*

          QUESTION 91: DE LEGUM DIVERSITATE   *148*
Article 1   *150*
Article 2   *155*
Article 3   *160*
Article 4   *166*
Article 5   *172*
Article 6   *178*

          QUESTION 92: DE EFFECTIBUS LEGIS   *185*
Article 1   *185*
Article 2   *192*

          QUESTION 93: DE LEGE AETERNA   *199*
Article 1   *199*
Article 2   *206*
Article 3   *210*
Article 4   *215*
Article 5   *222*
Article 6   *227*

QUESTION 94: DE LEGE NATURALI   *235*
Article 1   *235*
Article 2   *241*
Article 3   *251*
Article 4   *256*
Article 5   *264*
Article 6   *270*

QUESTION 95: DE LEGE HUMANA SECUNDUM SE   *276*
Article 1   *276*
Article 2   *283*
Article 3   *289*
Article 4   *296*

QUESTION 96: DE POTESTATE LEGIS HUMANAE   *305*
Article 1   *305*
Article 2   *311*
Article 3   *316*
Article 4   *321*
Article 5   *329*
Article 6   *336*

QUESTION 97: DE MUTATIONE LEGUM   *342*
Article 1   *343*
Article 2   *348*
Article 3   *353*
Article 4   *360*

ABOUT THE TRANSLATOR   *367*

NOTES ON STYLE

1. Every paragraph is numbered throughout Part A of the book so that every paragraph has its own number. Internal references will always be to the paragraph numbers, unless stated otherwise. The style of reference will be [149] or [150–165].

2. In Part B the text is divided according to St. Thomas's methodology. Therefore, internal references to the text of the *Treatise* will refer to these divisions, thus, *q.* 91, *a.* 2, *c.*

3. I have tried to avoid footnotes as much as possible. If anything is important, I put it in the text; if it's unimportant for my purpose I omit it.

4. When I refer to other authors I will give the author's name, the title and the page references in the text.

5. For brevity's sake, I refer to the *Summa Theologiae* simply by its subdivisions, thus, I-II *q.* 90 or I-II, *q.* 96, *a.* 2, etc.

6. Whenever I use a Latin expression, I will translate in brackets, thus, *Logica Vetus* [The *Old Logic*]. But, for convenience and clarity, some Latin terms will be used (after first introduction) as part of the regular terminology of the book.

PREFACE

When, some years ago, I began to study and teach jurisprudence, I was surprised to find how much attention modern jurisprudence paid to the legal philosophy of St. Thomas Aquinas. However, I became convinced that these jurisprudents, because of a lack of appropriate historical and doctrinal background, did not really understand St. Thomas.

This conviction was confirmed during many years of explaining St. Thomas to law students. I gradually devised ways of supplying their lack of background by a selective briefing of the most necessary points in that background.

More recently it occurred to me that my presentation of background and a corresponding commentary might be of help to all students and scholars in jurisprudence. This book is my effort to carry out that project. If I achieve my purpose, I will have produced a unique book. I know of no similar book in English philosophical or jurisprudential literature.

Although my main purpose has been to enable jurists to read St. Thomas more easily and with better understanding, it seems to me that a book like this would be a useful text for a course introducing Graduate Students in philosophy to the text of St. Thomas. For this reason I have included the Latin text and some other matters that might be of secondary interest to jurists.

A surgeon was once asked how long it took him to perform a certain operation. He replied, "All my life." In a similar sense I have been composing this book all my life. And so I am indebted to many wonderful teachers, brilliant scholars, stimulating colleagues, and students. I am grateful.

And there are some whose help has been so direct and so important that I must acknowledge them individually.

For financial assistance I most gratefully thank Greg and Jane McCarthy, their daughter Ann, and the Loyola Foundation, the Missouri Province of the Society of Jesus, the Jesuit Community at Saint Louis University, and Saint Louis University.

And to the staff of the University of Notre Dame Press, especially to its director, James Langford, and to editors E. Anne Rice and Jeannette Morgenroth, for their encouragement and cooperation my most appreciative thanks.

There are two cherished friends whose help exceeds all possible thanks. Patricia Lepore, my research assistant and secretary, patiently deciphered my kinesthetic handwriting, corrected my grammar and spelling, typed and retyped various versions, and gave me the benefit of her critical judgment and literary sensitivity. Father Linus Thro, S.J., went over the entire manuscript with the meticulous eye of a skilled editor and a philosophical scholar. Without the help and encouragement of these two friends this book would not exist.

Finally, to God, whose Eternal Law contains the exemplar even of this book and whose Providence has ever guided me, thanks and praise. *Sit Deus benedictus in aeternum.*

R. J. Henle, S.J.
Professor Emeritus of
Philosophy and Jurisprudence
St. Louis University
1991

INTRODUCTION

The primary purpose of this book is to provide the background and the explanations necessary for an intelligent and understanding reading of St. Thomas's *Treatise on Law*. It is primarily intended for law students, lawyers, judges and legal scholars. For this reason, I frequently relate points of doctrine in St. Thomas to modern jurisprudential discussions. However, the book would assist anyone interested in St. Thomas's legal philosophy to read him with understanding. It would thus be of some interest to political scientists, theoretical sociologists, cultural historians, etc. For philosophers, especially beginners in medieval philosophy, it could serve, at least in a supplementary way, as an introduction to the text of St. Thomas.

The book is *not* an introduction to the whole of St. Thomas's philosophy or theology. That is beyond the scope of this book. It would require not a book but a series of books. Besides, in order to understand the *Treatise* reasonably well, one does not have to know the entire thought of St. Thomas. Based on my own experience of teaching and studying jurisprudence, I have selected those points of doctrine, of methodology and of general background that I have found to be both useful and necessary to enable legally trained persons to read the *Treatise*.

The book is not intended simply to be read. It presents materials for study and thought. One who wants to profit most from this book will find it necessary not only to study it carefully but also to move back and forth so as to have each section illumine the others.

The book is organized as follows. After this introduction, Part A, the first major section of the book, presents selected historical, doctrinal and methodological explanations that are necessary for the understanding of the *Treatise*.

In Part B, the Latin text of the *Treatise* is presented unit by unit, each being followed immediately by an English translation and, when appropriate, by a comment. The translation is my own. I have tried to maintain the technical accuracy of St. Thomas's formal style even at the expense of stylistic nicety in the English.

Again, my primary purpose is to help students and scholars to understand St. Thomas aright. Then, if they agree with St. Thomas, they will be agreeing with his genuine thought and, if they disagree, they will not be making criticisms that are pointless.

I have tried to maintain a level of sound scholarship while keeping the baggage of scholarship at a minimum. There are few footnotes. If anything is relevant, I have inserted it in the text itself.

There is no index. Instead, I offer a detailed table of contents which will, to some extent at least, serve the same purpose of an index without the annoyance of multiple minute references.

Background for
St. Thomas's *Treatise on Law*

CHAPTER I
INTRODUCTION TO ST. THOMAS

SECTION 1:
ST. THOMAS AQUINAS

A. HIS LIFE

[001]   St. Thomas (1224–1274) was born in the castle of Roccasecca in the Kingdom of Sicily. His family was of the nobility and active in the political and military struggles of the age. One of his brothers became a soldier and was executed for plotting to kill Frederick II.

[002]   St. Thomas's parents had plans for the future of the family, and Thomas was very much in those plans. After his fifth year, his parents presented him to the Abbey of Monte Casino as an oblate, to receive an elementary education and be trained in piety and the Benedictine way of life. They hoped that he would become Abbot of Monte Casino, a position of considerable power and influence. In those days a boy reached his majority at age 14, and thereafter was independent of his parents and could make his own decisions. At about that age Thomas withdrew from the Abbey and went to Naples to study in the Faculty of Arts at the University there. It was at Naples that he became acquainted with the Dominicans, officially called the Order of Friars Preachers. He admired their way of life, their poverty and simplicity, their zeal for study and for souls, and their avoidance of ecclesiastical honors. There, too, he entered the Dominicans. His Superiors decided to send him to Paris. As he was traveling along a road north of Rome, his mother, who found out where he was, had him abducted forcibly by his brother (perhaps brothers) and some soldiers. These latter brought him to Roccasecca where he was confined by his family for about a year or more. During this time they did everything possible to persuade him to leave the Dominicans. His mother, Theodora, did not object to a religious vocation. She opposed his entering the Dominicans, since, because of the nature of the Order, he would hardly ever reach a position of prestige and power which was part of her plans. But nothing broke his determination, so, after a year or so he either escaped or was

"let go." He rejoined the Friars and went on to Paris. There he probably stayed three years, studying, not this time at the University but at the Dominican house there.

[003]   The rest of his life was filled with constant intellectual and religious activity. In 1274, on his way to attend the Council of Lyons, he fell ill and, after a brief illness, died.

[004]   Thomas was canonized on July 18, 1323. On April 11, 1567, St. Thomas was proclaimed a Doctor of the Church by Pope Pius V. Both before and after this event St. Thomas received numerous commendations from Popes, Councils, Bishops, theologians, and scholars.

B. ST. THOMAS'S WORK

[005]   About 455 the Roman Empire in the West collapsed and the barbarians from the East surged across the Rhine. They destroyed the Roman order and reduced Western Europe to physical and intellectual shambles. In the centuries that followed, the Church, largely through the Bishops, some outstanding missionaries, and the universal spread of monasteries, slowly Christianized and civilized the new masters of the West. This movement, briefly in flower under Charlemagne, suffered a serious setback with the incursion of the marauding Norsemen who once again plundered, burned and destroyed. But by the eleventh century, Western Europe was well on the way to a recovery of ancient culture and a creation of a new civilization and culture.

[006]   By the thirteenth century, St. Thomas's century, Europe was in an intense ferment of spiritual, intellectual, political, and commercial activity. It was the birth time of the great universities, the age of the cathedrals and palaces, of renewed commerce, urban growth, and the Guilds. Ancient culture was being recovered by an intense translation activity, the Moslem culture was entering Christian European science and philosophy.

[007]   St. Thomas was an active participant in this surge of intellectual life. He was not a monk working quietly in a mountain top monastery. He studied and lectured at the foremost centers, the universities, the courts of kings and popes. He was aware of the currents of change and was in the forefront of intellectual developments and controversies. As we would say today, he was at the "cutting edge."

[008]   All the great Western traditions, Classical Greek and Roman, Jewish, Arabic, and early medieval, flowed into the revitalized West and became sources for St. Thomas. He could quote Maimonides (1135–1204) (the greatest of Jewish philosophers), criticize the Arabic scholar Averroes (1126–1198), mine the *Corpus Juris Civilis,* explain the Scriptures and comment on Aristotle, line by line.

[009]   All this gave St. Thomas's work a richness, a universality, and a classical cosmopolitanism that explains his enduring influence throughout subsequent ages.

C. HIS WRITINGS

[010]   St. Thomas died at age 49 or 50, yet his literary output is simply astonishing. James Weisheipl (*Friar Thomas d'Aquino,* pp. 355–405) took fifty pages just to list and identify his writings. This list contains 101 items.

[011]   The breadth of his intellectual and religious interests can be gathered by scanning the classification used by Weisheipl (but originated by Eschmann and also used in *The New Catholic Encyclopedia*). Thus,

Theological Syntheses
Academic Disputations
Expositions of Holy Scripture
Expositions on Aristotle
Other Expositions
Polemical Writings
Treatises on Special Subjects
Expert Opinions
Letters
Liturgical Pieces and Sermons
Works of Uncertain Authenticity

SECTION 2:
ST. THOMAS AND JURISPRUDENCE

[012]   When, some years ago, I began to work in jurisprudence, I was surprised to find how much attention was paid to St.

Thomas in modern jurisprudence. This is all the more surprising since St. Thomas was not a lawyer, a judge, or a jurist. His *Treatise on Law* was not addressed to lawyers or jurists but to beginning students of theology.

[013]   Thus, today, we find St. Thomas present in the textbooks prepared for the teaching of jurisprudence in American law schools, in the world of legal scholarship, and in judicial decisions.

A. TEACHING MATERIALS IN JURISPRUDENCE

[014]   These materials range over a spectrum from books which are simply selected readings like Jerome Hall's *Readings in Jurisprudence* to books which contain a large amount of didactic text written by the authors themselves. In books of readings which span the entire history of jurisprudence, almost always selections of St. Thomas are given. There are, indeed, some books of readings which explicitly ignore ancient and medieval writers and begin with Hobbes or Locke or some other more recent author. In such books we do not find texts from St. Thomas though sometimes he is discussed by the authors quoted. There is one interesting exception. M. P. Golding, in his *Nature of Law,* states in his preface that he has limited himself to recent or contemporary authors but with one exception. This exception is St. Thomas Aquinas. He explains that, while St. Thomas has many distinguished followers today, he finds that none of them explains Natural Law better than St. Thomas himself. For this reason he gives, along with contemporary authors, an abridged account of the *Treatise on Law* (I–II, qq. 90–97).

[015]   In the didactic type of textbook in jurisprudence, St. Thomas is almost always discussed and, to some extent, quoted.

B. IN SCHOLARSHIP

[016]   St. Thomas has also been accepted by legal scholars as a serious authority in jurisprudence. His views may be approved or rejected, but, in any case, they are discussed. Major works like John Finnis' *Natural Law and Natural Rights,* strongly Thomistic in substance, have appeared and have received wide attention. Some

learned journals like *The American Journal of Jurisprudence* (published by the Natural Law Institute at Notre Dame University) and *Vera Lex* (published at Pace University) regularly publish studies in St. Thomas.

C. IN COURT DECISIONS

[017]   It was almost a natural result of St. Thomas's reappearance in legal discussion that he should be cited by judges. Nonetheless, I was surprised to find him quoted as a modern *auctor* [474–483]. I illustrate judicial use with a modern case (*Louis v. Nelson*, 344 F. Supp. 973 (1982)). This case concerned a regulation of the U.S. Immigration and Naturalization Service. The judge declared the regulation void because it was not properly promulgated. He based his decision on St. Thomas's article on promulgation (I–II, *q.* 90, *a.* 4), from which he quoted the entire argument.

[018]   The study of St. Thomas's jurisprudence is not merely an archeological or historical enterprise.

[019]   St. Thomas's most direct contribution to jurisprudence and the one most frequently cited by modern jurisprudents is his *Treatise on Law* which is, in fact, a section of the *Summa Theologiae* (I–II, *qq.* 90–97). His treatment of justice (II–II, *qq.* 57–62) and injustice (II–II, *qq.* 63–79), though less well known, is very important as are his commentaries on the *Nicomachean Ethics* and the *Politics* of Aristotle. There is also the opusculum *De Regimine Principum* (*On the Rule of Princes*). Many of his general philosophical doctrines are relevant to the enterprise of jurisprudence (as I hope to show in this study).

[020]   Almost from the moment of its first publication, St. Thomas's *Treatise on Law* became a classic point of departure for discussions of law among the Scholastic philosophers of the Universities of Europe until well into the seventeenth century. Thus, Suarez began his monumental *De Legibus* (*Concerning Laws*) with a lengthy and careful examination of St. Thomas's definition of law.

[021]   However, in the eighteenth century St. Thomas disappears from Anglo-American jurisprudence. There is no reference to him in Sir William Blackstone's *Commentaries on the Common Law of England*.

[022]   I suspect that the explanation of this neglect of St. Thomas may include the following:

1. the increasing hostility of Protestant England to things Catholic;
2. the contempt for Medieval culture resulting from the Renaissance and the Reformation;
3. The fact that before the 1920s there was no English translation of the Summa Theologiae.

[023]   In the 1920s the English Dominicans translated the *Summa,* thus providing an English version of the *Treatise.* Almost at once St. Thomas reappeared in jurisprudence and rather quickly recovered his place in jurisprudential discussions.

SECTION 3:
ON READING ST. THOMAS

[024]   For a variety of reasons, which I will discuss here, St. Thomas's writings are difficult for modern readers.

[025]   1) St. Thomas was primarily a theologian. His magistral work, the *Summa Theologiae* is a summary of theology intended for beginning students in that discipline. Therefore, if one wishes to develop a Thomistic philosophy of Natural Law (or of anything else) he must extricate the philosophical principles from the theological doctrine with which they are intertwined. Such an undertaking is possible because St. Thomas's principal intellectual instrument was philosophy, a philosophy derived from but not identical with that of Aristotle. Moreover, he had a mature mastery of the philosophy with which he worked.

[026]   The *Treatise on Law* occurs within the *Summa Theologiae.* It is not addressed to jurists or lawyers but to students of theology. It has a theological purpose; it is part of St. Thomas's moral theology. In the course of presenting his moral doctrine, St. Thomas investigated all the intrinsic and extrinsic influences that play upon human decisions and guide human acts as such. Among the extrinsic

influences he found the various types of laws. Because of his controlling purposes he defined and discussed laws as rules and measures directing human conduct. He simply was not interested, at this point, in defining a legal system. He knew, of course, that legislators, administrators, and judges were necessary adjuncts of laws in the primary sense. Fortunately for the present purpose, the *Treatise* is more philosophical and empirical than some other parts of the *Summa*.

[027]   2) As indicated above, the *Treatise* was addressed to students of theology. These students would have had a thorough course in Aristotle as well as a comprehensive course in Sacred Scripture. St. Thomas could assume this background and make use of it by brief references. The students would have recognized the context and force of these references.

[028]   The modern reader, unless he has specialized in Medieval Philosophy and Theology and in Sacred Scripture, lacks this background. This creates a formidable obstacle. I hope in this work to supply the immediately relevant background that will enable the reader to understand the text of the *Treatise*.

[029]   3) Also, as indicated above, the *Treatise* is found well along in the *Summa*. The *Summa* is a highly architectonic work. St. Thomas continuously builds on what has gone before as the frequent references to the earlier parts of the *Summa* indicate. The proper way to study the *Summa* is to start at the very beginning and work one's way through, question by question. This is obviously not feasible for most modern readers. Consequently, here also I will try to supply the relevant data from the earlier parts of the *Summa*.

[030]   4) St. Thomas, along with other scholars of the period, accepted the physical science of his day. He sometimes uses illustrations or examples drawn from medieval science, much of which is now obsolete and quite unknown to the average modern reader. These illustrations from medieval science usually are no part of the argument and are intended merely as clarifications or illustrations. Thus, what St. Thomas intended as a clarification often is a baffling obfuscation to the modern reader.

[031]   An instance occurs at the end of the *Corpus* of the first article of Question 90, where St. Thomas wrote, "Now that which is the principle in any genus is the rule and measure of that genus, for instance, . . . the first movement in the genus of movements."

[032]   This refers to the Aristotelian cosmology according

to which the universe is structured as follows. At the center of the universe is the spherical earth. From the moon upwards the universe consists of a series of concentric spherical shells that are transparent and indestructible. The moon and each planet are set in one of these shells and for each one there is a number of shells which determine the apparent path and speed of the heavenly body. All these shells are moving, but they all depend on the outermost shell which is the first mover and causes all the movements of the others. Hence, the first mover is the "rule and measure" of all the other movements.

[033]   The principle illustrated here can be seen in a simpler example. Think of a locomotive pushing a number of boxcars. Each boxcar pushes the car in front of it, but all the movement of the boxcars is produced by the locomotive. In this series, the locomotive is the first mover and therefore is the "rule and measure" of the movements of the boxcars.

[034]   St. Thomas's students would have read all this in Aristotle's own account of his cosmology. The modern reader can ignore this example without injury to the argument.

[035]   5) In common with all other medieval writers, especially theological and religious writers, St. Thomas constantly quoted Scripture. The Latin Bible was so well-known to literate persons that it was a common store and source of wisdom, doctrine, and illustration. (To be literate in the thirteenth century was to be able to speak, read, and write Latin; standardized national languages were only in the process of development.) To the medieval reader the references to Scripture were intelligible and illustrative. The modern reader finds them sometimes irrelevant or puzzling. The important point, sometimes a difficult one, is to determine whether the scriptural quotations are part of the argument, or are only illustrative, confirmatory, or decorative. Most of the scriptural references in *qq.* 90–97 fall into these latter categories. Clarification of the biblical quotations in the *Treatise* will be given in the commentary.

[036]   6) St. Thomas wrote a highly technical medieval Latin. He is terse rather than expansive, precise rather than florid, and is a master of the brilliant lapidary expressions to which Latin lends itself. For these reasons, it is extremely difficult to translate St. Thomas into English.

[037]   Unfortunately, many of the existing translations are unsatisfactory and sometimes positively misleading. I have tried, in

the English text given later on, to present at least a basically correct translation.

[038]   7) St. Thomas, in accordance with the custom of his day, frequently uses quotations from authors generally recognized as experts in their own fields, such as Aristotle in philosophy, St. Augustine in theology, and Boethius in musical theory. The modern reader sometimes finds this practice confusing or misleading. I will discuss this practice at greater length later [Chap. IV].

SECTION 4:
THE STRUCTURE OF THE SUMMA THEOLOGIAE

A. THE STYLE OF THE *SUMMA*

[039]   The two principal means of teaching in the medieval universities were the *lectio* and the *disputatio*.

[040]   The *lectio* was conducted in the following fashion. The basis was an important book such as the *Nicomachean Ethics* of Aristotle or St. Paul's Epistle to the Romans. The Master started by indicating to the class the divisions in the text to be read. He then read the text paragraph by paragraph. At each paragraph he explained the meaning of the text and the intent of the author. Next, he commented on the paragraph, raising questions, pointing out difficulties, etc. In the comment the Master set forth his own views, his own creative interpretation.

[041]   The *disputatio* was an elaborate debate, conducted according to the rules of logic, in which the medieval students were well trained. The disputation was an intellectual fencing match which aroused in the students the partisanship and enthusiasm and general excitement associated with football or basketball in modern universities.

[042]   The disputations were of various types. Sometimes a student defended, at other times a Master conducted them. We have many transcriptions of disputations presented by St. Thomas himself.

[043]   The articles in the *Summa* are stylized imitations of the *disputatio*. A question is raised, e.g., "Is law something related

to reason?" The problem is opened up by presenting arguments or *auctoritates* [474–483] against the position to be taken by St. Thomas. This is followed by some general statement in favor of his opinion (the *Sed Contra*). Next St. Thomas gives his own opinion (in the *Corpus* or "body" of the article). Then St. Thomas replies to the objections one by one. This highly formalized way of scholarly writing seems strange to modern readers. Yet, there is some similarity in the scholarly writing of our own time. Presentations often begin with a review of the literature on the subject and of the opinions of experts in the field (= the objections). The author then presents his own view (the *Corpus*) and finally discusses difficulties and objections (= reply to objection).

B. THE STRUCTURE OF THE *SUMMA*

[044]   The *Summa* has three Parts (*Partes*) and a Supplement. Thus:

1. The First Part (*Prima Pars*)
2. The Second Part (*Secunda Pars*) subdivided into two parts:
   The First Part of the Second Part (*Prima Secundae*),
   the Second Part of the Second Part (*Secunda Secundae*)
3. The Third Part (*Tertia Pars*)
4. Supplement (*Supplementum*).

[045]   Each Part is subdivided into Questions (*Questiones*) which in turn are subdivided into Articles (*Articuli*).

[046]   The Article is the basic unit of presentation. It has parts but it is not subdivided. The parts are integrated into a logical unit. In fact, each Article is a miniature *disputatio*.

[047]   As given in 2 above, the structure of the Article is as follows:

1. The Question
   e.g., "Whether Law Is Something Pertaining to Reason?" (*q.* 90, *a.* 1).
2. Objections
   Arguments against the position to be taken in the *Corpus*.
3. On the Contrary (*Sed Contra*) [In this text I am translating

Sed Contra as "On the Contrary."]
A general statement or argument favoring the position to
be taken in the *Corpus*.
4. The Body (*Corpus*)
Presentation of St. Thomas's position.
5. Replies to the Objections [In this text I am using "Reply"
instead of the standard "ad."]
Given in 2 above.
6. Occasionally a comment on the *Sed Contra* (the On the
Contrary).

[048]   Modern readers often find it easier to begin by reading the *Corpus* and then reading each objection with its reply.

C. THE STYLE OF REFERENCE

[049]

1. To refer to a Question:
S.T., I-II, *q.* 90
2. To refer to an Article:
S.T., I-II, *q.* 90, *a.* 1
3. To refer to an objection:
S.T., I-II, *q.* 90, *a.* 1, *obj.* 2
4. To refer to a *sed contra:*
S.T., I-II, *q.* 90, *a.* 1, *sed contra*
5. To refer to the *Corpus:*
S.T., I-II, *q.* 90, *a.* 1, *c.*
6. To refer to a Reply:
S.T., I-II, *q.* 90, *a.* 1, *ad* 1.

D. THE COMPOSITION OF THE *SUMMA*

[050]   The *Summa Theologiae* (also called the *Summa
Theologica*) was St. Thomas's masterpiece. Like all great scholars
and thinkers, St. Thomas continued to learn and develop intellectually
all his life. Thus, since the *Summa* is the last work St. Thomas wrote,
it presents his mature thought. In fact, he died without completing

it. His disciples tried to complete his work by adding a *Supplement* to the *Third Part,* which was largely pieced together by selecting sections from his earlier works. However, the Treatise on Law is the work of St. Thomas himself.

[051]   The *Summa* is a didactic work, intended, as St. Thomas himself said, for beginners in theology. It is tightly organized and integrated. It is progressive, each section building on and using what goes before it, as St. Thomas often indicates by saying "as was stated above" ("ut supra dictum est"). In this, it somewhat resembles Euclid's Geometry.

[052]   Ideally, therefore, one should begin with the first Articles of the *Prima Pars* and read up to the *Treatise on Law.* In lieu of this, I am offering these notes.

SECTION 5:
SCHOLASTICISM

A. INTRODUCTION

[053]   St. Thomas was a Scholastic theologian and philosopher. In fact, he is often called the "Prince of the Scholastics." Therefore, some introduction to Scholasticism may help one understand St. Thomas's methodology.

[054]   Scholasticism is the name given to the sort of philosophy the European university scholars practiced from the twelfth to the seventeenth centuries. It was thus distinguished from the philosophies that arose outside the universities. A Scholastic was thus a School-man, a university professor of philosophy or theology.

[055]   Although there was a wide diversity of opinions among the Scholastics and much controversy, the Scholastics developed a fairly uniform methodology and a common set of questions and points of inquiry. These common features enable us to place Scholasticism, not only in an historical line of development, but in a common intellectual tradition.

[056]   This common methodology embodied a mastery, in theory and practice, of Aristotelian logic. In addition, however, the

Scholastics introduced original methods of their own, such as the use of *auctoritates* [Chap. IV].

[057]   When the medieval intellectual renaissance began in the eleventh and twelfth centuries, western scholars had very little access to Aristotelian texts. They had the *Categories,* the *De Interpretatione* (On Interpretation) and relevant commentaries by Porphyry and Boethius. From the study of these works they developed what was later called the *Logica Vetus* (the *Old Logic*). From this logic the controversy over the status of universals arose, a controversy in which Abelard (1079–1142) was a principal contender. He defended a position called "Moderate Realism" which was essentially the position taken by St. Thomas in the next century. Abelard's method of teaching and his great dialectical skill helped to develop the disputatious character of both medieval university education and of medieval scholarly writings, a style illustrated by the *Treatise.* Abelard's work, *Sic et Non* (*Yes and No*), contributed to his influence. It was a compilation of apparently contradictory statements from earlier theologians which challenged the skill of the Scholastics and contributed to the development of the method of drawing distinctions.

B. METHODOLOGY

[058]   The following methods are characteristic of the Scholastics and were used by St. Thomas.

1. The Method of Distinguishing

[059]   Making careful distinctions was a standard part of Scholastic method. Modern critics sometimes ridicule this practice, calling it "splitting hairs." To this Chesterton's riposte was: "There is nothing wrong with splitting hairs. The problem is to split the right hairs." No doubt the method was abused by lesser men, but, in the hands of a genius like St. Thomas, it became a powerful instrument for solving difficulties and for clarifying thought.

[060]   Thus, St. Thomas often begins a discussion with some such formula as "X can be in Y in two ways" or "X can be said to be Y in two ways." He then carefully explains the two ways. In the process contradictions disappear, difficulties dissolve, and truths become evident.

[061]   There is a statement that goes back at least as far as Cicero, namely, that unjust laws are not laws. St. Thomas quotes it from Augustine. [*q. 96, a.* 4.] Positivists have criticized it as being an obvious contradiction. This statement talks of unjust laws, not some other unjust things, but laws. In the predicate it denies that these laws are laws.

[062]   St. Thomas deals with a slightly different form of the proposition, to wit, "Tyrannical laws are not laws." [*q.* 92, Reply 4.] Tyrannical laws are contrary to reason and so are not laws *properly speaking.* Yet they have the appearance of laws as being ordinances made by a superior to his subjects with the aim of being obeyed. The subject of the statement is talking about laws *secundum quid,* that is, in only a partial sense; the predicate is talking about *laws simpliciter,* that is, in the full sense. The contradiction disappears.

[063]   Another example is found in *q. 95, a.* 2. St. Thomas there maintains that every human law is derived from the Natural Law. But an objection is raised: If this is so, since the Natural Law is the same for all human beings, human laws would be the same in all countries. This is obviously false. St. Thomas explains that laws are derived from the Natural Law in two different ways. One by way of conclusion (as it were). Thus, from the general precept "Harm no person" the prohibition of murder can be deduced. The second way is by way of determination. Thus, reckless driving is against the Natural Law since it endangers life and limb. But what sort of traffic regulations should be made and what punishments should be imposed must be "determined" by the human lawgiver. Laws derived by way of determination can therefore be diverse in different jurisdictions. The objection loses its force.

2. *The Use of Auctoritates*

[064]   This is treated elsewhere [Chap. IV].

3. *The Disputation Method*

[065]   A question is asked; a point of inquiry is raised. The author presents arguments against his own position and

balances them by favorable arguments or opinions. By examining the main arguments advanced on either side, both in themselves and in the light of other relevant knowledge, the author then works out his own answer or solution. Finally, he carefully replies to each opposing argument.

[066]   This method is illustrated in the *Treatise*. In the *Summa Theologiae* there are usually only three or four objections and one *sed contra*. This is probably because St. Thomas is writing for beginners. In more elaborate works there are often many more objections and *sed contras* than in the *Summa Theologiae*.

SECTION 6:
ST. THOMAS'S APPROACH TO THE STUDY OF LAW

[067]   The subject matter of modern Anglo-American jurisprudence is generally taken to be positive law and positive legal systems. It is not a study restricted to Anglo-American law but rather to law in its generality, both with respect to the various nations of the world and also to underdeveloped and developed countries. The aim of this jurisprudence is to describe, explain, and therefore understand law and legal systems as accurately and profoundly as possible.

[068]   St. Thomas was neither working nor writing as a jurist, a lawyer, a judge or even merely as a philosopher. He was working and writing as a theologian, indirectly as a philosopher. His *Treatise* appears in the *Summa Theologiae* in the section where he is developing his moral theology. The precise context of his treatment of law is the section in which he deals with all the external factors which influence or bear upon human acts or human decision making. One of these external influences is, obviously, law. Hence, St. Thomas is not interested in elaborating a description or a theory of a legal system. He, of course, knows that there have to be legislators, enforcers, judges, prisons, and so forth. On appropriate occasions he will discuss the

various parts of a legal system, but his major interest at this point does not lie there.

[069]   For the same reason, his study of law is not limited to human positive law but embraces a variety of *kinds* of law. Thus, in Question 91 he identifies six kinds of la w: Article 1, The Eternal Law; Article 2, Natural Law; Article 3, Human Positive Law; Articles 4 and 5, Divine Law; Article 6, The Law of Sin (*fomes peccati*).

[070]   Although the basic definition given briefly in *q*. 90, *a*. 4 at the end of the *Corpus* was constructed mainly from a consideration of Human Positive Law, it nonetheless applies properly although analogously to all of these laws except the Law of Sin. It is properly applied because these various laws do fulfill the essential elements of the definition. It is analogous because they fulfill these elements in quite different ways. With regard to the Law of Sin which is concupiscence insofar as it leads to sin, the definition does not apply properly. To call the law of the members, to which St. Paul refers, a law is an improper application of the term. In *q*. 90, *a*. 1, *obj*. 1, St. Thomas raises the question of this Law of Sin. In his Reply he states that law is predicated *per participationem*, by way of participation. Participation in St. Thomas's language means that some characteristic exists somewhere essentially and per se while in other places it exists by a similitude and in a deficient degree or manner. So, although the Law of Sin is improperly called law, there is a similarity between the law of the members and law properly so called.

[071]   A simple reading of St. Thomas's list of the various kinds of law makes it clear that in his investigation of law he must not only use philosophy of law and juristic thinking but must also draw from Revelation (the Bible), theology, metaphysics, ethics and most of the branches of philosophy. Thus he produced a synthesis that transcends the scope of any single one of these various disciplines.

[072]   Despite the synthetic unity of St. Thomas's presentation, the basic arguments and positions within the synthesis which can be properly designated as jurisprudential are not logically dependent on Revelation (the Bible), theology, or even

some general a priori principles of philosophy. The jurisprudential arguments, positions, principles developed in the *Treatise*
are not derived a priori from Revelation, theology, and philosophy; they can all stand on their own evidence rationally and
experientially arrived at. However, the tight unity of St. Thomas's synthesis makes it difficult to compare his jurisprudence
point by point with modern systems of jurisprudence. There is
also another complicating factor. St. Thomas rarely directly con-
fronts any of the main positions of modern Positivists. The
reason for this is quite simple: In the thirteenth century there
were no Positivists like John Austin, Bentham, Kelsen or H. L.
A. Hart. Again, the fact that St. Thomas constantly quotes from
the Bible often masks the fact that the determining argument
or evidence is derived from a philosophy that is based on reason
and experience. The fact is that in many cases the quotation
from Scripture simply illustrates, confirms, explains or embellishes the Thomistic text. In many cases the quotation from
Scripture could be omitted from the text without interfering in
the line of argumentation at all. (In a late section of this book
[Chap. IV] I will discuss the use of these quotations which in
medieval terminology were called *auctoritates*).

[073]   In view of all this, anyone who wishes to do a
serious study of the *Treatise* should do two things. First, he
should study the entire *Treatise* and the entire Thomistic synthesis, including the theological and other such aspects. Secondly, he should try to extricate from that synthesis those
positions and arguments which can be directly focused on the
problems dealt with by modern jurisprudents. In some cases a
position or argument of St. Thomas must be expanded and
further developed in order to apply it to these modern problems.
I hope to assist the reader in doing this.

CHAPTER II
THE NATURE OF DEFINITION
AND THE ART OF DEFINING

SECTION 1:
INTRODUCTION

[074]   One of the basic questions in jurisprudence is the question of the definition of law. Almost every jurisprudent since St. Thomas has tried to work out an acceptable definition. H. L. A. Hart begins his *Concept of Law* (p. 6) with this statement: "We shall distinguish here three such principal recurrent issues, and show later why they come together in the form of a request for a definition of law or an answer to the question 'What is law?' or in more obscurely framed questions such as 'What is the nature (or the essence) of law?'"

[075]   In I-II, *q*. 90 St. Thomas works out a definition of a law (taken to be a statute or the equivalent). As far as I can discover, his definition was the first pregnant and concise definition of *a* law in jurisprudence or the philosophy of law.

[076]   Every serious definition of law encapsulates the particular jurisprudent's whole philosophy of law. Rolf Sartorius in "Hart's Conception of Law", pp. 132–135 gives four different meanings for the question "What is Law", that is, he elaborates four different but compatible definitions. Then he adds (p. 36): "We have, then delimited four forms of the question 'What is law?', and noted that a unified answer to these questions, such as Austin's, may be said to constitute a philosophical theory of law."

[077]   That is, an analysis of a jurist's definition of law will display the basic ideas of his philosophy of law.

[078]   Despite the recognized importance of defining law, a law, or a system of law, very few jurists have given attention to the epistemological nature of definition in general. Many of the problems that arise when different definitions of law are compared are due to the fact that different jurists use different types of definitions or are defining different aspects of law. It is one thing to define *a* law, as St. Thomas did, and quite another thing to give a comprehensive descriptive definition of a legal system as John Finnis did. It is one

thing to define an aspect of the practice of law as Oliver Wendell Holmes did and quite another thing to define the ongoing creation of law as Lon Fuller did.

[079]   Moreover, quite aside from the study of jurisprudence or the understanding of St. Thomas's definition of law, the nature and art of defining is a matter of importance for any practicing lawyer or sitting judge. Many cases turn on the definition of a term in a statute or a definition created by legislators or judges. Cases have turned on the definition of a tomato, an automobile, a pedestrian, etc.

[080]   However, our immediate purpose—the understanding of the *Treatise on Law,* of the nature of law—is of prime importance, since the entire *Treatise* is based on the definition of a law worked out in *q.* 90, *a.* 4, *c.*

[081]   For all these reasons, we begin our investigation by considering the nature and art of defining.

SECTION 2:
THE NATURE OF DEFINITION

[082]   In general a definition states what something is. What is a triangle? It is a three-sided plane figure. Or: "What is the essential intelligibility of a triangle?" The answer is the same, a definition. A definition is based on an analysis of the nature or essential intelligibility of the thing to be defined.

[083]   However, not every thing can be analyzed. Consequently, not everything can be defined. For example, everyone knows what it means to be conscious, but consciousness can only be understood from experience and cannot be analyzed into simpler or broader intelligibilities. Moreover, if everything had to be defined, there would be an infinite regress in defining.

[084]   Some people, who have not reflected on the matter, think that everything has one true or correct definition. This, of course, is not the case. First, as we shall see, there are different epistemological types of definition. Secondly, definitions may vary with the point of view (e.g., philosophical, scientific) or the purpose.

SECTION 3:
TYPES OF DEFINITION

[085]   We will now examine different types of definition.

A. THE LOGICAL MODE OF DEFINING

[086]   First, we will examine the traditional logical mode of defining *per genus et differentiam specificam* (through genus and specific difference) which goes back at least as far as Aristotle. An example will explain this mode.

[087]   Consider the traditional philosophical definition of a human being, to wit, that a human being is a rational animal. In this definition the genus is animal, the specific difference is rationality. Human beings share the genus with the other animals, but rationality specifies human nature as such and so distinguishes it from all other animals.

[088]   This definition fits into a classifying scheme as follows:

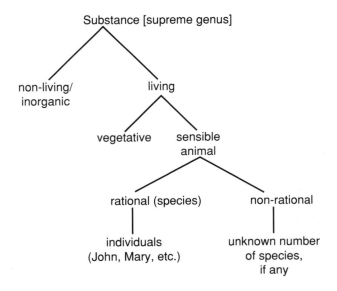

[089]   Note that below the species there are only individuals.

[090]   Now we can expand the definition of human nature thus: a human being is a substance, living, sensitive, and rational.

[091]   The definition *per genus et differentiam specificam* is thus also a system of classification.

[092]   The same method of definition can be used in geometry. For example, we can take "triangle" as a genus under which there are various species of triangles, i.e., isosceles, right-angle, equilateral, scalene, etc., all differentiated by a specific difference.

[093]   This method of definition presupposes that we know the essential nature of the thing to be defined. But, in fact, we know the truly essential nature of very few specific things. Therefore, in most cases, we must use some other type of definition.

[094]   John Austin made use of the logical type in defining law. He started with the genus "wish" which he divided into (1) an expression of a wish backed by threats and (2) types of expressed wishes not backed by threats, e.g, "Please pass the butter;" expression of wish backed by threats, he called a "command." He then divided "command" into two species namely (1) *general* commands and (2) *particular* commands, thus generating the following scheme:

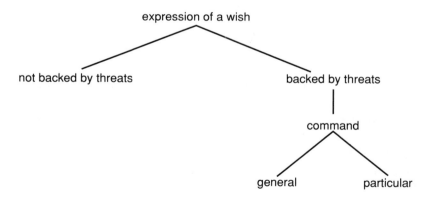

A law was a *command,* a general command backed by threats.

B. THE DESCRIPTIVE MODE OF DEFINING

[095]   In many cases, where the essence is unknown, a *descriptive* definition is used. This is the type of definition that traditional botany used. Botanists did not know whether there is an

essential difference between a rosebush, e.g., and a tree, but they could observe a variety of features that distinguishes them. Thus the tree has bark, a wooden core, and a large natural size, none of which a rosebush has. On the other hand, the botanist observed similarities, e.g., between a rosebush and a strawberry plant. On the basis of these accidental, selective features, the botanists set up a system of pseudo-genera and species and so were able to classify hundreds of plants.

[096]   H. L. A. Hart used this type of definition in framing his definition of a legal system. In this type of definition, the basic problem is selecting the features that are general and important. As John Finnis points out, this selection presupposes a method or principle of evaluation and selection.

C. THE EXPLANATORY MODE OF DEFINING

[097]   A third type of definition is called the *explanatory* definition. This is one that is based on the Aristotelian-Thomistic Doctrine of the Four Causes. This doctrine will be explained in detail later, since it is the type used by St.Thomas in Question 90.

D. THE CONSTRUCTURAL MODE OF DEFINING

[098]   The next type is what I call a *constructural* definition. I distinguish constructural concepts from ontological concepts. An ontological concept is one that simply transcribes the intelligibility of something into the order of knowledge. Thus the shape of a cube of sugar or ice or a box 8 in. on each side is understood without any addition or manipulation by the mind. On the other hand, a constructural concept is one that ultimately relates to reality but has been given an additional intelligibility by the mind. Thus the concept of *average speed* in mechanics rests on real distance and real time, but there is no reality that is *average* speed. That concept is the result of a simple mathematical manipulation of measures of distance and of time. Thus, if you cover 50 miles in 2 hours, $50/2 = 25$ mph = average speed. Or, in sociology, we might say that the average American family consists of 3.1 persons. There is no such actual

family. It is produced by statistical manipulation of measures of the sizes of real families.

[099]   Hence, when a constructural concept is used in a definition, the definition does not simply state the nature of a reality. It defines a concept based on reality but as modified by the mind.

[100]   This type is used frequently in physical science, psychology, sociology, etc. However, it seems to be inappropriate in jurisprudence, at least, in philosophical jurisprudence.

E. DEFINITION BY INSTANCES

[101]   When defining by the usual methods is very difficult, impractical or controversial, the understanding of a term or a nature is sometimes given by listing some more or less clear instances. In the Act establishing the National Endowment for the Humanities, the following definition is given.

> §952. Definitions
> As used in this chapter—
> (a) The term "humanities" includes, but is not limited to, the study of the following: language, both modern and classical; linguistics; literature; history; jurisprudence; philosophy; archeology; comparative religion; ethics; the history, criticism, theory, and practice of the arts; those aspects of the social sciences which have humanistic content and employ humanistic methods; and the study and application of the humanities to the human environment with particular attention to the relevance of the humanities to the current conditions of national life.

[102]   It is impossible to get any group of scholars to agree on an essential definition of "humanities." Hence, Congress used a rather lengthy list of instances. Such a definition, though necessary, gives rise to problems of judgment on borderline cases. For example, how is one to determine when sociology has humanistic content?

F. PARTIAL DEFINITIONS

[103]   All previous types are standard modes of defining. There are other answers to the "what" questions that can be considered partial definitions, framed in view of a special purpose, point of view, or situation. We can call some of these *identifying* definitions.

[104]   When, for example, a hiker asks, "What is poison ivy?", he doesn't want the scientific definition [a climbing plant of the sumac family that is especially common in the eastern and central U.S., that has ternate leaves, greenish flowers, and white berries, and that produces an acutely irritating oil causing a usually intensely itching skin rash (from *Webster's New Collegiate Dictionary*)]. The hiker simply wants to identify poison ivy so he can avoid it. If an instructor in a science class asked a student to define poison ivy, he would expect the scientific definition.

[105]   A cook wants a chocolate cake defined in terms of familiar ingredients, flour, chocolate, eggs, etc. He doesn't want or need a chemical definition of chocolate. To a cook, salt is a condiment; to a chemist it is NaCl.

[106]   Thus, there are many partial definitions, many definitions of the same thing because of different viewpoints, purposes, and methodologies.

[107]   Oliver Wendell Holmes' definition of law as "a prediction of what the courts will do" is framed from the standpoint of the "bad man" and defines a lawyer's advice to the bad man. Because of the limited point of view, the definition is inadequate. Lon Fuller's definition, "the enterprise of bringing human conduct under the governance of rules" may be regarded as a partial definition.

SECTION 4:
THE AMBIGUITY OF WORDS

[108]   Now we must consider a point of great importance in jurisprudence. Definitions have a twofold function. They express what something is and also give us the meaning of a word. The chemist says water is H_2O. Thus, H_2O is the scientific meaning of the term "water": It is also a scientific statement of what water in itself really is. This double function would cause no problem if each word had one meaning and corresponded to one definition. But this is not the case. Many words can have different meanings in different contexts. If, for example, without a context, I simply say "bat", you could not be certain of my meaning. I may be thinking of the little

flying animal. Such words are, by themselves, ambiguous. The ambiguity of words creates confusion and mistakes, unless one is very
careful in their use.

A. EQUIVOCAL, UNIVOCAL AND ANALOGOUS TERMS

i. Equivocal Terms

[109]   Terms are used equivocally when, in two or more
contexts, the term (remaining the same in spelling or phonetics or in
both) is used with totally different meanings (concepts or definitions).

[110]   Thus, in the statements:

> "The player threw his *bat* at the umpire"

and

> "I chased a *bat* out the window"

the term "bat" is used in two completely unrelated meanings. There
is nothing in common except the spelling and sound of the terms.

[111]   In the following statements:

> "I went *to* the supermarket"

and

> "I bought *two* dozen eggs"

and

> "The grapefruit were *too* expensive"

there is only an *oral* equivocation. As soon as we write the statements,
there are different terms as well as three different meanings.

[112]   These examples, and many others, are quite clear and
would deceive no one, but, in a long discussion or in complicated
matters, people are deceived by an insensible shift into equivocation.
A pro-life speaker once said that a basic question was, "When does
human life begin?" In answer, another speaker later said, "No one
knows when human life first began."

[113]   In the first case, the speaker was talking about the
beginning of the life of an individual human being. In the second
case, the speaker was talking about the first appearance of human
life on earth.

[114]   An example more relevant to jurisprudence is the
following:

"A Missouri *law* requires the payment of income tax"

and

"The *law* of gravitation applies to all pieces of matter."

[115]   The term "law" is equivocal. In the first case the law is prescriptive; in the second case it is descriptive.

[116]   Jurisprudence deals with law in the first sense, not with law in the second sense.

ii. Univocal Terms

[117]   A univocal term is one that is used, in two or more contexts, in exactly the same sense, that is, with the same meaning or definition.

[118]   When I say of this shape: [⎽⎽⎽⎽⎽] that it is *oblong* and, when I say of this shape: [⎽⎽⎽⎽⎽] that it is *oblong,* I am using the term in exactly the same sense. The differences in size and colorations are irrelevant.

[119]   In the statements:

"George Washington was a *human being*"

and

"Nancy Reagan is a *human being*",

the term "human being" has the same definition in each case, namely, "rational animal."

[120]   In the following statements:

"Boatmen's *Bank* has many outlets in St. Louis"

and

"The First National *Bank* is a solvent institution",

the term "bank" is used univocally. [Remember that in definition by genus and species, the genus and the species must be univocal with reference to the population to which each refers.]

[121]   Univocal terms are used in exactly the same sense; equivocal terms are used in radically different senses. Analogous terms may be said to fall on an extended spectrum between the extremes of equivocation and univocity.

iii. Analogous Terms

[122]   An analogous term is one, that in two or more contexts, is used in a sense that is partly the same and partly different

and *the partly-same and partly-different are inseparable in a given context.*

[123]   The standard example, which seems to have been first used by Aristotle and has been used ever since (it occurs in H. L. A. Hart, *The Concept of Law,* pp. 15–16), is that of the term "healthy."

[124]   Consider the following statements;

> "Mary is healthy."
> "Mary's complexion is healthy."
> "This food is healthy."
> "Moderate exercise is healthy."

[125]   The original and only proper meaning for "healthy" is "having the proper state of a living thing." This meaning is expressed in the first statement. Mary's complexion is called "healthy", not because it has the proper disposition of a living thing, but because it *manifests* health. Food is called "healthy" because it *produces* health. All the meanings in the last three statements are derived from a relationship to health properly so called and would have no meaning without that relationship.

[126]   Note that the derived meanings are complex: "manifesting-health", "producing-health", "promoting-health." The complexity cannot be separated without producing nonsense. We cannot say:

> "Mary's complexion is manifesting."

or

> "Mary's complexion has the proper state of a living thing."

[127]   Compare a complex term like "red house."

> "There is a red house there."
> "There is a house there."
> "There is a red thing there."

The division does not produce nonsense. Hence, "red house" is not an analogous term. For analogy, the part that is different and the part that is the same are inseparable.

[128]   There are many types of analogy. The type just examined (namely, "healthy") is called an analogy of "extrinsic attribution" because the derived meanings do not contain intrinsically real

"health" but have "health" attributed to them only because of a relation to health properly so called.

[129]   In analogies of extrinsic attribution, the proper case is called the primary analogate, the derivative cases are called the secondary analogates.

[130]   There are many different forms of analogy. All metaphors are based on simple analogies. Thus:

"Every man is a wolf to every other man."

(Hobbes)

[131]   The comparison here can be set up as a simple proportion:

Wolf		man
is to	as	is to
other animals		other men

that is, they are both predators.

[132]   This is an analogy of intrinsic proportion, intrinsic because both the wolf and the man are really (intrinsically) predators. Legal arguments from analogy are often based on this sort of analogy. When the Court extended the statute defining the liability of innkeepers to the operators of passenger boats on the Mississippi, the analogy was:

innkeepers		operators of
are to	as	*passenger boats*
guests		*are to*
		live-in passengers

[133]   An understanding of the three modal uses of terms will help one understand many controversies in Jurisprudence.

[134]   Both H. L. A. Hart and John Finnis criticize the earlier Positivists for attempting to develop a univocal definition of "law." They maintained that the effort to achieve a univocal definition ended in distorting the given data of legal systems. Kelsen, for example, in order to reduce all laws (Hart's primary rules, private empowering rules and public empowering rules) to a common form, proposed to rewrite all laws as directives, not to citizens, but to officials, ordering them that if x, then they should do y. This seems to most jurists to be a tortuous distortion of the actual features of laws.

[135]   Hart expressly rejects the use of the logical mode of

definition (*per genus et differentiam specificam*) because this mode requires *univocal* concepts.

[136]   Univocal definition is quite widely used in science and mathematics wherein so many things are fully determined and distinct. Thus, H_2O is a univocal definition of water; "three-sided plane figure" is a univocal definition of a geometrical triangle.

[137]   It is very difficult, often impossible, to formulate univocal definitions of human institutions, such as corporations, contracts, trusts, felonies and law. All chemists agree on the definition of water as H_2O. They do so because chemical analysis of water forces that definition on them. There are no schools of chemists which have different definitions of water.

[138]   Jurisprudents are generally well aware of the basic facts about law, yet they advance various definitions. This is the case because they are applying to those facts different principles, either from different disciplines (e.g., sociology, psychology, anthropology, etc.) or from different philosophies (e.g., Positivism, Kantianism, Thomism, Utilitarianism, etc.), or because of using a different mode of defining. Hence, a jurist's definition of law reveals his basic philosophy. Therefore, a critique of a jurisprudential position must proceed from the facts of laws and legal systems and from a critique of the underlying philosophical (or other) principles.

SECTION 5:
THE CENTRAL CASE

[139]   Some jurisprudents, faced with the diversity of legal systems, have attempted to reach a univocal definition by looking for the lowest common denominator. Thus we can ask, with Kelsen, what is common to the Constitution of the Swiss Republic and to the rule of a tyrannical African chieftain? The result may be a univocal definition but one that is so jejune and limited as to be of little explanatory value. Others have taken the approach of elaborating, what they call, "the Central Case." They examine the most highly developed legal systems and select the most relevant and important features and put them together in a Central Case definition of a legal

system. Such Central Case definitions can be fully verified in the systems of most modern nation-states, such as England, Germany, France, the United States and others. Primitive systems and only partially developed systems will verify only some of these features and, on that account, can be called a "legal system" in a deficient sense.

[140]   H. L. A. Hart, Lon Fuller, and John Finnis have all used this procedure in framing their definitions of a "legal system." This procedure not only produces a concept that can be applied analogously to a wide range of societies, but it also produces an ideal by which other systems can be evaluated.

[141]   Scholastic philosophers (following Aristotle) used a simple vocabulary which deals with this situation. Thus, if the Central Case is found to be fully verified, say in Canada, Canada is said to have a legal system *simpliciter* (i.e., without qualification), while those tribes, say the Watusi, who have a limited legal system are said to have a legal system *secundum quid* (i.e., in some respect).

[142]   Hart frequently illustrates one of the difficulties of definition by asking, "How many hairs must a man have in order to be haired, not bald?" or "How few hairs must a man have to be bald?" There is no possible answer to these questions. But we can clarify the matter by identifying the Central Cases. A man is *simpliciter* haired when he has a full head of hair with no bald spots. A man is *simpliciter* bald when he has no head hair at all, only smooth skin from ear to ear and from forehead to back of the skull. All mixed cases can be identified simply as *secundum quid* cases.

[143]   Let us apply this distinction to one of the celebrated arguments in jurisprudence. St. Augustine wrote, "An unjust law seems to be no law at all." St. Thomas repeats this doctrine as do many other Natural Law Thinkers. But the retort comes, "This statement is a plain self-contradiction. In the subject 'laws' are spoken of; in the predicate they are denied the name 'law.'"

[144]   What is the situation? Here is a statute, passed by a properly constituted legislative body, signed by a properly elected or appointed chief executive and promulgated in accordance with some Constitution, Grundnorm, or Basic Law. In all these respects it is like any other law.

[145]   On examination, however, it is found to be unjust and, therefore, to fail in a point, according to Natural Law jurists,

esssential to a law, hence it is not a law. Now, what shall we call it? An unjust *what?*

[146]   The law has many of the features of a law and resembles nothing else, yet fails to verify the full essence of a "law." It is, therefore, a law *secundum quid*. Since it fails in an essential point of jurisprudential legality, it is not a law *simpliciter*. The contradiction disappears. Note that there is a similar situation when a Court declares a law "invalid"; we speak of an "invalid law."

SECTION 6:
A FURTHER NOTE ON THE AMBIGUITY
OF WORDS

[147]   We can only determine whether an ambiguous word is being used equivocally, univocally or analogously when it is used at least twice in a given context. But it should be noted that ambiguous words in some contexts may be equivocal, in others univocal and, yet in others, analogous.

[148]   We have seen that in a given context "bat" is equivocal. Consider the following context:

> "*Bats* are flying mammals that live in caves and other dark places.
> *Bats* have a sonar system which enables them to fly free of obstacles."

In this context "bats" is a univocal term.

[149]   We have seen the univocal use of "bank." Consider:

> "Boatmen's *Bank* has many outlets in St. Louis."

and

> "I sat on the *bank* of the Mississippi and fished all afternoon."

Here "bank" is equivocal.

[150]   We have discussed the use of "healthy" as an analogous term. Consider:

"Mary is *healthy.*"
"My dog is *healthy.*"

In this context, "healthy" is a univocal term.

[151]   Thus, when words are ambiguous, the context should remove the ambiguity. This is especially important in the drafting of legislation and in writing judicial decisions.

SECTION 7:
ON ANALYZING AND EVALUATING A DEFINITION OF "LAW"

A. INTRODUCTION

[152]   Some guidelines may be suggested for analyzing and evaluating different definitions of "law."

[153]   Such guidelines will constitute a method for the critique of the various definitions as well as a basis for understanding them as their authors understood them. This method also will guide the comparison of the competing definitions.

B. WHAT IS THE AUTHOR DEFINING?

[154]   The first point is to determine what aspect of "law" the author intends to define or is actually defining. Most modern jurisprudents seek to define *a system of law,* the complete organization of law as found in modern civil societies. This is what H. L. A. Hart attempts to do in *The Concept of Law.* On the other hand, many older jurisprudents defined *a* law, a statute or its equivalent (e.g., a decree, an ordinance, a Court decision). St. Thomas formulated a definition of *a* law, of a statute, etc. as it occurs in all the varieties of laws which he recognized (e.g., divine, natural, ecclesiastical, etc.). Lon Fuller defines the making and administering of laws, the whole *enterprise* of bringing human conduct under rules (emphasis added). St. Thomas (*q. 90, a.* 1, Reply 2) gives an example of these two

approaches when he speaks of distinguishing the "building of a house" from the "house built."

[155]   Lon Fuller is defining the "building" of the law: St. Thomas is defining the "law built." When we make this distinction, we may come to see that the two definitions, though at first sight quite different, may be fundamentally in agreement or, at least, compatible. John Austin, like St. Thomas, was defining a law, but, despite this similarity, his definition is sharply opposed to that of St. Thomas.

C. WHAT METHODOLOGY DOES THE AUTHOR USE?

[156]   One of the factors that determines the mode of defining is the methodology used by the individual jurisprudents.

[157]   One of the features that distinguishes disciplines among themselves is the methodology appropriate to or created by the various disciplines. Thus, physics is particularly distinguished from history because physics has an overall mathematical method and aims at formulating mathematical equations and definitions which will express, explain, and control matter and motion or matter and energy; while history may use dates and borrow scientific methods of dating, it is not itself mathematical. Again, physics is partially distinguished from mathematics itself because physics uses an experimental hypothetical-deductive method for discovery, explanation, and verification, whereas geometry is not experimental at all. The geometer does not experiment with cubes and triangles.

[158]   Now the methodology of a discipline determines what it can deal with and what kind of answers it can get. A chemist can analyze the pigment and canvas of a painting, but he cannot determine whether it is trash or a great work of art. Art critics and art historians must do that. Physics cannot answer moral questions or say anything about the existence or non-existence of God.

[159]   Similarly, the methodology adopted by a jurisprudent will determine his mode of defining and what features can or cannot be included in his definition. If, for example, one uses a value-free, descriptive, sociological method as H. L. A. Hart does, one's definition cannot include a moral element or a moral reference. Moreover, such a method has the difficulty of selecting the relevant feature of a

law or a legal system. For a critical discussion of this type of methodology, see John Finnis, *Natural Law and Natural Rights,* pp. 3–22.

[160]   If one adopts a "pure" theory of law, as Hans Kelsen does, one excludes all methodologies of any external discipline, such as psychology, philosophy, science, political science, etc. One must use a logical analysis of a legal system in a purely legalistic manner. This results in the conclusion that the *content* of law is irrelevant.

[161]   St. Thomas uses the Aristotelian methodology of explanation known as the Doctrine of the Four Causes. (We shall study this method in detail later.) In this method, the jurisprudent has an outline of the questions, answers to which will constitute a complete essential definition of the definiendum.

[162]   So, when one studies any proposed definition of law, he should try to determine the methodology used.

D. WHAT ARE THE SUBSTANTIVE POSITIONS AND PRINCIPLES OF THE AUTHOR?

[163]   All jurisprudents are well acquainted with the obvious facts and operations of a system of laws. They have had approximately the same technical courses in law and have observed approximately the same legal and judicial activities. Yet, they differ widely in their second-level understanding of a law, the law, and/or a legal system. As already explained, part of the reason for this is the particular methodology chosen by each jurisprudent. But the broader principles held by each jurisprudent are also determinative of his jurisprudence.

[164]   If one thinks that, in a state of nature, every man is an enemy of every other man and that every man has the right and will to do whatever is necessary for survival and self-satisfaction, then the jurisprudent thinks of the role of law as the suppression by force of man's aggressiveness. This is what Hobbes did.

[165]   If one holds there is no connection between morality and law, he will be unable to hold that there is a moral obligation to obey laws. He will have to look elsewhere for an explanation of legal obligation. Thus, John Austin found it in the fear of punishment, of sanction. Sanction then becomes an essential element of all law. This was the position of John Austin.

[166]   If one believes that men are basically ordered to good and have a natural tendency to love and cooperate with other men, then he will see law as precisely directive to the Common Good. Sanctions will then not be of the essence of law but only a necessity consequent on the fact that some people, evil people, do not observe the law except under compulsion. This was the view of St. Thomas.

[167]   If one believes in participatory democracy, then one will hold that the people have a right to remove their rulers and change their government. This was the position of Robert Bellarmine.

[168]   If, however, one believes in the Divine Right of Kings, one will not recognize any limits to the King's power and will deny the people any right to rebel. This was the view of James I of England who consequently had the work of Robert Bellarmine burned and banned in England.

[169]   It is thus clear that some of the basic reasons for the difference in definition sometimes lie outside the field of jurisprudence proper. The argument must often be extended to matters involved in the broader debate.

CHAPTER III
GENERAL DOCTRINAL BACKGROUND
FOR THE *TREATISE*

SECTION 1:
INTRODUCTION

[170]   In this Chapter I will present and briefly explain the doctrinal background necessary to understand the *Treatise*. St. Thomas developed an impressive synthesis of philosophy and theology. No part of this synthesis is wholly self-explanatory. This is especially true of the parts of the *Summa Theologiae,* the architectonic structure of which has been admired by thinkers of almost all persuasions ever since. The *Treatise* is a part of the *Summa* and its integration into the whole is clearly indicated by St. Thomas's frequent references to previous parts of the *Summa.*

[171]   It is impossible, however, to give even a brief complete exposition of a synthesis and world view of which the *Summa* itself is only a summary. My method in this Chapter, therefore, is to select essential topics and arrange them in a somewhat pedagogical order. I am uncomfortably aware that, on the one hand, I will not do justice to the depth and beauty of Thomism and that, on the other hand, I will not satisfy the high standards of professional Thomists. However, I am writing mainly for those who neither are nor wish to be Thomistic scholars.

PRELIMINARY CLARIFICATION OF KEY TERMS

i. Positive Law

[172]   Positive law (variously called "human law," "man-made law," "civil law," "municipal law") is the law produced by human legal institutions. Thus the statutes of the state of Missouri or those passed by the "Queen in Parliament" are Positive laws. The term "positive" is here philosophically neutral and is used, in the sense here indicated, by all schools of jurisprudence.

ii. Positivism

[173]   "Positivism" names a jurisprudential or philosophical position. It rejects Natural Law and maintains that there is no necessary connection between Positive Law and morality. H. L. A. Hart summarizes the Positivistic position thus:

> The expression 'positivism' is used in contemporary Anglo-American literature to designate one or more of the following contentions: (1) that laws are commands of human beings; (2) that there is no necessary connexion between law and morals, or law as it is and law as it ought to be; (3) that the analysis or study of meanings of legal concepts is an important study to be distinguished from (though in no way hostile to) historical inquiries, sociological inquiries, and the critical appraisal of law in terms of morals, social aims, functions, &c; (4) that a legal system is a 'closed logical system' in which correct decisions can be deduced from predetermined legal rules by logical means alone; (5) that moral judgments cannot be established, as statements of fact can, by rational argument, evidence or proof ('non cognitivism in ethics'). Bentham and Austin held the views expressed in (1), (2), and (3) but not those in (4) and (5); Kelsen holds those expressed in (2), (3), and (5) but not those in (1) or (4). Contention (4) is often ascribed to 'analytical jurists' but apparently without good reason.

iii. Natural Law

[174]   Both Natural Law and the Law of Nature have two very different meanings. In science the laws of nature, like the law of gravitation, are generalizations or theories about the way physical nature operates. From the Positivistic viewpoint, such laws merely describe natural happenings; for others these laws reveal a necessity in nature.

[175]   But Natural Law, as used in philosophy, ethics, and jurisprudence, consists of a set of principles and precepts, worked out by human insight and reflection, based on the concrete nature and activities of human beings which ought to guide human conduct.

iv. Positive Morality

[176]   Positive morality is the de facto morality of any given society, i.e., the complex of rules and customs which the society accepts as being the obligatory way for human beings to act.

v. Moral Relativism

[177]   Moral relativism maintains that there are no moral absolutes, no moral principles that have universal value. The positive morality of any society is simply in function of *that* society and cannot be used to criticize the morality of any other society. Natural Law thinkers, on the other hand, maintain that there are some moral precepts that have universal force in all human societies. Thus Aristotle said that the principles of justice were the same in Athens and in Persia.

SECTION 2:
THE DOCTRINE OF THE FOUR CAUSES

A. INTRODUCTION

[178]   As stated above [097], St. Thomas uses an explanatory mode of defining based on the Doctrine of the Four Causes. It is, therefore, necessary to explain that Doctrine.

[179]   Aristotle gave the Doctrine its classical formulation, though, of course, he used ideas from previous thinkers. He presented it primarily as a method of explanation, but, precisely because it is a method of explanation, it can be used as a method of defining.

[180]   The result of an explanation is understanding. When can we say that we understand some entity or some event? When we exhaust all our questions about them, we say we understand. For example: Someone says, "I don't understand a word processor." Someone undertakes to explain it to him. Finally the expositor asks, "Do you understand or do you have some more questions?" The person so addressed may reply, "I don't quite understand this or that." The explanation resumes. Or, he may say, "I now *understand* it."

[181]   Thus understanding can be translated into the answering of questions. Now, Aristotle pointed out that all questions that could be asked at the universal level, that is, at the level of scientific and philosophical investigation, could be reduced to four basic categories of questions and that these categories were radically different and were mutually irreducible.

[182]   First, it must be noted that in this Doctrine the term "cause" is used in a wider sense than in modern English. When we speak today of a cause, we almost always mean an Efficient Cause. In the Doctrine "cause" means any factor that is necessary to bring about an effect through an intrinsic relationship to that effect. The causes can also be used to explain the continued existence of an entity.

B. THE FOUR CAUSES

[183]   To enable the reader to follow the exposition, we list the four basic categories and then explain each one of them in detail. The four categories are: 1. The Material Cause; 2. The Efficient Cause; 3. The Final Cause; and, 4. The Formal Cause.

1. The Material Cause

[184]   An old-fashioned watchmaker sits at his workbench. In front of him are boxes of wheels, screws, jewels, springs, etc. These various items do not constitute a watch. They are, however, necessary for the making of a watch. If his boxes were empty, the watchmaker could not make a watch. When he puts them together to make a watch, they remain in the result, that is, in the watch and are part of its reality.

[185]   These materials are the things out of which the watch is made. They are called the Material Cause of the watch.

[186]   Now let us consider another case. A sculptor has before him a block of marble. The block is not a statue but is essential for the production of a statue. The sculptor cannot produce a statue unless he has something to make it out of.

[187]   When the statue is made, marble remains in the effect, that is, it is an intrinsic and necessary part of the statue. The marble is called the Material Cause of the statue.

[188]   Out of these examples, by induction, we generalize the following definition.

[189]   The Material Cause is that out of which or in which the effect is produced.

[190]   Note that in this definition, "material" is not, as the examples might suggest, used in the sense in which we contrast

material beings or physical matter with spiritual entities or intellectual abstractions.

2. The Efficient Cause

[191]   Looking back at our examples, we can see that the watchmaker plus the materials in his boxes do not account for the final watch nor do they constitute a watch. Clearly, he must put the parts together. Thus he contributes to the result, i.e., the watch, by *doing something, by activity.* He is called the Efficient Cause (or the agent) because he effects the result by *acting* (from Latin *agere* [to act]).

[192]   Now, consider the sculptor. The same reflection makes clear that the sculptor must do something, if there is to be a statue. The sculptor is the agent, the Efficient Cause.

[193]   So again, by induction, we generalize the definition: The Efficient Cause is the cause that contributes to the effect by *activity.*

3. The Final Cause

[194]   If we now consider the agent, namely, the watchmaker or the sculptor, what explains their doing or making? Of course they must have the appropriate skills but that alone does not explain why they actually make watches or statues. They act for a purpose.

[195]   According to St. Thomas all acting or making is ordered to a purpose. Thus, the watchmaker may make watches in order to make money or as a hobby. It is the purpose that moves the agent to act. It contributes to the effect through the Efficient Cause *by being desired.* It is called the Final Cause. It is essential to the acting of the agent.

[196]   So we generalize the following definition: The Final Cause is the cause that contributes to the effect *by being desired.*

[197]   An analysis of human activity supports the dictum that all intelligent agents, when positing *human* acts as such, act for an end (purpose).

[198]   We might note here that human beings direct their human acts to a Final Cause or private goods of their personal choosing while law directs certain human acts (positive or negative) to the Final Cause of society, the Common Good [393–404].

4. *The Formal Cause*

[199]   Now, what is the difference between the watch and the materials in the boxes (the Material Cause of the watch)? The watch is not just a heap of metal bits. Is it not the structure or the organization of these parts that make the watch be a watch? This factor is called the Formal Cause of the watch. It "forms" the parts into a watch in a way analogous to the way the shape of a statue makes it to be a statue of St. Thomas rather than just a block of marble or a statue of St. Francis.

[200]   Hence the definition: The Formal Cause contributes intrinsically to the effect by being in it and *making it to be the kind of thing it is*. Note that both the Material Cause and the Formal Cause are in the effect and, in some sense, remain in it.

[201]   The examples used here are rather simple cases, deliberately chosen for that reason. But there are other widely analogous uses. One of these is in the formulation of St. Thomas's definition of law.

[202]   In order to complete the explanation of the Doctrine of the Four Causes—though it may not be relevant to our present purpose—I must indicate that there are several subdivisions in some of the categories of causes.

[203]   In the category of Final Cause, we can distinguish the Final Cause of the thing done and the Final Cause or purpose of the agent. For example, the intrinsic Final Cause of a watch (the thing done) is to tell time. If some instrument is made that looks like a watch, if it does not indicate time, it isn't a watch. The Final Cause of the *watchmaker's activity* may differ from the intrinsic Final Cause of the watch made. Thus he may make watches for money, for fun (i.e., as a hobby), to have gifts for his friends, and so forth. A statue may be simply a work intrinsically ordered to aesthetic enjoyment, while the sculptor's purpose might be quite different, e.g., to make money, to honor a saint, or to please his wife.

[204]   [This distinction between the finality of the thing made and the finality of the maker is extremely useful in areas other than jurisprudence. Thus, in any economic system the intrinsic Final Cause of a shoe factory is to make shoes, while the Final Cause of the activity of the workers and owners is to make money; in a slave economy the purpose of the workers is to get food and avoid a

whipping; in an idealistic Mao Tse-tung economy it is to serve the necessity of the society.]

[205]   In the category of Efficient Causality, we distinguish the primary Efficient Cause from instrumental Efficient Causes. Thus, in the making of a statue, the sculptor is the primary Efficient Cause while his instruments—hammer, chisel, etc.—are instrumental causes. The total Efficient Cause is the sculptor plus his tools. The primary cause imparts, as it were, effectiveness to the instrumental cause, whereas the instrumental cause increases the capability of the Primary Efficient Cause.

[206]   In the category of Formal Cause, we distinguish the internal Formal Cause from the extrinsic Formal Cause. Thus, in the building of a bridge, the intrinsic Formal Cause is the arrangement and integration of the steel, concrete, etc. The extrinsic Formal Cause is the plan of the bridge in the mind of the engineer and in the blueprint. The extrinsic Formal Cause may also begin as a real entity, when, for example, an artist paints the picture of a certain cathedral or a portrait of an individual. Then, the extrinsic Formal Cause is the cathedral or the person whose appearance is painted.

[207]   For obvious reasons, the extrinsic Formal Cause is also called the Exemplar Cause.

[208]   Explanation by means of the Four Causes dominated Medieval science, philosophy and theology from the thirteenth century well into the seventeenth century. In the seventeenth century it confronted modern science and was theoretically ignored. But it still influenced thought even up to the present time. William Wallace in his *Causality and Explanation* has made the continuity of causal explanation clear, as he tracks its course from Aristotle to the present.

[209]   Not all disciplines use all four causes. Modern physics does not use the Final Cause. This is a methodological choice. On the other hand, Geometry, because of its very nature, that is, because it deals with the formalities of continuous quantity, cannot use the Efficient Cause or the Final Cause. There is no place for the Efficient Cause, because there are no happenings, no changes in its subject matter. Since the Final Cause causes through the Efficient Cause, there can be no Final Cause.

[210]   In order to maintain the relevance and the internal unity of this extended background presentation, I provide a brief preview of how the Doctrine of the Four Causes is used in St.

Thomas's definition of law: Law is a promulgated dictate of reason for the Common Good made and promulgated by him who has the care of the community (*q.* 90, *a.* 4, *c.*). Promulgated dictate of reason is the (intrinsic) Formal Cause of law (*q.* 90, *a.* 1 and *a.* 4). The Common Good is the Final Cause (*q.* 90, *a.* 2). The one who has the care of the community and makes and promulgates the law is the Efficient Cause (*q.* 90, *a.* 3 and *a.* 4). The community or human acts within society are the Material Cause (*q.* 90, *aa.* 1 through 4).

[211]   Note that promulgation appears with two different causes. Since promulgation is essential to law, promulgating is part of the activity of the Efficient Cause. The act of promulgation results in a promulgated dictate and so promulgation becomes part of the Formal Cause. In *q.* 90, *a.* 1, Reply 2, St. Thomas illustrates this kind of distinction by the example of building a house and the house built.

[212]   John Finnis (*Natural Law and Natural Rights,* pp. 3–22) has criticized Positivists for not providing a criterion for selecting the important or the elucidating features of law. The Doctrine of the Four Causes provides a set of questions the answers to which constitute an elucidation of the essence or nature of law. The Doctrine thus supplies the missing basic principle.

SECTION 3:
ST. THOMAS'S WORLD VIEW

A. INTRODUCTION

[213]   St. Thomas wrote as a Catholic theologian and as a medieval scholar. He therefore accepts Divine Revelation as presented in the Bible and in the traditions of the Church, including also the development of the Faith through Christian experience and reflection. At the same time, he accepts many of the philosophical positions adopted by Aristotle. His theology is thus a synthesis of Christian belief and human understanding. This union of Faith and reason is indicated by the fact that the three main sources for *auctoritates* in the *Treatise* are the Bible, Aristotle, and St. Augustine. In common

with other medieval scholars, St. Thomas saw in Aristotle the only example of a rather complete rational system of philosophy, developed without benefit of a real or alleged religious revelation.

[214]   Now St. Thomas not only developed a philosophical jurisprudence, he also integrated it into his comprehensive view of reality. It is true that a great deal of St. Thomas's jurisprudence can be extricated from his synthesis and presented in its own evidence. But, if one wishes to understand the *Treatise,* he must have some knowledge of the broader context. Hence I present here two brief outlines of St. Thomas's world view. The first is more theological, the second more philosophical. Since these two outlines are combined in St. Thomas, there will be some overlapping.

B. THE THEOLOGICAL OUTLINE

[215]   In St. Thomas's theology God is, of course, the infinite Being, the Creator of all things. But in the universe thus created by God, the human creature has a unique position. The human creature, alone in the world we know, is made to the very "image and likeness" of God Himself; he alone can understand, can know and appreciate, and he alone can consciously experience and respond to God's love. All other things are determined by physical laws; man alone is free. Therefore man has an eternal destiny transcending the material world.

[216]   Now St. Thomas distinguishes two levels of reality, a natural order and a supernatural order. The natural order includes all those things which exist and operate according to their own nature; fish swim, fire burns, man reasons and loves. But God has given human beings not only their nature but a new level of life which flows not from man's nature but from the Divine Life. Thus man, who can naturally know and love God from the outside, is now introduced into the very internal life of the Blessed Trinity.

[217]   So when our first parents were created, they were also endowed with this participation and were also given special gifts of grace. But they turned against God and thereby lost both their sharing His divine life as well as those special gifts.

[218]   God, in His mercy, sent the Second Person of the Trinity into the world, incarnate in Christ Jesus. Christ, through his

life and sufferings, won for all good people access to the Divine Life. The special gifts were not restored.

[219]   St. Thomas, though accepting the Doctrine of Original Sin (the sin of our first parents), did not believe that that sin had intrinsically destroyed man's reason or his natural ordination to good. This is an important point for understanding the *Treatise*, for St. Thomas frequently refers to man's inclination to good. This may be better appreciated when one remembers that in some non-Catholic theologies man is considered as completely depraved by Original Sin.

[220]   St. Thomas believes that all laws, in one way or another, help man attain his destiny in God.

C. THE METAPHYSICAL OUTLINE

[221]   God is an infinite, perfect being, intelligent, free, and all-powerful. He necessarily exists and exists without dependence on any other being.

[222]   All other beings in the universe are contingent, that is, they do not exist in their own right and cannot explain their own existence. They are dependent upon God for their existence and for their continuance in existence.

[223]   God is thus the creator of all things. "Creator" is here used in the strict metaphysical sense. In this sense, creation is the production of being without any preexisting matter or being (except God). Creation is not a change. A change presupposes something that changes. All the productions of which we are aware in this world are changes. We have to make things out of preexisting things. We have thus no direct experience of creation.

[224]   All the things in the universe are, therefore, totally dependent on God and totally derived from Him.

[225]   St. Thomas analyzes the relationship of created things to God in accordance with the Doctrine of the Four Causes.

[226]   God is the ultimate Efficient Cause of all created things. God produces the totality of every being. Despite this fact, created things really exist and really exercise causality, a limited causality to be sure, but, nonetheless, a real causality.

[227]   God is also the ultimate Exemplar Cause (external Formal Cause) of all things. Since God is infinite reality, all created

realities must, in some way, mirror God. We can distinguish the ultimate exemplarity which is the nature of God from the proximate exemplarity in the mind of God which is the determined exemplar for this universe. This latter exemplar is called the Eternal Law (*q.* 91, *a.* 1).

[228]   In divine efficiency there is no pre-existing material cause (as the marble pre-exists the statue). God concreates the internal material cause in finite beings.

[229]   In one sense, God Himself is the final cause of the universe. All things necessarily show forth the perfections of God and God Himself is the ultimate term of all desire.

[230]   The *finis operantis,* the motive of God, if we can so speak of divinity, is love. Because of His perfection God creates intelligently, freely, and lovingly.

[231]   St. Thomas often says that created things "participate" in God's perfections. This term thus expresses the fact that perfection in created things resembles the corresponding perfection in God (exemplarity) but in a deficient manner (as the finite falls short of the infinite) and is derivative (by efficient causality) from God. Thus St. Thomas says that the Natural Law, which exists in us, is a participation in the Eternal Law, which is in the mind of God (*q.* 91, *a.* 2, *c.*). The term "participation" in Thomistic language is a very pregnant expression. Since it is understood in relation to the Four Causes, it has lost its various Platonic and Neo-Platonic meanings.

SECTION 4:
"NATURE" AND "ESSENCE"

[232]   There are two reasons why it is necessary to clarify the Thomistic meanings of these two terms. The first is that, in the basic initial Question of the *Treatise,* St. Thomas poses the question, "What is the essence of law?" The second reason is that the Thomistic understanding of human nature, the essence or nature of man, underlies St. Thomas's philosophy of man, his ethics, and his philosophy of law.

[233]   Most Positivists deny that there is any such thing as an "essence" or "nature." They assert that a question like, "What is the nature or essence of law?" is uselessly vague or even meaningless.

[234]   In St. Thomas, however (and in the Scholastics in general), these terms have a very precise and explicit meaning. It is true that, like so many philosophical terms, they are used in a variety of senses. Here I will discuss only the meaning directly relevant to the *Treatise*.

[235]   I will attempt to explain the meaning of "essence" by describing it in three different ways. First of all, essence is related to existence. Essence consists of those realities (a Positivist might say "those characteristics") which are necessary and sufficient for the existence of the kind of thing under study. Thus, the essential definition of a triangle as "a three-sided plane figure" provides the fundamental realities necessary and sufficient to have a triangle exist. If one of these elements, e.g., "*three*-sided" is missing, there simply is no triangle. But, if all these elements are present, no matter what other elements may be present, there is a triangle. Hence we say that the elements expressed in the definition of a triangle are "essential" to a triangle.

[236]   Secondly, the essence also distinguishes one kind of thing from another kind of thing. Thus, a triangle is clearly distinguished from a square since three-sidedness is included in its essence, whereas a square is essentially four-sided.

[237]   Thirdly, the essence consists of the elements that are basic to the object in question. Thus, we distinguish two sets of elements in an object, those that are basic to the object and those which, though necessary, are derivative from the basic elements.

[238]   The essence consists of the basic and primary elements and intelligibility of the kind of thing under discussion. The essence is thus differentiated from other necessary but secondary and derivative characteristics. These latter characteristics are called "properties." Thus, the primary elements and intelligibility of a triangle are expressed in the definition of a triangle as a "three-sided plane figure." These elements cannot be derived from any more primitive elements or intelligibilities. The definition is derived from immediate consideration and analysis of a triangle. But given this basic understanding of a triangle, other elements or characteristics of triangle can be derived in various ways. Thus, geometers establish that "the

sum of the angles of a triangle is equal to the sum of two right angles." This is a property of triangle and is derived from the essence of triangle.

[239]   Thus, the whole of trigonometry is a display of the properties of triangle and their logical mode of derivation from the essence.

[240]   Now, besides constitutive elements and properties, there is a third class of qualifications called "accidents." Thus, it is of the essence of a triangle that it have sides and that these sides have length, but that a side of a triangle be *three* inches long is neither part of the essence nor necessarily derivative from it. Yet it is a qualification of this particular triangle. Hence, that a side be *three* inches long is accidental.

[241]   Thus St. Thomas had a methodology for analyzing the inner structure of any given kind of thing. Additionally, he could distinguish accidental qualifications of an instance of this kind of thing which are appropriate for this sort of thing though not necessary to it.

[242]   Let us apply this methodology, briefly, to one of St. Thomas's primary interests, human beings.

[243]   The traditional definition of man, accepted by St. Thomas, the Scholastics, and many others is "rational animal." This is an essential definition since it expresses the two elements of the essence of man.

[244]   Whenever we find a being that is an animal and yet possesses the ability to understand and to reason, we know we are dealing with a human being. As anthropologists and missionaries found different tribes and groups, however different their customs (exotic to us), they were able to identify them as human beings. Thus, the presence of these two elements is necessary and sufficient for the existence of a human being. Moreover, these elements adequately distinguished human beings from all other kinds of beings.

[245]   Moreover, all the proper characteristics of human beings are derived from or necessarily connect with these essential elements.

[246]   Because man has a universalizing intellect, he can consider a range of possible goods or choices and, after such consideration, can determine freely, to a certain extent, the particular good or choice that he deliberately makes his "own." He has the

power to make, within limits, free choices and so escapes the determinism of nature. He can construct sciences and set up legal systems because he is rational. Throughout the history of philosophy, risibility, the ability to laugh, has often been recognized as a property of man. In order to laugh one must have an intelligence to recognize humor and a body to express this recognition. Neither brute animals nor angels can laugh. Likewise, we can distinguish many accidents that can modify individuals or groups of individuals. Thus *brownness* of skin is neither an essential element nor a property of human nature.

[247]   Human beings in the concrete are extremely complex; yet the analysis into essence, properties, and accidents can deepen our understanding of human life and human activities.

[248]   When, therefore, St. Thomas posits the question, "What is the essence or nature of law?" he isn't presenting some vague obscure question but a very clear and precise one.

[249]   I have already pointed out that St. Thomas's definition of law is an "explanatory" one, worked out in accordance with the methodology of the Four Causes. I now assert that it is an essential definition, i.e., it expresses all the essential elements of a law.

[250]   "A dictate of [practical] reason [= a rule and measure of human acts], for the Common Good, made by him who has the care of the community, and promulgated."

[251]   If any one of these elements is missing, no law exists. Perhaps a thing resembling a law in some ways may exist and, therefore, be called a "putative" law or a law *secundum quid,* i.e., in some limited or partial sense. If all these elements are present, a law exists—*simpliciter,* i.e., in the full sense, without qualification. Thus, if a piece of legislation has been passed by Congress and signed by the President, it can be called a law. But, if it fails in some other respect, e.g., if it is contrary to the Common Good, it is not a law *simpliciter* but only *secundum quid.*

[252]   St. Thomas establishes his definition of law, which is both an explanatory and an essential definition, in the First Question of the *Treatise.* There are, however, six further questions in the *Treatise.* What is St. Thomas doing in these questions? How does he further develop his investigation of law?

[253]   In order to answer these questions, I return to our primary example, namely, the triangle.

[254]   After establishing his definition, the geometer does

three things. First, he works out the properties of triangle as such. Thus he shows that, given the essence of triangle, the sum of the three angles of a triangle is equal to the sum of two right angles. No one would think that this theorem, though true and necessarily so, defines a triangle. Then, the geometer expands the list of theorems, setting forth the properties of triangle as such. Also, since triangle is a genus and not a species, it includes different kinds of triangles which differ essentially among themselves and not merely as individuals.

[255]   Thus the geometer identifies the right triangle as a species or kind of triangle. Its definition is developed by recognizing an essential element (one right angle) that does not appear in the definition of triangle in general. A right triangle differs essentially from an equilateral triangle and not merely individually as one right triangle differs from another right triangle.

[256]   The geometer then determines the properties of the species of triangles. Thus, that the square of the hypotenuse of a *right* triangle is equal to the sum of the squares on the other two sides is a property of a *right* triangle, necessarily derived from its essence, yet not identical with that essence.

[257]   In a somewhat different order, St. Thomas does much the same thing. In Question 91 he distinguishes four different species of law which, analogously at least, fulfill the definition of law worked out in Question 90, but he does not separate the properties of law in general from the properties of the different species of law. This must be determined from the context.

[258]   There are two listings of properties of law as such, one of which (that of St. Isidore (*Etymologies,* V. 21) is expressly approved by St. Thomas (*q.* 95, *a.* 3), and the other of which (that of Lon Fuller, *The Morality of Law,* pp. 46–90) can easily be reconciled with both Isidore and St. Thomas.

[259]   A final note. In many cases we cannot discover the true essences of things. We then use a group of apparent properties or a selection of recurrent accidents to function in knowledge as essences. Thus we define "gold" by carefully examining it empirically and by describing some of its characteristics: a heavy, yellow, inert, metallic chemical element with a high degree of ductility and malleability (*Webster's New World Dictionary*).

[260]   Likewise, in defining a "rose" we put it under a

pseudo-genus described through selected characteristics: any of a genus (*Rosa*) of shrubs of the rose family, characteristically with prickly stems, alternate compound leaves, and five-parted, usually fragrant flowers of red, pink, white, yellow, etc. having many stamens (*op. cit.*). How many of these characteristics are true properties or elements of an essence, we do not know. But St. Thomas believes that, in the case of geometrical entities, human nature, and the law, we can discover true essences and at least some real properties in the strict sense.

[261]   When we examine any concrete or individual instance of any essence, we discover a variety of qualifications appropriate to such a kind of thing but which are neither part of the essence nor derived from the essence as properties. I have already instanced "brown-colored skin." An animal has to have some color, but whether it be green, black, or brown is not necessary to it. I now give a more relevant example.

[262]   From the analysis of a law—according to St. Thomas: Promulgation is of the essence of law. From this the property of clarity can be deduced. It is rightly listed among Lon Fuller's "principles of legality" or "principle of the inner morality of the law" (*The Morality of Law*, pp. 65–69), and among Isidore's "qualities" of the law (*Etymologies*, v. 21; *q. 95, a. 3*).

[263]   But, whether this promulgation is achieved by the posting of the law in the Forum or by being read at designated points by the town crier or published in a Federal Register or by broadcast over official radio is a matter of indifference to the essence and properties of law and will be determined by factors outside the nature of law. Thus, if 99 percent of the populace were illiterate, printed publication would hardly be promulgation; likewise, if the common language of the people were German, publication in Latin would hardly be promulgation. Thus the factors determining the mode of publication are outside the nature of law.

[264]   Thus, the methodological analysis of things into essence, properties, and accidents makes it possible to determine the intelligible interrelationship between the "features" or "elements" of a law or a legal system which are obscured by the simple listing of such features in descriptive definitions like those of the "central case" or the comprehensive descriptions like that of John Finnis's definition of a legal system (*Natural Law and Natural Rights*, pp. 276–281).

[265]   St. Thomas's definition of a law (I–II, *q*. 90, *a*. 4, *c*.) is both an explanatory and an essential definition.

SECTION 5:
HUMAN NATURE

A. INTRODUCTION

[266]   In the last Section I discussed St. Thomas's method of analysis of different kinds of substances. In this Section I use this analysis to present some aspects of St. Thomas's view of human nature. We must investigate the understanding of man because all Natural Law thinkers, in one way or another, base their theories on the nature of man.

B. THOMISM VS. MATERIALISM

[267]   Some people think that evolutionary theory has shown human beings to be simply animals, more cunning and clever than the other animals, but, nonetheless, simply another species of ape. From the standpoint of Thomistic epistemology, this is a mistaken application of scientific methodology beyond its competence. Modern physical science is limited by its formal nature, its presuppositions and its methodology to dealing only with material reality. It is unable even to raise the question of spiritual reality. Hence it can say nothing, either positively or negatively, about a spiritual element in man. To attempt to extend the methodology of physical science to spiritual questions is like trying to prove the existence of God from mathematics or like trying to paint a picture with a violin.

[268]   Scientific evolutionary theory did not exist in the science of the thirteenth century, but I think we can safely assert that St. Thomas would have left the matter to the scientists insofar as it concerned the material world and so also the material element in man. However, St. Thomas's epistemology would have rejected the extension of scientific methodologies to man as spiritual. The spiritual

nature of man requires quite different modes of investigation. And, according to these modes of investigation, man has a spiritual soul.

C. INTELLIGENCE, WILL, AND FREE CHOICE

[269]   The general principle for identifying different sorts of beings is that their operations, and their capabilities, both active and passive, reveal their distinctive natures. We distinguish animals from plants by the special operations which animals display and plants do not. So also we distinguish human beings from animals by their special attributes. The special attributes of human beings are summed up in the word "rational" which contrasts sharply with the other animals which are "non-rational." Human beings possess a cognitive power which enables them to universalize, to grasp meaning, to reason logically, to understand relationships, to perform perfect self-reflection, and to understand the real as such. Moreover, since man's intellect is universalizing and man is ordered to the good in general, human beings can consider a range of choices and deliberately choose one to the exclusion of the others, that is, human beings are capable, at least to some degree, of making free choices.

[270]   These operations cannot be reduced to sense-level activities and none can be explained by neurology, materialistic psychology or, least of all, by physics. Man is therefore said to have a spiritual intellect and a spiritual will.

D. THE SOUL

[271]   Intellect and will are powers or faculties, not substances, and so must be supported by a substantive principle in the nature of man. This substantive principle is called the soul.

[272]   Thus man is a union of two substantive principles, a spiritual one (the soul) and a material one (the body). In Thomistic doctrine, this union is substantial, not accidental, and is therefore a complete unity in being; man is one substance, not two substances conjoined in some extrinsic manner. All this is congruent with our natural experiential knowledge of ourselves and is expressed in the pronoun "I."

[273]   This view is in sharp contrast to the position of Plato and of Descartes. For both of these philosophers, the soul is a complete substance in itself, but for Plato the body is like a temporary garment for the soul, while for Descartes the body is a machine controlled by the soul through the pineal gland. For St. Thomas the unity of man is so intimate that he thinks of it in terms of Aristotle's Doctrine of the Four Causes; the body is the material cause of man, the soul is the formal cause which makes the body to be human. Hence, the spiritual intellect and the physical brain can cooperate in man's conscious life.

[274]   According to St. Thomas, then, alone in the known universe man has intelligence, will, and free choice in the strict sense, and, since he alone has a spiritual soul, he is unique in the known universe.

[275]   Man transcends the limits of matter; he alone asks the cosmic questions, the ultimate whys; he alone can understand and explain. Since his soul is spiritual, he escapes the mortality to which all other creatures are doomed. His destiny transcends the material universe and reaches into eternity. His ultimate quest is God and, in reaching God, he will reach fulfillment and happiness.

E. THOMISTIC DOCTRINE AND RELIGION

[276]   All this, St. Thomas believes, can be established by reason. For him, as for all Catholics (and many other Christians), religion, Revelation, and theology add incredibly much more. However, St. Thomas's total theology is not strictly necessary to understand the *Treatise* so I will not attempt even a brief summary. When theological points appear in the *Treatise* they will be explained in the commentary *ad locum*.

F. MAN'S ORIENTATION TO THE GOOD

[277]   St. Thomas believes that, since the first self-evident principle of the moral order is that good should be done and evil avoided, man has a basic orientation to the good. This places St. Thomas in opposition to various other views of man. Thus many

Protestant theologians believe that Original Sin has completely destroyed the orientation to the good. St. Thomas does not accept this negative view of Fallen Man. Likewise, St. Thomas is in sharp disagreement with Hobbes who held that man is naturally aggressive and has to be restrained by an all-powerful ruler. St. Thomas rejects this pessimistic view of man. For St. Thomas, law is primarily a rule that presupposes man's orientation to good. For St. Thomas, sanctions and punishments are only extrinsically connected with law.

SECTION 6:
THE NATURE OF HUMAN ACTS

[278]   In the *Corpus* of *q.* 90, *a.* 1, St. Thomas states that law is a rule and measure of human acts. What does he understand by this phrase? What is a human act? St. Thomas uses the phrase in a strictly formal meaning, namely, human acts qua human acts; that is, acts which are posited in a way that is specifically and distinctively human. Now, what specifically distinguishes human beings from all other animals? According to St. Thomas it is that the specific nature of man consists in his ability to reason, to deliberate, and to make free choices. Therefore, a human act is one that is posited with knowledge or understanding, deliberation or intention, and freely.

[279]   Such acts are distinguished from what are called merely acts of human beings. These latter are acts over which people have no conscious control such as digesting one's food, scratching one's head absent-mindedly, carrying out some habit without thinking and so forth. This distinction is important because it precisely determines responsibility. Human beings are responsible only for those acts over which they have conscious control. For this reason human acts are sometimes called "imputable" acts.

[280]   The degree of guilt or responsibility is determined both morally and legally in accordance with the degree of knowledge, deliberation, and freedom with which the act is posited. Many factors may reduce the conscious control and thereby reduce responsibility and guilt. For example, a man who kills another in a spontaneous drunken brawl is not as guilty as a man who cold-bloodedly plans

the murder of his wife. A man who is out of his mind completely is considered not to be guilty at all. There are other factors such as fear or confusion, which reduce the quality of a human act and therefore also guilt. St. Thomas develops a very careful analysis of the factors that reduce the voluntariness of human acts (*S. T.,* I–II, *q.* 6, *aa.* 1–8).

[281]   Lon Fuller points out that the Anglo-American legal tradition (as does every legal tradition) presupposes this view of human acts. He writes:

> I come now to the most important respect in which an observance of the demands of legal morality can serve the broader aims of human life generally. This lies in the view of man implicit in the internal morality of law. I have repeatedly observed that legal morality can be said to be neutral over a wide range of ethical issues. It cannot be neutral in its view of man himself. To embark on the enterprise of subjecting human conduct to the governance of rules involves of necessity a commitment to the view that man is, or can become, a responsible agent, capable of understanding and following rules, and answerable for his defaults. (*The Morality of Law,* p. 162)

He also points out that there are today philosophers (like Edgar Wilson) and psychologists (like B. F. Skinner) who simply deny that human beings have the ability to make free choices. They sometimes portray human beings simply as more complicated animals that need to be programmed rather than directed in their actions. Sometimes human beings are portrayed as being a kind of biological machine. If this philosophy or psychology is taken seriously, the entire legal system would have to be revamped or perhaps totally replaced.

[282]   Although law directs human acts, civil or human law cannot direct all human acts. The civil law can only direct acts in society and such as can be dealt with in a public forum. Therefore, civil law can deal only with the external acts of the human being. It cannot deal with purely private acts nor with the internal dispositions, motives, and attitudes which lie back of the external act. As the old saying has it, the law can require a man to bare his head when the queen is passing by, but it cannot require him to love and respect her in his heart.

[283]   Human acts, according to St. Thomas, constitute the

material cause of law. That is to say that the law, in directing human acts, in fact forms them in a way that is analogous to the way in which a sculptor forms a statue so that it receives the shape of George Washington. Sometimes the material cause of law is stated to be the community which is also a feasible way of saying that it would include all the subjects and their human acts in this limited sense.

SECTION 7:
"RULE AND MEASURE"

[284]   In *q.* 90, *a.* 1, St. Thomas says that a law is a "rule and measure of human acts." H. L. A. Hart asserts that the problem of defining rules and explaining the different kinds of rules is one of the persistent questions of modern jurisprudence (*The Concept of Law,* pp. 8–13).

[285]   For St. Thomas, the nature of a rule was not problematic. A rule is a general directive for action. If I say to my assistant, "Send this letter to the President of the United States," I'm not setting up a rule for guiding her action; I am asking her to do a single act. If I have to characterize that, I will say it's a request or a gentle order, but it's not a rule. If, however, I tell my cook that I want breakfast served every morning at 7 A.M., I am setting up a rule for his repetitious action and a general directive, consequently a rule.

[286]   Lon Fuller says (*The Morality of Law,* p. 47) simply that there must be rules and that rules must be general. Likewise, H. L. A. Hart (*The Concept of Law,* pp. 20–22) makes the same point in his criticism of John Austin's use of the "gunman model." He also says that a legal system consists of a combination of different sorts of rules.

[287]   There seems to be no serious debate as to whether a law is a rule for action.

[288]   "Measure" is, first of all, a quantitative measure. We measure distance in miles, we measure liquids in gallons, and so forth. However, it is extended to qualitative things as well. Aristotle, for example, extended it to any kind of standard. St. Thomas refers to Aristotle's discussion of measure as the conception of measure

which he himself is using. In the present case, therefore, measure is a standard by which we judge human acts. The rule is prospective; it directs future action. The measure is applied to human acts which have already been performed. Therefore, when the court is applying a rule of law, it is also measuring whatever it is applying that rule to and it is using that rule precisely as a measure.

[289]   In the definition of law (*q.* 90, *a.* 4, *c.*) the "rule and measure of human acts" is translated into a "dictate of reason," a translation which is achieved in Article 1. However, in subsequent parts of the *Treatise,* over and over again St. Thomas repeats his description of a law as a rule and measure of human acts and uses it as a basis for developing many other points in his theory of law.

[290]   St. Thomas's assertion that law is a rule and measure of human acts is an inference from the observed way that laws actually do function. It is an empirical fact that laws bind men either to do or to abstain from doing something. This function can clearly, at least by inference, be said to be that of a rule or measure.

SECTION 8:
HABIT

A. INTRODUCTION

[291]   The term "habit" has been used in a variety of meanings. Perhaps the most common meaning in English is the repetition of certain acts with little deliberation and sometimes with no conscious attention at all. Of the first sort we may instance the habit of brushing one's teeth after breakfast; of the second sort is scratching one's head while thinking of something else. St. Thomas refers to the habit of unconsciously stroking one's beard (*barbam fricare*).

B. AN IMPORTANT MEANING OF "HABIT" IN THOMISTIC PHILOSOPHY

[292]   Now, in Thomistic philosophy, "habit" has a much more profound and important meaning. In this meaning "habit" may

be defined as a development or perfection of an operative faculty that enables that faculty to deal with its object in a correct and effective manner.

[293]   An example may clarify this definition.

[294]   We have seen that human beings have an intellect, a knowing faculty fundamentally related to being as such. As soon as it begins to operate as a Speculative Intellect, it immediately understands being and certain general principles of being such as the principle of contradiction, which states that no being can both be and not be at the same time under the same aspect. Since the Speculative Intellect is ready to immediately grasp these principles, the intellect is said to have *by nature* a habit of first principles of the Speculative Reason. Since we know these principles by nature, we do not have *to learn* how to know them. We do that naturally.

[295]   But, although the Speculative Intellect is ordered to all knowledge, we do not immediately know all the disciplines that we have developed in the centuries following Plato. We can immediately recognize the difference between being and non-being, but we cannot immediately solve equations, prove the Pythagorean Theorem, or diagnose glaucoma. We have to learn *how* to do these things. Thus, for example, we must acquire the habit of geometry, which is a stable perfection of the Speculative Intellect by which we can perform geometrical acts correctly, easily, and with pleasure. This habit is acquired, not by mechanical repetition of acts, but by insightful repetition of acts that are formally geometrical acts.

[296]   If one carefully considers the description of "habit" just given, it will be evident that we must make a careful distinction between, on the one hand, the *habit of geometry by which* a person is able to do geometry and to learn geometrical knowledge and, on the other hand, the knowledge so gained and *held habitually* by that habit. This distinction plays a key role in *q*. 90, *a*. 1, obj.-reply 2 and in *q*. 94, *a*. 1, *c*.

[297]   A very similar analysis could be made of the Practical Intellect. There is a natural habit of first principles by which the basic principle of the moral law is known, i.e., "Good is to be done and evil avoided." There are moral habits dealing with specific kinds of moral acts. These are called "virtues" and will be considered later [322–360]. They can be thought of as analogous in the moral order

to the individual disciplinary habits (like the habit of geometry) in the speculative order.

SECTION 9:
THE SPECULATIVE INTELLECT, THE PRACTICAL INTELLECT, AND RIGHT REASON

A. INTRODUCTION

[298]   As stated above, St. Thomas accepted the traditional definition of human beings as "rational animal." This means that human beings have a spiritual, universalizing intellect through which they can grasp reality, understand and explain it and, in contrast to the instinctive activity of animals, can intelligently guide their actions.

[299]   They also have a will, a faculty ordered to action and to the good. Through the interplay of intellect and will, human beings are able to make free choices (that is, imputable choices). Thus they are more or less responsible for their actions.

[300]   The intellect operates in two very different, though rational, ways which I will now explain.

B. THE SPECULATIVE INTELLECT

[301]   When the intellect is used to obtain knowledge, to understand and to explain reality, it is called the Speculative Intellect. In this way, the intellect gives rise to the knowledge disciplines (what St. Thomas calls the "speculative" or "demonstrable" sciences) such as philosophy, physics, geometry, optics, etc.

[302]   The Speculative Intellect operates through definitions, judgments, and syllogisms. When the speculative disciplines are fully developed, they are organized under general definitions, generalizations and principles, all tied together in a deductive system. This pattern is clearly displayed in geometry.

[303]   Now, according to St. Thomas, all the activities of the Speculative Intellect are grounded in and regulated by certain

self-evident (indemonstrable) principles. These principles are immediately understood implicitly as soon as the intellect grasps any reality whatever. These principles can be formulated as follows: "Being is", "Being is what it is", "It is impossible to affirm and deny the same thing", "Things equal to a third thing are equal to each other." These principles are, first of all, concerned with reality (*ens*, "being") and consequently are also principles of all deductive or demonstrative reasoning. Hence, the Speculative Intellect deals only with the knowledge of what is. It is not involved in the making of moral decisions or prudential moral judgments. The Speculative Intellect deals with the "is" in Hume's "is / ought" dichotomy.

C. THE PRACTICAL INTELLECT

[304]   When the intellect is used to make a decision with regard to action, it is called the Practical Intellect.

[305]   The Speculative Intellect deals only with what is; it seeks the truth of things and so operates solely as a knowing faculty. Since the Practical Intellect deals not with what is but with what is to be done, it requires the cooperation of the will. St. Thomas's analysis presented in the *Corpus* of *q.* 90, *a.* 1 interrelates the Practical Intellect with human moral activity and so interrelates the intellect and the will with human acts to be done. Hence the "good" or the "human good" as such is involved. The relationship of reason and will in Practical Reason is explicitly indicated: "I answer that, All law proceeds from the reason and will of the lawgiver; the Divine and natural laws from the reasonable will of God; the human law from the will of man, regulated by reason . . . "(*q.* 97, *a.* 3, *c.*).

[306]   Since the Practical Reason is ordered to action, and all action is purposeful, the Practical Reason argues in a different mode from that of the Speculative Intellect. Practical Reason begins with the end (the good / happiness). By the same reasons, the first principles of the Practical Reason are different from those of the Speculative Intellect.

[307]   The first principle of the Practical Reason and of the moral order is, "Good is to be done and evil avoided." This principle is called the first principle of the moral order not because any particular moral precept can be deduced from it or any individual moral

decision can be produced by it, but because it is the formal pattern of all moral precepts and all moral decisions. It states the basic principle of moral obligation, based on the attractive power of the good. No proposition or principle of the Speculative Intellect carries any obligatory moral content.

[308]   There have been Natural Law thinkers who thought that the moral order could be deduced from an abstract theoretical knowledge of human nature. Against this position Hume's assertion that no "ought" can be deduced from an "is" has valid logical force. However, the objection fails completely as against St. Thomas's position, for he draws the obligation of the moral law from an immediate self-evident principle of the moral order—the primitive grasp of the obligatory nature of the good.

[309]   Now, when St. Thomas says (*q. 90, a. 4, c, ad fin.*) that law is a dictate of reason, he means a dictate of Practical Reason.

D. RIGHT REASON

[310]   When St. Thomas says that law is a dictate of Practical Reason, he is assuming that the dictate of Practical Reason is correctly guided by the Natural Law. It is a fact that human beings can come to a final decision, in a given case, that is contrary to the moral law. This is so because human beings are free and are under many pressures towards immorality, such as passions, evil habits (vices), unhappy family life, etc. If a person had completely good will, fortified by the moral virtues and especially by insightful judgment, such a one would freely choose the good.

[311]   Hence, in interpreting the Thomistic definition, one should understand that the dictate therein contained is a dictate of *right* Practical Reason.

[312]   From St. Thomas's standpoint, it is absurd to try to distinguish what law *is* from what law *ought to be*. Of course, civil law can be contrary to what ought to be. Almost everyone agrees that law is a rule and measure (a standard) of human acts, if law does not have a *standard distinguishing what is from what ought to be,* if law contains no standard, it cannot be a measure and hence would lack an essential function of law or of Practical Reason.

SECTION 10:
VOLUNTARISM VS. PRACTICAL REASONABLENESS

[313]   Human beings have two basic faculties, the will and the intellect. The will is ordered to the good and the good involves the notion of a purpose and therefore of action. The will moves all the faculties of man to action. The intellect is a knowing faculty; through it human beings learn, understand, and reason. Of itself it does not move to action, just as the will does not know. It is obvious that these two faculties are in close association and must work together in man's life.

[314]   For St. Thomas, the most intimate cooperation of these two faculties occurs in Practical Reason. The act of Practical Reason is a composite one and involves an interplay of will and intellect.

[315]   In the long discussion of morality and law there are two conflicting opinions concerning the relevant collaboration of intellect and will in the making of laws and moral rules. The question is: Which faculty has the primacy in these discussions?

[316]   According to St. Thomas, law is a dictate of Practical Reason. This "dictate," although requiring will, is formally and primarily an act of the intellect. This position is asserted in the first article of the *Treatise* (q. 90, a. 1). In this article the emphasis falls on reason, though the contribution of the will is not excluded. More expressly, in q. 97, a. 3, c., St. Thomas refers to the source of obligation as being "reasonable will" and "will regulated by reason." The emphasis on reason as the source and measure of law runs through the whole of the *Treatise*. And the same doctrine recurs in the history of Natural Law.

[317]   Now the opposite opinion is likewise a venerable one that is found in the discussion in ancient Greece. In Plato's *Republic* Thrasymachus declared that justice is the will of the stronger. In Roman Law the imperial principle was stated thus: "What pleases the prince has the force of law." In the Middle Ages an extreme position of irrationality appears in Ockham (1300?–49?). Referring to God as a lawgiver, he said that God, *if he so willed,* could make blasphemy, murder, rape acts of virtue and therefore requirements for admission to heaven. The medieval controversy went on and is

discussed in Suarez's *De Legibus* (*Concerning Laws*) in which he opted for a moderate voluntarism. (The best account of this Medieval development is *The Nature of Law* by Thomas Davitt, S.J.)

[318]   As in Thrasymachus' blunt statement, voluntarism is usually associated with force. Spinoza said that tyrants had a natural right to rule as long as they could control the people.

[319]   The founder of modern Anglo-American Positivism, John Austin, was a Voluntarist, though not often so called. According to him, law is a general command backed by threats made by a sovereign who has the physical power to carry out those threats. There is no rational test by which the legality of a law can be judged from the law's contents.

[320]   It is easy to see why Positivism must include sanctions or punishment as an essential element of law.

[321]   St. Thomas faced this voluntaristic position in the very first article in the *Treatise*. In the Third Objection he presents an argument for the primacy of will based on the nature of will. He backed it up with the classic Roman Imperial principle, "What pleases the prince has the force of law." In reply he does not exclude the will, but he sets up the criterion of reasonableness. What pleases the prince has the force of law if what pleases the prince is according to reason (i.e., right Practical Reason). Hence, it is not enough that some lawgiver has commanded a law; the content of law, which is generally of no moment to Positivism as such, must meet the demands of Practical Reason and so be just and for the Common Good (not simply for social control by force or pressure).

SECTION 11:
THE VIRTUES

A. INTRODUCTION

[322]   The doctrine of the virtues is central to St. Thomas's moral theology and moral philosophy. It also has a significant importance for understanding his jurisprudence (see, for example, *q*. 96, *a*. 3, "Whether human law is competent to direct all acts of virtue?").

[323]   The doctrine was developed by Plato, the Stoics, and especially Aristotle (in his great ethical work, *The Nicomachean Ethics*). St. Thomas adopted, expanded, and refined the doctrine. Plato introduced the problem in this manner. He said that we know what the excellence ("virtue") of a lutenist is; it is to play the lute well. So also the excellence of the shipbuilder is to build seaworthy ships; of the cook, to prepare good meals.

[324]   But now, is there a virtue of human beings simply as human beings, not as lutenists, shipbuilders and cooks? Who is the good person? Who is the just man? Who is the happy man? The doctrine of the virtues was developed to answer (at least partially) these questions.

B. THE VIRTUES IN GENERAL

[325]   A virtue is defined as an interior disposition or skill (a habit) by which a person can do the right things, correctly, easily and with pleasure. As we shall see, some virtues are innate, some infused, and some are acquired. Virtues are distinguished and specified by the objects with which they deal. We will see how this works out with respect to the different virtues.

[326]   A virtue is thus a perfection of an active power, a natural inclination or desire of man. Thus the virtue of Justice is a perfection of a man's relationship with others in regard to goods and services.

[327]   Now, before we deal with the cardinal moral virtues, we must take a brief comprehensive view of the different sorts of virtues recognized by St. Thomas. (Although I have dealt with some of this material before, I am repeating it in this new context in order to give a balanced understanding of the virtues).

[328]   St. Thomas distinguished four types of virtues (or good habits).

C. THE THEOLOGICAL VIRTUES

[329]   St. Thomas recognizes three theological virtues, so called because they relate man directly to God.

[330]   The first of these is Faith, by which man, trusting in God, believes what God has revealed. The second is Hope, by which, trusting in God, we expect salvation and the means to reach it. The third is Love, by which we love God for his own sake and all others for God's sake. The good towards which the theological virtues enable us to move is thus expressed by Christ: "You shall love the Lord your God with all your heart, with all your soul, with all your strength, with all your mind; and your neighbor as yourself" (Luke 10:27).

[331]   It is through these theological virtues that man reaches his complete fulfillment and his ultimate happiness. But they presuppose and foster the development of a strong moral character through the acquisition of the moral virtues.

D. THE INTELLECTUAL VIRTUES

[332]   The second type of virtues is those that perfect the Speculative Intellect. The Speculative Intellect has the basic power of grasping reality, of insight, understanding, and reasoning. But it is naturally in possession of a habit, called the habit of the first indemonstrable (self-evident) principles. The most important principle thus held through this habit is the principle of contradiction, "A thing cannot both be and not be, under the same aspect, at the same time." St. Thomas sometimes quotes this principle in its logical form, "The same thing cannot be both affirmed and denied." This principle governs all thinking and all reasoning. It guarantees the certitude of a valid syllogism.

[333]   Human beings implicitly know this principle as soon as they intellectually confront reality. Hence, the habit of the first principle does not have to be acquired.

[334]   There are, however, many other more particular and specific habits that perfect the Speculative Intellect but must be acquired. We are not born knowing how to do geometry. We must acquire the ability to think about and understand geometry. Once this habit is acquired, a person can gain geometrical knowledge which he thereafter holds habitually. St. Thomas refers to the habit of the grammarian by which he makes proper speech (q. 94, a. 1, c.).

[335]   This list of virtues, other than the moral virtues, is not complete but it is adequate to understand the Treatise.

E. THE MORAL VIRTUES

[336]   In accord with the main tradition, St. Thomas identifies four basic virtues which, because they are basic, are called the four cardinal moral virtues. In addition to these cardinal virtues, there are very many other virtues subordinate and attached to them. For our purpose here we will deal only with the Cardinal Virtues. St. Thomas lists them thus: 1. Temperance, 2. Fortitude, 3. Justice, 4. Prudence.

[337]   All these virtues assist in the making of good moral choices and the placing of good human acts. Hence they fall under the Practical Intellect since the first principle of the Practical Intellect is, as stated above [304–309], "Good is to be done, evil avoided."

[338]   I will now discuss each of the cardinal virtues.

1. Temperance

[339]   Temperance is the virtue by which we regulate our sensual appetites, our desire for food and drink, for sexual pleasure, and for sensual comfort.

[340]   Today, temperance is often limited to the use of alcoholic drinks and often means total abstinence. That is not its meaning here. The virtue of temperance enables us to make the right use of our sensual appetites. It is a moderating power, not a totally negative one.

[341]   This virtue is self-regarding; it deals with one's desires, the sensual appetites of one's self.

[342]   For this reason, the judgments of temperance are proportionate to individuals and so may vary from person to person. For example, an ordinary well-regulated individual may make a moderate use of alcohol; for such a one drinking a moderate amount of champagne at a wedding reception may be an act of virtue. For a confirmed alcoholic total abstinence may be the only temperate act possible. Again, what would not be gluttony in a full-grown adult would be so for a child.

[343]   Insofar as Temperance is a personal virtue, the state cannot legislate it, but, when a lack of temperance results in external acts, such as drunken brawling or drunken driving, the state may impose an external temperance (*q. 96, a. 3*).

2. Fortitude

[344]   Fortitude is the virtue that enables us to face up to dangers and difficulties in order to do the right thing or, for the same reason, to endure with patience sufferings and hardship. It orders what Plato called the "spirited" part of man. It controls anger and fear, not that it eliminates fear but that it helps to act despite fear.

[345]   Fortitude is often thought of as the characteristic virtue of policemen, and firefighters, but, in fact, everyone needs it, for the way of virtue is beset with difficulties, pains, and obstacles.

[346]   Fortitude often supports the other virtues. Thus to stand up for justice may entail risking one's life or facing torture.

[347]   Fortitude is a balanced virtue rejecting both recklessness and cowardly behavior.

[348]   The state may order external acts of Fortitude when the Common Good requires it. Thus a captain may order his men to take a fortified hill (q. 96, a. 3).

3. Justice

i. Introduction

[349]   Justice is *the* social virtue and is therefore the virtue most closely related and relevant to the law, since law always directs a society or a community. Our ordinary ways of talking indicate this close connection. We call our courts "Courts of Justice." People say they go to the law or the Courts to get justice; they don't say they go to Court to get temperance or courage. We call Court decisions or laws "just" or "unjust." We criticize unjust social arrangements. For these reasons, we must examine Justice more closely than Temperance or Fortitude. Another reason for studying Justice more carefully is the complexity of the relationships involved in achieving justice.

ii. Justice in General

[350]   There is a well established definition of Justice, expressed in imperative forms as, "Give every man his due" or "Give every man what is his own." St. Thomas acknowledges this formula but in fact substitutes a more complex and, I think, a more accurate one. Justice is the right relation between human beings with regard to goods and services. This definition presents Justice as a three-term relationship which may be diagrammed as follows:

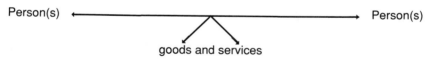

goods and services

This definition also emphasizes why Justice is the social virtue; it displays the patterns of human relations underlying Justice.

[351]   Today we have translated most justice relationships into "rights" language. Thus I say, "I have a right to this piece of property." The inadequacy of this statement can be seen by asking what it would mean if there were no other people. In order to understand a justice relationship it is necessary to identify two human terms in the given relationship.

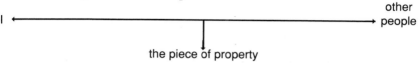

the piece of property

[352]   The simplification of a justice relationship into a two-term relationship and "rights" language did not exist in the thirteenth century. However, by Suarez's time (1548-1617) the rights language was widely accepted, though what we call a "right" was then called a "subjective right" (*jus subjectivum*). Thus, all the rights enumerated in the Universal Declaration of Human Rights issued by the U.N. can be restated in the three-term pattern. The rights language is so well established in all modern languages and so easy to use that no one would dream of rejecting it.

[353]   However, since I am trying to clarify St. Thomas's position, I will continue to use his analysis, which, moreover, I consider philosophically more accurate and enlightening than the two-term analysis.

[354]   Because it involves two human terms, Justice is a more objective virtue, that is, the just thing (*justum*) can be objectively discussed in itself. Thus we can speak of a just contract, a just compensation, a just law. The objectivity of Justice makes it easy to make Justice part of a legal system and to deal with it in the public forum.

[355]   There are different kinds of Justice which we will now consider.

iii. Commutative Justice

[356]   In Commutative Justice the relationship is between two individual persons or groups of individual persons, and the basic form of the relationship is one of arithmetical equality. For example, a person buys a candy bar for fifty cents. If the price is just, the candy bar and the fifty cents are equal in value and each person is satisfied. The same would apply if a person bought a car from a corporation (= a group of individuals).

[357]   If a person buys an object represented by the seller as a genuine diamond and pays the price usual for such an object, when, in fact, the object is an imitation, the transaction is not equal and is unjust. It can easily be seen that Commutative Justice is the Justice basis for all commercial transactions and, as such, is largely incorporated into commercial law.

iv. Distributive Justice

[358]   Distributive Justice orders the relationship between individuals or groups of individuals and the whole community or the state. It has to do with the distribution of goods, benefits, burdens, etc. to the citizens of the state. This type of Justice regulates the sharing in the Common Good. The pattern of Justice here requires a proportionate distribution rather than the arithmetical equality of Commutative Justice. Thus, taxes should be levied proportionately to the ability to pay. Medicare benefits (or any other public health benefits) should be proportionate to the needs of each individual. An economic system which keeps some citizens living in poverty while others live in high luxury is an unjust system. If a judicial system is harsh on blacks or Latinos but goes easy on whites or the rich, that judicial system violates Distributive Justice.

v. Contributive Justice

[359]   Contributive Justice is, in a sense, the reverse of Distributive Justice, since it deals with the obligations of individual citizens or groups of citizens to contribute to the Common Good, the community, or the State. Thus the requirements of this Justice are also proportionate. For example, in times of war, different sorts of persons make different kinds of services to the war effort. Able-bodied young men serve in the armed forces; older men may form a Home Guard as was done in the towns of England when a Nazi invasion was feared. In the second World War, women worked in munitions

plants; scientists were exempted from military service to work on weapons systems, etc. The obligation to pay taxes comes under Contributive Justice as does the obligation of the rich to contribute to charitable enterprises.

vi. Social Justice

[360]   Social Justice is a modern term which is used in various senses by different authors. In general, it seems to be a combination of Distributive and Contributive Justice under the concept of the common good. It embraces all the Justice relationships found in a society (political, economic, social, etc.). For St. Thomas Social Justice is not a special kind of Justice.

vii. Right Relationship

[361]   It should be noted that all forms of Justice include the notion of a "right" relationship but do not supply a calibrated standard by which the "right" relationship can be determined. The rightness must be determined by Prudential Judgment of Practical Reason. In many cases injustice can readily be recognized. For example, if one man is executed for drunken driving while another, equally guilty, is merely reprimanded, it is clear that Justice has miscarried. More complicated cases can only be determined by a person possessing not only a good ethical or jurisprudential education but also a strong virtue of Prudence. This is why Aristotle said that the judge should be Justice Personified. Many of the judicial principles which Ronald Dworkin stresses so much are simply generalized prudential judgments of Justice. For example, "No one should profit from his crime." An appeal to "Natural Justice" requires the same sort of prudential insight.

4. Prudence

[362]   In modern English "Prudence" often has a pejorative meaning, connoting extreme caution, timidity in acting and playing it safe. These interpretations must be rejected if one is to understand the cardinal moral virtue of Prudence.

[363]   Prudence is the acquired skill of making the right moral choice in individual cases, of properly applying a general moral rule to an individual case, or of selecting the right means to a good end. It is a perfection of the Practical Reason and so provides the rational elements in the other virtues. Without Prudence, there can

be no Temperance, no Fortitude, and no Justice. Without Prudence we cannot regulate our sensual appetites aright, we cannot distinguish courageous acts from rash and foolhardy ones; without Prudence our decisions in matters of Justice will be confused and erratic.

[364]   As we have seen, each of the other virtues (Temperance, Fortitude, and Justice) has a distinctive set of proper objects. Thus Temperance deals with our sensual appetites while Justice deals with relationships between human beings. Prudence cooperates in every moral decision. That is why Prudence is a perfection of the Practical Reason which is ordered to action and to the good.

[365]   The activity of the virtue of Prudence results in the prudential judgment. The process leading to the prudential judgment may be quite simple or very complex, but, in any case, Prudence makes use of insight.

[366]   Insight is the direct apprehension of an intelligibility, whether of fact or of value. There are no rules for the development of an insight. One can only reflect on and consider a variety of factors until understanding emerges. A simple case may illustrate this: A $1,000 fine for parking ten minutes overtime in a metered parking place is clearly a violation of Distributive Justice. But there is no calibrated standard, no mathematical formula to prove that.

[367]   Some consider "insight" to be simply a gut reaction or an expression of feeling or of prejudice. Such reactions do happen, but they are not instances of insight.

[368]   In order to make a genuine prudential judgment one must possess the other virtues. One who has a disordered sex life cannot make sound judgments in such matters. Passion, infatuation, anger blind the eye of judgment. Thus there is a two-way relationship between Prudence and the other virtues.

[369]   Though insight is characteristic of prudential judgments, the process of moral judgment is generally more complex. One must have knowledge of all the relevant facts, of the moral principles and precepts involved. One may find it necessary to consult experts and persons who are skilled in such matters.

[370]   Some persons have a natural disposition conducive to the development of the virtue of Prudence. But, in any case, experience and practice, study and reflection, consultation and discussion and basic self-honesty are necessary to acquire prudential skill.

[371]   In straightforward cases the prudential judgment may be easy to achieve. There are clear cases of murder or fraud. It is in the hard and complicated cases where Prudence is especially needed. In such cases there are generally a number of heterogeneous factors which have no common denominator and yet must be taken into account. In such cases logic fails and insight must take over.

[372]   In the first instance Prudence is the virtue of each individual who must take responsibility for his own moral decisions. But it can also be used to judge the actions of others. In this way, Prudence becomes the virtue of the counsellor, the confessor, and the spiritual advisor.

[373]   More to our purpose here, we can say that, at least in a sense, Prudence is *the* virtue of the good judge. The judge has to apply the law and judicial doctrine—including "Natural Justice" to individual cases. Reasoning, factual investigation, etc. must precede the judicial prudential judgment, but, in the last analysis, the judge must judge. There are no rules for rule application, otherwise there would be an infinite regress of rules.

[374]   The ancient tradition said that judges should be "Justice Personified." We may add that the judge should be "Prudence Personified."

F. FINAL NOTE ON THE VIRTUES

[375]   As stated above, Prudence is necessary for the other virtues to be truly virtues. But actually all the virtues work together. A judge may make a correct prudential judgment, but it may take considerable courage (Fortitude) to announce it in face of threats from organized crime. One who violates Temperance by using "crack" can hardly make correct prudential judgments. And so forth.

[376]   The possession of all the virtues in some substantial degree constitutes a sound and strong moral character. In part, this answers Plato's question seeking an excellence of human nature as such.

[377]   However, the moral virtues do not constitute the complete perfection of man. From St. Thomas's Christian perspective, human beings achieve full perfection only when they achieve the understanding, appreciation for God in an ultimate loving union. In

this life the love of God and of other human beings is the highest perfection and, at the same time, happiness (though imperfect).

[378]   However, the moral virtues are prerequisite for such a fullness of knowledge and love.

SECTION 12:
HAPPINESS, THE LAST END OF MAN

[379]   St. Thomas says (q. 90, a. 2, c.) that the last end of human beings is happiness. He uses this doctrine as part of the basis for arguing that all laws must be directed to the Common Good.

[380]   An immediate warning is in order. This doctrine is not hedonism. St. Thomas is not thinking of simply a surfeit of pleasures, fulfillment of unbridled sensual appetites, or total self-regarding and selfish actions. In fact, the happiness that St. Thomas was thinking of may involve acceptance of pain, self-denial, self-sacrifice, or even of death. There is a long philosophical tradition that the just or good man is the happy man. Plato said that the just man is happy even when he is being unjustly tortured. There is indeed a seeming paradox here as there was in Christ's statement, "He who saves his life shall lose it and he who loses his life shall save it." The ordination to happiness is the intrinsic finality of human living. Everyone desires to be happy. At the same time, human beings also have an ordination to the good, to not merely private and personal good but to good in general. We are able to applaud the man who, at the risk of his life, rescues children from a burning building. We can condemn a brutal dictator even though he doesn't touch us personally in any way. We can give time, effort, money to drives for shelter for the poor, food for the hungry, and so forth.

[381]   In the long run the ordination to the good and the desire of happiness converge. Happiness turns out to be the fulfillment of human nature in its noblest aspirations.

[382]   Thus, while we have an intrinsic drive to happiness, we also guide our human actions according to what is right and what is wrong, according to generosity and love, according to the fulfillment of our desire for knowledge and love. Therefore, throughout

our lives we are faced with making many decisions in which the motivation must be the objective good and not simply the desire for happiness.

[383]   The fulfillment of our various appetites can contribute to our happiness only if they are regulated by reason and controlled through grace. Then, in the first instance, they will achieve goodness, both personal and objective.

[384]   The acquisition of the moral virtues to a high degree is, in fact, the development of a strong moral character. The moral perfection of man, the level of the moral virtues, is not, of course, the complete fulfillment of human nature. But the moral virtues make it possible for a person to resist those vices which destroy human nature and prevent any further fulfillment.

[385]   But the highest realization of man's potentialities, the highest fulfillment of human nature, lies in the achievement of knowledge and love. We are able to know, understand, appreciate; we are able to love in a reciprocal but unselfish love. The highest fulfillment, knowledge and love, consists of the understanding and love of other persons, most eminently, of course, in the knowledge and love of the most loveable, most knowable, most magnificent thing in all existence, namely God. This achievement gives us the highest happiness, but it's a happiness that is not fundamentally self-regarding because both knowledge and love are attached to objects which, for the most part, are other.

[386]   In St. Thomas's doctrine, in this life we are only capable of achieving imperfect happiness (*beatitudo imperfecta*) and to achieve happiness in this life we need many things besides the per se fulfillments which I've just mentioned. For example, in order to live a virtuous life and in order to achieve knowledge and love we have to have energy, we have to have time; consequently, we need a great deal of temporal support. Still, even in this life, a loveless life is an unhappy life. Aristotle has said, and St. Thomas agrees, "No man can be happy without friends."

[387]   Perfect happiness (*beatitudo perfecta*) can only be achieved in the next life through knowing, understanding, and loving union with God. We are destined to participate in the mysterious life, the active knowing and loving of the Holy Trinity itself. And that will be perfect happiness and perfect unselfishness because we

will be completely focused on the object of our knowledge and love and the source of our happiness.

[388]   Now to return to *q*. 90, *a*. 2: every member of the temporal civil society desires happiness. Society comes into being to provide for the temporal happiness of its members and so the common desire or the common purpose of all members of the temporal civil society is to reach happiness, at least the imperfect happiness of which St. Thomas speaks. Thus, society is ordered not to the happiness of some people and not others, but to the happiness of every member of that society. The society is ordered to the common happiness and this is what is meant by the Common Good. The happiness to which the society is ordered is not an aggregate happiness; that is to say, St. Thomas would reject the often stated goal of the greatest happiness of the greatest number. For this goal could be achieved through extreme happiness on the part of some while others, at the other end of the spectrum, may be living in misery. Nor is the common happiness and therefore the Common Good to which society is ordered a state as something superior to, over and above the individual members of that state. Thus, the fascist elevation of the state and subordination of all citizens to it is rejected by Thomistic doctrine.

[389]   Of course, the civil state cannot and should not try to provide all the things that its individual members need in order to fulfill themselves and achieve temporal happiness. Many things must be left to the individual citizen who must enjoy a large measure of self-determination and freedom. This also is necessary for happiness. But the Common Good provides things that individuals by themselves or in voluntary organizations cannot achieve. Thus, St. Thomas says that there are many things in the Common Good and among them are peace and order. Clearly, experience shows us that individuals or groups of individuals within society cannot guarantee the peace and order of that society. This has to be done by a central authority operating through laws designed to maintain peace and order. Peace and order are primary requisites for human happiness and well-being. Nobody can fulfill himself and achieve happiness if he is living in anarchy in which there is daily danger of being injured, oppressed, robbed, tortured, or even killed.

[390]   Therefore, not everything requisite for human temporal happiness can be the object of civil positive law. But every civil

positive law has to be ordered to the common happiness of the citizens.

[391]   Civil positive law cannot command people to have the proper internal disposition or to act for the right motives. Yet, St. Thomas believes that by repressing vices and ordering the acts of some of the virtues, positive law can lead people to accept and develop virtues, which, he believes, is, in fact, the ultimate intent of every lawgiver (*q.* 96, *a.* 3, reply 2). Since virtue is requisite for man's ultimate happiness, the civil positive law can, in this way, contribute to his eternal fulfillment.

[392]   Moreover, civil positive law can help provide a community culture within which individuals can more easily work towards their own excellence and happiness (cf. Lon Fuller, *The Morality of Law,* p. 5).

SECTION 13:
THE COMMON GOOD

[393]   In *q.* 90, *a.* 2, St. Thomas teaches that the final cause, the intrinsic finality or purpose of law is the "Common Good." By establishing the Common Good as the final cause of law, he also made it part of his definition of law, since his definition is an explanatory type consisting of the four causes.

[394]   But what is the Common Good? A society's Common Good, in its broadest sense, includes all those things which everyone in the society needs, desires or shares in, either actually or potentially, directly or indirectly (*q.* 94, *a.* 1).

[395]   The citizens share in the Common Good by proportionate justice, that is, they share in the Common Good proportionately to their need or capacity. Thus, Medicare is part of the Common Good, but citizens actually share in it only as they need it. Education is part of the Common Good, but not everyone can be admitted to a Ph.D. program. Police protection is part of the Common Good, but those who are at greater risk like the President of the United States or a judge sentencing leaders of organized crime need more protection than the average citizen.

[396]   There are some things that are always present in the Common Good of any society, however simple or primitive, such as peace and order. But the actual content of the Common Good depends on many factors and can vary from society to society or from time to time in the same society. Universal free education is part of the Common Good of a modern developed country. It would have been impossible in ninth-century France. The country could not have afforded it and only a few would have been able to attend.

[397]   Modern developed societies try to provide universal health care because the people demand it.

[398]   The Common Good of a society is more comprehensive than that portion of it that law can or should provide. It is generally better, whenever possible, that the Common Good be served by private initiatives, whether by individuals or groups. There are many institutions in society that serve the Common Good, such as private universities, medical societies, national organizations of professional people, private foundations, churches, etc. Even private business serves the Common Good—if it fails to, the State can regulate it. The legal system is an instrument of society for the promotion of the Common Good under certain limitations.

[399]   Now the Common Good is the Common Good of all the citizens. It is not the public good of the political state understood in a Fascist manner as something distinct from the people and to which the citizens are ordained.

[400]   The Common Good is not the same as the aggregate of a society's happiness, the greatest happiness of the greatest number. Such an end could leave some of the citizens in great misery. The utilitarians do not envision a true Common Good.

[401]   The Thomistic Common Good is quite different from "social control" which Positivists frequently hold to be the purpose of law. St. Thomas's view is that the coercive force of law is required not to control society as a whole but to force the wicked to do the acts of virtue ordered by the law. Even coercive power is not aimed merely at control. It has the general effect of leading people to acquire the virtue itself by becoming habituated to performing the acts of virtue.

[402]   The law cannot and should not try to direct every aspect of the Common Good. As mentioned above, there are many other institutions and organizations (including voluntary ones) that

contribute in some way or other to the Common Good. However, the law does supervise, in a general way, these other contributions to the Common Good. Thus, while law cannot dictate the detail or the operation of the economic system, it can ensure that the economic system is just.

[403]   The theory of the Common Good has been criticized as being too vague. In St. Thomas the concept of the Common Good is perfectly clear, but its practical realization is open ended. The achievement of the Common Good requires the selection of means which must be flexible to fit the varying changes in human culture. Production and distribution of food is part of the Common Good, but the laws (or customs) regulating this aspect of the Common Good in a hunting and gathering society like that of the pygmies of Africa is very different from the laws which regulate it in a complex advanced civilization like that of the United States. But in each case the effect is to serve the Common Good. An experienced investigator of what legislatures and lawgivers actually do confirms the fact that the Common Good is the final cause of human law.

[404]   The reader may, at this point, find it interesting to re-examine the Preamble to the United States Constitution as stating the final cause of that Constitution and detailing the Common Good envisioned for the Federal Government. "We, the people of the United States, in order to form a more perfect Union, establish justice, insure domestic tranquility, provide for the common defense, promote the general welfare, and secure the blessings of liberty to ourselves and our posterity, do ordain and establish this Constitution for the United States of America."

SECTION 14:
OBLIGATION

[405]   Universally all normal people have a sense or an awareness of *obligation* in the sense that they are bound to, obliged to do certain things and not to do certain other things. Every language has words like *should, ought to, obliged to,* etc. Sometimes the obligation is clearly instrumental. "You have a high fever—you ought

to see your doctor", "You want to get into medical school? Then you ought to take a pre-med program and get high grades." But other obligations bind to actions that are simply good, simply the right thing for human beings to do. "It's wrong to kill your mother." "Keep your promises." Many anthropologists have recognized the universality of obligation. Thus Robert Redfield states: "Everywhere there are recognized obligations, commitments, sentiments and judgments of what is good and what is bad. If we let 'morality' stand for all such judgments and commitments as to what it is felt right or wrong to do, not because it is merely prudential or expedient but because it is in itself right and obligatory, then morality is universal" ("Anthropology's Contribution to the Understanding of Man", p. 16).

A. THE QUESTIONS ABOUT OBLIGATION

[406]   A universal phenomenon requires a universal explanation. This phenomenon is a human phenomenon. Animals do not have obligations; they are programmed to act in certain ways. They act from instinct and in determinate ways. Since the phenomenon of obligation is exclusively a human matter, it must be grounded in or related to something in human nature.

[407]   The nature and source of obligation have been discussed by thinkers of every persuasion, and widely different answers have been given to the questions thereby raised. I will here first discuss the (or a) Thomistic view of the matter. Then I will compare it with some other jurisprudential views.

B. THE THOMISTIC VIEW OF OBLIGATION

[408]   According to St. Thomas, human beings have a natural inclination to the good. This inclination becomes conscious and rational in the first principle of Practical Reason, namely, "Good is to be done; evil is to be avoided." This principle is self-evident and becomes implicitly operational as soon as a human being makes reasonable choices.

[409]   The good which creates the moral obligation is that which is rightly desired, approved, or loved. Subjectively it is the good that is rightly chosen by Right Practical Reason; objectively it

is the good that goes beyond the good of any individual and creates an objective obligation such as the obligation to work for the Common Good whence (in particular) the moral obligation of positive (human) law derives its obligation.

[410]   Some have thought that the substantive precepts of the Natural Law can be deduced or derived from this principle. This is not so. The principle is a formal principle which provides the obligatory force of all the precepts of the Natural Law and all the judgments of Prudence. The most general precepts of the Natural Law—"Harm no person", "Give every person his due", "Maintain moderation in sensual appetites" are self-evident in their own right. From them more particularized precepts can be logically derived. Thus, in *q. 95, a. 2, c.,* St. Thomas states that "Thou shalt not kill" can be derived from the more general precept, "Do no harm to any man." Thus, also, one might derive from the general principle, "Give every man his due" the more limited precept, "Keep your promises."

[411]   Others think the first principle is a tautology. If you define the "good" as that which should be done, the principle at least appears to be a tautology. But the "good" is that which is rightly desired; the principle imposes on this conception of the good the additional idea of "obligation." Thus obligation arises from the attraction of the Good. The explanation just given pertains to the epistemological explanation.

[412]   Metaphysical explanations ultimately terminate in God. And so it does here. In *q. 91, a.* 1, St. Thomas establishes that there exists in God an Eternal Law which is God's master plan for the whole universe and everything in it. All created things are thus a participation in the Eternal Law. By metaphysical "participation" St. Thomas means that the created reality analogously imitates the Divine original, that it is derived from the Divine Model through efficient causality and is ordered to God as to a final cause. Thus, since God is the perfect good, the most desirable good in the universe, every human obligation is based on and is a participation in the primordial obligation to choose and seek the highest Good—God Himself.

C. MORAL OBLIGATION AND POSITIVE (HUMAN) LAW

[413]   In a tight and pregnant article (*q. 96, a.* 4) St. Thomas establishes that just human laws "bind in conscience," that is, that

human laws impose a moral obligation to obey them. The immediate corollary of this is that unjust laws do not per se impose a moral obligation. The reason is that unjust laws fail in an essential element of law. Unjust laws are simply not laws. What the moral law forbids an individual to do cannot be imposed on a group of human beings by positive law.

[414]   John Austin places human law entirely outside of the moral order. The only motive for obeying the law arises from fear of threats of unpleasant consequences if the law is disobeyed. The power of the sovereign is simply the power to carry out those threats. If the people find the laws of the sovereign unbearable, they will rebel. If the revolution succeeds, the sovereign thereby loses his power to make laws. This is in line with Spinoza's doctrine that a tyrant has a natural right to govern as long as he can control his subjects. It is also consonant with Hobbes' theory that the only natural law is the requirement that men enter society and establish an absolute ruler who will restrain by physical power the aggressiveness innate in human beings.

[415]   In John Austin the law itself is referred to simply as an "order" or a "command", thus characterizing it by reference to the sovereign, thus by extrinsic denomination. No intrinsic quality is requisite for a valid law. Thus, the whole nature of the law, as law, is reducible to the sovereign and to his power. The sovereign can make any action legally obligatory. This is why some Positivists maintained that Hitler's laws against the Jews were valid laws and therefore obligatory.

[416]   This emphasis on the physical power runs through the whole history of Anglo-American Positivism, though sometimes softened and muted. In H. L. A. Hart moral obligation arises from social pressure (*The Concept of Law,* pp. 79–88).

[417]   In contrast, St. Thomas maintains that a law, formally and intrinsically, must be a dictate of Practical Right Reason. This means that to be a law, that is, to have binding force or be obligatory, a law must conform to the moral law (i.e., to the Natural Law). No amount of power possessed by a lawgiver can empower him to enact obligatory laws that are intrinsically unjust (*q.* 96, *a.* 4).

[418]   Again, the lawgiver, according to St. Thomas, has the right to make laws only insofar as he represents the people. All legitimate legislative authority comes from the people (*q.* 90, *a.* 3;

q. 97, a. 3, reply 3). The legitimate lawgiver has (moral) authority that rests neither on "habit" nor on physical power.

[419]   For St. Thomas law must be ordered to the Common Good while for Positivists something like social control is often stated as the purpose of rules (both legal and moral). Here again "control" connotes physical force.

[420]   Both St. Thomas and Positivists agree that only valid laws impose obligations. But Positivists have only a technical formalistic requirement for validity, namely, that the law be made by one who has the physical power to punish those who disobey, or is made according to the formal technical requirements established by a *Grundnorm,* a set of general rules or a tradition.

SECTION 15:
A SYNOPSIS OF ST. THOMAS'S DOCTRINE OF NATURAL LAW

A. INTRODUCTION

i. Prenote

[421]   Now that we have covered some of the principles and terminology of Thomistic philosophy, we are in a position to give a preliminary synopsis of St. Thomas's doctrine of Natural Law.

[422]   I accept John Finnis' distinction between Natural Law as a fact of human life and theories or explanations of Natural Law.

[423]   As a fact of human life, Natural Law can be found, at least implicitly and at least in its most general precepts, even in underdeveloped and unreflective societies. In such cases, Natural Law is not formulated or distinguished from mere custom or historical developments. Thus, in a primitive society, the tribal way of life, in which elements of Natural Law can be found, is simply accepted as a *total* way of life.

[424]   When the ancient Greeks developed cosmopolitan travel and trade, they were struck by the great variety of languages, social structures, and customs. The first reflective result was a simplistic relativism. Many philosophers, notably Plato and Aristotle,

reacted against this relativism. They undertook the task of sorting out those things which were of intrinsic value and applied to all human beings and all human societies and, on the other hand, those things which were idiosyncratic to individual societies and were determined simply culturally. Thus, they concluded, for example, that the basic principles of justice were the same in Athens and in Persia—a conviction expressed dramatically in the Greek play *Antigone*—while styles of dress and rules of table etiquette were variable and were morally indifferent.

[425]   What St. Thomas offers us in the *Treatise* is a sophisticated philosophical explanation which emerges from reflection on human life in the light of many major philosophical and religious traditions.

[426]   However, St. Thomas does not provide a complete or detailed defense of Natural Law. There are two major reasons for this.

[427]   First, in the thirteenth century Natural Law was not a matter of controversy; all the leading scholars of Western Europe accepted the Natural Law position.

[428]   Secondly, all of St. Thomas's primary sources maintained Natural Law positions—the Bible, Aristotle, St. Augustine, the *Corpus Juris Civilis*, the Stoics, and the Platonists. However, Natural Law is constantly presupposed throughout the *Treatise* and explicitly dealt with in *q*. 91, *a*. 2 and *q*. 94.

[429]   Nonetheless, St. Thomas is universally recognized as a classic exponent of Natural Law theory.

[430]   The outline offered here is intended as a general introduction which must be filled in by study of St. Thomas's *Treatise*.

[431]   I will use the methodology of the Four Causes to organize this synopsis in a way parallel to St. Thomas's definition of law (in general) developed by him in Question 90.

B. THE PRINCIPLES AND PRECEPTS OF THE NATURAL LAW (THE FORMAL CAUSE)

[432]   The Formal Cause of law as stated in St. Thomas's definition of law is the dictate of Practical Reason promulgated. Viewed as the totality of such dictates, law consists formally of a set of principles and precepts which are promulgated.

[433]   Promulgation is reducible to two categories of causes. Viewed as active promulgating, it is part of the activity of the lawgiver and so belongs to the efficient cause. Viewed as the result of the activity of the efficient cause, it is reducible to the formal cause, the state of being promulgated. In other words, after the activity of promulgating, the result remains promulgated. Because of this double function of promulgation, I do what St. Thomas did, namely, treat promulgation in a separate unit.

[434]   Of this set of rules, the primary principle is that good is to be done and evil avoided. This is the first principle of Practical Reason and so of the entire moral order. It is a product of the Practical Intellect of human beings in the second stage of promulgation.

[435]   This is not the first principle in the sense that any secondary principles or precepts can be derived or deduced from it. Rather, it is so called because it supplies the obligatory character to the entire moral order [405–406].

[436]   General substantive precepts of the Natural Law are likewise self-evident. These precepts are such as, "Do no harm to any person," "Give every man his due." Many other precepts can be derived by a quasi-deductive process from the general substantive principles.

[437]   Many more particularized precepts are derived by combining a contingent factor with a secondary precept. These can be changed as circumstances change. Thus the moralist's view of taking interest changed after the medieval period in Europe because of the change in Europe's financial system.

[438]   The application of general precepts to individual cases requires a special ability called the virtue of Prudence. In many cases application can be made only by a prudential judgment. This is an extension of the insight into Natural Law [362–374].

[439]   In fact, changing circumstances often require the elaboration of new secondary principles. The effect of the vast expansion of medical procedures on moral discussion furnishes a good example.

C. THE COMMON GOOD OF THE NATURAL LAW
(THE FINAL CAUSE)

[440]   St. Thomas's definition of law requires that the essential purpose (= final cause) of law be the Common Good. To

what Common Good, then, is the Natural Law ordered? According to St. Thomas, the Natural Law is *intrinsically* ordered to the Common Good of all human beings. This Common Good is happiness, imperfect happiness in this life, and perfect happiness in the next life.

[441]   It is important to note that the Natural Law is not a sort of extrinsic test imposed by God for which God then gives a reward, much as a parent might say, "If you graduate with an A average, I will buy you a sports car." The Natural Law is intrinsic to human beings and is a simple recognition that, if a human being wishes to grow to full stature of personal excellence, the rules according to which one must achieve his own personal excellence and happiness [379–393] and so also contribute to the universal Common Good, he must observe the rules. One of the many misunderstandings of Natural Law that occurs in the Positivist critique is precisely viewing Natural Law as an arbitrary creation of God which conflicts with the private purposes of human beings (H. L. A. Hart, *The Concept of Law,* p. 186).

[442]   Certainly, within the ambit of the Natural Law, there are many possible personal choices. But it is obvious that, if a person chooses a purpose such as a life of drug addiction or as a member of Murder Inc., he will be destroying his humanity and so violating the Natural Law, or, conversely, one can say that he is violating the Natural Law and so destroying his humanity and his happiness. According to St. Thomas, God adds a penalty, as in legal sanctions, to be sure that human beings are motivated to work for their own good. This situation is similar to that of a parent who tells a child that he will be spanked if he does not brush his teeth. The real *reason* for brushing one's teeth is to protect one's teeth; the *motive* is avoiding the spanking.

[443]   So also the real reason for discovering and obeying the Natural Law is love of the good—ultimately—of God and for one's own realization of personal good. In the good human being, this *reason* becomes the *motive*. "Love casts out fear."

D. THE MATERIAL CAUSE OF NATURAL LAW

[444]   What is it that the Natural Law "forms" in a way analogous to the way in which the arrangement of the watch forms

the parts into a watch or to the way in which the shape of Lincoln's head "forms" the marble, making it a statue? A human act that is conformed to a precept of the Natural Law is thereby molded or formed into a moral act and a moral act of a definite kind.

[445]   In civil (human) law, the Material Cause is human acts *in society* and insofar as they can be dealt with in the public (external) forum. It should be remembered that St. Thomas's definition of law is analogous as referring to the major types of law (Eternal, Divine, Natural, Positive).

E. THE EFFICIENT CAUSE OF NATURAL LAW

[446]   Since the Natural Law arises from the consideration of human beings in their full experiential concrete reality, and since God, through creation, is the Efficient Cause of human beings, the remote Efficient Cause of Natural Law is God himself. God, however, does not imprint on the intellect or "heart" of man the precepts of the Natural Law but, instead, endows man with a Practical Reason by which man can recognize and formulate the basic principles and general precepts of the Natural Law. Man himself is the immediate Efficient Cause of the Natural Law.

[447]   The Natural Law is, therefore, not to be compared to the instincts of the animals which are blindly carried out. Man has an insightful and conscious recognition of the Natural Law and of the good to which he is ordered by nature. He freely conforms his human acts to the Natural Law or freely refuses to do so.

F. PROMULGATION OF THE NATURAL LAW

[448]   According to St. Thomas, promulgation belongs to the essence of law. Natural Law, therefore, must be promulgated to all human beings, as they are all under the jurisdiction of God.

[449]   Promulgation of the Natural Law takes place in two phases. First, God establishes the basis of the Natural Law when he creates human beings, for the Natural Law is simply a formulation, the rules of which are the appropriate guides for a free rational creature.

[450]   Note that the Natural Law is not a code extrinsically imposed on man, an external law, the observance of which will result in an extrinsic reward. The Natural Law is intrinsic to human beings and guides them according to their own nature to the full development of them as human beings.

[451]   The second phase of promulgation consists in man's recognition and formulation of the principles implied by the existence of human beings. Man, in part, promulgates the Natural Law to himself. Thus, human beings become aware, implicitly or explicitly, of the basic principle of the Natural Law, that "good is to be done; evil is to be avoided" as well as the most general precepts of the Natural Law, such as, "Harm no innocent person." According to St. Thomas, these general principles and precepts cannot totally be abolished from the mind of man (q. 94, a. 6). The less general precepts, the applications of Natural Law, can be abolished from the mind of man and, indeed, are explicitly known only to the wise and learned.

[452]   A bad disposition, vices, and a bad education can obfuscate much of the Natural Law.

[453]   None of this should be taken to imply that human beings have formal innate moral ideas or moral principles. What is innate is the Practical Intellect and the habit of first principles. Guided by these primary precepts, human beings have to work out the detailed and particularized rules. And, finally, in applying these rules to individual cases, one needs the virtue of Prudence.

[454]   For a full explanation of the Natural Law, St. Thomas reduces it back to God as its creator and first propagator. But ordinary people, in knowing the Natural Law in its self-evident principles, do not necessarily refer the Natural Law to God. In fact, even at the philosophical level, the reference to God need not appear. Aristotle, for example, worked out a complete Natural Law ethic without formal reference to God or religion.

[455]   St. Thomas maintains that a complete explanation requires that God must be seen as the ultimate source of the Natural Law inasmuch as this law is a participation in the Eternal Law, its model, in the mind of God (q. 91, a. 2).

[456]   There has been a tendency among some Natural Law thinkers to identify the Natural Law with the Divine Law which is the Law revealed by God in the Old and New Testaments. St. Thomas keeps the Natural Law and the Divine Law distinct as arising, as far

as human beings are concerned, from two different acts of God, though, of course, many precepts appear in both.

[457]   John Austin identified Natural Law and the Divine Law, denying human beings an independent access to Natural Law and also by excluding both Divine Law and Natural Law from the province of jurisprudence.

G. THE EXEMPLAR CAUSE OF NATURAL LAW

[458]   According to St. Thomas, God created the universe, intelligently, freely, and lovingly. Since He creates intelligently, and since the range of possible universes is infinite, God chooses the universe He intends to create and so produces in His mind a pattern of all the details of the universe He actually creates. This pattern is called the Eternal Law, which is somewhat misleading since it contains many things (types of things) that are not laws properly so called. However, it does include the prototype of all laws.

[459]   St. Thomas then distinguishes the Divine Law, the Natural Law, and the Positive (or human, man-made) Law.

[460]   The Divine Law is that part of the Eternal Law that is revealed in the Bible, e.g., in the Ten Commandments, the Sermon on the Mount, etc.

[461]   The Natural Law is also derived from the Eternal Law by way of creation of human nature and recognition by the human Practical Reason. This is why St. Thomas calls the Natural Law a "participation" in the Eternal Law.

[462]   Human Law is derived from the Natural Law and so also indirectly from the Eternal Law. However, the Human Law is derived from the Natural Law in two very different ways. Human laws embody, almost directly, the general precepts of the Natural Law, e.g., in the statutes against murder, fraud, etc. But there are many things that the Natural Law, in its high generality, does not determine. These are left to the active determination by the human lawgiver. Thus the Natural Law has nothing determinate to say about driving on the right or left, speed limits, income tax percentages, the requirements for a valid will, etc., although the Natural Law does require that all human determinations be just and serve the Common Good.

[463]   To repeat, the primary Exemplar Cause (extrinsic formal cause) of Natural Law is the Eternal Law; the proximate Exemplar Cause is the recognition and formulation of the principles and precepts of the Natural Law in the human Practical Reason.

H. NATURAL LAW AND POSITIVE LAW

[464]   Natural Law is the "rule and measure" of all human acts. Now, Positive Law is made by men through their human acts, and Positive Law is also a "rule and measure" of some human acts. Hence, Positive Law, in its development and in its precepts, must conform to Natural Law. For example, the Natural Law requires that human acts be just; therefore the human lawgiver must act justly and human laws must be just.

[465]   In a sense, therefore, all Positive Laws are derived from the Natural Law. All political and legal institutions have a moral basis. However, Positive Law is derived from Natural Law in two quite different ways.

[466]   The first way is by a substantively quasi-deduction. For example, the legal statute against murder can be derived from the general precept of the Natural Law, "Do no harm to any man." In modern legal codes this sort of derivation is very limited when compared to the second way.

[467]   The second way of deriving Positive Law from Natural Law is by way of what St. Thomas calls "determination." The Natural Law is very general in its substantive precepts. The human lawgiver must take care of a wide variety of particular and detailed needs. Thus the Natural Law says nothing about right- or left-hand driving; it determines no speed limit; it does not specify the legal requirements for a valid contract. There is an enormous number of such "determinations" and they depend immediately on the authority of the human lawgiver and his Practical Reason. Of course, such determinations must conform to the general requirements of Natural Law. Thus the human lawgiver determines the income tax scale, but a scale placing a heavy burden on the very poor while lightly touching the rich would violate Distributive Justice (q. 95, a. 2, c.).

[468]   Of course, the scope of Positive Law is restricted in other ways. Positive Law must serve the Common Good, not the

good of an individual or of a favored class. Nor can Positive Law regulate the internal life of man, his motives, attitudes, and thoughts (*q.* 96, *a.* 3, Reply 1).

I. NATURAL LAW AND NATURAL RIGHTS

[469]   One may be surprised that in a treatise dealing with law and justice there is no mention of "rights." All modern political and legal documents that are in any way concerned with fundamental Natural Law speak "rights" language.

[470]   The Declaration of Independence speaks of "unalienable rights," of the right to "life, liberty, and the pursuit of happiness." Blackstone identified the three basic rights of "free Englishmen" as life, liberty, and property. The U.N. issued a *Declaration of Universal Human Rights.*

[471]   The historical fact is that in the thirteenth century the use of the term "right" in this sense did not exist. "Rights," as we call them, were expressed in precepts, principles, and relationships. The "right to life" appears in the precept, "Do not kill innocent people." Justice rights were described as "the right relationship between persons."

[472]   In the thirteenth century, the term "right" (*jus*) was generally used in an objective sense, the just thing. The modern usage was well-established by the time of Suarez (1548–1617), though at first, in the new usage rights were called subjective rights (*jus subjectivum*) since they seemed to inhere in a subject, that is, in the person who can say, "I have a right. . . ." Today, Natural Law theorists accept the modern rights language and have no difficulty in deriving human rights from their foundation in St. Thomas and in other earlier Natural Law theorists. (See John Finnis, *Natural Law and Natural Rights,* pp. 199–205.)

[473]   Today, therefore, one of the distinguishing positions of Natural Law is that human rights are "unalienable" rights possessed by human beings, precisely because they are human beings and possessed prior to any society or Positive Law, while Positivists derive rights from social pressure or Positive Law.

CHAPTER IV
ST. THOMAS'S SOURCES
AND HIS USE OF THEM

SECTION 1:
THE USE OF AUCTORITATES

A. INTRODUCTION

[474]   When one looks into a medieval text for the first time, he is usually surprised by the constant quotation of other authors. One might expect frequent quotations from the Bible, but the quotations range through a comparatively remarkable list of writers, Christian, pagan, and Jewish and books originally in various languages—Latin, Greek, Arabic, and Hebrew. These quotations were called *auctoritates,* that is, authoritative quotations, and those who produced them were called *auctores,* that is, authorities outstanding in their own fields; thus, in theology, the primary *auctores* were the biblical authors, the Fathers of the Church, and, above all, St. Augustine; in philosophy, Aristotle (who was so highly regarded that he was referred to simply as "the Philosopher"); in music, Boethius; in geometry, Euclid; in medicine, Galen, and so forth.

[475]   To a superficial reader this method appears as a slavish subservience to human authority. "Aristotle said it, therefore it's true; St. Augustine said it, therefore I believe it." Actually, it is nothing of the sort. St. Thomas knew exactly what he was doing in his handling of *auctoritates.* A scholarly study of his works displays this clearly. But he also explicitly said that philosophy was not about the opinions of men but about the truth of reality.

[476]   In evaluating the evidential value of *auctoritates,* St. Thomas makes a sharp distinction between those drawn from the Bible and those derived from the writings of human scholars like Aristotle or St. Augustine.

[477]   In theology, since it depends not on human data but on data revealed by God, *Auctoritates* from the records of that Revelation, namely the biblical writings, are decisive. The *auctoritates* that are of solely human origin yield the weakest of all arguments.

[478]   Let us express this in St. Thomas's own words: . . .

. . . to argue from *auctoritates* is most proper to this discipline [i.e., to theology], for the principles of this discipline are known by Revelation and therefore *auctoritates* of those to whom the Revelation was made must be believed. Nor does this derogate from the dignity of the discipline for, although arguments from human *auctoritates* are the weakest of all arguments, arguments drawn from an *auctoritas* based on Revelation are the most effective." (*S. T., q.* 1, *a.* 8, Reply 2)

[479]   Some additional quotations stating the same evaluation are cited in *Toward Understanding Saint Thomas* (p. 139):

The source arising from authority based on human reason [is] the weakest" (*Ia Pars,* q. 1, a. 8, ad 2um). "To prove by means of authority is not to prove demonstratively, but to form an opinion on a thing through faith . . ." (*Quodl.* III, a. 31, ad 1um). "When sacred doctrine utilizes philosophical writings, it does not admit of them because of the authority of those who wrote them, but rather because of that which they formally contain" (*In De trin.,* q. 2, a. 3, ad 8um). And in the same vein WILLIAM OF AUVERGNE: "Because I know the source arising from authority to be solely dialectic, and to produce faith only . . ." (*De an.,* c. 1). ALBERT THE GREAT: "In theology, the source arising from authority is inspired by the Spirit of truth...; in the other sciences, the source arising from authority is weak, weaker than the others" (*Summa theol.,* Ia Pars, q. 5, m. 2, in *AMOO* [sic.], XXXI (1895), 24 B). ". . . Otherwise, if the master determines the question on the strength of bare authorities, the auditor, to be sure, will have a certainty that the thing is so, but he will have acquired no science or understanding and he will leave empty in mind." (*Quodl.* IV, a. 18)

[480]   We may now illustrate this doctrine.

[481]   With regard to human science, I may believe that the sum of the angles of a triangle is equal to two right angles because a recognized geometrician tells me to (*ex auctoritate*) without my knowing how to prove it. When one learns how to prove it then one really knows the matter scientifically. But, when I am dealing with the doctrine of the Holy Trinity, I can only know this through *auctoritates* from the Bible, not by human reason.

[482]   If now we make a cursory examination of the four articles of *q.* 90, we discover that although in the total Question

there are *auctoritates,* in the *Corpora* (where St. Thomas establishes his own doctrine) there is only one *auctoritas* and this one is not used as a part of a decisive argument but rather as an *unde* type of *auctoritas* [493–495].

[483]   Now we will analyze the various principal ways in which *auctoritates* function in St. Thomas's writings, using examples from the *Treatise.* The reader should follow the discussion with parallel reading of the portions of the *Treatise* referred to.

B. THE FUNCTION OF *AUCTORITATES* IN ARGUMENTATION

[484]   One of the primary uses of *auctoritates* is to serve as a basis for argumentation. In this use, the *auctoritas* serves as a major, or, less frequently, as a minor in deductive reasoning, i.e., in a syllogism. For this purpose, the *auctoritas* is taken, at least tentatively, to be true and certain.

[485]   This probative use of *auctoritates* is most frequent in the Objections. This is most appropriate since the Objections present arguments from other *auctores* and traditions which St. Thomas must take into account. Also, the appearance of apparently divergent views in the Objections enables St. Thomas to add nuanced explanations in the Replies which clarify and extend the positive presentation of the *Corpora.*

[486]   I have just said that the truth and certitude of the *auctoritas* is, at least tentatively, assumed. St. Thomas, as we shall see, has various techniques for dealing with objections based on *auctoritates,* but here we must make a distinction between Scriptural *auctoritates* and those arising from human opinion. In the latter case the truth of the *auctoritas* itself may be challenged but, with regard to Scriptural *auctoritates,* it is the interpretation or application that can be questioned, and, to this extent, even a Scriptural *auctoritas* has a "wax nose."

[487]   *Q. 93, a. 2, obj.* 1 provides an example:

> It seems that the Eternal Law is not known to everyone. For, as the Apostle says (1 Corinth., ii, 11), "the things that are of God, no one knows except the Spirit of God." But the Eternal Law is an idea in the divine mind. Therefore, it is unknown to everyone except God alone.

The Scriptural *auctoritas,* "The things that are of God, no man knows, but the Spirit of God" is the major of the argument. When the minor is added, "But the Eternal Law is something existing in the mind of God," the conclusion follows, "The Eternal Law is not known to all but only to God."

[488]   In replying, St. Thomas distinguishes thus: We cannot know the things of God in themselves, but we can know them in their effects. He supports his distinctions with another Scriptural *auctoritas.* Thus the Scriptural texts stand firm, but their opposition to St. Thomas's doctrine is removed. Here is the text itself:

> We cannot know the things that are of God, as they are in themselves; but they are made known to us in their effects, according to Rom. i. 20: *The invisible things of God . . . are clearly seen, being understood by the things that are made.*

[489]   In *q.* 94, *a.* 1, *obj.* 1 we find an example in which an Aristotelian *auctoritas* is the basis of the argument:

> It would seem that the natural law is a habit, because, as the Philosopher says (*Ethic.* ii. 5), "There are three things in the soul, power, habit, and passion." But the natural law is not any power of the soul nor is it one of the passions, as can be seen by going through them one by one. Therefore, the natural law is a habit.

[490]   The argument rests on taking the Aristotelian text to mean that there are *only* three things in the soul. Thus, if the natural law is not the power or a passion, it must be a habit.

[491]   In the Reply, St. Thomas says that Aristotle intended the text quoted to list only those things that are in the soul *as principles of human acts.* There are other things in the soul and so the argument fails. (The same point is made in *q.* 90, *a.* 1, *obj.* and reply 2.)

C. A NON-EVIDENTIAL USE OF *AUCTORITATES*

[492]   St. Thomas has one highly stylized use of *auctoritates* in which they play no logical role in any argument and which is easily identified.

[493]   The common pattern for this use consists of the following elements: First, there is an argument or explanation that is

logically complete in itself, based simply on reasons without the support of any *auctoritas*. Second, there is a verbal signal that indicates that the following *auctoritas* is based on the reasons just presented in the argument. The commonest verbal signals are these: *unde* ("hence" or "wherefore"), *et ideo* ("and therefore"), *et propter hoc* ("and for this reason"). These indicators are not always so used, but, in this pattern, there is always an indicator of this sort. Third, there follows an *auctoritas* that repeats or amplifies the conclusion of the argument just presented. The *auctoritas* often has a rhetorical or even poetical quality that not only confirms the conclusion but embellishes it, much as English writers used to use apt quotations from the "Bard," i.e., Shakespeare. Fourth, because of the nature of the pattern here developed, the *auctoritas* comes at the end of a *Corpus* or of a significant unit within the *Corpus*. Now, the following example is from *q.* 97, *a.* 2, *c.* First there is a reasoned argument (without any supporting *auctoritas*) that concludes as follows:

> ... human law is rightly changed insofar as the Common Good is thereby promoted. However, a change in law, simply in itself, is somewhat detrimental to the common welfare inasmuch as the observance of law is greatly supported by custom, since what is done against a common custom, even though trivial of itself, is looked upon as quite serious. Hence, when law is changed, the binding power of law is diminished inasmuch as the custom is abolished. Hence, human law should not be changed unless the damage done thereby to the common welfare is compensated for by some other benefit. And this happens when some very great and most evident benefit comes from the new law, or when there is the greatest necessity or when either the customary law clearly contains injustice or when its observation is extremely harmful.

[494]   The complicated reasoned argument is now complete, with its own demonstrative evidence.

[495]   Next there follows a verbal indicator *unde* ("Hence" or "Wherefore"), then an *auctoritas* from the "Jurist" (from the *Corpus Juris Civilis*) which states the conclusion just reached in different words. And with this, the *Corpus* is concluded.

[496]   As stated above, this use of *auctoritates* is most common in the *Corpora*. Yet it is found also in Objections and in Replies;

in fact, the very first Article of *q.* 90, *obj.* 3 furnishes a clear example: "Further, the law moves those who are subject to it to act aright. But it belongs properly to the will to move to act, as is evident from what has been said above [*q.* 9, *a.* 1]. Therefore law pertains, not to the reason, but to the will." Up to this point the argument is based on the nature of the will and is logically complete. However, St. Thomas adds: ". . . according to what the Jurist also says (*Lib. i. ff., De Const. Prin. leg.* i.): Whatever pleases the sovereign has force of law," a well-known and famous principle drawn from the *Corpus Juris Civilis* which, in fact, simply repeats the conclusion of the argument without itself being part of the argument. Thus the *auctoritas* not only repeats and confirms the conclusion in a striking phrase, but it ties the objection into the whole tradition of imperial rule (which, in a Christian context, becomes the doctrine of the Divine Right of Kings).

[497]   I have called this use "non-evidential" because it is quite clear that the *auctoritas* is not part of the argument. It is much more difficult to identify the positive contribution made by the *auctoritas*. Generally, it appears to confirm the argument and to add emphasis, dignity, and embellishment to a rather jejune text.

[498]   This use also makes us aware of how little St. Thomas depends on *auctoritates* when he is establishing non-theological conclusions. Thus, in the four *Corpora* that constitute *q.* 90, there is only one *auctoritas*. The reason for this is that the definition of law which is the upshot of these four *Corpora* is non-theological. The definition is derived by applying philosophical principles to the empirical data found in legal systems.

D. ST. THOMAS'S TECHNIQUE IN DEALING WITH *AUCTORITATES* PRESENTED IN THE OBJECTIONS

[499]   It is obvious that what is done in a Reply is, to some extent, dictated and controlled by what has been presented in the corresponding objection. When an *auctoritas* is the logical basis for the objection, St. Thomas is forced to deal with the *auctoritas* itself.

St. Thomas respects *auctoritates* because of the standing of their *auctores*. He therefore tends to give them a "reverential" or "benign" interpretation. Moreover, his dialectical method leads him to look for some truth even in objections. Hence, he has a variety of techniques for dealing with various *auctoritates*.

[500]   St. Thomas frequently uses a technique that is distinctive of Scholastic scholars, namely, making relevant distinctions. Thus, in the very first objection of *q*. 90, *a*. 1, an *auctoritas* from St. Paul is used to show that law does not pertain to reason. St. Thomas distinguishes two different meanings for the term "law," an essential meaning which defines law as he is dealing with it in the *Corpus* and a derivative (by participation) meaning which is used in the *auctoritas*. Thus the standing of the *auctoritas* is protected but its adversarial force is eliminated.

[501]   Again, in *q*. 93, *a*. 2, *obj*. 1, St. Thomas argues that we cannot know the things of God. St. Thomas replies with a distinction: We cannot know the things of God in themselves (this validates the *auctoritas*), but we can know them in their effects (this maintains St. Thomas's position).

[502]   Sometimes St. Thomas points out and denies an assumption made in the objection. In *obj*. 2 of *q*. 90, *a*. 1, the argument assumes that when Aristotle says that there are three things in the soul, Aristotle meant there are only these three things in the soul. St. Thomas argues that there are many other things in the soul, hence denying the validity of the argument while explaining that, in the text, Aristotle is listing only those things that are principles of human acts, thus explaining why, in this text, Aristotle mentions only three things. Thus, the integrity of the text is maintained while its logical relevance is removed.

[503]   Sometimes St. Thomas adds a qualification to the text of the objection without denying the positive assertion of the objection. Thus, in replying to *q*. 90, *a*. 1, *obj*. 3, St. Thomas grants the *auctoritas* provided what is willed by the sovereign is in accordance with reason. Again, the *auctoritas* is saved but its adversarial force is eliminated.

[504]   Sometimes St. Thomas appeals to the context of an *auctoritas* to confirm his own analysis. Thus in *q*. 90, *a*. 3, Reply 1, after distinguishing the *auctoritas* presented in the objection, he

says, hence the same text goes on to say, "Who shows the work of the law, written in their hearts."

E. THE USE OF *AUCTORITATES* IN THE ON THE CONTRARY

[505]   The purpose of the On the Contrary is to present a preliminary indication that there is traditional or rational support for the position to be taken by St. Thomas in the *Corpus*. The On the Contrary is thus a kind of counterbalance to the Objections.

[506]   St. Thomas sets forth the On the Contrary in one of three ways.

[507]   First, he frequently simply presents an *auctoritas* without comment or development ("Simple Authority" technique). "Here is what Aristotle (or Augustine or Isidore) said."

[508]   For example, in *q.* 90, *a.* 2, On the Contrary he simply quotes from Isidore, a recognized *auctor* in many classical matters, such as Roman Law: Isidore says (*Etym.* v. 21) that "law is enacted for no private benefit but for the common utility of the citizens."

[509]   Second, sometimes St. Thomas uses an *auctoritas* as a basis for or as a part of argumentation, drawing from it an inference or a formal syllogistic conclusion ("argumentation" technique). For example, *q.* 95, *a.* 1, On the Contrary.

> Isidore says (*Etym.* v. 20) "Laws were made that, through fear thereof, human audacity might be repressed, and that innocence might be safe in the midst of the wicked, and that the wicked themselves might, by fear of punishment, be restrained from doing harm." But these are extremely necessary for the human race. Therefore, it was necessary to make laws. [See also, *q.* 93, *a.* 4, On the Contrary.]

[510]   This is a formal syllogism ("but . . . therefore . . . ") in which an *auctoritas* serves as the major premise.

[511]   Third, much less frequently, St. Thomas sets forth, in the On the Contrary, a simple argument without benefit of a supporting *auctoritas*. Thus, in *q.* 90, *a.* 1, we find the following On the Contrary: "It belongs to reason to order and to prohibit. But

to command belongs to reason, as was shown above [*q.* 17, *a.* 1]. Therefore, law is a thing of reason."

[512]   In the Objections and the On the Contrary the original question has been opened up. A number of opinions and arguments have been, as it were, put on the table. Now the *Corpus* will present the *determinatio* (the authoritative discussion of the Master).

[513]   St. Thomas seems never to incorporate the On the Contrary into the *Corpus* or even to use it. While the On the Contrary indicates the general direction St. Thomas will take, it should not be used in explaining St. Thomas's personal doctrine.

[514]   Very rarely (there are only two examples in the *Treatise*) St. Thomas adds, after the replies to Objections, a comment on the On the Contrary.

> However, with regard to what is objected to the contrary: Sometimes a person cannot use that which he habitually possesses because of some impediment; for example, a person cannot use the habit of science because of sleep. Likewise, a child, because of his age, cannot use the habit of the understanding of the first principles or even the Natural Law, both of which he habitually possesses. (Q. 94, *a.* 1, *ad fin.*)

[515]   The On the Contrary, taken by itself, is usually too simple, too ambiguous and open to too many interpretations to be taken as a definitive statement of a position. The ambiguities are removed in the *Corpus* and, therein also, St. Thomas defines his own interpretation of the *auctoritas* in the On the Contrary.

F. A CONCLUDING COMMENT

[516]   We have now taken a brief look at the principal ways *auctoritates* were used in medieval scholarship in general and by St. Thomas in particular. There are other uses and some subtle refinements that would be more appropriately studied in a more specialized account. For example, in *q.* 97, *a.* 1, *c.* a long quotation from St. Augustine supplies an example of the corruption of a political state that calls for drastic reformation.

[517]   However, the analysis offered in this Section will generally be adequate for the understanding of the Thomistic text. Besides, there will be further clarifications throughout the Commentary.

SECTION 2:
THE AUCTORES *QUOTED IN THE* TREATISE

[518]   There are 141 *auctoritates* in the *Treatise*. These are drawn from 13 *auctores*.

[519]   There are four *auctores* from whom the majority of the *auctoritates* are drawn. These are the Bible (58 references), Aristotle (35 references), St. Augustine (26 references), St. Isidore (15 references), 135 in all.

[520]   These figures may be compared with Chenu's similar count (without biblical references) of the *auctoritates* in the first 12 Questions of the *Summa Theologiae* (*Toward Understanding St. Thomas*, p. 127): Aristotle 55, St. Augustine 44, Dionysius 25, the Latin Fathers 23, the Greek Fathers 4, and secular authors 9—in all 160.

[521]   These two sets of figures illustrate two things. First, they indicate St. Thomas's major general sources which appear constantly in his works, namely, the Bible, Aristotle, and St. Augustine. Secondly, they illustrate the fact that other sources vary with the subject matter. The *Treatise* deals with the nature and properties of law. Hence, Isidore, who left a summary of classical Roman ideas about law, appears as a major source. The first part of the *Summa Theologiae* deals with the nature of Theology and the nature of God, a much more theological context. Hence, Isidore does not appear, but Dionysius, who wrote of God, becomes a major source.

[522]   In the following pages I identify for the convenience of the reader the *auctores* of the *Treatise*.

[523]   The first sections under the rubric "A" include the major *auctores* in order of descending number of references. The second list under rubric "B" identifies the rest of the *auctores* in alphabetical order.

A. THE MAJOR SOURCES

A1: *The Bible*

[524]   The Bible was and is The Book in the Western world. Even today in the United States, in a secularizing society, the Bible

is the bestseller. Moreover, commentaries, reflections, meditations based on the Bible are flowing from our printing presses by the dozens. But in Medieval society the Bible was even more important; its culture was saturated with Biblical ideas, themes and scenes. Every parish was required to have a Bible at the entrance to the Church. It was, of course, chained—for the same reason telephone directories are chained in public places. A Bible was very valuable both because of the short supply and because of the man-hours required to print it out by hand. The windows of the great cathedrals portrayed, in brilliant and jewel-like colors, scenes from the Bible and the lives of the Saints. These windows were part of the religious instruction for the illiterate. Of course, the illiterate learned of the Bible from sermons, week after week, delivered in churches all over Europe. Many of the most important events of Biblical narration were dramatized in the churches, making the churches sacred theater. Churches and monasteries were decorated with carvings and statues portraying the heroes of the Bible and the Saints of the Church. Statues and pictures of Christ and of the Virgin with the Christ child were everywhere.

[525]   Every Medieval writer frequently quoted the Bible. Of course, a theologian like St. Thomas quotes the Bible constantly. However, the *Treatise,* though an integral part of a theological treatise and ordered to a theological purpose, is basically, in its explanation and argumentation, with a few exceptions (such as *q*. 91, *a*. 6) philosophical.

[526]   A brief review of the history of the Bible may be helpful here. The Hebrew Scriptures were written and compiled over many centuries B.C. It was produced by many authors and contains a wide diversity of writing—historical, poetic, prophetic, and other. The official list of the Books of the Hebrew Scriptures was established at Jamnia A.D. 90.

[527]   The early Christians, regarding Christ as the Messiah, foretold and described in the Hebrew Scriptures, and regarding these Scriptures as a preparatory Revelation, simply continued the Jewish acceptance of these Scriptures. According to the Christians, the Scriptures contain a covenant between the Hebrews and God, a covenant replaced by the new covenant established by Christ for all time. Hence, the Hebrew Scriptures entered the Christian Bible as the Old Testament. There was some difficulty concerning certain

positive perceptions of the Old Law such as circumcision, but these difficulties did not destroy the authority of the Old Testament in religious matters. So St. Thomas treats *auctoritates* from the Old Testament with the same respect as he does those from the New Testament.

[528]   In the early Christian churches the custom grew up of reading not only the accepted Gospels but also other Christian writings such as the letters of St. Paul, of St. Clement of Rome, and so forth. In fact, a considerable body of Christian writings was produced, some of which were authentically Apostolic, some not Apostolic but orthodox, some heretical, some actually silly, and some simply forgeries to which the authors attached names of Apostles and other prominent Christians. The Churches decided that an approved list of orthodox Christian writings should be drawn up. Thus the Canon (or official list) of the writings of the New Testament was established. The Christian Bible, consisting of the Old and New Testaments, was thus finalized. The Church maintained the authority of the Bible and promulgated it through the subsequent centuries. In the scriptoria (writing rooms) of the monasteries hand printed copies, some of great beauty, were lovingly reproduced. The copies of the Bible in medieval Europe were in Latin, since that was the only standardized common language of Western Europe during that period. And so the Bible came down to St. Thomas in the approved Latin version known as the "Vulgate."

[529]   St. Thomas himself knew almost no Greek or Hebrew though he did have available translations of many of the Greek Fathers of the Church and the Latin commentaries of St. Augustine. He also seems to have consulted William Moerbeke, O.P., former Archbishop of Corinth in Greece and a prolific translator of Greek texts.

[530]   St. Thomas was a thorough student of the Bible, having gone through the extensive biblical studies required at the University of Paris and having written a large number of Commentaries on various sections of the Bible.

[531]   In most of St. Thomas's writings, the Bible is the primary source of *auctoritates*. In principle an *auctoritas* from the Bible is decisive in theological matters. But the matter is complicated by the problem of interpretation and the many controversies that have arisen concerning the authentic meaning of the Scriptures. Thus St.

Thomas often has a Scriptural text in Objections and, in the corresponding reply, deals with the difficult problem of interpretation. References in the *Treatise:* 58

A2: Aristotle

[532]   Aristotle (384–322 B.C.) was born at Stagira in Macedonia. His father was a medical doctor, a fact that is reflected in Aristotle's great interest in biology. Aristotle entered Plato's Academy and was for a time a follower of that thinker. His early writings were said to be Platonic, but only fragments of those writings are extant. Later he became a severe critic of his former master, while still developing many Platonic views. He opened his own school in Athens where he remained until the anti-Macedonian movement forced him to flee.

[533]   Aristotle is universally regarded as one of the greatest minds in western history. Coming as he did, towards the end of the great age of classical Greek culture, he was able brilliantly to organize and synthesize, to criticize and further develop the central themes of that culture. But at the same time he opened up new questions and new disciplines. His systematic treatment of logic (*The Prior* and *Posterior Analytics*) was the first comprehensive treatise in that field and became the methodological basis of medieval learning. He wrote magistral works in metaphysics, psychology, physics, politics and biology. These works likewise became the primary philosophical sources for medieval scholars. There are literally hundreds of extant medieval commentaries on his works.

[534]   After the fall of the Roman Empire Aristotle's works disappeared in the Latin West. They were reintroduced in the West in the twelfth and thirteenth centuries. At first the Church was alarmed by the spread of Aristotelianism, especially since the Averroistic commentaries were widely used. But the reinterpretation of Aristotle by St. Albert the Great and St. Thomas incorporated Aristotle into Christian philosophy and theology. By the end of the thirteenth century the study of the Aristotelian writings was required in all the Universities of Western Europe.

[535]   For St. Thomas Aristotle was the philosopher par excellence, though he reworked Aristotle's basic positions, producing an original Christian philosophy. Yet, Aristotle is the major source of philosophical *auctoritates* for St. Thomas. Thus, in the *Treatise,*

Aristotle is quoted 35 times. St. Thomas frequently refers to Aristotle simply as the "Philosopher" or only by the title of an Aristotelian treatise.

[536]   Franz Brentano called St. Thomas Aristotle's greatest disciple, but this is a case in which the disciple went, in some areas, far beyond the master. For this reason Etienne Gilson said that St. Thomas used Aristotelian language to say non-Aristotelian things.

A3: St. Augustine, Bishop of Hippo (North Africa)

[537]   St. Augustine (354–430), a Doctor of the Church, was born in Tagaste (North Africa). He studied at Carthage where he led a licentious life and became a master of classical rhetoric. He moved to Rome where he taught rhetoric with great success. There he became a Manichean. He moved to Milan where he was deeply influenced by St. Ambrose, Bishop of that city. He became a Christian and returned to Tagaste where he was eventually chosen Bishop of Hippo. He died while the city was under siege by the Vandals.

[538]   St. Augustine is regarded as the greatest theological writer in the Western Church between the Bible and St. Thomas. He wrote numerous works on a wide variety of topics, biblical exegesis, systematic theology, polemical works and letters. His greatest theological work, De Trinitate (On the Trinity) formed the traditional explanation of the Trinity in Western theology. De Civitate Dei (The City of God) presented a magnificent view of God's working in the history of mankind. His Confessions is a spiritual autobiography which ranks with the greatest spiritual writings of all time.

[539]   Though St. Thomas criticized some of the Neo-Platonic elements in Augustine's thought, St. Augustine was one of Thomas's principal theological sources (an auctor in the technical sense). There are 26 references to St. Augustine in the Treatise.

A4: St. Isidore of Seville

[540]   St. Isidore (c. 560–636), Bishop of Seville (Spain) and Doctor of the Church, was famous for his service of the poor, his support of farmers, his holy life and his voluminous writings on a surprising variety of topics. His most important work was his Etymologies, an encyclopedic dictionary in which he attempted to record all the basic elements of classical learning. It was a primary

source of classical learning for the scholars of the Middle Ages. There were, of course, few books of similar scope available to them. St. Thomas, too, used Isidore's *Etymologies* as a valuable source of information. In the *Treatise,* St. Thomas frequently quotes from Isidore's treatment of law. There are 15 references to St. Isidore in Thomas's *Treatise,* and, in fact, St. Thomas devotes two Articles (*q.* 95, *aa.* 3 and 4) to Isidore.

B. THE SECONDARY SOURCES

B1: St. Basil the Great

[541]   St. Basil the Great (c. 330–379), Doctor of the Church, was one of the greatest theologians of the early Eastern Church. He wrote a famous Monastic Rule which became the basis for the life of Basilian monks and strongly influenced St. Benedict.

[542]   He was regarded as a principal defender of orthodoxy in the Eastern Church and was highly regarded as a theological *auctor* by medieval theologians in the West. Number of references in the *Treatise:* 1

B2: Anicius Manlius Severinus Boethius

[543]   Boethius (c. 475–525 A.D.) was an outstanding Roman philosopher and statesman. While in prison on false charges of treason, he wrote his most famous work, *De Consolatione Philosophiae* (*On the Consolation of Philosophy*). He translated a number of Greek philosophical works and commented on them, thereby transmitting some Greek sources to the early Middle Ages.

[544]   St. Thomas wrote a commentary on his *De Trinitate* (*On the Trinity*). Number of references in the *Treatise:* 1

B3: Julius Caesar [102?–44 B.C.]

[545]   In the *Treatise* St. Thomas makes one reference to Julius Caesar. He uses Caesar's report that among the Germans theft was not considered wrong to illustrate the possibility that some precepts of the Natural Law can be lost or obscured in certain societies.

[546]   We do not know if St. Thomas had access to the original text of the *Gallic Wars.* I suspect the report comes from a

secondary source, perhaps from Augustine. Number of references in the *Treatise:* 1

B4: *Marcus Tullius Cicero*

[547]   Cicero (106–43, B.C.) was the greatest of Roman orators and a master of the Latin language. He was a practicing lawyer, an active politician and a statesman as well as a philosopher. His philosophy was largely Stoic and fully in the Natural Law tradition. He wrote voluminously on a wide variety of topics. Of special interest to jurisprudence are his treatises on law and *On the Republic.*

[548]   He was executed by his victorious political opponents in 43 B.C. Number of references in the *Treatise:* 3

B5: *Damascene*

[549]   Under this name St. Thomas refers to St. John of Damascus (c. 675–c. 749). St. John was a Father and Doctor of the Church. He wrote many theological works; of these his *De Fide Orthodoxa (Concerning the Orthodox Faith)* was well known to the Scholastics and highly esteemed as a summary of the teachings of the Eastern Fathers of the Church. St. Thomas made considerable use of this work. Number of references in the *Treatise:* 2

B6: *The Decretals*

[550]   The Decretals were collections of the decrees of the Popes. The first collection was made in the twelfth century. This is the collection to which St. Thomas refers. Subsequently, from time to time, other collections were made until they were all replaced by the 1918 codification of Canon Law. Number of references in the *Treatise:* 3

B7: *The Glosses*

[551]   A gloss was an annotation inserted in a manuscript by some scholar or commentator. They were written in the margin or inserted between the lines of the original text. The glosses were sometimes actually copied into the text itself by subsequent scribes.

[552]   Since they often contained useful explanations, the glosses themselves were often quoted as *auctoritates.* Number of references in the *Treatise:* 4

B8: Gratian

[553]   Gratian (fl. 1140 A.D.) was an Italian monk and a famous legal scholar. He taught law at his monastery in Bologna. His fame rests on the fact that he was the founder of Roman Catholic Canon Law. Working within the renaissance of Roman Law and the study of the *Corpus Juris Civilis* in Bologna, he, in fact, structured Canon Law after the model of Roman Law and incorporated in it the basic principles of Roman jurisprudence.

[554]   His *Decretum* was a systematic presentation of Canon Law with emphasis on the basic principles of Canon Law. Subsequent Popes made use of the *Decretum* and all subsequent Canon Law is based on it. Number of References in the *Treatise:* 1

B9: St. Hilary of Poitiers (315–367?)

[555]   St. Hilary, Bishop of Poitiers and a Doctor of the Church, figured prominently in the fight against Arianism. He wrote a number of theological works, the most famous of which was his *De Trinitate* (*On the Trinity*). It is from this latter work that St. Thomas drew the only citation from Hilary in the *Treatise*. Number of references in the *Treatise:* 1

B10: The "Jurist"

[556]   Under this rubric St. Thomas quotes from the *Digest,* the third part of the *Corpus Juris Civilis*. He uses this mode of reference since he was quoting from the excerpts recorded in the *Digest* and taken from the great Roman jurists such as Ulpian, Gaius, and Papinian.

[557]   A brief explanation of the *Corpus Juris Civilis* is appropriate.

[558]   Justinian I (483–565 A.D.) decided that it was time, after 1000 years of practice, to correct, codify, and summarize the Roman law. For this purpose he appointed various commissions, the most important of which was headed by the famous jurist, Tribonian. It is said that these commissions read two million cases of Roman law in order to produce the *Corpus Juris Civilis*. The *Corpus* eventually had three parts plus a supplement (variously arranged): 1) *The Institutes,* a handbook of Roman legal practice and procedure intended for students and practitioners of Roman law; 2) the *Codex Juris Civilis*

which consisted of a codification of all laws still in force at that time. This involved the deletion of many obsolete and contradictory laws; 3) the *Digest* which was a summary of Roman jurisprudence. Here appear long excerpts from the leading jurists of the past, men such as Ulpian and Gaius. The *Digest* was intended to establish the only authoritative general principles for Roman law.

[559]   It was providential that just at the time that the Roman Empire was breaking up Justinian I arranged for this mammoth presentation of Roman law. It is considered the most outstanding and magnificent presentation of any large legal system in the history of the world. As the Western empire continued to fall apart, Roman law in the West was almost entirely forgotten. When medieval Europe was recovering from the devastation of the tribal invasions and the incursions of the Norsemen, the *Corpus Juris Civilis* was rediscovered in Italy in the 11th century. It created a tremendous impression which developed into a full-scale movement of study and use of the Roman law. Several brilliant teachers like Gratian appeared to give direction and rationality to this development.

[560]   The Roman law thus presented to a rapidly developing Europe became the foundation of all the subsequent legal systems on the Continent. It influenced but it did not replace the Common Law of England.

[561]   The civilizing influence of this rediscovery of the Roman law can hardly be overestimated. It brought reason and order into the legal systems of Europe and strongly influenced the Canon Law of the Roman Catholic Church.

[562]   It is obvious why St. Thomas quoted from the *Digest* for he was primarily interested in the nature of law and of its basic principles. Number of references in the *Treatise:* 6

B11: Peter Lombard

[563]   Peter Lombard (c. 1100–1160 A.D.) was a celebrated theologian and churchman. He was a successful teacher and, for a time, Archbishop of Paris. His great contribution, however, was his *Sentences,* a compilation of the opinions of earlier theologians on basic Catholic Doctrine. This book became a standard theological text in the universities of the Middle Ages. It was widely commented on, and one of St. Thomas's earliest works was just such a commentary. Number of references in the *Treatise:* 1

B12: Pope Urban II

[564]   Pope Urban II (c. 1042–1099), is referred to in *q.* 96, *a. 5, obj.* and reply 2. He was a reforming Pope (1088–1099) who traveled widely in order to promote renewal and reform in the Church. Number of references in the *Treatise:* 1

St. Thomas Aquinas
The Treatise on Law

[BEING *SUMMA THEOLOGIAE,* I–II, QQ. 90 THROUGH 97]

with
Latin Text, English Translation,
Introduction, and Commentary

INTRODUCTION

Part B consists of the Latin Text directly associated with the corresponding English translation and comments. The comments are of two kinds. Some are general, as, for example, the Introductory Comment for *q.* 91; others are directed to specific texts, as, for example, the comment on the *Sed Contra* in *q.* 90, *a.* 1.

I have taken some liberty with the arrangement of the text. Instead of the original order of objection, *sed contra, Corpus,* and replies to the objections, I have paired the replies with the corresponding objections. I have done this for two reasons. First, it facilitates the direct comparison of the reply with the corresponding objection. Secondly, since any *ad locum* comment must refer both to the objection and to its reply, it focuses the comment directly with the pair objection-reply, thus producing a neat unit of study.

There is, of course, a disadvantage in this arrangement, since frequently the reply presupposes the *Corpus* and cannot be fully understood by itself. However, Part B is not intended simply for reading; it provides a basis for study, which, in turn, requires a back-and-forth perusal of the text. I believe the advantage of this arrangement for the modern reader in any case outweighs this disadvantage. I try to reduce this disadvantage by referring to the *Corpus* in the comment.

The translation is my own. I have tried for accuracy and clarity rather than stylistic elegance.

I emphasize again that St. Thomas is not doing jurisprudence per se; he is not writing for jurists or judges. He is writing as a theologian and for "beginners" in that discipline. He is studying everything that bears on the human act, the act for which human beings are responsible agents. Among these influences he finds law.

For these reasons St. Thomas is interested in all types of law that are properly (but analogously) so-called. Modern jurisprudence focuses on Positive Law and deals with Natural Law only inasmuch as it may influence Positive Law.

Yet, St. Thomas's *Treatise* was accepted as a classic in all subsequent Scholastic discussion of law or government. It is still recognized in modern jurisprudence as a classic source of Natural Law.

I remind the reader that references like [138–145] are to paragraph numbers in Part A.

DE LEGE
CONCERNING LAW

Consequenter considerandum est de principiis exterioribus actuum. Principium autem exterius ad malum inclinans est diabolus, de cujus tentatione in Primo dictum est. Principium autem exterius movens ad bonum est Deus, qui et nos instruit per legem et juvat per gratiam. Unde primo de lege, secundo de gratia dicendum est. Circa legem autem,

primo, oportet considerare de ipsa lege in communi;
secundo, de partibus ejus.

Circa legem autem in communi tria occurrant consideranda,

primo quidem, de essentia ipsius;
secundo, de differentia legum;
tertio, de effectibus legis.

[Being Summa Theologiae, I–II, qq. 90–97]

Consequently, we must consider the extrinsic principles of human acts. Now, the external principle inclining to evil is the devil concerning whose temptation we discussed in the First Part. But the extrinsic principle moving us to good is God Who instructs us through law and helps us through grace. Wherefore, we must first speak of law and secondly about grace. However, with regard to law, we will consider

first, the nature of law in general (*qq.* 90–92)
secondly, the different types of Law.

Now, concerning law in general, there are three points to consider,

first, the essence of law itself (*q.* 90);
secondly, the various types of Law (*q.* 91);
thirdly, the effects of law (*q.* 92).

QUESTION 90
DE ESSENTIA LEGIS
CONCERNING THE ESSENCE OF LAW

Circa primum quaeruntur quatuor:

1. utrum lex sit aliquid rationis;
2. de fine legis;
3. de causa ejus;
4. de promulgatione ipsius.

Question 90

Concerning the first topic, there are four points of inquiry:

1. whether law is something pertaining to reason;
2. concerning the end of law;
3. concerning its cause;
4. concerning its promulgation.

Introductory Comment

In this Question St. Thomas develops his general definition of law. An understanding of this Question is therefore a prerequisite for the understanding of the rest of the *Treatise* as St. Thomas himself makes clear by his constant references to the elements of the definition throughout the *Treatise*. The reader is therefore urged to study Question 90 thoroughly before proceeding to the rest of the *Treatise*.

The definition is framed in terms of the Aristotelian Doctrine of the Four Causes, one of Aristotle's most important contributions to the methodology of Western philosophy, theology, and science [178–210]. St. Thomas's definition is the first concise yet comprehensive definition in the history of jurisprudence.

ARTICLE 1
UTRUM LEX SIT ALIQUID RATIONIS?
WHETHER LAW IS SOMETHING PERTAINING TO REASON?

OBJECTION 1

Videtur quod lex non sit aliquid rationis. Dicit enim Apostolus, *Video aliam legem in membris meis,* etc. Sed nihil

118

quod est rationis est in membris, quia ratio non utitur organo corporali. Ergo lex non est aliquid rationis.

Objection 1

It would seem that law is not something pertaining to reason. For the Apostle says (Rom. vii. 23): *I see another law in my members,* etc. But nothing pertaining to reason is in the members; since the reason does not make use of a bodily organ. Therefore law is not something pertaining to reason.

REPLY 1

Ad primum ergo dicendum quod, cum lex sit regula quaedam et mensura, dicitur dupliciter esse in aliquo. Uno modo sicut in mensurante et regulante; et quia hoc est proprium rationis, ideo per hunc modum lex est in ratione sola. Alio modo sicut in regulato et mensurato; et sic lex est in omnibus quae inclinantur in aliquid ex aliqua lege; ita quod quaelibet inclinatio proveniens ex aliqua lege potest dici 'lex' non essentialiter, sed quasi participative. Et hoc modo inclinatio ipsa membrorum ad concupiscendum 'lex membrorum' vocatur.

Reply 1

Since law is a kind of rule and measure, it may be in something in two ways. First, as in that which measures and rules: and, since this is proper to reason, it follows that, in this way, law is in the reason alone. Secondly, as in that which is measured and ruled. In this way, law is in all those things that are inclined to something by reason of some law, so that any inclination arising from a law, may be called a "law," not essentially but by a kind of participation. And thus the inclination of the members to concupiscence is called the "law of the members."

Comment

Briefly, the problem here is that St. Paul is using "law" to apply to something that has nothing to do with "reason," while St. Thomas, on the other hand, asserts in the *Corpus* that law pertains to "reason."

Hence, St. Thomas must, on the one hand, justify the *auctoritas* from Scripture while, on the other hand, removing it as an objection to his own position.

Briefly, the answer consists of pointing out that there are two different ways of using the term "law." The first use is the essential use in which law is in the reason, functioning as regulating something else. This is St. Thomas's usage. The other way is to use the term "law" to refer to *what* is regulated. This is a derivative use which is therefore called "by way of participation." There is one unsolved problem in this Reply. What is the proper law from which St. Paul's use is derived? St. Thomas devotes an entire Article to the problem in *q.* 91, *a.* 6. I will postpone a fuller explanation to that Article.

Now some clarification: By "member" St. Paul means the body. In the body he finds desires for food, drink, sex, and sensible comfort; these constitute "concupiscence." In itself concupiscence is good, but it does lead us into sin and so is at war with the law of the mind. Concupiscence, viewed precisely *as* leading to sin, is called the *fomes peccati,* "that which foments or promotes sin."

According to St. Thomas's philosophy of human nature, "reason" (the "intellect") is a spiritual faculty that cannot be reduced simply to a physical organ (i.e., the brain); hence the "law in the member" has nothing to do with reason.

OBJECTION 2

> Praeterea, in ratione non est nisi potentia, habitus, et actus. Sed lex non est ipsa potentia rationis; similiter etiam non est aliquis habitus rationis, quia habitus rationis sunt virtutes intellectuales, de quibus supra dictum est; nec etiam actus rationis est, quia cessante rationis actu lex cessaret, puta, in dormientibus. Ergo lex non est aliquid rationis.

Objection 2

Further, in the reason there is nothing else but power, habit, and act. But law is not the power itself of reason. In like manner, neither is it a habit of reason, because the habits of reason are the intellectual virtues of which we have spoken above (*q.* 57). Nor, again, is it an act of reason, because then law would cease, when the act of reason ceases, for instance, while we are asleep. Therefore, law is nothing pertaining to reason.

REPLY 2

Ad secundum dicendum quod, sicut in actibus exterioribus est considerare operationem et operatum, puta, aedificationem et aedificatum, ita in operibus rationis est considerare ipsum actum rationis, qui est intelligere et ratiocinari, et aliquid per hujusmodi actum constitutum; quod quidem in speculativa ratione primo quidem est definitio; secundo, enuntiatio; tertio, vero syllogismus vel argumentatio. Et quia ratio etiam practica utitur quodam syllogismo in operabilibus, ut supra habitum est (*q.* 12, *a.* 3; *q.* 76, *a.* 1), secundum quod Philosophus docet in *Ethic.* vii, 3, ideo est invenire aliquid in ratione practica quod ita se habeat ad operationes sicut se habet propositio in ratione speculativa ad conclusiones; et hujusmodi propositiones universales rationis practicae ordinatae ad aciones habent rationem legis: quae quidem propositiones aliquando actualiter considerantur, aliquando vero habitualiter a ratione tenentur.

Reply 2

Just as, in external action, we may consider the act of working and the work done, for instance, the work of building and the house built; so in the acts of reason, we may consider the act itself of reason, i.e., to understand and to reason, and something produced by this act. With regard to the Speculative Reason, this is first of all the definition; secondly, the proposition; thirdly, the syllogism or argument. And since the Practical Reason also makes use of a kind of syllogism in respect of the work to be done, as stated above (*q.* 12, *a.* 3; *q.* 76, *a.* 1), and as the Philosopher teaches (*Ethic.* vii, 3), hence we find in the Practical Reason something that holds the same position in regard to operations, as, in the Speculative Intellect the proposition holds in regard to conclusions. Such universal propositions of the Practical Intellect that are directed to actions have the nature of law. And these propositions are sometimes under our actual consideration, while sometimes they are habitually retained in the reason.

Comment

The Objection assumes that there are only three things in the reason, namely, the power of reason itself, the habits that perfect the reason, and acts of reason. Law is not the power itself, it is not a habit, it is not an act. Therefore it is not in the reason. The basic answer is that there is another thing, a fourth thing in the intellect, namely, general propositions produced by reason and governing human action. Thus propositions are retained habitually in the reason, being sometimes actually considered and sometimes not. St. Thomas returns to this discussion of habit and law in *q. 94, a. 1*. For "habit" see [291–297].

St. Thomas places this answer in a consideration of the Speculative Intellect and the Practical Reason. St. Thomas will frequently refer to this distinction. The reader should become familiar with it [298–309].

OBJECTION 3

Praeterea, lex movet eos qui subjiciuntur legi ad recte agendum. Sed movere ad agendum proprie pertinet ad voluntatem, ut patet ex praemissis (*q. 60, a. 1*). Ergo lex non pertinet ad rationem, sed magis ad voluntatem, secundum quod etiam Jurisperitus dicit (*Lib. I, De Const. Prin. Leg.* i), *Quod placuit principi, legis habet vigorem.*

Objection 3

Further, the law moves those who are subject to it to act aright. But it belongs properly to the will to move to act, as is evident from what has been said above (*q. 60, a. 1*). Therefore, law pertains not to the reason but to the will, according to what the Jurist also says (*Lib. 1, De Const. Prin. Leg.* i), "Whatever pleases the sovereign has the force of law."

REPLY 3

Ad tertium dicendum quod ratio habet vim movendi a voluntate, ut supra dictum est (*q. 17, a. 1*). Ex hoc enim quod aliquis vult finem, ratio imperat de his quae sunt ad finem. Sed voluntas de his quae imperantur, ad hoc quod legis rationem habeat, oportet quod sit aliqua ratione regulata; et hoc modo intelligitur quod *voluntas principis habet* vigorem legis: alioquin voluntas principis magis esset iniquitas quam lex.

Reply 3

Reason has its power of moving from the will (*q*. 17, *a*. 1), for it is due to the fact that one wills the end, that reason issues its commands as regards things ordained to the end. But in order that the volition of what is commanded may have the nature of law, it needs to be in accord with some rule of reason. And in this sense is to be understood the saying that the will of the sovereign has the force of law, for otherwise, the will of the sovereign would rather be injustice than law.

Comment

In the history of jurisprudence there has been a radical difference in the explanation of the origin of law from the lawgiver. The first of these is called voluntarism because it holds that the will of the lawgiver is primary in the making of the law. This position is presented in the Objection in the words of the Jurist in the *Corpus Juris Civilis*.

St. Thomas carefully corrects this position by adding the requirement that the will of the lawgiver be regulated by reason.

Neither side totally rejects the alternate position. The difference lies in which power is given the primacy, the will or the reason.

St. Thomas develops his position more clearly in *q*. 97, *a*. 3, *c*., where he carefully interrelates the action of will and reason while giving the reason primacy as the *regulator* of the action of the will.

ON THE CONTRARY

Sed contra est quod ad legem pertinet praecipere et prohibere. Sed imperare est rationis, sicut supra habitum est (*q*. 17, *a*. 1). Ergo lex est aliquid rationis.

On the Contrary

It belongs to law to order and to prohibit. But to command belongs to reason, as was shown above (*q.* 17, *a.* 1). Therefore, law is a thing of reason.

Introductory Comment to the Corpus

The Corpus falls into two main divisions. In the first Section St. Thomas explains the relationship of law to reason. In the second Section he applies a general principle to the primacy of reason. I will analyze each Section independently.

CORPUS
[SECTION 1]

Dicendum quod lex quaedam regula est et mensura actuum, secundum quam inducitur aliquis ad agendum vel ab agendo retrahitur. Dicitur enim lex a ligando, quia obligat ad agendum. Regula autem et mensura humanorum actuum est ratio, quae est principium primum actuum humanorum, ut ex praedictis patet (*q.* 1, *a.* 1, Reply 3). Rationis enim est ordinare ad finem, qui est primum principium in agendis secundum Philosophum.

Corpus
[Section 1]

Law is a rule and measure of acts whereby man is induced to act or is restrained from acting. . . . for *lex* (law) is derived from *ligare* (to bind), because it binds one to act.

Now, the rule and measure of human acts is the reason, which is the first principle of human acts, as is evident from what has been stated above (I–II, *q.* 1, *a.* 1, *ad* 3) for it belongs to the reason to direct to the end, which is the first principle in all matters of action according to the Philosopher (*Phy.* ii, 9).

Comment

In the first sentence St. Thomas sets forth the empirical starting point of his investigation of law, namely, that law binds men to act or not to act. This is the most obvious and universal aspect of law. Whether you look at the laws of ancient Rome, the decrees of the

Pharaohs, the customs of the Iroquois Nations, or the regulations of a Swiss canton, there are always rules telling people to do certain things and to avoid doing certain other things.

In the same sentence St. Thomas makes his first inference about law, namely, that "law is a rule and measure of acts."

This is not simply a restatement of the empirical fact; it is already a philosophical inference. Law is a *rule,* that is, a general directive for action. It is a *measure,* that is, a standard for judging acts. [On these two points, see 284–290.]

When St. Thomas uses "acts" in this context, he means *human* acts as such [278–283]. Throughout the *Treatise* St. Thomas will frequently appeal to the essential characteristics of law.

Medieval writers (as do some modern writers) often used the etymology of a word to explain an idea or bolster a statement. These etymologies were not scientific; they even used conflicting etymologies for different purposes. St. Thomas himself, later on in the *Treatise* [*q.* 90, *a.* 4, Reply 3], refers to Isidore's derivation of law (*lex*) from *legere* (to read), so used because laws are written.

The "reason" that is the first principle of all human acts is the Practical Reason [304–309]. Whenever St. Thomas, throughout the Treatise, refers to Practical Reason, one should understand that he is assuming that it is also Right Reason [310–312]. Now, all human activity is purposeful, i.e., all human acts are directed to an end, so the end is also a first principle of human acts. The reason directs to the end and dictates the means to that end.

The Practical Reason is the efficient cause of human acts; the end is the final cause of the human act [for the Causes, see 183–210].

Since reason is the rule and measure of all human acts, and law is a rule and measure of some human acts, law must pertain to reason.

This Section 1 establishes the basis for Reply 3.

CORPUS
[SECTION 2]

In unoquoque autem genere id quod est primum principium est mensura et regula illius generis; sicut unitas in genere numeri, et motus primus in genere motuum. Unde relinquitur quod lex sit aliquid pertinens ad rationem.

Corpus
[Section 2]

Now, that which is the principle in any genus is the rule and measure of that genus, for example, unity in the genus of numbers, and the first mover in the genus of movements. Consequently, it follows that law is something pertaining to reason.

Comment

St. Thomas introduces a new principle and illustrates it. One (*unitas*) is the first principle in the genus of number. Two is two ones, three is three ones, and each number is measured by "one." When he speaks of the first mover, he is undoubtedly thinking of the Aristotelian cosmology, according to which the moon, the sun, the planets, and the stars are fixed in crystalline hollow concentric spheres which are moving in dependence on the First Mover, the outermost sphere.

But, without this obsolete science, the principle can be illustrated by a simple modern example. A locomotive is pushing a train of boxcars. They are all moving but the locomotive is the rule of the motion of the cars and is the measure of their motion. Reason is the first principle of human acts and is therefore their rule and measure.

In this Article St. Thomas has argued that, since it is obvious that law is a certain rule and measure of human acts and since Practical Reason is the rule and measure of all human acts, law must pertain to reason. Reason makes laws. But the question remains: "Whose reason can make laws?" This question is answered in *a.* 3. It is not the reason of just any man but, basically, and initially, the reason of all the people or, reductively, of their vicegerent. All this is in the order of efficient causality.

However, human acts are directed to an end. So the question remains: "What is the final cause of human acts and so of those human acts governed by law?" This question is answered in *a.* 2.

So the full understanding of *a.* 1 will only be achieved in *a.* 4 wherein all the results of *aa.* 1 through 4 are summarized in St. Thomas's formal definition of law.

In this Article St. Thomas also rejects Voluntarism. He also denies that law is a habit and so identifies law as a set of propositions (principles and precepts of action) held in the Practical Reason habitually.

ARTICLE 2
UTRUM LEX ORDINETUR SEMPER AD BONUM COMMUNE?
WHETHER LAW IS ALWAYS ORDERED TO THE COMMON GOOD?

Introductory Comment

The question raised here has to do with the final cause (the end or the purpose) of law. [For the Final Cause, see 194–197; for the Common Good, see 393–204.] St. Thomas's answer that law is always ordered to the Common Good sharply distinguishes his philosophy of law from that of the Positivists, Utilitarians, Realists and similar philosophies. To say that the Common Good is the final cause of law is to say, in accordance with the Doctrine of the Four Causes, that ordination to the Common Good is part of the essence of law. Laws which serve the interests of rulers or of privileged groups, may indeed be called laws *secundum quid,* but they are not laws in the full sense or *simpliciter* since they fail in an essential point.

OBJECTION 1

Videtur quod lex non ordinetur semper ad bonum commune sicut ad finem. Ad legem enim pertinet praecipere et prohibere. Sed praecepta ordinantur ad quaedam singularia bona. Non ergo semper finis legis est bonum commune.

Objection 1

It seems that law is not always ordered to the Common Good as to an end. For it belongs to law to command and to prohibit. But precepts are ordered to certain singular goods. Therefore, the end of law is not always the Common Good.

REPLY 1

Ad primum ergo dicendum quod praeceptum importat applicationem ad ea quae lege regulantur. Ordo autem ad bonum commune, qui pertinet ad legem, est applicabilis ad singulares fines. Et secundum hoc etiam de particularibus quibusdam praecepta dantur.

Reply 1

A precept implies application to those things that are regulated by law. However, the ordination to the Common Good which pertains to law is applicable to singular ends. And, according to this, precepts are given also with regard to certain particulars.

Comment

The basic argument is that laws sometimes deal with particular matters or particular ends. St. Thomas agrees but explains that the law does this by way of application to a singular case and only by this application brings the singular case under a law which is ordered to the Common Good. For example, the law sets a general rule regarding traffic. The state trooper applies this rule to Mr. Smith who has violated it. It is clear that this particular case is thus brought under the ordination to the Common Good of society, which, in this case, is safety for all citizens. The law is a rule and measure and rules and measures are always general. Lon Fuller remarks (*The Morality of Law,* p. 46), "The first desideratum of a system for subjecting human conduct to the governance of rules is an obvious one. There must be rules. This may be stated as the requirement of generality."

OBJECTION 2

Praeterea, lex dirigit hominem ad agendum. Sed actus humani sunt in particularibus. Ergo et lex ad aliquod particulare bonum ordinatur.

Objection 2

Further, law directs a man to act, but human acts deal with particulars. Therefore, the law also is ordered to some particular good.

REPLY 2

Ad secundum dicendum quod operationes quidem sunt in particularibus; sed illa particularia referri possunt ad bonum commune—non quidem communitate generis vel speciei, sed communitate causae finalis, secundum quod bonum commune dicitur finis communis.

Reply 2

Operations indeed deal with particular matters, but those particular matters can be referred to the Common Good—not indeed as coming under a common genus or species but as sharing a common final cause inasmuch as the Common Good is said to be the common end.

Comment

Law is directive of human acts. But human acts are always the singular acts of individuals. Therefore, law also deals with particular acts. A fairly clear objection. The Reply, however, points out that these particular acts can be referred to the Common Good by a Law. St. Thomas points out that these acts are not thereby brought under a common genus or species, i.e., they are not the same *kind* of things; they do not share a common Formal Cause but are related only by sharing a common end, namely the ultimate end which is the Common Good.

OBJECTION 3

Praeterea, Isidorus dicit (*Etym.* v, 3), *Si ratione lex constat, lex erit omne quod ratione constiterit.* Sed ratione consistit non solum quod ordinatur ad bonum commune, sed etiam quod ordinatur ad privatum bonum unius. Ergo lex non ordinatur solum ad bonum commune sed etiam ad bonum privatum unius.

Objection 3

Isidore says (*Etym.* v, 3), "If law is established by reason, then whatever is established by reason will be a law." But reason founds not only what is ordered to the Common Good but also what is ordered to the private good of an individual. Therefore, law is not ordained solely to the Common Good but also to the private good of an individual.

REPLY 3

Ad tertium dicendum quod, sicut nihil constat firmiter secundum rationem speculativam nisi per resolutionem ad prima principia indemonstrabilia, ita firmiter nihil constat per rationem practicam nisi per ordinationem ad ultimum finem, qui est bonum commune. Quod autem hoc modo ratione constat legis rationem habet.

Reply 3

Just as nothing stands firm according to Speculative Reason unless it is reduced to the first indemonstrable principles, so nothing stands firm according to Practical Reason unless it is ordered to the last end which is the Common Good. However, whatever is based on reason in this way has the nature of a law.

Comment

Isidore said that whatever is made firm by reason is law. By what reason? There are two basic modes of human reason [299–309]. The Speculative Reason, which is ordered to knowledge, has basic self-evident principles which govern (make firm) all the reasonings of the Speculative Reason. But the Speculative Reason does not order acts to the good. Hence, it is not the Speculative Reason that establishes (makes firm) law.

The Practical Intellect directs acts to an end. The basic principle is, "Good is to be done, evil avoided." All human acts are ordered by the Practical Intellect to the good, ultimately to the Common Good of all mankind. Anything that is established (made firm) by this ordination has the force of law.

ON THE CONTRARY

Sed contra est quod Isidorus dicit (*Etym.* v, 21) quod *lex est nullo privato commodo, sed pro communi utilitate civium conscripta.*

On the Contrary

Isidore says (*Etym.* v, 21) that "law is enacted for no private benefit but for the common utility of the citizens."

Introductory Comment to the *Corpus*

The *Corpus* is divided into three Sections. In Section 1 St. Thomas establishes that law must principally be concerned with happiness. In Section 2 he shows the law must be ordered to the common happiness, the Common Good. In Section 3 he offers a confirmation of the conclusion.

CORPUS
[SECTION 1]

Dicendum quod, sicut dictum est (*a.* 1), lex pertinet ad id quod est principium humanorum actuum, ex eo quod est regula et mensura. Sicut autem ratio est principium humanorum actuum, ita etiam in ipsa ratione est aliquid quod est principium respectu omnium aliorum: unde ad hoc oportet quod principaliter et maxime pertineat lex. Primum autem principium in operativis, quorum est ratio practica, est finis ultimus. Est autem ultimus finis humanae vitae felicitas vel beatitudo, ut supra habitum est (*q.* 2, *a.* 7; *q.* 3, *a.* 1). Unde oportet quod lex maxime respiciat ordinem qui est in beatitudine.

Corpus
[Section 1]

As stated above (*a.* 1), law pertains to that which is a principle of human acts because it is their rule and measure. However, just as reason is the principle of human acts, so also in reason itself there is something that is the principle with respect to all the others. Hence, it is to this that law must principally and mainly pertain. Now, the first principle of practical matters which are the object of Practical Reason is the last end. The last end of human life is felicity or happiness as was shown above (*q.* 2, *a.* 7; *q.* 3, *a.* 1). Hence, the law must principally look to the ordination to happiness.

Comment

The Practical Intellect is the intellect making decisions with regard to human acts. This activity of the Practical Intellect is complex. Now, since human acts are always purposeful, they are ordered to some end. If there is no purpose, there are no human acts. Hence, what starts the whole process of the Practical Intellect is the end, i.e., the Final Cause. Hence, the Final Cause is the first principle of human acts. Now what is the Final Cause of all human acts? It is happiness [379–392]. Since law pertains to Practical Reason, it must be principally concerned with happiness.

CORPUS
[SECTION 2]

Rursus cum omnis pars ordinetur ad totum sicut imperfectum ad perfectum, unus autem homo est pars communitatis perfectae, necesse est quod lex proprie respiciat ordinem ad felicitatem communem. Unde et Philosophus, praemissa definitione legalium, mentionem facit de felicitate et communione politica: dicit enim in *Ethic.* v, 1, quod *legalia justa dicimus factiva et conservativa felicitatis et particularium ipsius politica communicatione,* perfecta enim communitas civitas est, ut dicitur in *Politic* v, 1.

Corpus
[Section 2]

Again, since every part is ordered to the whole as the imperfect to the perfect and one man is part of the perfect society, it is necessary that the law properly regard the order to the happiness of the society. Hence, also the Philosopher, after having defined legal matters, mentions happiness and the political society. For he says (*Ethic.* v, 1) that "we call those legalities just which produce and preserve happiness and its components for the political society." For the perfect community is the state, as he says in *Polit.* v, 1.

Comment

In Section 1 St. Thomas argued that law is directive of human acts and since human acts are ordered to human happiness, law must be principally concerned with happiness. In Section 2 he argues that, since the good of an individual part of society is subordinate to the good of the whole perfect society, law must be directed to the common happiness of the society, i.e., to the Common Good or what John Finnis calls "human flourishing" [*Natural Law and Natural Rights,* passim]. (It should be remembered that the Common Good is the good of all members of society, not the good of the society viewed as a Fascist State.)

However, this argument has created problems for some Thomists inasmuch as it seems to totally subject man to the state. There are, I think, two reasons for this. First, St. Thomas, since he is writing what he considers a simplified theological textbook, does not put in all the qualifications a longer treatment would include. Secondly, he presupposes all that he has said in the first questions of the *Prima Secundae* wherein he dealt with the transcendent destiny of man.

If we balance this text with others, we know that human beings, according to St. Thomas, cannot, for example, be treated unjustly for any good of the state, real or pretended.

Jacques Maritain handled the problem by distinguishing man as an individual from man as a person. As an individual unit, man is indeed simply a part of the whole society. As a person, he is independent of society and transcends the human city. After all, St. Thomas said that person is the most perfect thing in the universe. Human beings, taken in their fullness, are persons.

CORPUS
[SECTION 3]

In quolibet autem genere id quod 'maxime' dicitur est principium aliorum, et alia dicuntur secundum ordinem ad ipsum: sicut ignis, qui est maxime calidus, est causa caliditatis in corporibus mixtis, quae intantum dicuntur calida inquantum participant de igne. Unde oportet, cum lex maxime dicatur secundum ordinem ad bonum commune, quod quodcumque aliud praeceptum de particulari opere non habeat rationem legis nisi secundum ordinem ad bonum commune. Et ideo omnis lex ad bonum commune ordinatur.

Corpus
[Section 3]

Moreover, in any genus, that which is called the greatest, is the principle of all the other instances and these others are named with reference to that greatest, just as fire, which is the hottest of all things, is the cause of heat in mixed bodies which are called hot insofar as they have a share of fire. Hence, since law is most of all ordered to the Common Good, it is necessary that any other precept concerning a particular matter must needs lack the nature of law except insofar as it is ordered to the Common Good. And therefore every law is ordered to the Common Good.

Comment

The general principle with which this argument begins seems to be regarded as self-evident, not indeed self-evident to everyone but only to the wise and learned. It might be compared to H. L. A. Hart's idea of the Central Case of a legal system, that is, a fully developed legal system which other instances are called legal systems only to the extent that they have some of the features of a legal system or, as St. Thomas would say, only insofar as they participate in the Central Case.

The example, drawn from ancient and medieval science, is intended to give an inductive clarity to the principle. If one believed medieval science, it would be a good example.

The ancient Greeks tried to determine what the ultimate components of the things around us were. Thales said liquid was the basic element; Heraclitus chose fire. Eventually there was general agreement that there were four elements, namely, earth, air, fire and water and that all things were various combinations of these. They therefore were called "mixed bodies." If a thing was heavy, it had a high proportion of earth. If it was light, it had a high proportion of air.

One of the oddest things about this theory is the conception that fire is a substance (not a process).

There is an analogy in modern sciences, namely, the periodic table of elements and chemical combinations of composed substances. The question was the same and the explanations are analogous.

In any case, the conclusion seems, in view of the arguments in Sections 1 and 2, to be evident.

ARTICLE 3
UTRUM RATIO CUJUSLIBET SIT FACTIVA LEGIS?
WHETHER ANY PERSON'S REASON IS ABLE
TO MAKE LAW?

OBJECTION 1

Videtur quod cujuslibet ratio sit factiva legis. Dicit enim Apostolus (Rom. ii, 14) quod *cum gentes, quae legem non habent, naturaliter ea quae legis sunt faciunt, ipsi sibi sunt lex.* Hoc autem communiter de omnibus dicit. Ergo quilibet potest facere sibi legem.

Objection 1

It seems that the reason of any person can make a law, for the Apostle says (Rom., ii, 14) "When the Gentiles who do not have the law, naturally do the things of the law, they are a law unto themselves." But this he says generally about everyone. Therefore, any person's reason can make a law for himself.

REPLY 1

Ad primum ergo dicendum quod, sicut supra dictum est (*a.* 1, Reply 1), lex est in aliquo non solum sicut in regulante, sed etiam participative sicut in regulato. Et hoc modo unusquisque sibi est lex inquantum participat ordinem alicujus regulantis; unde et ibidem subditur, *Qui ostendunt opus legis scriptum in cordibus suis.*

Reply 1

As stated above (*a.* 1, Reply 1), a law can be in a person not only as in a ruler but also by participation as in the person ruled. And in this way each one is a law unto himself in so far as he participates in the ordination of some ruler. Hence, the same text adds "who display the work of the law written in their hearts."

Comment

St. Thomas used this distinction in *q*. 90, *a*. 1, Reply 1. To participate in something is to have it by derivation and imperfectly. Thus, the law that is written in men's hearts is derived from the law in God and is less perfect than the law in God.

When St. Paul says that the Gentiles do not have the Law, he is referring to the Law of Moses, the Jewish Law. When he says the Law is inscribed in their hearts he refers to the Natural Law. The phrase "inscribed in their hearts" is, of course, a metaphor and cannot by itself be reduced to a precise philosophical position. Those who believe in innate ideas find some support here, but that is not a Thomistic position [112–113].

St. Thomas maintains that all men know the primary precepts of the Natural Law but more or less clearly, and more or less extensively.

OBJECTION 2

Praeterea, sicut Philosophus dicit (*Ethic*. ii, 1), *intentio legislatoris est ut inducat hominem ad virtutem*. Sed quilibet homo potest alium inducere ad virtutem. Ergo cujuslibet hominis ratio est factiva legis.

Objection 2

Further, as the Philosopher says (*Ethic*. ii, 1), the lawgiver intends to lead men to virtue. But any man can lead another to virtue. Therefore, the reason of any man can make laws.

Comment

In *q*. 92, *a*. 1 St. Thomas discusses law as leading to virtue.

REPLY 2

Ad secundum dicendum quod persona privata non potest inducere efficaciter ad virtutem: potest enim solum monere; sed, si sua monitio non recipiatur, non habet vim coactivam, quam debet habere lex ad hoc quod efficaciter inducat ad virtutem, ut Philosophus dicit (*Ethic.*, x, 9). Hanc

autem virtutem coactivam habet multitudo, vel persona publica, ad quam pertinet poenas infligere, ut infra dicetur
(*q. 92, a. 2, Reply 3; q. 96, a. 5, c.*), et ideo solius ejus est
leges facere.

Reply 2

A private person cannot effectively lead another to virtue, for he
can only admonish, but, if his admonition is not heeded, he does not
have the coercive power which the law must have in order to lead a man
to virtue, as the Philosopher says (*Ethic.* x, 9). This coercive power is
vested in the whole people or in some public official to whom it belongs
to inflict punishment, as will be stated further on (*q. 92, a. 2,* Reply
3; q. 96, a. 5, 167c.). Therefore, it belongs to him alone to make laws.

Comment

While St. Thomas does not make sanction an element in the essence
of law, he does say that law should have coercive power in order to be
effective (*efficaciter*). The passages referred to above are sometimes mis-
interpreted as showing that St. Thomas held that sanction is part of the
essence of law. [See Jerome Hall, Foundations of Jurisprudence, p. 101.]
For St. Thomas laws must have coercive power, not because of the nature
of law but because of the imperfection of human beings. In general,
Positivists derive legal obligation from the sanction. The major premise
used in the Objection, namely, that the legislator intends to lead men
to virtue, is developed at greater length in *q. 92, a.* 1.

OBJECTION 3

Praeterea, sicut princeps civitatis est civitatis gubernator,
ita quilibet paterfamilias est gubernator domus. Sed princeps
civitatis potest in civitate legem facere. Ergo quilibet paterfamilias potest in sua domo facere legem.

Objection 3

Further, just as the prince of a state is the governor of that state,
so also any father is the governor of the home. But the prince of the
state can make law in the state, therefore any father can make law in
his own home.

REPLY 3

Ad tertium dicendum quod, sicut homo est pars domus, ita domus est pars civitatis; civitas autem est communitas perfecta, ut dicitur in *Polit.* i, 1. Et ideo, sicut bonum unius hominis non est ultimus finis sed ad commune bonum or-dinatur, ita etiam bonum unius domus ordinatur ad bonum unius civitatis quae est communitas perfecta. Unde ille qui gubernat aliquam familiam potest quidem facere aliqua prae-cepta vel statuta, non tamen quae proprie habent rationem legis.

Reply 3

As a man is part of a family, so the family is part of the state. The state, however, is a perfect society, as is said in *Polit.* i, 1. And, therefore, just as the good of one man is not the ultimate end but is ordered to the Common Good; so also the good of one family is ordered to the Common Good of the state, which is a perfect society. Hence he who governs a family can indeed make some precepts and statutes but not ones which properly have the nature of law.

Comment

The view of the family taken here is the ancient and medieval view that the father-husband was the head of the family and the final decision-maker. Even if we substitute the modern view that the parents are the decisionmakers, the argument holds, for, in either case, the family is part of a perfect society.

A "perfect society" according to Aristotle and St. Thomas is one that is supreme in some territory or for some group (such as a nomadic tribe) and independent of all other societies or authorities. Examples are the Greek city-state (*polis*) and the modern nation-state. In a federal nation like the United States, the individual states are imperfect societies.

ON THE CONTRARY

Sed contra est quod Isidorus dicit in *lib. Etymol.* v, 10 et habetur in *Decretis* (Gratian, *Decretum* I, II, I), *Lex est constitutio populi, secundum quam majores natu simul cum plebibus aliquid sanxerunt.* Non est ergo cujuslibet facere legem.

On the Contrary

Isidore says in the Fifth Book of the *Etymologies*—and it is found in Gratian, *Decretum* I, II, I: "Law is an ordinance of the whole people by which the elders together with the common people sanction something." Therefore, not everyone's reason can make law.

CORPUS

Dicendum quod lex proprie primo et principaliter respicit ordinem ad bonum commune. Ordinare autem aliquid in bonum commune est vel totius multitudinis vel alicujus gerentis vicem totius multitudinis. Et ideo condere legem vel pertinet ad totam multitudinem, vel pertinet ad personam publicam quae totius multitudinis curam habet; quia et in omnibus aliis ordinare in finem est ejus cujus est proprius ille finis.

Corpus

Law, properly speaking, regards first and principally the order to the Common Good. However, to order to the Common Good belongs either to the whole people or to one who represents the whole people. And therefore, to establish law belongs either to the whole people or to a public official who has the care of the whole community, because, as in all other matters, to order to an end belongs to him to whom that end most properly belongs.

Comment

In the first part of this Article St. Thomas simply explains the doctrine; the basic argument is contained in the last sentence. "He who has an end has the right to order himself to that end." As soon as one understands the Common Good of the people (*a.* 2), it is self-evident that the people have the right to determine their own ordination, through laws, to that Common Good. Today we call this right the right of self-determination. St. Thomas elaborates this doctrine further when discussing "custom" [*q.* 97, *a.* 3].

This is a clear statement that political power and authority are vested, first of all, in the people. Whereas John Austin said that the political superior was superior in power, St. Thomas says that the political superior represents the whole people and has care of them. St. Thomas also rejects the Divine Right of Kings which holds that the King's authority comes directly from God. St. Robert Bellarmine based a whole theory of democracy on St. Thomas's doctrine. His works were therefore banned and burned by the public executioner under orders from James I.

Elsewhere, St. Thomas will frequently say that all human law is a participation in the Divine Law. This is a metaphysical statement that all authority is ultimately derived from God and analogously resembles God's authority. This in no way contradicts the position taken here. Mortimer Adler (*The Development of Political Theory and Government*, p. 72) comments as follows:

> Here in Aquinas is one of the first clear statements of the doctrine of popular sovereignty. The voice of the people is the voice of God, but only when the people make just laws for the common good. Otherwise, popular sovereignty degenerates into the might of the majority, which is just another form of tyranny. But when, in addition to being made by duly constituted authority, the positive laws of the state are also based on the natural moral law and represent just regulations of human conduct, they speak with the authority of right, not just the force of might. While they exercise the sanction of coercive force over the bad man who obeys them only from fear of punishment, they bind the good man in conscience. In obeying them from the promptings of virtue he obeys them freely and not under coercion.

The Preamble to the U.S. Constitution is exactly in accordance with St. Thomas's view. "We, the people, . . . do ordain and establish this Constitution for the United States of America."

ARTICLE 4
UTRUM PROMULGATIO SIT DE RATIONE LEGIS?
IS PROMULGATION ESSENTIAL TO LAW?

Introductory Comment

This Article requires very little commentary. It is clear and straightforward and presents a position that is almost universally accepted and for which St. Thomas gives the classic argument. Note that there is no Scriptural or theological reference. The argument is strictly philosophical.

OBJECTION 1

Videtur quod promulgatio non sit de ratione legis. Lex enim naturalis maxime habet rationem legis. Sed lex naturalis non indiget promulgatione. Ergo non est de ratione legis quod promulgetur.

Objection 1

It would seem that promulgation is not of the essence of law. For the Natural Law is law in the fullest sense but needs no promulgation. Therefore, it is not of the essence of law that it be promulgated.

REPLY 1

Ad primum ergo dicendum quod promulgatio legis naturae est ex hoc ipso quod Deus eam mentibus hominum inseruit naturaliter cognoscendam.

Reply 1

The Natural Law is promulgated by the very fact that God has instilled it in the minds of men so as to be naturally known by them.

Comment

The argument, both in the Objection and in the Reply is clear. There is only one problem. What does "God instilled the Natural Law in the minds of men so as to be naturally known by them" mean? Certainly, people do not need Revelation or a supernatural illumination in order to know the primary precepts of the Natural Law. Clearly, as opposed to being supernaturally known, Natural Law is "naturally known." But the term "naturally" is still ambiguous and lies open to at least two interpretations.

One interpretation is to say that there are in our intellects, prior to reflection or experience, fully formed first principles of the Natural

Law and therefore of the moral order. It seems to me that this interpretation is not sustainable, since St. Thomas accepts the Aristotelian position that in the very beginning, prior to experience and reflection, the human intellect is a *tabula raza,* a blank page on which nothing is written.

The correct interpretation is as follows. The Practical Intellect has by nature the habit of the first principles of the Natural Law. This means that the Practical Intellect has the innate ability to recognize the first principles without previously *acquiring* the ability to do so. The habit is the ability to recognize the first principles, that is, by the habit the first principles are recognized without learning to do so, but the habit is not the first principles themselves. The distinction between the habit as that by which something is known and the things thereby known is fundamental [291–297].

OBJECTION 2

Praeterea, ad legem pertinet proprie obligare ad aliquid faciendum vel non faciendum. Sed non solum obligantur ad implendam legem illi coram quibus promulgatur lex, sed etiam alii. Ergo promulgatio non est de ratione legis.

Objection 2

Further, it properly belongs to law to oblige one to do or not to do something. But not only those are obliged to fulfill the law in whose presence the law is promulgated but others. Therefore, promulgation is not of the essence of law.

REPLY 2

Ad secundum dicendum quod illi coram quibus lex non promulgatur obligantur ad legem observandam, inquantum in eorum notitiam devenit per alios, vel devenire potest, promulgatione facta.

Reply 2

Those who are not present when a law is promulgated are obliged to observe the law in as far as it comes to their attention or can come to their attention through others, once the promulgation is made.

Comment

The problem is clear and more serious today. No ordinary citizen can possibly know all the statutes and Court decisions that constitute the law. Note that St. Thomas says "or *can* be brought to their attention through others." Today, these "others" are usually lawyers, or, in some cases, government agencies as when the IRS tried to educate all citizens about the new tax code. For a modern discussion, see Fuller, The *Morality of Law,* pp. 49–51.

OBJECTION 3

Praeterea, obligatio legis extenditur etiam in futurum, quia *leges futuris negotiis necessitatem imponunt,* ut *Jura* dicunt (*Cod.* I., tit. *De leg et constit.* leg. vii.). Sed promulgatio fit ad praesentes. Ergo promulgatio non est de necessitate legis.

Objection 3

Further, the obligation of a law extends into the future, since laws impose necessity on future affairs, as the Jurists say (*Cod.* I., tit. *De leg et constit.* leg. vii.). But promulgation is directed to those present. Therefore, promulgation is not necessary for a law.

REPLY 3

Ad tertium dicendum quod promulgatio praesens in futurum extenditur per firmitatem scripturae, quae quodammodo semper eam promulgat. Unde Isidorus dicit (*Etym.* ii, 10; v, 3) quod *lex a legendo vocata est, quia scripta est.*

Reply 3

Present promulgation extends into the future through the durability of writing which, in a way, promulgates the law forever.

Hence, Isidore says (*Etym.* ii, 10; v, 3) that the word "law" (*lex*) is derived from "reading" (*legendo*), because it is written down.

Comment

St. Thomas is dealing with the problem of promulgation to future citizens. This is not the same as H. L. A. Hart's problem of the "persistence of law through time." Hart's question concerns the continuing obligatory character of a law after the original lawgiver is gone and the citizens no longer habitually obey him. [See *The Concept of Law*, pp. 60–64.] The quotation from Isidore is not part of the argument.

ON THE CONTRARY

Sed contra est quod dicitur in *Decretis* (*Decret.* I, iv) quod *leges instituuntur cum promulgantur.*

On the Contrary

It is stated in the *Decretals* (*Decret.* I, iv) that "laws are established when they are promulgated."

Introductory Comment to the Corpus

The *Corpus* of this Article has two quite distinct parts.

The first section deals with the particular subject of the Article, namely, promulgation as an essential element of law.

The second section is a summary of the results of the four Articles of this Question.

CORPUS
[SECTION 1]

Dicendum quod, sicut dictum est (*a.* 1), lex imponitur aliis per modum regulae et mensurae. Regula autem et mensura imponitur per hoc quod applicatur his quae regulantur et mensurantur. Unde ad hoc quod lex virtutem obligandi obtineat, quod est proprium legis, oportet quod applicetur hominibus qui secundum eam regulari debent. Talis autem applicatio fit per hoc quod in notitiam eorum deducitur ex

ipsa promulgatione. Unde promulgatio ipsa necessaria est ad
hoc quod lex habeat suam virtutem.

Corpus
[Section 1]

As stated above (*a.* 1) a law is imposed on others as a rule and
measure. Now a rule or measure is imposed by being applied to those
who are to be ruled and measured by it. Hence, in order for a law to
obtain the power of obligating, which is proper to law, it must be applied
to those who are to be directed by it. This application takes place by
being made known to them by promulgation. Therefore promulgation
is necessary for law to have its binding force.

Comment

As stated above, St. Thomas here presents the intrinsic and classical
argument that establishes promulgation as an essential element of law.

A lawgiver may frame a law and intend it to be a law, yet, if he
does not make it known to those subject to it, it cannot function as a
rule and measure of human conduct. Hence it is not a law.

A U.S. Federal judge quoted this section of the Article as the basis
for declaring a regulation of the U.S. Immigration and Naturalization
Service invalid (*Louis v. Nelson,* 344 F. Supp. 973 (1982) I).

CORPUS
[SECTION 2]

Et sic ex quatuor praedictis potest colligi definitio legis,
quae nihil est aliud quam quaedam rationis ordinatio ad
bonum commune, ab eo qui curam communitatis habet,
promulgata.

Corpus
[Section 2]

We can now gather from the preceding four articles the definition
of a law which is nothing other than a certain dictate of reason for the
Common Good, made by him who has the care of the community and
promulgated.

Comment

Here, at the end of the last Article of Question 90, St. Thomas draws the results of his discussion together into his formal philosophical definition of *a* law. Since this definition is basic to the entire *Treatise,* a number of observations should be made about it.

1. St. Thomas is defining *a* law (statute, etc.), not a legal system.

2. The definition is of the explanatory type based on the methodology of the Four Causes. An analysis of the definition in these terms gives us:

a. The Formal Cause is the "dictate of reason."

b. The Final Cause is the "Common Good."

c. The Efficient Cause is "he who has the care of the community." The ultimate Efficient Cause is the "whole people."

d. The Material Cause is the community or, more precisely, the human acts of people in society. The dictate of reason *forms* the human acts of its subjects in a way analogous to the way the shape imposed on a block of marble forms the statue.

e. Promulgation must be viewed in two ways. As the act of promulgating it is part of the efficient cause; making the law includes promulgating it. If a lawgiver frames a law in his own mind and decides to make it a law, it is not really a law until he actually promulgates it. Prior to promulgation, it might be called an inchoative or potential law but not a law *simpliciter.* The second way of regarding promulgation is to view promulgation as enduring in the law as a permanent state. Thus, we could say that the Formal Cause is the promulgated dictate of reason. The distinction made here is the same as that used by St. Thomas himself (*q.* 90, *a.* 1, Reply 2) between the building of the house and the house built.

3. It should be noted that there is no mention of force or power and no mention of sanction or punishment. Most Positivists ultimately reduce legal obligation to fear of punishment created by the power of the lawgiver to do evil to the violater of his law.

4. By the same token, most Positivists make laws primarily dependent on the will of the lawgiver. St. Thomas rejected this view in *q.* 90, *a.* 1, Reply 3. The "dictate of reason" is not a dictate of Speculative Reason but of Practical Reason. Of course, Practical Reason includes a relation to the will but St. Thomas maintains that the dictate is primarily dependent on reason. He will constantly assert that a law or an action that is contrary to reason is not a valid law.

5. The definition is worked out within the analysis of entities in essence, properties, and accidents. Hence it is an essential definition [232–265].

6. This is a general definition of law. Since St. Thomas is interested in all types of law as influencing human conduct, he applies this definition not only to Positive Law but to the Natural Law, Divine Law, etc. These applications as made in *qq.* 91–92 show that the definition is analogous.

QUESTION 91
DE LEGUM DIVERSITATE
THE VARIETY OF LAWS

Deinde considerandum est de diversitate legum, et circa hoc quaeruntur sex:

1. utrum sit aliqua lex aeterna?
2. utrum sit aliqua lex naturalis?
3. utrum sit aliqua lex humana?
4. utrum sit aliqua lex divina?
5. utrum sit una tantum vel plures?
6. utrum sit aliqua lex peccati?

Question 91

Next we must consider the diversity of Laws, and on this Question there are six points of inquiry:

1. Whether there is an Eternal Law?
2. Whether there is a Natural Law?
3. Whether there is Human Law?
4. Whether there is a Divine Law?
5. Where there is one or more Divine Laws?
6. Whether there is a Law of Sin?

Introductory Comment

Having established the general definition of law, St. Thomas now identifies four different kinds of law, namely, the Eternal Law (*a.* 1), the Natural Law (*a.* 2), the Divine Law (*aa.* 3 and 4), and Positive (human) Law (*a.* 5).

Modern jurisprudents, at least since Austin, have considered Positive Law to be the proper subject of their discipline. They ignore the Eternal Law and the Divine Law and deal with Natural Law only insofar as it relates to Positive Law. But St. Thomas, as we have seen, is not writing as a jurisprudent but as a theologian, and, in this part of the *Summa,* he is sorting out all the factors, intrinsic and extrinsic, that bear on human moral decision-making and so on human acts as such. Among these external factors he finds law and so is interested in all law of whatever kind.

In this Question St. Thomas simply establishes and distinguishes these four types of law. Later he devotes an entire Question to each of three types, namely, the Eternal Law, the Natural Law, and the Positive Law. The fourth type, the Divine Law, being the law revealed in the Bible, is continuously explained throughout the *Second Part* of the *Summa* and so receives no special treatment here.

The reader will note that St. Thomas's definition, as applied to these four types of law is analogous, not univocal, inasmuch as each type fulfills some part(s) of the definition in a different but similar way.

St. Thomas not only identifies these laws; he also interrelates them.

The Eternal Law is the model in the mind of God of the total universe, including in itself, therefore, the prototype of all things in the universe, and so of all law. The Eternal Law is the exemplar cause of the universe.

All law, then, is derivative from the Eternal Law. The Divine Law (the law in the Bible) is derived by way of divine Revelation. The Natural Law is derived by way of creation. God lays the foundation for Natural Law in creating human nature and enables man to work out the Natural Law by endowing him with practical reason. The Positive Law is derived from the Natural Law by human reason but in two quite different ways, as St. Thomas explains in *q. 95, a. 2*.

It is important to note that this order of derivation is not the order in which we come to know the various laws. For example, we do not derive the *knowledge* of the Natural Law from *knowledge* of the Eternal Law. We can discover the basic requirements of justice without first referring to God.

St. Thomas made a clear distinction between the Natural Law and the Divine Law. Of course, since they were both derived from the Eternal Law and both related to human well-being, there is a congruence of content. The Decalogue has "Thou shalt not kill," while St. Thomas cites "Do no harm to any person" as one of the principles of the Natural Law. In fact, all the Ten Commandments are also dictates of practical reason except the determination of the Sabbath as the day of worship. That is a determination of divine Positive Law.

Unfortunately, Blackstone, a rather rigid Natural Law thinker, identified the Natural Law with the law of Moses, without, however, intending to deprive Natural Law of its rational base. This view was common among the Founding Fathers. John Austin also identified the Natural Law with the Divine Law and then concluded that the Natural Law could be known to us only by Revelation. Thus he eliminated both laws from the field of jurisprudence.

In the Sixth Article St. Thomas deals with a theological problem arising from a text of St. Paul. Those not interested in theology may omit Article 6 without loss to the understanding of St. Thomas's jurisprudence. This Article simply returns to *q.* 90, *a.* 1, Obj.–Reply 1.

ARTICLE 1
UTRUM SIT ALIQUA LEX AETERNA?
WHETHER THERE IS AN ETERNAL LAW?

OBJECTION 1

Videtur quod non sit aliqua lex aeterna. Omnis enim lex aliquibus imponitur. Sed non fuit ab aeterno cui aliqua lex posset imponi: solus enim Deus fuit ab aeterno. Ergo nulla lex est aeterna.

Objection 1

It seems that there is no Eternal Law. For a law must be imposed on someone but there was no one from eternity on whom the Law could be imposed, since only God exists eternally. Therefore, no law is eternal.

REPLY 1

Ad primum ergo dicendum quod ea quae in seipsis non sunt, apud Deum existunt, inquantum sunt ab ipso cognita et praeordinata, secundum illud *Rom., Qui vocat ea quae non sunt tanquam ea quae sunt.* Sic igitur aeternus divinae legis conceptus habet rationem legis aeternae, secundum quod a Deo ordinatur ad gubernationem rerum ab ipso praecognitarum.

Reply 1

Those things which do not exist in themselves do exist with God who knows and prearranges them, according to the text (Rom. iv, 17), "Who calls those things that are not, just as he does those things that are." Thus, then, the eternal concept of the divine law has the nature of an eternal law, inasmuch as it is ordered by God to the governance of the things foreknown by Him.

Comment

The objection is based on the fact that promulgation is of the essence of law, and that promulgation implies the existence of subjects to whom the law can be promulgated. Although the Eternal Law exists in God from eternity, it is law beause it is related to things foreknown by God as coming under the Eternal Law. Thus, the requirement of promulgation is analogously verified in respect to the Eternal Law.

OBJECTION 2

Praeterea, promulgatio est de ratione legis. Sed promulgatio non potuit esse ab aeterno, quia non erat ab aeterno cui promulgaretur. Ergo nulla lex potest esse aeterna.

Objection 2

Further, promulgation belongs to the essense of law, but there was no one existing from eternity to whom the law could be promulgated. Therefore, no law is eternal.

REPLY 2

Ad secundum dicendum quod promulgatio fit et verbo et scripto; et utroque modo lex aeterna habet promulgationem ex parte Dei promulgantis, quia et Verbum divinum est aeternum, et scriptura libri vitae est aeterna. Sed ex parte creaturae audientis aut inspicientis non potest esse promulgatio aeterna.

Reply 2

Law can be promulgated both by the spoken word and by writing. The Divine Word is from eternity and so is the writing of the Book of Life. But on the part of the creature promulgation cannot be from eternity.

Comment

Here St. Thomas clarifies his position by distinguishing promulgation on the part of God from promulgation to creatures. Thus, the nature of the analogous promulgation of the Eternal Law is clarified.

The Second Person of the Trinity is called the Divine Word inasmuch as He is the Father's expression of Himself. The Book of Life is considered as God's foreknowledge of those to be saved. Thus, on the part of God, promulgation is analogously effected both in word and in writing. The concept of the Book of Life raises a serious theological question which we need not discuss here, since our focus is not constructing a theology but only to understand St. Thomas's use of theology in explaining law.

OBJECTION 3

Praeterea, lex importat ordinem ad finem. Sed nihil est aeternum quod ordinetur ad finem: solus enim ultimus finis est aeternus. Ergo nulla lex est aeterna.

Objection 3

Law implies an ordination to an end. But nothing that is eternal is ordered to an end. For only the ultimate end is eternal. Therefore no law is eternal.

REPLY 3

Ad tertium dicendum quod lex importat ordinem ad finem active inquantum scilicet per eam ordinantur aliqua in finem; non autem passive, idest quod ipsa lex ordinetur ad finem, nisi per accidens in gubernante cujus finis est extra ipsum, ad quem etiam necesse est ut lex ejus ordinetur. Sed finis divinae gubernationis est ipse Deus, nec ejus lex est aliud ab ipso: unde lex aeterna non ordinatur in alium finem.

Reply 3

Law implies an ordination to an end actively, that is, inasmuch as it directs someting else to an end but not passively, that is, the law itself is not directed to an end, except *per accidens* when the law is distinct from the lawgiver and it is necessary for him to direct the law to that end. But the end of the Divine governance is God Himself, and there is no other end distinct from God. Therefore, the Eternal Law is not directed to any other end.

ON THE CONTRARY

Sed contra est quod Augustinus dicit, *Lex quae summa ratio nominatur non potest cuipiam intelligenti non incommutabilis aeternaque videri.*

On the Contrary

Augustine says (*De Lib. Arb.* i, 6), "That law which is the supreme norm cannot be understood as other than unchangeable and eternal."

CORPUS

Dicendum quod, sicut supra dictum est, nihil est aliud lex quam dictamen practicae rationis in principe qui gubernat aliquam communitatem perfectam. Manifestum est autem, supposito quod mundus divina providentia regatur, ut in *Prima* habitum est, quod tota communitas universi gubernatur ratione divina. Et ideo ipsa ratio gubernationis rerum in Deo sicut in principe universitatis existens legis habet rationem. Et quia divina ratio nihil concipit ex tempore, sed habet aeternum conceptum, ut dicitur Proverb., inde est quod hujusmodi legem oportet dicere aeternam.

Corpus

As stated above (*q.* 90, *a.* 4, *c.*), law is nothing else than a dictate of practical reason in a ruler who governs some perfect society. Now it is clear that, granted that the world is governed by Divine providence, as was established in the *First Part* (*q.* 22, *aa.* 1 and 2), that the whole community of the universe is governed by Divine Reason. And, therefore, the very idea of the governance of things as it exists in God has the nature of a law and, since the Divine reason conceives nothing from time, that conception must be eternal, as is said (Proverb. viii, 2). Hence it is that this sort of law must be called eternal.

Comment

In order to show that the supreme norm existing in the mind of God has the nature of law, he must establish that it fulfills the definition of law given in *q.* 90, *a.* 4, *c.* and that it is eternal.

1. Law is a dictate of reason. The supreme norm is a dictate of God's reason.
2. Law must be made by him who has the care of the community. The supreme norm is made by God who has the care of all mankind.
3. Law must be made for the Common Good. The supreme norm is for the benefit of all mankind.
4. Law must be promulgated. The supreme norm is promulgated through God's foreknowledge of those whom it will regulate.
5. Since everything in God is eternal, the supreme norm is eternal. Therefore, there is an Eternal Law.

Some of the difficulties in this Article arise from the problem of understanding eternity. We are creatures of time; we possess our existence minute by minute, spread out in a sequence from past into the future, with an ever-changing "now." Eternity is an existence that is perfect, complete all at once; it has a single "now." People often think of eternity as a sequence that has no beginning and no end. But there is no sequence in eternity; it cannot be clocked. Hence, God can relate His plan to creatures in time without having a common date.

The Greeks had no concept of eternity; it belongs strictly and solely to Theistic Metaphysics.

ARTICLE 2
UTRUM SIT IN NOBIS ALIQUA LEX NATURALIS?
WHETHER THERE IS A NATURAL LAW IN US?

Introductory Comment

This Article will surprise and disappoint the modern reader. After reading the title of the Article, the modern reader would expect St. Thomas to argue for the existence of the Natural Law against Positivists or, at least, their medieval equivalents. The problem with which St. Thomas deals is a twofold theological one. He distinguishes the Natural Law from the Eternal Law. This problem is set in the first Objection wherein it is argued that the Eternal Law is adequate and no Natural Law is needed. Secondly, he relates the Natural Law to the Eternal Law. The Eternal Law is the supreme exemplar cause of all things in the universe and exists in the mind of God. Therefore, it is eternal, infinite and perfect. The Natural Law exists in human beings and is derivative from the Eternal Law. The term St. Thomas uses to express the relationship of things to the exemplar cause in God is "participation." Participation means that the participating entity has something that resembles the exemplar cause, though in a limited, deficient or imperfect way and that the participating entity is derived from the exemplar by efficient causality. Hence, St. Thomas concluded that, from this viewpoint, the Natural Law is a participation in the Eternal Law (the supreme exemplar).

The reason St. Thomas does not simply establish the existence of the Natural Law is that its existence was no problem for the philosophers and theologians of the thirteenth century. There were no Positivists in western Europe in that century. All leading thinkers agreed on the existence of a Natural Law, although their theoretical explanations varied. St. Thomas could simply take its existence for granted. In Question 94 St. Thomas investigates the Natural Law in detail. For a preliminary outline of Natural Law, see [421–473].

OBJECTION 1

Videtur quod non sit in nobis aliqua lex naturalis. Sufficienter enim homo gubernatur per legem aeternam. Dicit

enim Augustinus (*De Lib. Arb.*, i) quod *lex aeterna est qua
justum est ut omnia sint ordinatissima.* Sed natura non abun-
dat in superfluis, sicut nec deficit in necessariis. Ergo non est
homini aliqua lex naturalis.

Objection 1

It seems that there is no Natural Law in us. For man is sufficiently
governed by the Eternal Law. For Augustine says (*De Lib. Arb.*, i), "the
Eternal Law is that by which it is right that all things are most orderly."
But nature does not abound in superfluities, just as it does not fail in
necessities. Therefore, man does not have a Natural Law.

REPLY 1

Ad primum ergo dicendum quod ratio illa procederet si
lex naturalis esset aliquid diversum a lege aeterna. Non autem
est nisi quaedam participatio ejus, ut dictum est in corp. art.

Reply 1

That argument would succeed if the Natural Law was something
different from the Eternal Law. But Natural Law is a participation in
us of the Eternal Law, as is said in the *Corpus* of this Article.

OBJECTION 2

Praeterea, per legem ordinatur homo in suis actibus ad
finem, ut supra habitum est (*q.* 90, *a.* 2). Sed ordinatio
humanorum actuum ad finem non est per naturam, sicut
accidit in creaturis irrationalibus, quae solo appetitu naturali
agunt propter finem, sed agit homo propter finem per rationem et voluntatem. Ergo non est aliqua lex homini naturalis.

Objection 2

Further, through law man is ordered in his acts towards the end,
as was stated above (*q.* 90, *a.* 2). But the ordination of human acts to
an end is not through nature as happens in irrational creatures which

act for an end solely by natural appetite. For man acts for an end through reason and will. Therefore, there is no Natural Law in man.

REPLY 2

Ad secundum dicendum quod omnis operatio rationis et voluntatis derivatur in nobis ab eo quod est secundum naturam, ut supra habitum est (*q*. 10, *a*. 1). Nam omnis ratiocinatio derivatur a principiis naturaliter notis, et omnis appetitus eorum quae sunt ad finem derivatur a naturali appetitu ultimi finis; et sic etiam oportet quod prima directio actuum nostrorum ad finem fiat per legem naturalem.

Reply 2

Every operation through reason and will is derived in us from what is according to nature, as was said above (*q*. 10, *a*. 1). All ratiocination is derived from principles that are naturally known. And every appetite for those things which are for the end is derived from the natural appetite for the final end, and thus it is also necessary that the first direction of our acts to the end be through the Natural Law.

OBJECTION 3

Praeterea, quanto aliquis est liberior tanto minus est sub lege. Sed homo est liberior omnibus aliis animalibus propter liberum arbitrium, quod prae aliis animalibus habet. Cum igitur alia animalia non subdantur legi naturali, nec homo alicui legi naturali subdetur.

Objection 3

Further, the freer one is, the less he is under the law. But man is freer than all other animals because of his power of free choice which he possesses beyond all other animals. Since, then, the other animals are not subject to the Natural Law, neither is man subject to any natural law.

REPLY 3

Ad tertium dicendum quod etiam animalia irrationalia participant rationem aeternam suo modo, sicut et rationalis

creatura. Sed, quia rationalis creatura participat eam intel-
lectualiter et rationaliter, ideo participatio legis aeternae in
creatura rationali proprie lex vocatur: nam lex est aliquid
rationis, ut supra dictum est (*q.* 90, *aa.* 1 and 4). In creatura
autem irrationali non participatur rationaliter: unde non potest dici lex nisi per similitudinem.

Reply 3

Even irrational creatures participate in the eternal reason in
their own way as also the rational creature does. But, because the
rational creature participates in the eternal reason intellectually and
rationally, the participation of the rational creature is properly called
a law, for law is something pertaining to reason as was said above
(*q.* 90, *aa.* 1 and 4). The irrational creature's participation is not
rational, therefore it cannot be called a law except metaphorically.

ON THE CONTRARY

Sed contra est quod super illud (Rom. ii, 14), *Cum
gentes, quae legem non habent, naturaliter ea quae legis sunt
faciunt,* dicit glossa quod *si non habent legem scriptam, habent tamen legem naturalem, qua quilibet intelligit, et sibi
conscius est quid sit bonum et quid malum.*

On the Contrary

A gloss on Rom. ii, 14, "When the Gentiles who do not have the
law, do the things of the law . . .", says, "Although they have no written
law, they do have the Natural Law by which each one knows and is
conscious of what is good and what is evil."

CORPUS

Dicendum quod, sicut supra dictum est (*q.* 90, *a.* 1,
Reply 1), lex, cum sit regula et mensura, dupliciter potest
esse in aliquo: uno modo sicut in regulante et mensurante;
alio modo sicut in regulato et mensurato, quia inquantum

participat aliquid de regula vel mensura sic regulatur vel mensuratur, unde, cum omnia quae divinae providentiae subduntur a lege aeterna regulentur et mensurentur, ut ex dictis (*a.*
1) patet, manifestum est quod omnia participant aliqualiter
legem aeternam, inquantum scilicet ex impressione ejus habent inclinationes in proprios actus et fines.

Inter caetera autem rationalis creatura excellentiori quodam modo divinae providentiae subjacet, inquantum et ipsa
fit providentiae particeps, sibi ipsi et aliis providens. Unde et
in ipsa participatur ratio aeterna per quam habet naturalem
inclinationem ad debitum actum et finem, et talis participatio
legis aeternae in rationali creatura 'lex naturalis' dicitur.

Unde, cum Psalmista dixisset (Ps. iv, 6), *Sacrificate sac-*
rificium justitiae, quasi quibusdam quaerentibus quae sunt
justitiae opera, subjungit, *Multi dicunt, Quis ostendit nobis*
bona? Cui quaestioni respondens, dicit, *Signatum est super*
nos lumen vultus tui, Domine; quasi lumen rationis naturalis,
quo discernimus quid sit bonum et quid malum, quod pertinet
ad naturalem legem, nihil aliud sit quam impressio luminis
divini in nobis.

Unde patet quod lex naturalis nihil aliud est quam participatio legis aeternae in rationali creatura.

Corpus

As was said above (*q.* 90, *a.* 1, Reply 1), law, since it is a rule
and measure, can be in something in two different ways; one way, as
in the one regulating and measuring; in another way, as in the thing
regulated and measured, which, inasmuch as it participates in something
of the rule or measure, is thus regulated and measured. Hence, since
everything that is subject to Divine Providence is regulated and measured
by the Eternal Law, as is clear from what has been said (*a.* 1), it is
evident that everything participates in some manner in the Eternal Law,
inasmuch as, by the imprinting of the Eternal Law, it has an inclination
to its own proper acts and ends.

Compared to others, the rational creature is subject to Divine Providence in a more excellent way, inasmuch as it participates in Divine
Providence by providing for itself and others. Hence, it participates in
the eternal plan through which it has a natural inclination to its due act
and end. And this sort of participation in the Eternal Law by the rational

creature is called the Natural Law. Hence, after the Psalmist had said (Ps. iv, 6), "Offer up a sacrifice of justice" he adds, as though responding to some who asked what the works of justice are, "Many say, who shows us good things?" He answers this question by saying, "The light of your countenance, Lord, is signed upon us," as though the light of natural reason, by which we discern what is good and what is evil—which pertains to the Natural Law—is nothing other than an impression in us of the divine light.

And from this it is evident that the Natural Law is nothing other than a participation in the Eternal Law by the rational creature.

Comment

The emphasis here on the difference between the participation by irrational creatures and that of rational creatures is noteworthy. Not only does the rational creature participate in the Eternal Law in a more excellent way, but it also participates in the carrying out of the Eternal Law (the Divine Plan) by actively and freely providing for itself and others. Human beings are partners of God in Divine Providence.

ARTICLE 3
UTRUM SIT ALIQUA LEX HUMANA?
WHETHER THERE IS SOME HUMAN LAW?

Introductory Comment

Having established the existence of an Eternal Law and a Natural Law, the question now arises whether these two laws, by themselves, are adequate to guide men in their own affairs. The first Objection puts the question; the Reply argues that some additional human determinations are necessary. The Question of the Article has a certain vagueness, for it asks about "some" (*aliqua*) human law.

What the Article asserts is that some additional determinations are necessary and that these determinations must be worked out by human Practical Reason. The Article does not itself lay out *how* these determinations are to be made. It points out that *some* human development is necessary, but it leaves open the precise nature of that human intervention. This vagueness makes it possible for St. Thomas to begin his in-depth discussion of Positive (man-made) Law by asking whether human *laws* are useful or whether the determination spoken of here could better be handled by judges (*q.* 95, *a.* 1). Some human intervention is necessary (this Article), and it is useful that this intervention take place through man-made *laws* (*q.* 95).

As St. Thomas does so often, he here uses a comparison and contrast between the Speculative Intellect and the Practical Intellect. The reader is advised to review [298–309].

In order to understand St. Thomas's reference to demonstrative science, one should think of geometry in which each theorem is a deductive presentation leading to a true and absolutely certain conclusion.

OBJECTION 1

Videtur quod non sit aliqua lex humana. Lex enim naturalis est participatio legis aeternae, ut dictum est (*a.* 2). Sed per legem aeternam *omnia sunt ordinatissima,* ut Augustinus dicit (*De Lib. Arb.* i, 6). Ergo lex naturalis sufficit ad omnia humana ordinanda. Non est ergo necessarium quod sit aliqua lex humana.

Objection 1

It seems that there is no human law. For the Natural Law is a participation in the Eternal Law, as was stated above (*a.* 2). But, through the Eternal Law "all things are very well ordered," as Augustine says (*De Lib. Arb.* i, 6). Therefore, the Natural Law is sufficient to order all human affairs. Therefore, it is not necessary that there be a human law.

REPLY 1

Ad primum ergo dicendum quod ratio humana non potest participare ad plenum dictamen rationis divinae, sed suo modo et imperfecte. Et ideo, sicut ex parte rationis speculativae per naturalem participationem divinae sapientiae inest nobis cognitio quorumdam communium principiorum, non autem cujuslibet veritatis propria cognitio, sicut in divina sapientia continentur, ita etiam ex parte rationis practicae

naturaliter homo participat legem aeternam secundum quaedam communia principia, non autem secundum particulares
directiones singulorum, quae tamen in aeterna lege continentur. Et ideo necesse est ulterius quod ratio humana procedat
ad particulares quasdam legum sanctiones.

Reply 1

The human reason cannot participate fully in the dictate of Divine
Reason, but only in its own way and imperfectly. Therefore, just as in
the Speculative Reason, by a natural participation in divine wisdom,
there is in us a knowledge of certain general principles, not, however,
proper knowledge of every truth that is contained in divine wisdom, so
also on the part of Practical Reason, man naturally participates in the
Eternal Law in respect to certain general principles, not, however, in
respect to the particular determinations of individual cases which are
nonetheless contained in the Eternal Law. Therefore, it is necessary, in
addition, for human reason to establish certain legal sanctions for particular cases.

OBJECTION 2

Praeterea, lex habet rationem mensurae, ut dictum est
(*q.* 90, *a.* 1). Sed ratio humana non est mensura rerum, sed
potius e converso, ut in *Meta.* x, text 5 dicitur. Ergo ex
ratione humana nulla lex procedere potest.

Objection 2

Further, law has the nature of a measure, as was stated above (*q.* 90,
a. 1). But, human reason is not the measure of things but rather the
reverse is true, as is stated in *Meta.* x, text 5. Therefore, no law can
come from human reason.

REPLY 2

Ad secundum dicendum quod ratio humana secundum
se non est regula rerum, sed principia ei naturaliter indita
sunt regulae quaedam generales et mensurae omnium eorum

quae sunt per hominem agenda, quorum ratio naturalis est
regula et mensura, licet non sit mensura eorum quae sunt a
natura.

Reply 2

Human reason by itself is not the rule of things, but principles
naturally instilled in man are certain general rules and measures of all
things to be done by man, and of these things natural reason is the rule
and measures although it is not the measure of things that come from
nature.

Comment

St. Thomas is a direct realist. He holds, with Aristotle, that reality—
things as they are—determines and measures human knowledge. Kant's
reversal is rejected in advance by St. Thomas. However, human beings
are equipped with reason and naturally discovered principles which enable them to determine and measure the things they themselves do.

OBJECTION 3

Praeterea, mensura debet esse certissima, ut dicitur in
Meta. x, text 13. Sed dictamen humanae rationis de rebus
gerendis est incertum, secundum illud Wis. ix, 14, *Cogita-
tiones mortalium timidae, et incertae providentiae nostrae.*
Ergo ex ratione humana nulla lex procedere potest.

Objection 3

Further, a measure ought to be most certain, as is stated in *Meta.*
x, text 13. But the dictate of human reason concerning what should be
done is uncertain according to Wis. ix, 14, "The thoughts of mortals
are uncertain, and our counsels are uncertain." Therefore, no law can
proceed from human reason.

REPLY 3

Ad tertium dicendum quod ratio practica est circa operabilia, quae sunt singularia et contingentia, non autem circa

necessaria sicut ratio speculativa. Et ideo leges humanae non
possunt illam infallibilitatem habere quam habent conclusiones demonstrativae scientiarum. Nec oportet quod omnis
mensura sit omnino infallibilis et certa, sed secundum quod
est possibile in genere suo.

Reply 3

Practical Reason concerns operations which deal with individual
and contingent matters, not, however, with necessary things as the Speculative Reason does. Therefore, human laws cannot have that infallibility
that the demonstrated conclusions of the sciences have. Nor must every
measure be totally infallible and certain but only to the degree possible
in its own genus.

Comment

The closer one comes to the complex situations of real life, the
more difficult becomes the proper prudential judgment [362–378]. The
general principles of the moral order (of the Natural Law) are self-evident
and certain. [See *q*. 94, *a*. 4, *c*.] There is here an unstated reference to
a well-known statement of Aristotle (*Nic. Ethics,* I, iii, 5) to the effect
that it is the mark of an educated mind to expect only the degree of
certitude possible in a given subject matter.

ON THE CONTRARY

Sed contra est quod Augustinus (*De Lib. Arb.* i, 6) ponit
duas leges, unam aeternam, et aliam temporalem, quam dicit
esse humanam.

On the Contrary

Augustine (*De Lib. Arb.* i, 6) distinguishes two kinds of law, eternal
law and temporal law, which he calls human.

CORPUS

Dicendum quod, sicut supra dictum est (*q*. 90, *aa*. 1
and 4), lex est quoddam dictamen practicae rationis. Similis

autem processus esse invenitur rationis practicae et speculativae: utraque enim ex quibusdam principiis ad quasdam conclusiones procedit, ut superius habitum est (*q.* 90, *a.* 1, Reply 2). Secundum hoc ergo dicendum est quod sicut in ratione speculativa ex principiis indemonstrabilibus naturaliter cognitis producuntur conclusiones diversarum scientiarum, quarum cognitio non est nobis naturaliter indita sed per industriam rationis inventa, ita etiam ex praeceptis legis naturalis, quasi ex quibusdam principiis communibus et indemonstrabilibus, necesse est quod ratio humana procedat ad aliqua magis particulariter disponenda.

Et istae particulares dispositiones adinventae secundum rationem humanam, dicuntur 'leges humanae', observatis aliis conditionibus quae pertinent ad rationem legis, ut supra dictum est (*q.* 90). Unde Tullius dicit in sua Rhet. (*De Invent. Rhet.* ii), quod initium juris est a natura profectum; deinde quaedam in consuetudinem ex utilitatis ratione venerunt; postea res a natura profectas, et consuetudine probatas legum metus et religio sanxit.

Corpus

As stated above (*q.* 90, *aa.* 1 and 4), law is a dictate of Practical Reason. However, Practical and Speculative Reason are found to involve a similar process, for each moves from some principles to conclusions, as was stated above (*q.* 90, *a.* 1, Reply 2). Accordingly, we must say that, just as from indemonstrable principles Speculative Reason produces conclusions of the various sciences that are not known naturally but have been discovered through the diligent activity of reason, so also from the precepts of the Natural Law, as from universal and indemonstrable principles, human reason must proceed to things that must be dealt with more in particular.

And these particular determinations, devised by human reason, are called "human laws" provided they fulfill the other conditions which belong to the nature of law, as described above (*q.* 90). Hence, Cicero says in his *Rhetoric* (*De Invent. Rhet.* ii), that the beginning of law comes from nature; then certain things become customary because of their usefulness; afterwards, what had come from nature and was approved by custom was sanctioned by fear and reverence of the laws.

Comment

The nature of these "determinations" is explained at length in *q.* 95, *a.* 2.

ARTICLE 4
UTRUM FUERIT NECESSARIUM ESSE
ALIQUAM LEGEM DIVINAM?
WHETHER IT WAS NECESSARY THAT
THERE BE A DIVINE LAW?

Introductory Comment

This Article is basically theological. It presupposes the distinction made by St. Thomas between the natural order and the supernatural order.

Man is naturally ordered to happiness [see 379–392]. If he were left to his natural powers, he could, by these powers alone, achieve some degree of happiness proportionate to his nature. In this case, the Natural Law and Human Law would be adequate to guide him in his human acts.

However, God, in his great love, has given man a new and higher end, a happiness he could not achieve by his natural powers. This new end is an eternal, intimate union with God in knowledge and love, the Beatific Vision, a sharing in the inner life of God Himself. Such an end is a gratuitous gift of God and cannot be reached by human powers alone. Hence, it is called a *supernatural* end. To reach this end man needs new powers (grace) and new guidance (the Divine Law).

Note that the Article establishes a special meaning for "Divine Law." Obviously, in ordinary language, the Eternal Law can be called a "Divine Law." But, in the usage set forth here, the Divine Law is the law given man in Biblical Revelation.

This Article also has a certain vagueness which leads to the next Article in which "some" Divine Law is specified as the law revealed by God.

The Article is neatly organized. The first part of the *Corpus* gives four distinct reasons for the need of a Divine Law. Then, St.

Thomas finds all four reasons summarized in a single scriptural quotation (*auctoritas*). The argument is complete without the *auctoritas* [492–498].

OBJECTION 1

Videtur quod non fuerit necessarium esse aliquam legem divinam, quia, ut dictum est (*a*. 2), lex naturalis est quaedam participatio legis aeternae in nobis. Sed lex aeterna est lex divina, ut dictum est (*a*. 1). Ergo non oportet quod praeter legem naturalem, et leges humanas ab ea derivatas, sit aliqua lex divina.

Objection 1

It seems that it was not necessary that there be a Divine Law because, as has been stated (*a*. 2), the Natural Law is a participation of the Eternal Law in us, as stated above (*a*. 1). But, the Eternal Law is the Divine Law. Therefore, there was no need for a Divine Law in addition to the Natural Law and its derivative, human law.

REPLY 1

Ad primum ergo dicendum quod per naturalem legem participatur lex aeterna secundum proportionem capacitatis humanae naturae. Sed oportet ut altiori modo dirigatur homo in ultimum finem supernaturalem. Et ideo superadditur lex divinitus data, per quam lex aeterna participatur altiori modo.

Reply 1

Through the Natural Law we participate in the Eternal Law in proportion to the capacity of human nature. But man should be directed in a higher manner to his last supernatural end. Therefore, there is, in addition, a law given by God through which man participates in the Eternal Law in a higher manner.

OBJECTION 2

Praeterea, Ecclus. xv, 14 dicitur quod *Deus dimisit hom-*
inem in manu consilii sui. Consilium autem est actus rationis,
ut supra habitum est (*q.* 14, *a.* 1). Ergo homo dimissus est
gubernationi suae rationis. Sed dictamen rationis humanae
est lex humana, ut dictum est (*a.* 3). Ergo non oportet quod
homo aliqua lege divina gubernetur.

Objection 2

Further, it is said (Ecclus. xv, 14) that "God left man in the hand of
his own counsel." However, counsel is an act of reason, as was said above
(*q.* 14, *a.* 1). Therefore, man was left to the guidance of his own reason.
But the dictate of human reason is human law, as stated above (*a.* 3).
Therefore, it is not necessary for man to be guided by some Divine Law.

REPLY 2

Ad secundum dicendum quod consilium est inquisitio
quaedam, unde oportet quod procedat ex aliquibus principiis.
Nec sufficit quod procedat ex principiis naturaliter inditis,
quae sunt praecepta legis naturae, propter praedicta in corp.
art.; sed oportet quod superaddantur quaedam alia principia,
scilicet praecepta legis divinae.

Reply 2

Counsel is a sort of investigation. Hence, it must proceed from
some principles. Nor is it enough that it proceed from naturally known
principles as is explained in the *Corpus,* other principles must be added,
namely, the precepts of the Divine Law.

OBJECTION 3

Praeterea, natura humana est sufficientior irrationalibus
creaturis. Sed irrationales creaturae non habent aliquam legem divinam praeter inclinationem naturalem eis inditam.

Ergo multo minus creatura rationalis debet habere aliquam legem divinam praeter naturalem legem.

Objection 3

Further, human nature is more self sufficient than irrational creatures. But irrational creatures have no Divine Law beyond the inclination given them by nature. Much less, then, should the rational creature have some Divine Law besides the Natural Law.

REPLY 3

Ad tertium dicendum quod creaturae irrationales non ordinantur ad altiorem finem quam sit finis qui est proportionatus naturali virtuti ipsarum. Et ideo non est similis ratio.

Reply 3

Irrational creatures are not ordered to an end higher than the end that is proportioned to their own natural powers. Therefore, the comparison fails.

ON THE CONTRARY

Sed contra est quod David expetit legem a Deo sibi poni, dicens (Ps. 118, 33) *Legem pone mihi, Domine, viam justificationum tuarum.*

On the Contrary

David asked God to set a law for him, saying (Ps. 118, 33), "Set for me a law, Lord, the way of your justifications."

CORPUS

Dicendum quod praeter legem naturalem et legem humanam, necessarium fuit ad directionem humanae vitae habere legem divinam. Et hoc propter quatuor rationes.

Primo quidem, quia per legem dirigitur homo ad actus

proprios in ordine ad ultimum finem. Et, si quidem homo
ordinaretur tantum ad finem qui non excederet proportionem
naturalis facultatis hominis, non oporteret quod homo haberet
aliquid directivum ex parte rationis supra legem naturalem
et legem humanitus positam, quae ab ea derivatur. Sed, quia
homo ordinatur ad finem beatudinis aeternae, quae excedit
proportionem naturalis facultatis humanae, ut supra habitum
est (*q. 5, a. 5*), ideo necessarium fuit ut, supra legem naturalem et humanam, dirigetur etiam ad suum finem lege
divinitus data.

Secundo, quia propter incertitudinem humani judicii,
praecipue de rebus contingentibus et particularibus, contingit
de actibus humanis diversorum esse diversa judicia, ex quibus
etiam diversae et contrariae leges procedunt. Ut ergo homo
absque omni dubitatione scire possit quid ei sit agendum et
quid vitandum, necessarium fuit ut in actibus propriis dirigetur per legem divinitus datam, de qua constat quod non
potest errare.

Tertio, quia de his potest homo legem facere de quibus
potest judicare. Judicium autem hominis esse non potest de
interioribus actibus qui latent, sed solum de exterioribus mo-
tibus qui apparent, et tamen ad perfectionem virtutis requiritur quod in utrisque actibus homo rectus existat. Et ideo lex
humana non potuit cohibere et ordinare sufficienter interiores
actus, sed necessarium fuit quod ad hoc superveniret lex
divina.

Quarto, quia, sicut Augustinus dicit (*De Lib. Arb.* i, 5,
6), lex humana non potest omnia quae male fiunt punire vel
prohibere; quia, dum auferre vellet omnia mala, sequeretur
quod etiam multa bona tollerentur, et impediretur utilitas
boni communis, quod est necessarium ad conversationem humanam. Ut ergo nullum malum improhibitum et impunitum
remaneat, necessarium fuit supervenire legem divinam, per
quam omnia peccata prohibentur.

Et istae quatuor causae tanguntur in Ps. cxviii, ubi
dicitur, Lex Domini immaculata, idest nullam peccati turpi-
tudinem permittens, convertens animas, quia non solum exteriores actus sed etiam interiores dirigit, testimonium Domini

fidele, propter certitudinem veritatis et rectitudinis, sapientiam praestans parvulis, inquantum ordinat hominem ad supernaturalem finem et divinum.

Corpus

Besides the Natural Law and human law, it was necessary for the direction of human life to have a Divine Law. And this for four reasons.

First, because by law man is directed to perform acts proper for his ordering to his last end. And, indeed, if man were ordered solely to a last end that did not exceed the natural powers of man, there would be no need for man to have any other directive for his reason besides the Natural Law and human law which is derived from the Natural Law. But, because man is ordered to the end of eternal happiness which exceeds the natural power of man, as was shown above (*q. 5, a. 5*), therefore, it was necessary that, in addition to Natural Law and human law, man be directed to his end by a law given by God.

Secondly, on account of the uncertainty of human judgment, especially about contingent and individual things, it happens that different people have different judgments about human acts which also produce different and contradictory laws. Therefore, in order that man might know, without any doubt at all, what he must do and what he must avoid, it was necessary that he be guided in his proper acts by a law given by God concerning which there can be no mistake.

Thirdly, because man can make a law only about those things which he is able to judge. Now, man cannot judge about interior acts which are hidden but only about exterior movements which are visible, and, yet, for the perfection of virtue man is required to act rightly in both kinds of acts. Therefore, human law cannot adequately restrain and order the interior acts but for this it was necessary that a Divine Law be added.

Fourthly, as Augustine says (*De Lib. Arb.* i, 5, 6), human law cannot punish or forbid all evil deeds, for, while it aims at repressing all evils, it would follow that many good things would be lost and the service of the common good, which is necessary for human association, would be impeded. Therefore, that no evil would remain unprohibited and unpunished, it was necessary that there be a Divine Law which would prohibit all sins. All four of these causes are touched upon in Ps. cxviii, where it says, "The law of God is immaculate," that is, allowing no turpitude of sin, "converting souls," because it directs not only exterior acts but also interior ones, "the testimony of the Lord is faithful," because of the certitude of truth and rectitude, "giving wisdom to little ones," by directing man to an end that is supernatural and divine.

Comment

The Fourth Reason should be compared with *q*. 96, *a*. 2, *c*.

ARTICLE 5
UTRUM LEX DIVINA SIT UNA TANTUM?
WHETHER THERE IS ONLY ONE DIVINE LAW?

Introductory Comment

The problem of this Article is strictly a religious or theological one. The Catholic Bible consists of two major parts called the Old Testament and the New Testament respectively. In both Testaments God communicated precepts and commandments. These precepts constitute Divine Laws.

To review, the Eternal Law exists in the mind of God and is the supreme exemplar for the created universe. The Natural Law is a partial participation in the Eternal Law. The Natural Law is naturally known to human beings and exists in their minds. St. Thomas has already established (*a*. 4) that a Divine Law was necessary because man has a supernatural end to which the Natural Law is an inadequate directive.

The problem now faced is this. Is the Old Law (given in the Old Testament) the same as the New Law (given in the New Testament) or, are there two Divine Laws? St. Thomas asserts that there are two Divine Laws. They are not specifically distinct but they are distinct only as the imperfect is distinct from the perfect. The Old Law is a preparation for the coming of Christ and the New Law.

There is considerable agreement between the Natural Law and the Divine Law. They have a common ultimate source in the Eternal Law but are derived in different ways; the one through man's natural power, the other by God's revelation.

John Austin identified the Natural Law with the Divine Law and so made the Natural Law dependent on Revelation. He thus eliminated any possibility of man's discovering the Natural Law for himself and made it irrelevant for modern jurisprudence.

For the believing Christian, the independent extensive agreement of the Natural Law with the Divine Law is mutually confirmatory.

OBJECTION 1

Videtur quod lex divina sit una tantum. Unius enim regis in uno regno est una lex. Sed totum humanum genus comparatur ad Deum sicut ad unum regem, secundum illud Ps. xlvi, 8, Rex omnis terrae Deus. Ergo est una tantum lex divina.

Objection 1

It seems that there is only one Divine Law. For of one King in one kingdom there is only one law. But the human race is related to God as to one king, according to Ps. xlvi, 8, "God is king of all the world." Therefore, there is only one Divine Law.

REPLY 1

Ad primum ergo dicendum quod, sicut paterfamilias in domo alia mandata proponit pueris et alia adultis, ita etiam unus rex Deus in uno suo regno aliam legem dedit hominibus adhuc imperfectis existentibus, et aliam perfectiorem jam manu-ductis per priorem legem ad majorem capacitatem divinorum.

Reply 1

Just as a father of a family gives different commands to children and to adults, so the one King, God, in His one kingdom gave one law to men who were still imperfect and another more perfect law to those who, trained by the previous law, were already brought to a greater capacity for divine things.

OBJECTION 2

Praeterea, lex omnis ordinatur ad finem quem legislator intendit in eis quibus legem fert. Sed unum et idem est quod Deus intendit in omnibus hominibus, secundum illud I ad Tim. ii, 4, *Vult omnes homines salvos fieri, et ad agnitionem veritatis venire.* Ergo una tantum est lex divina.

Objection 2

Further, every law is ordained to the end which the legislator intends for those for whom he makes the law. But God intends one and the same end for all men according to I Tim. ii, 4, "He wills all men to be saved and to come to the recognition of the truth." Therefore, there is only one Divine Law.

REPLY 2

Ad secundum dicendum quod salus hominum non poterat esse nisi per Christum, secundum illud Act. iv, 12, *Non est aliud nomen datum hominibus in quo oporteat nos salvos fieri.* Et ideo lex perfecte omnes ad salutem inducens dari non potuit nisi post Christi adventum; antea vero dari oportuit populo ex quo Christus erat nasciturus legem praeparatoriam ad Christi susceptionem, in qua quaedam rudimenta salutaris justitiae continentur.

Reply 2

The salvation of men cannot be achieved except through Christ, according to Acts iv, 12, "There is no other name given to men in which we must be saved." Therefore, the law that perfectly leads all men to salvation could not be given before the coming of Christ. However, before that, it was necessary to give to the people from whom Christ was to be born a law preparatory for His reception which contained some rudiments of saving righteousness.

OBJECTION 3

Praeterea, lex divina propinquior esse videtur legi aeternae, quae est una, quam lex naturalis, quanto altior est

revelatio gratiae quam cognitio naturae. Sed lex naturalis est
una omnium hominum. Ergo multo magis lex divina.

Objection 3

Further, the Divine Law seems to be closer to the Etenal Law,
which is one, than the Natural Law is, since the revelation of Grace is
higher than the knowledge of nature. But there is one Natural Law for
all men. Therefore, much more must there be only one Divine Law.

REPLY 3

Ad tertium dicendum quod lex naturalis dirigit hominem
secundum quaedam praecepta communia, in quibus conveniunt tam perfecti quam imperfecti; et ideo est una omnium.
Sed lex divina dirigit hominem etiam in particularibus quibusdam, ad quae non similiter se habent perfecti et imperfecti;
et ideo oportuit legem divinam esse duplicem, sicut jam dictum est in corp.

Reply 3

The Natural Law directs men through certain universal precepts
which are the same for both perfect and imperfect men. Hence, there is
only one Natural Law for everybody. But the Divine Law directs men
also in cetain detailed matters which are not the same for the perfect
and the imperfect, and, therefore, it was necessary for the Divine Law
to be twofold, as has already been explained in the *Corpus* [of this
Article].

ON THE CONTRARY

Sed contra est quod Apostolus dicit, ad Heb. v, ii, 12,
Translato sacerdotio, necesse est ut legis translatio fiat. Sed
sacerdotium est duplex, ut ibidem dicitur, scilicet sacerdotium
leviticum et sacerdotium Christi. Ergo etiam duplex est lex
divina, scilicet Lex Vetus et Lex Nova.

On the Contrary

The Apostle said (Heb. v, ii, 12), "When there is a change in the priesthood, there must be a change in the law as well." But the priesthood is twofold, as is said in the same place, namely, the Levitical priesthood and the priesthood of Christ. Therefore, the Divine Law must be twofold as well, namely, the Old Law and the New Law.

CORPUS

Dicendum quod, sicut in Primo (*q*. 30, *a*. 3) dictum est, distinctio est causa numeri. Dupliciter autem inveniuntur aliqua distingui: uno modo, sicut ea quae sunt omnino specie diversa, ut equus et bos; alio modo, sicut perfectum et imperfectum in eadem specie, sicut puer et vir. Et hoc modo lex divina distinguitur in legem veterem et legem novam. Unde Apostolus (Gal. iii, 24), comparat statum veteris legis statui pueri existentis sub paedagogo; statum autem novae legis comparat statui viri perfecti, qui jam non est sub paedagago.

Attenditur autem perfectio et imperfectio utriusque legis secundum tria quae ad legem pertinent, ut supra dictum est.

Primo enim ad legem pertinet ut ordinetur ad bonum commune sicut ad finem, ut supra dictum est (*q*. 90, *a*. 2). Quod quidem potest esse duplex, scilicet bonum sensibile et terrenum. Et ad tale bonum ordinabat directe lex vetus: unde statim, Exod. iii, 8, 17, in principio legis invitatur populus ad regnum terrenum Chananaeorum. Et iterum bonum intelligibile et coeleste; et ad hoc ordinat lex nova: unde statim Christus ad regnum coelorum in suae praedicationis principio invitavit, dicens Matt., iv, 17, *Paenitentiam agite, appropinquabit enim regnum coelorum.* Et ideo Augustinus dicit, *Contra Faust.* iv, quod temporalium rerum promissiones in Testamento veteri continentur, et ideo 'vetus' appellatur; sed aeternae vitae promissio ad novum pertinet Testmentum.

Secundo, ad legem pertinet dirigere humanos actus secundum ordinem justitiae, in quo etiam superabundat lex nova legi veteri, interiores actus animi ordinando, secundum illud Matt., v, 20, *Nisi abundaverit justitia vestra plus quam*

Scribarum et Pharisaeorum, non intrabitis in regnum coelo-rum; et ideo dicitur quod lex vetus cohibet manum, lex nova animum.

Tertio, ad legem pertinet inducere homines ad obser-vantiam mandatorum, et hoc quidem lex vetus faciebat timore poenarum; lex autem nova facit hoc per amorem, qui in cordibus nostris infunditur per gratiam Christi, quae in lege nova confertur, sed in lege veteri figurabatur. Et ideo dicit Augustinus (*Contra Adimant. Manicab. discip.* xviii) quod brevis differentia est legis et Evangelii, timor et amor.

Corpus

As was said in the *Prima Pars* (*q.* 30, *a.* 3), distinction causes number. But things are found to be distinguished in two ways. One way is the distinction between things that belong to entirely different species, as between a horse and a cow. The second way is the distinction between the perfect and the imperfect in the same species, as between child and adult. And in this way, the Divine Law is divided into the Old Law and the New Law. Hence, the Apostle (Gal. iii, 24) compares the status of the Old Law to the status of a child who is subject to a tutor, but he compares the status of the New Law to an adult man who is no longer subject to a tutor.

Now, we must consider the perfection and imperfection of these two laws with reference to three elements that belong to law, as was stated above (*q.* 90).

First, it belongs to law to be ordered to the Common Good as to its end, as was said above (*q.* 90, *a.* 2). The Common Good can be twofold; it may be a sensible and terrestrial good. And to this sort of end the Old Law directly ordered men. Hence, at the very outset of the Law, the people were invited to the terrestrial kingdom of the Canaanites (Exod. iii, 8, 17). Or, again, the Common Good may be an intelligible and celestial one. And to this end the New Law directs men. Hence, in the very beginning of his preaching, Christ invited men to the Kingdom of God, saying (Matt. iv, 17), "Do penance for the Kingdom of Heaven is at hand." And, therefore, Augustine says (*Contr. Faust.* iv) that "the promises of material things were contained in the Old Testament, and, for that reason, it was called 'Old', while the promise of eternal life belongs to the New Testament."

Secondly, it belongs to law to direct human acts in accordance with the order of righteousness, in which the New Law surpasses the Old Law by ordering the internal acts of the soul, according to Matt. v, 20, "Unless your righteousness abounds more than that of the scribes and Pharisees, you will not enter the Kingdom of Heaven." And, therefore, it is said that the Old Law controlled the hand, but the New Law controls the soul.

Thirdly, it belongs to law to bring men to the observance of the commandments. The Old Law did this through fear of punishment, but the New Law does it through love which is poured into our hearts by the grace of Christ which the New Law actually gives us while it is only prefigured in the Old Law. Hence, Augustine says (*Contra Adimant. Manicab. discip.* xviii), "The difference between the Old and the New Testament is, in short, the difference between fear and love."

ARTICLE 6
UTRUM SIT ALIQUA LEX FOMITIS?
WHETHER THERE IS A LAW
IN THE FOMES PECCATI?

Introductory Comment

In the previous Articles of this Question, St. Thomas dealt with laws, properly so-called, i.e., laws which fulfill, however analogously, the esential definition established in *q.* 90, *a.* 4, *c.*

In this Article he returns to the Pauline text discussed briefly in *q.* 90, *a.* 1, *obj.* 1 and Reply 1. He there indicates that St. Paul was using the term "law" in a quite different sense from the one he uses in the *Corpus* of *a.* 1. Yet, he indicates a basis for St. Paul's usage; he indicated that whereas he was using "law" in an essential sense, St. Paul's usage was "by participation." However, he did not, in that place, explain the basis in detail. In this Article he gives a lengthy explanation.

This explanation often seems complex and somewhat contrived to modern readers. Those readers who are not interested in theology may omit this Article without serious loss to the understanding of the *Treatise.* The important conclusion of the discussion is that St. Paul uses the term "law" for something that does not pertain to reason and so uses it in a different sense than St. Thomas does.

The term *fomes peccati* means anything that foments or leads to sin. In this Article it refers to human sensuality insofar as that sensuality leads to sin. Human sensuality refers to our sensitive appetites—called "inclinations"—in this context. Included are our desires for drink, food, sex, and sensible pleasures.

One must remember that, according to Catholic theology, Adam was created with all the powers and inclinations proper to human nature but that, in addition, he was given special gifts which enlightened his mind and strengthened his will so that he could not "be taken by surprise" by his sensual inclinations. But Adam sinned and thereby, through an act of Divine Justice, he was punished by losing these special gifts. Hence, he was unable to pass these special gifts on to his posterity. Thus, human sensuality, which is good in itself, became a *fomes peccati*. Since this came about through a punishment from God's justice and therefore as the result of a Divine Law, the *fomes* itself participated in the Divine Law through God's justice and so can be called a "law." Thus St. Thomas illustrates this by citing the example of a nobleman condemned to slave labor for some crime. This condemnation being an act of a just law can be called a "law" insofar as it participates in the just law.

Note that the law proper to man is that he act according to reason so that reason should control his sensuality. When he fails to so control his sensuality, he acts against his own basic law.

OBJECTION 1

Videtur quod non sit aliqua lex fomitis. Dicit enim Isidorus quod *lex in ratione consistit*. Fomes autem non consistit in ratione, sed magis a ratione deviat. Ergo fomes non habet rationem legis.

Objection 1

It seems that there is no law in the *fomes peccati*. For, Isidore says (*Etym.*, v) that "law is based on reason." But the *fomes peccati* is not based on reason but rather deviates from it. Therefore, the *fomes peccati* does not have the nature of a law.

REPLY 1

Ad primum ergo dicendum quod ratio illa procedit de fomite secundum se considerato, prout inclinat ad malum: sic

enim non habet rationem legis, ut dictum est in corp. art.,
sed secundum quod sequitur ex divinae legis justitia: tanquam
si diceretur lex esse quod aliquis nobilis propter suam culpam
ad servilia opera induci permitteretur.

Reply 1

That argument considers the *fomes peccati* simply in itself, insofar
as it leads men into sin. In this respect the *fomes peccati* does not have
the nature of a law, as was explained in the *Corpus,* but it has the nature
of law only insofar as it follows from the justice of the Divine Law. It
is as though we would call it a law that a nobleman would be permitted
to be condemned to slave labor for some crime.

OBJECTION 2

Praeterea, omnis lex obligatoria est, ita quod qui eam
non servant transgressores dicuntur. Sed fomes non constituit
aliquem transgressorem ex hoc quod ipsum non sequitur; sed
magis transgressor redditur si quis ipsum sequatur. Ergo
fomes non habet rationem legis.

Objection 2

Further, every law is obligatory so that whoever does not obey it
is called a transgressor. But the *fomes peccati* does not make one a
transgressor, if he does not follow it, but rather he becomes a transgressor,
if he does follow it. Therefore, the *fomes peccati* does not have the nature
of law.

REPLY 2

Ad secundum dicendum quod objectio illa procedit de
eo quod est lex quasi regula et mensura; sic enim deviantes
a lege transgressores constituuntur. Sic autem fomes non est
lex, sed per quamdam participationem, ut supra dictum est.

Reply 2

That objection considers law insofar as it is a rule and measure,
for those who deviate from the law thus understood are made trans-
gressors. But in that sense, the *fomes peccati* is not a law, but it is a

law through a sort of participation, as was said above [in the *Corpus* of this Article].

OBJECTION 3

Praeterea, lex ordinatur ad bonum commune, ut supra habitum est. Sed fomes non inclinat ad bonum commune, sed magis ad bonum privatum. Ergo fomes non habet rationem legis.

Objection 3

Further, law is ordered to the Common Good, as was stated above (*q.* 90, *a.* 2). But the *fomes peccati* is not ordered to the Common Good but rather to a private good. Therefore, it does not have the nature of law.

REPLY 3

Ad tertium dicendum quod ratio illa procedit de fomite quantum ad inclinationem propriam, non autem quantum ad suam originem. Et tamen, si consideretur inclinatio sensualitatis prout est in aliis animalibus, sic ordinatur ad bonum commune, id est ad conservationem naturae in specie vel individuo; et hoc est etiam in homine prout sensualitas subditur rationi: sed fomes dicitur secundum quod exit rationis ordinem.

Reply 3

That argument is based on a consideration of the *fomes peccati* with respect to its proper inclination, not, however, with respect to its origin. For, if the *fomes peccati* be considered as it is in other animals, it is indeed ordered to the Common Good, that is, to the conservation of nature in the species or in the individual. And this is true of human sensuality insofar as it is subject to reason, for it is called the *fomes peccati* only insofar as it strays from the order of reason.

In the other animals, sensuality is directed by natural inclination to the good of the species, but in man, sensuality must be controlled by reason and so directed to the good of the species and of the individual. But when the *fomes peccati* is considered according to its origin, as imposed by Divine Justice as a punishment, it participates in the Divine Law of justice and so can be called a "law" by this participation.

ON THE CONTRARY

Sed contra est quod Apostolus dicit, *Video aliam legem in membris meis repugnantem legi mentis meae.*

On the Contrary

The Apostle says (Rom. vii, 2), "I see another law in my members fighting against the law of my mind."

Comment

It should be noted that this is the same text as was used in *q.* 90, *a.* 1, *obj.* 1.

CORPUS

Dicendum quod, sicut supra dictum est, lex essentialiter invenitur in regulante et mensurante, participative autem in eo quod mensuratur et regulatur; ita quod omnis inclinatio vel ordinatio quae invenitur in his quae subjecta sunt legi participative dicitur 'lex', ut ex supra dictis patet. Potest autem in his quae subduntur legi aliqua inclinatio inveniri dupliciter a legislatore. Uno modo in quantum directe suos inclinat subditos ad aliquid, et interdum diversos ad diversos actus: secundum quem modum potest dici quod alia est lex militum, et alia est lex mercatorum. Alio modo indirecte, inquantum, scilicet, per hoc quod legislator destituit aliquem sibi subditum aliqua dignitate sequitur quod transeat in alium ordinem, et quasi in aliam legem: puta si miles ex militia destituatur transibit in legem rusticorum vel mercatorum.

Sic igitur sub Deo legislatore diversae creaturae diversas habent naturales inclinationes, ita ut quod uni est quodammodo lex, alteri sit contra legem; ut si dicam quod furibundum esse est quodammodo lex canis, est autem contra legem ovis vel alterius mansueti animalis. Est ergo hominis lex, quam sortitur ex ordinatione divina, secundum propriam conditionem ut secundum rationem operetur. Quae quidem lex fuit tam valida in primo statu ut nihil vel praeter rationem vel contra rationem posset subrepere homini. Sed dum homo a Deo recessit, incurrit in hoc quod feratur secundum impetum sensualitatis. Et unicuique etiam particulariter hoc contingit quanto magis a ratione recesserit: ut sic quodammodo bestiis assimiletur quae sensualitatis impetu feruntur, secundum illud Psalm., *Homo cum in honore esset, non intellexit; comparatus est jumentis insipientibus, et similis factus est illis.*

Sic igitur ipsa sensualitatis inclinatio, quae 'fomes' dicitur, in aliis quidem animalibus simpliciter habet rationem legis, illo tamen modo quo in talibus lex dici potest secundum directam inclinationem legis. In hominibus autem secundum hoc non habet rationem legis, sed magis est deviatio a lege rationis. Sed inquantum per divinam justitiam homo destituitur originali justitia et vigore rationis, ipse impetus sensualitatis, qui eum ducit, habet rationem legis inquantum est poenalis, et ex lege divina consequens hominem destitutum propria dignitate.

Corpus

As was stated above (*a*. 2; *q*. 90, *a*. 1, *ad* 1), law is essentially in the one regulating or measuring but is in that which is regulated and measured only by participation, so that every inclination or ordination that is found in those things that are subject to a law can be called "law" by participation.

Now, it is possible in those things which are subject to a law to find some inclination from the legislator, and this can be in two different ways.

This happens in the first way inasmuch as a lawgiver directly inclines his subjects to something, and sometimes inclines different sorts of subjects to different sorts of acts. According to this mode, the military law can be said to be different from the mercantile law.

The second mode comes about indirectly, inasmuch as the legislator deprives a subject of some dignity with the result that the subject passes into a different order and, as it were, becomes subject to a different law, as, for example, when a soldier is expelled from the army, he will come under the rural or the mercantile law.

Thus, therefore, under God's legislation different creatures have different natural inclinations so that what is, in a sense, law for one is against the law for another, as if I were to say that being ferocious is, in a sense, the law for a dog but not for a sheep or some other gentle animal. Hence, it is a law for man, which he has received from God, in accordance with his own proper natural condition, that he act according to reason. And this law was so effective in the primitive state that nothing either beside the law or against it could take man by surprise. But when man turned away from God, he came under the influence of his sensual impulse, and this happens to each one in particular the more he withdraws from reason. And so, in a way, he is likened to the beasts who are controlled by the impulses of their sensuality, according to Ps. xlviii, 21, "when man was in honor, he did not understand and has been compared to senseless animals and became like them."

Thus, therefore, the sensual inclination itself, which is called the *fomes peccati,* in other animals simply has the nature of law but only insofar as a law can be said to be in them in accordance with the direct inclination of the law. Accordingly, in men the sensual inclination does not have the nature of law but rather is a deviation from the law of reason. But, inasmuch as man has been deprived through divine justice of original justice and strength of mind inasmuch as it is a penalty following from the Divine Law and depriving man of his proper dignity.

QUESTION 92
DE EFFECTIBUS LEGIS
CONCERNING THE EFFECTS OF LAW

Deinde considerandum est de effectibus legis, et circa hoc quaeruntur duo:

1. utrum effectus legis sit homines facere bonos;
2. utrum effectus legis sint imperare, vetare, permittere, et punire, sicut Legisperitus dicit.

Question 92

Next we must consider the effects of law, and on this question there are two points of inquiry:

1. Whether the effect of law is to make men good;
2. Whether the effects of law are to order, to forbid, to permit and to punish, as the Jurist says (*Digest* I, III, 7).

ARTICLE 1
UTRUM EFFECTUS LEGIS SIT
FACERE HOMINES BONOS?
WHETHER THE EFFECT OF LAW
IS TO MAKE MEN GOOD?

Introductory Comment

This Article may seem puzzling to some. St. Thomas has already established that the final cause, the intrinsic finality of law, is the Common Good. Law thus must provide for and promote the Common Good. That seems to be the effect of law, and this might satisfy some jurists. But we must remember that St. Thomas is primarily interested in law precisely as it bears on human acts and so as it affects the moral development of those subject to law. What changes take place in the subjects of law when they obey the law? The answer is that obedience to the law develops virtue.

OBJECTION 1

Videtur quod legis effectus non sit facere homines bonos. Homines enim sunt boni per virtutem: virtus enim est quae *bonum facit habentem,* ut dicitur in *Ethic.* ii, 6. Sed virtus est homini a solo Deo: ipse enim *eam facit in nobis sine nobis,* ut supra dictum est in definitione virtutis (*q. 55, a. 4*). Ergo legis non est homines facere bonos.

Objection 1

It seems that the effect of law is not to make men good. For men are good through virtue; "for virtue is that which makes its possessor good," as is said in *Ethic.* ii, 6. But virtue comes to man only from God, for it is He who "makes virtue in us without us," as was said above in the definition of virtue (*q. 55, a. 4*). Therefore, the effect of law is not to make men good.

REPLY 1

Ad primum ergo dicendum quod duplex est virtus, ut ex supra dictis patet (*q. 63, a. 2*), scilicet acquisita et infusa. Ad utramque autem aliquid operatur operum assuetudo, sed diversimode; nam virtutem quidem acquisitam causat; ad virtutem autem infusam disponit, et eam jam habitam conservat et promovet. Et quia lex ad hoc datur ut dirigat actus humanos, inquantum actus humani operantur ad virtutem, intantum lex facit homines bonos. Unde et Philosophus dicit in *Polit.,* et *Ethic.* ii, 1, quod *legislatores assuefacientes faciunt bonos.*

Reply 1

There are two kinds of virtue, as is clear from what was said above (*q. 63, a. 2*), namely, acquired and infused. However, becoming accustomed to actions contributes something to both types of virtue, but in different ways, for it causes the acquired virtues and prepares man for the infused virtues and preserves and fosters them once they are possessed. And, because law is given for the purpose of directing human acts, insofar as human acts operate toward virtue, to that extent does law make men good. Hence, the Philosopher says (*Polit.* [this reference appears to be mistaken]; *Ethic.* ii, 1) that "Lawgivers, by habituating men to good acts, make men good."

Comment

In St. Thomas's theology, a distinction must be made between the natural order and the supernatural order. The natural order includes everything that belong to human nature in itself. To human nature belong the natural virtues, for example, the virtues of temperance, fortitude, justice, and prudence [322–378.]

But God has raised man to a higher level of being in which he has a goal (participation in the Divine Life of the Trinity) for which he requires supernatural powers, the infused virtues, which God gives with his grace and which man cannot acquire by his own power.

Human law makes man good by guiding him (its directive force) [see *q.* 96, *a.* 5, *c.*] and by accustoming the wicked to doing good acts. St. Thomas firmly believed in the teaching mission of law.

OBJECTION 2

Praeterea, lex non prodest homini nisi legi obediat. Sed hoc ipsum quod homo obedit legi est ex bonitate. Ergo bonitas praeexigitur in homine ad legem. Non igitur lex facit bonos homines.

Objection 2

Further, law does not benefit man unless he obeys the law. But man's obedience to the law comes from goodness. Therefore, goodness in man is prerequired for law. Therefore, law does not make men good.

REPLY 2

Ad secundum dicendum quod non semper aliquis obedit legi ex bonitate perfecta virtutis; sed quandoque quidem ex timore poenae, quandoque autem ex solo dictamine rationis, quod est quoddam principium virtutis, ut supra habitum est (*q.* 63, *a.* 1).

Reply 2

Law is not always obeyed out of the perfect goodness of virtue. Sometimes it is obeyed through fear of punishment, and, sometimes from a dictate of reason, which is a beginning of virtue, as was shown above (*q*. 63, *a*. 1).

OBJECTION 3

Praeterea, lex ordinatur ad bonum commune, ut supra dictum est (*q*. 90, *a*. 2). Sed quidam bene se habent in his quae ad commune pertinent qui tamen in propriis non bene se habent. Non ergo ad legem pertinet quod faciat homines bonos.

Objection 3

Further, law is ordered to the Common Good, as has been said (*q*. 90, *a*. 2). But there are some who are well-disposed toward the Common Good, yet are not well-disposed in their own personal lives. Therefore, it does not belong to law to make men good.

REPLY 3

Ad tertium dicendum quod bonitas cujuslibet partis consideratur in proportione ad suum totum: unde et Augustinus dicit in *Confess*. iii *quod turpis est omnis pars quae suo toti non congruit*. Cum igitur quilibet homo sit pars civitatis, impossibile est quod aliquis homo sit bonus nisi sit bene proportionatus bono communi; nec totum potest bene consistere nisi ex partibus sibi proportionatis. Unde impossibile est quod bonum commune civitatis bene se habeat nisi cives sint virtuosi, ad minus in illis quibus convenit principari. Sufficit autem quantum ad bonum communitatis quod alii in tantum sint virtuosi quod principum mandatis obediant. Et ideo Philosophus dicit in *Polit*. iii, 2 quod *eadem est virtus principis et boni viri; non autem eadem est virtus cujuscumque civis et boni viri*.

Reply 3

The goodness of every part is considered in its proportionate re-lationship to its whole. Hence, Augustine says (*Confess.* iii) that "every part that does not harmonize with its whole is bad." Now, every man is a part of the state, and, therefore, it is impossible for anyone to be good, if he is not well-proportioned to the Common Good, nor can a state be sound unless it is composed of parts proportionate to itself. Hence, it is impossible for the Common Good to be in good condition, unless the citizens "be virtuous, at least those who are the rulers." It is sufficient for the good of the community that others be virtuous at least to the extent that they obey the commands of the rulers. And, therefore, the Philosopher says (*Polit.* iii, 2) that "the virtue of the ruler is the same as the virtue of a good man, but the virtue of any citizen at all is not that of a good man."

OBJECTION 4

Praeterea, quaedam leges sunt tyrannicae, ut Philoso-phus dicit in sua *Polit.* iii, 6. Sed tyrannus non intendit ad bonitatem subditorum, sed solum ad propriam utilitatem. Non ergo legis est facere homines bonos.

Objection 4

Further, some laws are tyrannical, as the Philosopher says in *Polit.* iii, 6. But a tyrant does not aim at the goodness of the subjects but only at his own benefit. Therefore, it is not the business of law to make men good.

REPLY 4

Ad quartum dicendum quod lex tyrannica, cum non sit secundum rationem, non est simpliciter lex, sed magis est quaedam perversitas legis. Et tamen inquantum habet aliquid de ratione legis, intendit ad hoc quod cives sint boni; non enim habet de ratione legis nisi secundum hoc quod est dic-tamen alicujus praesidentis in subditis: et ad hoc tendit ut subditi legis sint bene obedientes; quod est eos esse bonos, non simpliciter sed in ordine ad tale regimen.

Reply 4

A tyrannical law, since it is not in accord with reason, is not a law in the full sense (*simpliciter*); rather, it is a perversion of law. Yet, it has something of the nature of law and aims at this that the citizen be good, for it would not have something of the nature of law except inasmuch as it is a dictate of a ruler given to his subjects and aims at making the subjects fully obedient to the law and this is to make them good, not in the full sense (*simpliciter*) but only in relation to such a government.

ON THE CONTRARY

Sed contra est quod Philosophus dicit in *Ethic.* ii, 1, quod *voluntas cujuslibet legislatoris haec est ut faciat homines bonos.*

On the Contrary

The Philosopher says (*Ethic.* ii, 1) that "it is the intention of every legislator to make men good."

CORPUS

Dicendum quod, sicut supra dictum est (*q.* 90, *a.* 4, *c.*), lex nihil aliud est quam dictamen rationis in praesidente quo subditi gubernantur. Cujuslibet autem subditi virtus est ut bene subdatur ei a quo gubernatur; sicut virtus irascibilis et concupiscibilis in hoc consistit quod sint bene obedientes rationi. Et per hunc modum *virtus cujuslibet subjecti est ut bene subjiciatur principanti,* ut Philosophus dicit in *Polit.* I, 5.

Ad hoc autem ordinatur unaquaeque lex ut obediatur ei a subditis. Unde manifestum est quod hoc sit proprium legis inducere subjectos ad propriam ipsorum virtutem. Cum igitur virtus sit quae facit bonum habentem, sequitur quod proprius effectus legis sit bonos facere eos quibus datur, vel simpliciter vel secundum quid.

Si enim intentio ferentis legem tendat in verum bonum, quod est bonum commune secundum justitiam divinam regulatum, sequitur quod per legem homines fiant boni simpliciter. Si vero intentio legislatoris feratur ad id quod non est bonum simpliciter, sed utile vel delectabile sibi, vel repugnans justitiae divinae, tunc lex non bonos facit homines simpliciter, sed secundum quid, scilicet in ordine ad tale regimen. Sic autem bonum invenitur etiam in per se malis; sicut aliquis dicitur bonus latro quia operatur accommode ad finem.

Corpus

As was said above (*q.* 90, *a.* 4, *c.*), law is nothing other than a dictate of reason of a ruler by which subjects are governed. Now, the virtue of anything that is subject is to be fully subordinate to that by which it is governed just as the virtue of the irascible and concupiscible faculties consists in their being fully obedient to reason. And in this way the "virtue of any subject is to be fully subjected to the ruler," as the Philosopher says (*Polit.* I, 5).

But every law is ordered to this that it be obeyed by its subjects. Hence, it is clear that it is proper to law to bring subjects to the virtues proper to themselves. Since, therefore, it is virtue that makes its possessor good, it follows that the proper effect of law is to make good those for whom it is made, either in the full sense (*simpliciter*) or only in some respect (*secundum quid*). For if the intention of the lawgiver is focused on true good which is the Common Good regulated by divine justice, it follows that through the law men become good in the full sense (*simpliciter*). But, if the intention of the lawgiver is not focused on what is good in the full sense (*simpliciter*), but is useful or pleasurable to himself or contrary to Divine justice, it follows that the law does not make men good in the full sense (*simpliciter*), but only with reference to such a government (*secundum quid*). In this way good is found even in things that are evil of themselves, as, for example, someone might be called a good robber because he acts in a way conducive to his purpose.

Comment

Lawgivers may be motivated in various irrelevant ways. A Congressman may vote for a bill to please a rich supporter. St. Thomas is talking of a lawgiver precisely as a law-giver. As such, the lawgiver wants his laws obeyed. Thus, he promotes the virtuous obedience of his subjects, and, if he is a good lawgiver who intends the true Common Good, by ordering his subjects to it, he also makes his subjects good *simpliciter*.

ARTICLE 2
UTRUM LEGIS ACTUS CONVENIENTER ASSIGNENTUR?
WHETHER THE ACTS OF LAW ARE PROPERLY ASSIGNED?

Introductory Comment

In medieval scholarship there were certain highly regarded *auctoritates* that were generally considered relevant to certain contexts. For example, the imperial principle, "What pleases the prince has the force of law" appears in most discussions of law and political authority. St. Thomas faced this principle in *q.* 90, *a.* 1, Reply 3. He approved the principle but attached a condition of reasonableness which harmonized it with his own doctrine. This method of giving *auctoritates* a "benign interpretation" was common practice.

In this Article St. Thomas deals with an *auctoritas* for which he gives two sources: Gratian (359–383 A.D.) and Isidore (560?–636 A.D.). Four acts are listed as proper to law, namely, to command, to forbid, to permit, and to punish. In dealing with an *auctoritas* that simply enumerates a set of properties, St. Thomas's technique is to find, in his own doctrine, a rational basis for the enumeration, thus both approving and explaining the enumeration.

This same technique appears in *q.* 95, *a.* 3 where St. Thomas reviews Isidore's listing of the "qualities of law."

Of course, dealing with this *auctoritas* gave St. Thomas an opportunity to further develop his general doctrine.

OBJECTION 1

Videtur quod legis actus non sint convenienter assignati in hoc quod dicitur (Gratian, *Decretum,* I, II, 4: Isidore, *Etym.* V, 19), quod legis actus est *imperare, vetare, permittere et punire.* Lex enim omnis praeceptum commune est, ut legisconsultus Papinianus dicit (*Digest* I, III). Sed idem est imperare quod praecipere. Ergo alia tria superfluunt.

Objection 1

It seems that the acts of law are not properly assigned inasmuch as it is said that the acts of law are "to command, to forbid, to permit and to punish" (Gratian, *Decretum,* I, II, 4: Isidore, *Etym.* V, 19). For "every law is a general precept," as the Jurist Papinian says (*Digest* I, III). But command and precept are the same thing. Therefore, the other three are superfluous.

REPLY 1

Ad primum ergo dicendum quod, sicut cessare a malo habet quandam rationem boni, ita etiam prohibitio habet quandam rationem praecepti; et secundum hoc, large accipiendo praeceptum, universaliter lex 'praeceptum' dicitur.

Reply 1

Just as ceasing to do evil is a kind of good, so prohibition is a kind of precept, and so, if we take precept in a broad sense, law in every respect is a precept.

OBJECTION 2

Praeterea, effectus legis est ut inducat subditos ad bonum, sicut supra dictum est (*a.* 1). Sed consilium est de meliori bono quam praeceptum. Ergo magis pertinet ad legem consulere quam praecipere.

Objection 2

Further, the effect of law is to bring its subjects to good, as was said above (*a.* 1). But counsel concerns a higher good than a command. Therefore, to counsel is a more appropriate act of law than to command.

REPLY 2

Ad secundum dicendum quod consulere non est proprius actus legis, sed potest pertinere etiam ad personam privatam, cujus non est condere legem. Unde etiam Apostolus, cum consilium quoddam daret, dixit (I Cor. vii, 12), *ego dico, non Dominus*. Et ideo non ponitur inter effectus legis.

Reply 2

To counsel is not an act proper to law, for it can be done even by a private person who cannot make a law. As the Apostle (I Cor. vii, 12), after giving a certain counsel, says, "I say this, not the Lord." And, therefore, counsel is not listed among the effects of law.

OBJECTION 3

Praeterea, sicut homo aliquis incitatur ad bonum per poenas, ita etiam et per praemia. Ergo sicut punire ponitur effectus legis, ita etiam et praemiare.

Objection 3

Further, just as someone is moved to good by punishment, so also by rewards. So, just as to punish is listed among the effects of law, so also to reward should be included.

REPLY 3

Ad tertium dicendum quod etiam praemiare potest ad quemlibet pertinere; sed punire non pertinet nisi ad ministrum legis, cujus auctoritate poena infertur: et ideo praemiare non ponitur actus legis, sed solum punire.

Reply 3

To reward also belongs to anyone at all, but to punish belongs only to the administrator of the law by whose authority the punishment is inflicted. Hence, to reward is not counted among the effects of law but only to punish.

OBJECTION 4

Praeterea, intentio legislatoris est ut homines faciat bonos, sicut supra dictum est (*a*. 1). Sed ille qui solo metu poenarum obedit legi non est bonus; nam *timore servili, qui est timor poenarum, etsi bonum aliquis faciat, non tamen aliquid bene facit,* ut Augustinus dicit in *Contra duas epist. Pelag,* ii. Non ergo videtur esse proprium legis quod puniat.

Objection 4

Further, the intention of the legislator is to make men good, as was said above (*a*. 1). But he who obeys the law only because of fear of punishment is not a good man. "Although someone may do something good out of servile fear of punishment, nonetheless he would not do well," as Augustine says (*Contra duas Epist. Pelag,* ii). Therefore, to punish is not an effect of law.

Comment

St. Thomas is talking about effects which belong exclusively to law. Thus only law can punish; hence, to punish is an exclusive proper effect of law. The law can reward, but so can other agencies and therefore to reward is not a proper effect of law.

REPLY 4

Ad quartum dicendum quod per hoc quod aliquis incipit assuefieri ad vitandum mala et ad implendum bona propter

metum poenae, perducitur quandoque ad hoc quod delecta-
biliter et ex propria voluntate hoc faciat. Et secundum hoc
lex etiam puniendo perducit ad hoc quod homines sint boni.

Reply 4

When someone begins to be accustomed to avoiding evil and doing
good through fear of punishment, he is sometimes led on to do this with
pleasure and out of his own will. In this way law, even by punishing,
leads men to become good.

Comment
This theme of the reforming effect of law is developed in *a*. 1 and
in *q*. 95, *a*. 1.

ON THE CONTRARY

Sed contra est quod Isidorus dicit *Etym.* v, 19, *Omnis
lex aut permittit aliquid, ut vir fortis praemium petat; aut
vetat, ut sacrarum virginum nuptias nulli liceat petere; aut
punit, ut qui caedem fecerit, capite plectatur.*

On the Contrary

Isidore says (*Etym.* v, 19), "Every law either permits something,
as that a brave man may seek a reward, or forbids something as that
no one may seek marriage with a consecrated virgin, or punishes as that
anyone who commits a murder should be put to death."

CORPUS

Dicendum quod, sicut enuntiatio est rationis dictamen
per modum enuntiandi, ita etiam lex per modum praecipiendi.
Rationis autem proprium est ut ex aliquo ad aliquid inducat.
Unde sicut in demonstrativis scientiis ratio inducit ut assentiatur conclusioni per quaedam principia, ita etiam inducit
ut assentiatur legis praecepto per aliquid.
Praecepta autem legis sunt de actibus humanis, in quibus

lex dirigit, ut supra dictum est (*q*. 90, *aa*. 1 and 2). Sunt autem tres differentiae humanorum actuum, nam, sicut supra dictum est (*q*. 18, *a*. 8), quidam actus sunt boni ex genere, qui sunt actus virtutum et respectu horum ponitur legis actus praecipere vel imperare: praecipit enim lex omnes actus virtutum, ut dicitur in *Ethic*. v, 1. Quidam vero sunt actus mali ex genere, sicut actus vitiosi; et respectu horum lex habet prohibere. Quidam vero ex genere suo sunt actus indifferentes et respectu horum lex habet permittere et possunt etiam indifferentes dici omnes illi actus qui sunt vel parum boni vel parum mali.

Id autem per quod inducit lex ad hoc quod sibi obediatur est timor poenae; et quantum ad hoc ponitur legis effectus punire.

Corpus

Just as an assertion is a dictate of reason by asserting something, so also is law by ordering something. For it is proper to reason that it lead from one thing to another. Just as in the demonstrative sciences reason, through certain principles, induces assent to a conclusion, so also by some means, reason induces assent to the command of the law.

Now, the precepts of the law are concerned with human acts which law directs, as was said above (*q*. 90, *aa*. 1 and 2). Now, there are three different kinds of acts. For, as was said above (*q*. 18, *a*. 8), some acts are generically good, and these are the acts of the virtues and in respect to these, to order or command is assigned as an act of law, for, as is said in *Ethic*. v, 1, "the law commands all acts of virtue." However, some acts are generically evil, such as the acts of vices and with respect to these, the law forbids. Some acts are generically indifferent, and with respect to these, the law permits. And all those acts which are partly good and partly evil can be called indifferent.

But that through which the law induces obedience is fear of punishment, and so to punish is counted as an effect of law.

Comment

In this Article St. Thomas takes a standard traditional listing of the acts of law, clarifies them and establishes a rational basis for them. The first three he derives from the nature of law as a rule directive of human-acts. By distinguishing three kinds of human acts, he distinguishes three different acts of law. Punishment is shown to be a general act of law as being necessary to ensure obedience, that is, to make law effective (*q*. 90, *a*. 3, Reply 2).

QUESTION 93
DE LEGE AETERNA
CONCERNING THE ETERNAL LAW

Circa primum quaeruntur sex:

1. quid sit lex aeterna;
2. utrum sit omnibus nota;
3. utrum omnis lex ab ea derivetur;
4. utrum necessaria subjiciantur legi aeternae;
5. utrum contingentia naturalia subjiciantur legi aeternae;
6. utrum omnes res humanae ei subjiciantur.

Question 93

On the first question there are six points of inquiry:

1. What is the Eternal Law?
2. Whether it is known to everyone?
3. Whether every law is derived from it?
4. Whether necessary things are subject to the Eternal Law?
5. Whether natural contingent things are subject to the Eternal Law?
6. Whether all human affairs are subject to it?

ARTICLE 1
UTRUM LEX AETERNA SIT SUMMA RATIO IN DEO EXISTENS?
IS THE ETERNAL LAW THE SUPREME EXEMPLAR IN GOD?

OBJECTION 1

Videtur quod lex aeterna non sit summa ratio in Deo existens. Lex enim aeterna est una tantum. Sed rationes rerum in mente divina sunt plures: dicit enim Augustinus (*Qq.* 83, *qu.* 46) quod *Deus singula fecit propriis rationibus.* Ergo lex aeterna non videtur esse idem quod ratio in mente divina existens.

Objection 1

It seems that the Eternal Law is not the supreme exemplar in God. For the Eternal Law is only one, whereas the exemplars of things in the Divine Mind are many. For Augustine says (*Qq.* 83, *qu.* 46) that "God makes each individual thing according to its own exemplar." Therefore, the Eternal Law does not seem to be the same as the exemplar in the Divine Mind.

REPLY 1

Ad primum ergo dicendum quod Augustinus loquitur ibi de rationibus idealibus, quae respiciunt proprias naturas singularum rerum; et ideo in eis invenitur quaedam distinctio et pluralitas, secundum diversos respectus ad res, ut in *Primo* (*q.* 15, *a.* 2) habitum est. Sed lex dicitur directiva actuum in ordine ad bonum commune, ut supra dictum est (*q.* 90, *a.* 2). Ea autem quae sunt in seipsis diversa considerantur ut unum secundum quod ordinantur ad aliquod commune; et ideo lex aeterna est una, quae est ratio hujus ordinis.

Reply 1

Augustine in that text is speaking of the ideal exemplars which correspond to the proper natures of individual things, and, therefore, there is found in them a certain distinction and plurality according to the different relations to things, as was established in the First Part (*q.* 15, *a.* 2). But law is said to be directive of acts toward the Common Good, as was said above (*q.* 90, *a.* 2). But things that are diverse in themselves are considered as one according to their ordination to something common. Therefore, the Eternal Law is one, that is the exemplar of this ordination.

Comment

St. Thomas here is putting together two aspects of Divine Exemplarity. There are in God exemplars of the proper nature of all singular created things. This plurality is in the order of extrinsic formal causality. But God's relationship to created things is not only in the order of formal causality. There is need also of a final cause and this is the ordination of all things to the final cause (the end) of all created things. This is the ordination of all things to the Common Good of creation which is the happiness of all mankind. Hence this ordination is also included in God's exemplarity and so unifies the plurality of formal causes.

OBJECTION 2

Praeterea, de ratione legis est quod verbo promulgetur, ut supra dictum est (*q.* 90, *a.* 4). Sed 'verbum' in divinis dicitur personaliter, ut in *Primo* habitum est (*q.* 34, *a.* 1); 'ratio' autem dicitur essentialiter. Non igitur idem est lex aeterna quod ratio divina.

Objection 2

Further, it is essential to law that it be promulgated by word, as was said above (*q.* 90, *a.* 4). But "Word" is a personal name in God, as was stated in the *First Part* (*q.* 34, *a.* 1), whereas "exemplar" refers to the essence of God. Therefore, the Eternal Law is not the same as the Divine exemplar.

REPLY 2

Ad secundum dicendum quod circa verbum quodcumque duo possunt considerari, scilicet ipsum verbum et ea quae verbo exprimuntur. Verbum enim vocale est quiddam ab ore hominis prolatum, sed hoc verbo exprimuntur quae verbis humanis significantur; et eadem ratio est de verbo hominis mentali, quod nihil est aliud quam quiddam mente conceptum quo homo exprimit mentaliter ea de quibus cogitat. Sic igitur in divinis ipsum Verbum, quod est conceptio Paterni intellectus, personaliter dicitur; sed omnia quaecumque sunt in scientia Patris, sive essentialia sive personalia sive etiam Dei opera, exprimuntur hoc Verbo, ut patet per Augustinum in *De Trin.*, xv, 14. Et inter caetera quae hoc Verbo exprimuntur etiam ipsa lex aeterna Verbo ipso exprimitur. Nec tamen propter hoc sequitur quod lex aeterna personaliter in divinis dicatur; appropriatur tamen Filio propter convenientiam quam habet ratio ad verbum.

Reply 2

Concerning any word whatever, two things can be considered, namely, the word itself and what the word expresses. For the spoken word is something that comes from the mouth of man and expresses what human words signify. And the same explanation applies to the human mental word, for the mental word is nothing else than the mental expression of what man is thinking about. And so likewise in God, the Word itself, which is the conception of the intellect of the Father, is a person, but everything whatever that is in the Father's knowledge, whether it has to do with the Persons or the essence or even the works of God, is expressed by this Word, as Augustine explains (*De Trin.*, xv, 14). And among the other things expressed by this Word, even the Eternal Law itself, is expressed by this very Word. And yet, it does not follow on this account that the Eternal Law names a Person in God. Yet, it is appropriated to the Son because of the relationship of concept to word.

Comment

This objection and its answer are, obviously, theological. They involve the Christian doctrine of the Holy Trinity in which the Son, the second Person of the Trinity, is called the "Word" in accordance with the opening of John's Gospel. St. Thomas is using the Augustinian explanation of the Trinity which is based on an analogy with human thinking. The Son is eternally "uttered" by the Father and is a total image of God the Father. Hence, everything that the Father knows is expressed in the Second Person, the Son. Hence, the Eternal Law is also expressed in the Divine Word without itself becoming another person.

OBJECTION 3

Praeterea, Augustinus dicit (*De Vera Relig.*, xxx), *Apparet supra mentem nostram legem esse, quae veritas dicitur. Lex autem supra mentem nostram existens est lex aeterna.*

Ergo veritas est lex aeterna. Sed non est eadem ratio veritatis et rationis. Ergo lex aeterna non est idem quod ratio summa.

Objection 3

Further, Augustine says (*De Vera Relig.*, xxx) that "there is a law above our minds which is called the truth." Now the law above our minds is the Eternal Law. Therefore, truth is the Eternal Law. But the idea of truth is not the same as the idea of an exemplar. Therefore, the Eternal Law is not the supreme exemplar.

REPLY 3

Ad tertium dicendum quod ratio intellectus divini aliter se habet ad res quam ratio humani intellectus. Intellectus enim humanus est mensuratus a rebus, ut scilicet conceptus hominis non sit verus propter seipsum, sed dicitur verus ex hoc quod consonat rebus. Ex hoc enim quod res est vel non est, opinio vera vel falsa est. Intellectus vero divinus est mensura rerum; quia unaquaeque res intantum habet de veritate inquantum imitatur intellectum divinum, ut in *Primo* (*q*. 16, *a*. 1) dictum est. Et ideo intellectus divinus est verus secundum se, unde ratio ejus est ipsa veritas.

Reply 3

The Divine reason is not related to things in the same way as human reason. For the human intellect is measured by things so that the human concept is not true of itself but is called true inasmuch as it conforms to reality. For, from the fact that a thing exists or does not exist, human judgment is either true or false. But the Divine intellect is the measure of things so that each thing has truth inasmuch as it imitates the Divine intellect, as was said in the *First Part* (*q*. 16, *a*. 1). And, therefore, the Divine Intellect is true of itself and its exemplarity is truth itself.

Comment

In Thomistic epistemology the truth of human propositions is determined by the relationship of the human propositions to reality. But created things are true only to the extent that they conform to the divine exemplarity, hence in God the idea of exemplarity and the idea of truth are the same. This, of course, places St. Thomas in direct opposition to Kant.

ON THE CONTRARY

Sed contra est quod Augustinus dicit (*De Lib. Arb.* i, 6) quod *lex aeterna est summa ratio, cui semper obtemperandum est.*

On the Contrary

Augustine says (*De Lib. Arb.* i, 6), "The Eternal Law is the supreme exemplar to which we must always conform."

CORPUS

Dicendum quod sicut in quolibet artifice praeexistit ratio eorum quae constituuntur per artem, ita etiam in quolibet gubernante oportet quod praeexistat ratio ordinis eorum quae agenda sunt per eos qui gubernationi subduntur. Et sicut ratio rerum fiendarum per artem vocatur ars, vel exemplar rerum artificiatarum, ita etiam ratio gubernantis actus subditorum rationem legis obtinet, servatis aliis quae supra (*q.* 90) esse diximus de legis ratione. Deus autem per suam sapientiam conditor est universarum rerum; ad quas comparatur sicut artifex ad artificiata, ut in *Primo* (*q.* 14, *a.* 8) habitum est. Est etiam gubernator omnium actuum et motionum quae inveniuntur in singulis creaturis, ut etiam in *Primo* habitum est. Unde sicut ratio divinae sapientiae, inquantum per eam cuncta sunt creata, rationem habet artis, vel exemplaris, vel ideae, ita ratio divinae sapientiae moventis omnia ad debitum finem obtinet rationem legis. Et secundum hoc lex aeterna nihil aliud est quam ratio divinae sapientiae, secundum quod est directiva omnium actuum et motionum.

Corpus

Just as in any artist there preexists an exemplar of those things made by his art, so also in any ruler there must preexist an exemplar of the order of those things that are to be done by those who are subject to the ruler. And just as the idea of the things done through art is called art or the exemplar of the things done by the artist, so also the idea of the one who governs the acts of his subjects has the nature of law, provided all the other elements of the nature of law mentioned above (*q.* 90) are present.

Now, God, through His wisdom, is the creator of all things to which He is related as an artist is to his artefacts, as was shown in the *First Part* (*q.* 14, *a.* 8). He is also the ruler of all the acts and movements that are found in each single creature, as was also shown in the *First Part* (*q.* 103, *a.* 5). Hence, just as the model in the Divine wisdom through which all things were created has the nature of an art or exemplar or idea, so the plan in the Divine wisdom which moves everything to its proper end has the nature of a law. And, accordingly, the Eternal Law is nothing other than the idea in Divine wisdom inasmuch as it directs all acts and movements.

Comment

When explanation through the Four Causes is applied to creation, God is discovered as the efficient cause which produces and preserves the totality of all things without any preexisting material cause. God is, therefore, a creator in the strict sense of the term. Now, God is also infinite intelligence and, therefore, creates intelligently. Hence, He has an idea of whatever He creates. This idea is thus exemplar cause of the universe, the exemplar cause being a subdivision of the formal cause and is sometimes called the "extrinsic formal cause." God continues to maintain all things in existence and directs them to their proper end, that is, ultimately to the Common Good of the universe. Thus, the idea in the mind of God has the nature of a law since it is a dictate of God's wisdom, directing everything to the Common Good of the universe, produced by God's intellect inasmuch as He is the ruler of the universe and has the care of all things and this law is promulgated by the act of creation itself. Therefore, the directive exemplarity is called the Eternal Law.

St. Thomas works from two analogies, that of the artist to his artefacts and that of a ruler to his subjects. The two analogies are woven together into the idea of the Eternal Law.

ARTICLE 2
UTRUM LEX AETERNA SIT OMNIBUS NOTA?
WHETHER THE ETERNAL LAW
IS KNOWN TO EVERYONE?

OBJECTION 1

Videtur quod lex aeterna non sit omnibus nota. Quia, ut dicit Apostolus (I Cor., ii, 11), *Quae sunt Dei, nemo novit nisi Spiritus Dei.* Sed lex aeterna est quaedam ratio in mente divina existens. Ergo omnibus est ignota, nisi soli Deo.

Objection 1

It seems that the Eternal Law is not known to everyone. For, as the Apostle says (I Cor., ii, 11), "the things that are of God, no one knows except the Spirit of God." But the Eternal Law is an idea in the divine mind. Therefore, it is unknown to everyone except God alone.

REPLY 1

Ad primum ergo dicendum quod ea quae sunt Dei, in seipsis quidem cognosci a nobis non possunt, sed tamen in effectibus suis manifestantur, secundum illud Rom. i, 20, *Invisibilia Dei per ea quae facta sunt intellecta* conspiciuntur.

Reply 1

The things that are of God cannot indeed be known by us in themselves, yet they are manifested to us by their effects, according to Rom. i, 20, "The invisible things of God . . . are clearly seen, being understood through the things that are made."

OBJECTION 2

Praeterea, sicut Augustinus dicit (*De Lib. Arb.* i, 6), *lex aeterna est qua justum est ut omnia sint ordinatissima.* Sed

non omnes cognoscunt qualiter omnia sint ordinatissima.
Ergo non omnes cognoscunt legem aeternam.

Objection 2

Further, as Augustine says (*De Lib. Arb.* i, 6), "The Eternal Law
is that by which it is right that all things should be most orderly." But
not everyone knows how all things are most orderly. Therefore, the
Eternal Law is not known to everyone.

REPLY 2

Ad secundum dicendum quod legem aeternam etsi unusquisque cognoscat pro sua capacitate secundum modum
praedictum, nullus tamen eam comprehendere potest: non
enim totaliter manifestari potest per suos effectus. Et ideo
non oportet quod quicumque cognoscit legem aeternam secundum modum praedictum, cognoscat totum ordinem rerum
quo omnia sunt ordinatissima.

Reply 2

Although each one knows the Eternal Law according to his own
capacity in the way explained [in the *Corpus* of this Article], no one
can fully comprehend it; it cannot be perfectly manifested through its
effects. And therefore it is not necessary that whoever knows the Eternal
Law in the way explained [in the *Corpus*] should know the entire order
of reality by which all things are most orderly.

OBJECTION 3

Praeterea, Augustinus dicit (*De Vera Relig.*, xxxi) quod
lex aeterna est de qua homines judicare non possunt. Sed,
sicut in I *Ethic.* dicitur, *unusquisque bene judicat quae cognoscit.* Ergo lex aeterna non est nobis nota.

Objection 3

Further, Augustine says (*De Vera Relig.*, xxxi) "the Eternal Law
cannot be judged by man." But, according to *Ethic.* i, "Any man can

judge well about what he knows." Therefore, the Eternal Law is not known by us.

REPLY 3

Ad tertium dicendum quod judicare de aliquo potest intelligi dupliciter. Uno modo, sicut vis cognitiva dijudicat de proprio objecto, secundum illud Job, xii, 11, *Nonne auris verba dijudicat, et fauces comedentis saporem?* Et secundum istum modum judicii Philosophus dicit, quod *unusquisque bene dijudicat quae cognoscit,* judicando scilicet an sit verum quod proponitur. Alio modo, secundum quod superior judicat de inferiori quodam practico judicio, an scilicet ita debeat esse, vel non ita; et sic nullus potest judicare de lege aeterna.

Reply 3

To judge of a thing may be understood in two ways. One way is when a cognitive power judges concerning its proper object, according to Job xii, 11, "Does not the ear judge words and the palate of him who eats, taste?" It is to this way of judging that the Philosopher refers when he says that "each one judges well concerning what he knows," as in judging whether what is proposed is true. Another way of judging is when a superior judges an inferior by a kind of practical judgment, for example, whether he should be such and such or not. And in this way of judging, no one can judge of the Eternal Law.

ON THE CONTRARY

Sed contra est quod Augustinus dicit (*De Lib. Arb.* i, 6) quod *aeternae legis notio nobis impressa est.*

On the Contrary

Augustine says (*De Lib. Arb.* i, 6), "knowledge of the Eternal Law is imprinted in us."

CORPUS

Dicendum quod dupliciter aliquid cognosci potest: uno modo in seipso, alio modo in suo effectu in quo aliqua similitudo ejus invenitur, sicut aliquis non videns solem in sua substantia cognoscit ipsum in sua irradiatione. Sic igitur dicendum est quod legem aeternam nullus potest cognoscere secundum quod in seipsa est, nisi solus Deus et beati qui Deum per essentiam vident; sed omnis creatura rationalis ipsam cognoscit secundum aliquam ejus irradiationem vel majorem vel minorem.

Omnis enim cognitio veritatis est quaedam irradiatio et participatio legis aeternae, quae est veritas incommutabilis, ut Augustinus dicit *De Vera Relig.,* xxxi; veritatem autem omnes aliqualiter cognoscunt, ad minus quantum ad principia communia legis naturalis; in aliis vero quidam plus et quidam minus participant de cognitione veritatis: et secundum hoc etiam plus vel minus cognoscunt legem aeternam.

Corpus

A thing can be known in two ways. One way, in itself, another way in its effect in which some similitude of it is found, as a person who does not see the sun in its substance knows it in its irradiation. So, therefore, we must say that no one can know the Eternal Law as it is in itself. Only God and the Blessed who see God in His essence can know the Eternal Law, but every rational creature knows it from some greater or smaller irradiation of it.

For all knowledge of truth is an irradiation or participation of the Eternal Law which is the unchanging truth, as Augustine says (*De Vera Relig.,* xxxi). Now, everyone knows something of the truth, at least the general principles of the Natural Law; and accordingly they also know more or less of the Eternal Law.

Comment

The Eternal Law exists in the mind of God and is known in itself only to God and the Blessed.

But the Eternal Law is the model, the exemplar cause of the universe and everything in it.

Hence the things that are, including the Natural Law, manifest something of the Eternal Law, and so men can know more or less of the Eternal Law through its effects. The Blessed referred to here are those in Heaven who, through a special gift of God, see *God as He is in Himself.*

ARTICLE 3
UTRUM OMNIS LEX A LEGE AETERNA DERIVETUR?
WHETHER EVERY LAW IS DERIVED FROM THE ETERNAL LAW?

OBJECTION 1

Videtur quod non omnis lex a lege aeterna derivetur. Est enim quaedam lex fomitis, ut supra dictum est (*q.* 91, *a.* 6). Ipsa autem non derivatur a lege divina, quae est lex aeterna: ad ipsam enim pertinet prudentia carnis, de qua Apostolus dicit (Rom. vii, 7) quod *legi Dei non potest esse subjecta.* Ergo non omnis lex procedit a lege aeterna.

Objection 1

It seems that not every law is derived from the Eternal Law. For there is a law of the fomes [*peccati*], as was said above (*q.* 91, *a.* 6). It is not derived from the Divine Law which is the Eternal Law. For to it belongs the "prudence of the flesh" of which the Apostle says (Rom. vii, 7) that "it cannot be subject to the law of God." Therefore, not every law proceeds from the Eternal Law.

REPLY 1

Ad primum ergo dicendum quod fomes habet rationem legis in homine inquantum est poena consequens divinam justitiam; et secundum hoc manifestum est quod derivatur a lege aeterna. Inquantum vero inclinat ad peccatum, sic contrariatur legi Dei, et non habet rationem legis, ut ex supra dictis patet (*q.* 91, *a.* 6).

Reply 1

The *fomes peccati* has the nature of a law inasmuch as it is a punishment coming from divine justice, and in this way it is clearly derived from the Eternal Law. However, insofar as it inclines to sin, it is contrary to the law of God and does not have the nature of law, as is clear from what was said above (*q.* 91, *a.* 6).

Comment

The *fomes peccati* is human sensuality insofar as it leads to sin. In Adam, before the Fall, sensuality was subject to reason because of a special gift from God. When Adam sinned, as a punishment for that sin Adam lost that special gift for himself and his posterity. Since then, the unbridled *fomes peccati* in us is a punishment for Adam's sin. It results from the justice of the Eternal Law and so participates in that law and so can be called a law by participation but not properly.

OBJECTION 2

Praeterea, a lege aeterna nihil iniquum procedere potest, quia, sicut dictum est (*a.* 2, *obj.* 2), *lex aeterna est secundum quam justum est ut omnia sint ordinatissima.* Sed quaedam leges sunt iniquae, secundum illud Isa. x, 1, *Vae qui condunt leges iniquas!* Ergo non omnis lex procedit a lege aeterna.

Objection 2

Nothing unjust can come from the Eternal Law, because, as was said above (*a.* 2, *obj.* 2), "The Eternal Law is that according to which it is right that all things be most orderly." But some laws are unjust, according to Isa. x, 1, "Woe to them that make wicked laws." Therefore, not every law is derived from the Eternal Law.

REPLY 2

Ad secundum dicendum quod lex humana intantum habet rationem legis inquantum est secundum rationem rectam;

et secundum hoc manifestum est quod a lege aeterna derivatur. Inquantum vero a ratione recedit sic dicitur lex iniqua;
et sic non habet rationem legis, sed magis violentiae cujusdam.
Et tamen in ipsa lege iniqua inquantum servatur aliquid de
similitudine legis, propter ordinem potestatis ejus qui legem
fecit, secundum hoc etiam derivatur a lege aeterna. *Omnis
enim potestas a Domino Deo est,* ut dicitur Rom. xiii, 1.

Reply 2

Human law has the nature of law insofar as it is in accord with
right reason, and it is clear that, according to this, it is derived from
the Eternal Law. However, inasmuch as it deviates from reason, it is
called an unjust law, and, thus it does not have the nature of law
but rather of a sort of violence. But even an unjust law retains some
semblance of the nature of law, since it was made by one in power
and in this respect it is derived from the Eternal Law. "For all power
is from the Lord God," as is said in Rom. xiii, 1.

OBJECTION 3

Praeterea, Augustinus dicit (*De Lib. Arb.,* i, 5) quod
*lex quae populo regendo scribitur, recte multa permittit quae
per divinam providentiam vindicantur.* Sed ratio divinae providentiae est lex aeterna, ut dictum est (*a.* 1). Ergo nec etiam
omnis lex recta procedit a lege aeterna.

Objection 3

Further, Augustine says (*De. Lib. Arb.,* i, 5), that "the law that
is written for the governance of the people rightly permits many things
that are punished by Divine Providence." But the model of Divine
Providence is the Eternal Law, as was said above (*a.* 1). Therefore,
not even every right law proceeds from the Eternal Law.

REPLY 3

Ad tertium dicendum quod lex humana dicitur aliqua
permittere, non quasi approbans sed quasi ea dirigere non

potens. Multa autem diriguntur lege divina quae dirigi non possunt lege humana: plura enim subduntur causae superiori quam inferiori. Unde hoc ipsum quod lex humana non se intromittit de his quae dirigere non potest ex ordine legis aeternae provenit. Secus autem esset, si approbaret ea quae lex aeterna reprobat. Unde ex hoc non habetur quod lex humana non derivetur a lege aeterna, sed quod non perfecte eam assequi possit.

Reply 3

Human law is said to permit some things not as approving them but as not being able to direct them. For many things are directed by the Eternal Law which cannot be directed by human law. For more things are subject to a higher cause than to an inferior one. But this very fact that human law does not meddle with things which it cannot direct itself comes from the ordination of the Eternal Law. However, it would be otherwise, if human law approved things which the Eternal Law condemned. Hence, from this it does not follow that human law is not derived from the Eternal Law but that it does not perfectly follow the Eternal Law.

Comment

This Reply should be compared with *q*. 96, *a*. 2. It should be recalled that the Eternal Law is the total plan (the *ratio*) of the universe, while Divine Providence is God's working out of that plan through time.

ON THE CONTRARY

Sed contra est quod Prov. viii, 15 divina Sapientia dicit, *Per me reges regnant, et legum conditores justa decernunt.* Ratio autem divinae Sapientiae est lex aeterna, ut supra dictum est. Ergo omnes leges a lege aeterna procedunt.

On the Contrary

Divine Wisdom says (Prov. viii, 15), "Through me Kings rule and the makers of law make just decrees." But the model of Divine

Wisdom is the Eternal Law. Therefore, all laws proceed from the Eternal Law.

CORPUS

Dicendum quod, sicut supra dictum est (*q*. 90, *aa*. 1 and 2), lex importat rationem quamdam directivam actuum ad finem. In omnibus autem moventibus ordinatis oportet quod virtus secundi moventis derivetur a virtute moventis primi, quia movens secundum non movet nisi inquantum movetur a primo. Unde in omnibus gubernantibus idem videmus, quod ratio gubernationis a primo gubernante ad secundos derivatur, sicut ratio eorum quae sunt agenda in civitate derivatur a rege per praeceptum in inferiores administratores, et in artificialibus etiam ratio artificialium actuum derivatur ab architectore ad inferiores artifices qui manu operantur.

Cum ergo lex aeterna sit ratio gubernationis in supremo gubernante, necesse est quod omnes rationes gubernationis quae sunt in inferioribus gubernantibus a lege aeterna deriventur. Hujusmodi autem rationes inferiorum gubernantium sunt quaecumque aliae leges praeter aeternam. Unde omnes leges inquantum participant de ratione recta intantum derivantur a lege aeterna; et propter hoc Augustinus dicit (*De Lib. Arb*. i, 6) quod *in temporali lege nihil est justum ac legitimum, quod non ex lege aeterna homines sibi derivaverint*.

Corpus

As was said above (*q*. 90, *aa*. 1 and 2), law denotes a directing of acts to an end. Now, in an ordered series of movers, it is necessary that the power of the second mover be derived from the power of the first mover because the second mover only moves insofar as it is moved by the first mover. We see the same thing in all governing powers, namely, that the plan of governing derives from the chief ruler to the subordinate rulers, just as the plan of the things that are to be done in a state are derived from the King's command to the inferior administrators. And also in the crafts we see that the plan of what is to be made is derived from the chief craftsman to the inferiors who work with their hands. Since, therefore, the Eternal Law is the plan of government in the supreme governor, all plans of government in inferior governors must be derived from the Eternal Law. However, such plans of the inferior governors are whatever laws there are besides the Eternal Law. Hence, all laws insofar as they participate in right reason are derived from the Eternal Law. And, therefore, Augustine says (*De. Lib. Arb.* i, 6), "In temporal law there is nothing just or lawful except what men have derived for themselves from the Eternal Law."

Comment

By an ordered series of movers, St. Thomas means a series in which all the inferior movements are derived from the first mover. This may be illustrated by the case of a locomotive pushing a line of freight cars. The engine pushes the first car and the first car, in virtue of that push from the locomotive, pushes the next car and so on through the whole series of cars.

However, the plan of the Eternal Law is communicated to all inferior human plans and laws, not mechanically but through right reason which is a participation in the Eternal Reason of God. For right reason, see 310–312.

ARTICLE 4
UTRUM NECESSARIA ET AETERNA SUBJICIANTUR LEGI AETERNAE?
WHETHER NECESSARY AND ETERNAL THINGS ARE SUBJECT TO THE ETERNAL LAW?

OBJECTION 1

Videtur quod necessaria et aeterna subjiciantur legi aeternae. Omne enim quod rationabile est rationi subditur. Sed voluntas divina est rationabilis, cum sit justa. Ergo rationi subditur. Sed lex aeterna est ratio divina. Ergo voluntas Dei subditur legi aeternae. Voluntas autem Dei est aliquid aeternum. Ergo etiam aeterna et necessaria legi aeternae subduntur.

Objection 1

It seems that necessary and eternal things are subject to the Eternal Law. For everything that is reasonable is subject to reason. But the Divine Will is reasonable, since it is just. Therefore, it is subject to reason. But the Eternal Law is the Divine Reason. Therefore, the Divine Will is subject to the Eternal Law. But the will of God is an eternal thing. Therefore, necessary and eternal things are subject to the Eternal Law.

REPLY 1

Ad primum ergo dicendum quod de voluntate Dei dupliciter possumus loqui. Uno modo quantum ad ipsam voluntatem; et sic, cum voluntas Dei sit ipsa essentia ejus, non subditur gubernationi divinae neque legi aeternae, sed idem est quod lex aeterna. Alio modo possumus loqui de voluntate divina quantum ad ipsa quae Deus vult circa creaturas; quae quidem subjecta sunt legi aeternae inquantum horum ratio est in divina sapientia; et ratione horum voluntas Dei dicitur rationabilis: alioquin ratione sui ipsius magis est dicenda ipsa ratio.

Reply 1

We may speak of the will of God in two different ways. First, with reference to the will itself, and, in this way, since the will of God is the very essence of God, it is not subject to either divine governance or the Eternal Law. In another way, we can speak of the Divine Will with reference to the things God wills concerning creatures, and these things are subject to the Eternal Law inasmuch as their model is in the Divine Wisdom. And because of these things the will of God is said to be reasonable, though, otherwise, by reason of itself, it should rather be called the model itself.

Comment

According to St. Thomas's metaphysics, God is the exemplar cause of all things. This causality, analyzed according to the human mode of thinking, is explicated in this way. God's nature is the exemplar of all things, for all created things in some way reflect that nature. But based on His nature, God understands the precise natures of the things He creates, i.e., the models (*rationes*) of all things are in the mind of God.

OBJECTION 2

Praeterea, quidquid subjicitur regi subjicitur legi regis. Filius autem, ut dicitur (I Cor. xv, 24, 28), *subjectus erit Deo et Patri, cum tradiderit ei regnum.* Ergo Filius, qui est aeternus, subjicitur legi aeternae.

Objection 2

Further, whoever is subject to a king is subject to the king's law. The Son, according to I Cor. xv, 24, 28, "will be subject to God the Father . . . when he shall have delivered up the kingdom to Him." Therefore, the Son who is eternal is subject to the Eternal Law.

REPLY 2

Ad secundum dicendum quod Filius Dei non est a Deo factus, sed naturaliter ab ipso genitus; et ideo non subditur divinae providentiae aut legi aeternae, sed magis ipse est lex aeterna per quamdam appropriationem, ut patet per Augustinum in lib. *De Vera Relig.,* xxxi dicitur autem esse subjectus Patri ratione humanae naturae, secundum quam etiam Pater dicitur esse major eo.

Reply 2

The Son of God was not made by God, but was naturally born of Him. Therefore, He is not subject to Divine Providence or the Eternal Law; rather He Himself is the Eternal Law, by a kind of appropriation, as is clear from Augustine (*De Vera Relig.,* xxxi). However, He is said to be subject to the Father because of His human nature in virtue of which the Father is also said to be greater than Him.

Comment

This Objection together with its Reply require a knowledge of the Christian doctrine of the Blessed Trinity. Although theologians call the Trinity a strict mystery, that is, it is beyond human understanding, the Church and theologians have worked out ways of thinking and speaking about the Trinity that give us some understanding of it.

The Godhead consists of three distinct, coequal and eternal persons, the Father, the Son and the Holy Spirit, who share a common nature. They are all God. By an eternal and continuous activity the Father generates the Son and the Father and Son give rise to the Holy Spirit.

If we consider the Trinity just in itself, it is clear that the Son, as the Second Person of the Trinity, is not subject to the Father or to the Eternal Law, since He is just as much God as the Father.

Now, in the Incarnation the Son assumed a human nature and so, in a sense, "became man." Now the Son, because of his human nature, that is Christ, is subject to the Father. There are places in the Gospels where Christ says the Father is greater than himself (Jo. xiv, 28). This is interpreted as a statement referring to his human nature.

OBJECTION 3

Praeterea, lex aeterna est ratio divinae providentiae. Sed multa necessaria subduntur divinae providentiae, sicut permanentia substantiarum incorporalium et corporum coelestium. Ergo legi aeternae subduntur etiam necessaria.

Objection 3

Further, the Eternal Law is the model for Divine Providence, but many necessary things are subject to Divine Providence, such as the permanence of incorporeal substances and of the heavenly bodies. Therefore, even necessary things are subject to the Eternal Law.

Comment

The "incorporeal substance" are human souls and angels which cannot be destroyed by any natural cause. The "heavenly bodies" were, in Aristotelian science, made of a matter quite different from the matter of the earth. Aristotle considered the heavenly matter to be indestructible. The elements of earthy substances were earth, air, fire, and water, out of which all composed substances were made. All these substances could be destroyed by natural causes. Since the matter of the heavenly bodies was radically different, their matter was called the *quinta essentia* (the fifth essence) in contrast to the four earthy elements.

REPLY 3

Tertium concedimus, quia procedit de necessariis creatis.

Reply 3

The third we concede, since it is arguing from created necessities.

ON THE CONTRARY

Sed contra, ea quae sunt necessaria, impossibile est aliter se habere, unde cohibitione non indigent. Sed imponitur homini lex ut cohibeatur a malis, ut ex supra dictis patet (*q.* 92, *a.* 2). Ergo ea quae sunt necessaria legi non subduntur.

On the Contrary

It is impossible for necessary things to be otherwise than they are, and so need no restraining. But law is imposed on man in order to restrain him from evil, as is clear from what has been said above (*q.* 92, *a.* 2). Therefore, necessary things are not subject to law.

ST. THOMAS'S COMMENT ON THE ON THE CONTRARY

[Quantum ad id quod in contrarium dicitur,] dicendum quod, sicut Philosophus dicit in *Meta.* v, 4, *quaedam necessaria habent causam suae necessitatis:* et sic hoc ipsum quod impossibile est ea aliter se habere habent ab alio; et hoc ipsum est cohibitio quaedam efficacissima. Nam quaecumque cohibentur in communi intantum cohiberi dicuntur inquantum non possunt aliter facere quam de eis disponatur.

St. Thomas's Comment on the On the Contrary

As the Philosopher says (*Meta.* v, 4), "Some necessary things have a cause of their necessity." And so the very impossibility of being otherwise, they have from another, and this is a very effective restraint. For whatever is restrained is restrained insofar as it cannot do otherwise than it is allowed to do.

CORPUS

Dicendum quod, sicut supra dictum est (*a*. 1), lex aeterna est ratio divinae gubernationis. Quaecumque ergo divinae gubernationi subduntur subjiciuntur etiam legi aeternae; quae vero gubernationi divinae non subduntur neque legi aeternae subduntur.

Horum autem distinctio attendi potest ex his quae circa nos sunt. Humanae enim gubernationi subduntur ea quae per homines fieri possunt; quae vero ad naturam hominis pertinent non subduntur gubernationi humanae, scilicet quod homo habeat animam, vel manum aut pedes. Sic igitur legi aeternae subduntur omnia quae sunt in rebus a Deo creatis, sive sint contingentia sive sint necessaria. Ea vero quae pertinent ad naturam vel essentiam divinam legi aeternae non subduntur, sed sunt realiter ipsa lex aeterna.

Corpus

As it was said above (*a*. 1), the Eternal Law is the model for Divine Governance. Therefore, whatever is subject to Divine Governance is subject to the Eternal Law; those things which are not subject to Divine Governance are not subject to the Eternal Law.

This distinction can be understood from the things around us. For those things that are produced by man, are subject to human governance, but those things that pertain to the nature of man are not subject to human governance, namely that a man should have a soul or hands or feet. Thus, therefore, everything that is in the things created by God, whether contingent or necessary, are subject to the Eternal Law. But whatever pertains to the nature or essence of God is not subject to the Eternal Law but is really the Eternal Law itself.

Comment

The discussion in the Article rests on a very important point of Thomistic metaphysics (and theology). The contingent is that which could be or can be otherwise than it is. The necessary is that which cannot be otherwise than it is. But St. Thomas, by distinguishing between the order of existence (*esse*) and the order of nature or essence (*essentia*) introduces the doctrine of contingent necessities.

God is absolutely necessary both in the order of existence and in the order of essence. He cannot not exist; He cannot have an essence other than the one He has. In Him existence is identical with His essence. But all the things that God creates are absolutely contingent in the order of existence; they need not exist and they remain in existence not because of their essence but because God preserves them. But, in the order of essence, there are necessities in created things. If a fire breaks out it *must* have a cause, a match, a spark, lightning or spontaneous combustion. Such necessities are called contingent necessities because, in the order of existence, they are contingent, yet in the order of essence they are necessary. They might be called conditional necessities; if lightning *exists,* if flammable material *exists* and if the lightning actually strikes the material, the material *necessarily* burns. If a man exists, he must have a soul.

Hence, St. Thomas can say that whatever is in created things, whether contingent or necessary (in the order of essence), is subject to the Eternal Law, but whatever pertains to the essence of God is not subject to the Eternal Law but is actually the Eternal Law.

This doctrine puts St. Thomas with Aristotle in opposing the extreme positions of Heraclitus and of Parmenides, the former maintaining that there are no points of stability, no necessities in the world, the latter holding that being is absolutely necessary as it is.

It also puts St. Thomas in opposition to Aristotle's position that necessities in the order of essence were absolute necessities; for him there were no existential contingencies. Thus, Aristotle maintained that the heavenly bodies, being composed of the indestructible matter, always existed and always will exist. It also puts St. Thomas in opposition to David Hume who maintained that there were no necessities in the world. Anything could be anything; anything could come from (he means "after") anything.

By introducing the idea of creation into metaphysics and grounding it on a rational analysis of the world, St. Thomas revolutionized Aristotelian thought in particular and Greek thought in general.

ARTICLE 5
UTRUM NATURALIA CONTINGENTIA SUBSINT LEGI AETERNAE?
WHETHER CONTINGENT THINGS IN NATURE ARE SUBJECT TO THE ETERNAL LAW?

OBJECTION 1

Videtur quod naturalia contingentia non subsint legi aeternae. Promulgatio enim est de ratione legis, ut supra dictum est (*q. 90, a. 4*). Sed promulgatio non potest fieri nisi ad creaturas rationales quibus potest aliquid denuntiari. Ergo solae creaturae rationales subsunt legi aeternae; non ergo naturalia contingentia.

Objection 1

It seems that the contingent things in nature are not subject to the Eternal Law. For promulgation belongs to the essence of law, as was said above (*q. 90, a. 4*). But promulgation can only be made to rational creatures to whom something can be announced. Therefore, only rational creatures are subject to the Eternal Law, not contingent things in nature.

REPLY 1

Ad primum ergo dicendum quod hoc modo se habet impressio activi principii intrinseci quantum ad res naturales sicut se habet promulgatio legis quantum ad homines, quia per legis promulgationem imprimitur hominibus quoddam directivum principium humanorum actuum, ut dictum est.

Reply 1

The relationship of the impression of an internal active principle into natural things is similar to the relationship of promulgation to men, for, the promulgation of a law imprints on men a certain directive principle of human acts, as was stated above (in the *Corpus*).

OBJECTION 2

Praeterea, *ea quae obediunt rationi participant aliqualiter ratione,* ut dicitur I *Ethic.* Lex autem aeterna est ratio summa, ut supra dictum est (*a.* 1). Cum igitur naturalia contingentia non participent aliqualiter ratione, sed penitus sint irrationabilia, videtur quod non subsint legi aeternae.

Objection 2

Further, "those things that obey reason participate somewhat in reason" as is said in *Ethic.* i. Now, the Eternal Law is the highest reason, as was said above (*a.* 1). Since, therefore, the contingent things in nature do not participate somewhat in reason but rather are completely irrational, it seems that they are not subject to the Eternal Law.

REPLY 2

Ad secundum dicendum quod creaturae irrationales non participant ratione humana, nec ei obediunt; participant tamen per modum obedientiae ratione divina: ad plura enim se extendit virtus rationis divinae quam virtus rationis humanae. Et sicut membra corporis humani moventur ad imperium rationis, non tamen participant ratione, quia non habent aliquam apprehensionem ordinatam ad rationem, ita etiam creaturae irrationales moventur a Deo, nec tamen propter hoc sunt rationales.

Reply 2

Irrational creatures do not participate in human reason, nor do they obey it. Yet, they participate, through obedience, in the Divine Reason. For the power of Divine Reason extends to more things than human reason does. And just as the members of the human body are moved by the command of reason, nonetheless they do not participate in reason for they have no understanding ordered to reason, so, also, irrational creatures are moved by God but are not, on this account, rational.

OBJECTION 3

Praeterea, lex aeterna est efficacissima. Sed in naturalibus contingentibus acccidit defectus. Non ergo subsunt legi aeternae.

Objection 3

Further, the Eternal Law is most effective. Yet, in the contingent things in nature, defects occur. Therefore, they are not subject to the Eternal Law.

REPLY 3

Ad tertium dicendum quod defectus qui accidunt in rebus naturalibus, quamvis sint praeter ordinem causarum particularium, non tamen sunt praeter ordinem causarum universalium, et praecipue causae primae, quae Deus est, cujus providentiam nihil subterfugere potest, ut in *Primo* dictum est (q. 22, a. 2). Et quia lex aeterna est ratio divinae providentiae, ut dictum est (a. 1), ideo defectus rerum naturalium legi aeternae subduntur.

Reply 3

The defects which occur in natural things, although they are outside the order of particular causes, yet, they are not outside the order of universal causes and especially of the first cause which is

God whose providence nothing can escape, as was said in the *First Part* (*q.* 22, *a.* 2). And, since the Eternal Law is the model of Divine Providence, as has been said (*a.* 1), therefore, the defects of natural things are subject to the Eternal Law.

ON THE CONTRARY

Sed contra est quod dicitur Prov. viii, 29, *Quando circumdabat mari terminum suum, et legem ponebat aquis, ne transirent fines suos.*

On the Contrary

It is written (Prov. viii, 29), "When he established the limits of the sea and set a law to the waters, that they should not pass over their limits. . . ."

CORPUS

Dicendum quod aliter est de lege hominis dicendum et aliter de lege aeterna, quae est lex Dei. Lex enim hominis non se extendit nisi ad creaturas rationales quae homini subjiciuntur. Cujus ratio est, quia lex est directiva actuum qui conveniunt subjectis gubernationi alicujus; unde nullus, proprie loquendo, suis actibus legem imponit. Quaecumque autem aguntur circa usum rerum irrationalium homini subditarum aguntur per actum ipsius hominis moventis hujusmodi res; nam hujusmodi irrationales creaturae non agunt seipsas, sed ab aliis aguntur, ut supra habitum est (*q.* 1, *a.* 2). Et ideo rebus irrationalibus homo legem imponere non potest, quantumcumque ei subjiciantur. Rebus autem rationalibus sibi subjectis potest imponere legem, inquantum suo praecepto vel denuntiatione quamcumque imprimit menti earum quamdam regulam, quae est principium agendi.

Sicut autem homo imprimit denuntiando quoddam interius principium actuum homini sibi subjecto, ita etiam Deus imprimit toti naturae principia propriorum actuum; et ideo

per hunc modum Deus dicitur praecipere toti naturae, secundum illud Ps. cxlviii, 6, *Praeceptum posuit, et non prae-
teribit.* Et per hanc etima rationem omnes motus et actiones
totius naturae legi aeternae subduntur. Unde aliquo modo
creaturae irrationales subduntur legi aeternae, inquantum
moventur a divina providentia; non autem per intellectum
divini praecepti, sicut creaturae rationales.

Corpus

We must speak differently of human law and of the Eternal
Law which is the law of God. For human law applies only to rational
creatures which are subject to man. The reason for this is that law
directs acts which are appropriate for those subject to someone's
governance. Hence—properly speaking, no one imposes a law on his
own acts. Now whatever is done concerning the use of irrational
things subject to man is done by an act of man himself moving such
things. For such irrational creatures do not act of themselves but are
acted upon by others, as was stated above (*q. 1, a. 2*). And therefore,
man cannot impose a law on irrational things, however much they
are subject to him. But he can impose a law on rational beings subject
to him, inasmuch as, by his command or some sort of communication,
he imprints on their minds a rule which is a principle of action.

Now, just as man, by a communication, imprints on a man
subject to him an internal principle of action, so God also imprints
on the whole of nature principles of their proper actions, and, in this
way, God is said to issue commands to the whole of nature, according
to Ps. cxlvii, 6, "He has made a decree and it shall not pass away."
And for this reason also, all movements and actions of the whole of
nature are subject to the Eternal Law. Hence, in some way, irrational
creatures are subject to the Eternal Law, inasmuch as they are moved
by Divine Providence but not through understanding the Divine precept as rational creatures are.

Comment

This Article presents emphatically the radical difference St.
Thomas sees between human beings who are rational and the rest
of creation which consists of irrational beings. It also points out a
radical difference between human and Divine law. Finally, it adds
clarification to the relationship of the Eternal Law to Divine Providence which, in God, are identical although the former can be thought

of as the supreme model for Divine Providence which can be considered as the carrying out of the Eternal Law.

ARTICLE 6
UTRUM OMNES RES HUMANAE SUBJICIANTUR LEGI AETERNAE?
WHETHER ALL HUMAN THINGS ARE SUBJECT TO THE DIVINE LAW?

OBJECTION 1

Videtur quod non omnes res humanae subjiciantur legi aeternae. Dicit enim Apostolus, Gal. v, 18, *Si Spiritu Dei ducimini, non estis sub lege.* Sed viri justi, qui sunt filii Dei per adoptionem, Spiritu Dei aguntur, secundum illud Rom. viii, 14, *Qui Spiritu Dei aguntur, hi filii Dei sunt.* Ergo non omnes homines sunt sub lege aeterna.

Objection 1

It seems that not all human things are subject to the Divine Law. For the Apostle says (Gal. v, 18), "If you are led by the Spirit of God, you are not subject to the law." But just men who are the sons of God by adoption are moved by the Spirit of God, according to Rom. viii, 14, "Whoever are led by the Spirit of God, they are the sons of God." Therefore, not all men are subject to the Eternal Law.

REPLY 1

Ad primum ergo dicendum quod illud verbum Apostoli potest intelligi dupliciter. Uno modo, ut esse sub lege intelligatur ille qui nolens obligationi legis subditur quasi cuidam ponderi: unde glossa ibidem dicit quod *sub lege est qui timore supplicii quod lex minatur, non amore justitiae a malo opere abstinet;* et hoc modo spirituales viri non sunt sub lege, quia per caritatem, quam Spiritus sanctus cordibus eorum infundit, voluntarie id quod legis est, implent. Alio modo potest etiam intelligi, inquantum hominis opera qui Spiritu sancto agitur magis dicuntur esse opera Spiritus sancti quam ipsius hominis. Unde, cum Spiritus sanctus non sit sub lege, sicut nec Filius, ut supra dictum est (*a.* 4, Reply 2), sequitur quod hujusmodi opera, inquantum sunt Spiritus sancti, non sint sub lege. Et huic attestatur quod Apostolus dicit, 2 Cor., iii, 17, *Ubi Spiritus Domini, ibi libertas.*

Reply 1

The Apostle's text can be understood in two different ways. One way, as a person is understood to be under a law when he is unwillingly under its obligation as under a great weight. And so, a gloss on the same text says that "a man is said to be under the law when he refrains from evil deeds through fear of the punishment threatened by the law and not through love of justice." In this way, spiritual men are not under the law because they voluntarily fulfill the law through love which the Holy Spirit pours into their hearts. The text can be understood in another way, namely, that the works of a man who is led by the Holy Spirit are said to be the works of the Holy Spirit rather than of the man himself. Hence, since the Holy Spirit is not under the law, just as the Son is not, as stated above (*a.* 4, Reply 2), it follows that works of this sort, inasmuch as they belong to the Holy Spirit, are not under the law. And the Apostle testifies to this when he says (2 Cor., iii, 17), "Wherever the Spirit of the Lord is, there is liberty."

Comment

St. Thomas treats the problem of this objection-reply at greater length in *q.* 96, *a.* 5.

OBJECTION 2

Praeterea, Apostolus dicit, Rom. viii, 7, *Prudentia carnis inimica est Deo; legi enim Dei subjecta non est.* Sed multi homines sunt in quibus prudentia carnis dominatur. Ergo legi aeternae, quae est lex Dei, non subjiciuntur omnes homines.

Objection 2

Further, the Apostle says (Rom. viii, 7), "The prudence of the flesh is hostile to God, for it is not subject to the law of God." But there are many men who are dominated by the prudence of the flesh. Therefore, not all men are subject to the Eternal Law which is the law of God.

REPLY 2

Ad secundum dicendum quod prudentia carnis non potest subjici legi Dei ex parte actionis, quia inclinat ad actiones contrarias legi divinae; subjicitur tamen legi Dei ex parte passionis, quia meretur pati poenam secundum legem divinae justitiae. Nihilominus tamen in nullo homine ita prudentia carnis dominatur quod totum bonum naturae corrumpatur; et ideo remanet in homine inclinatio ad agendum ea quae sunt legis aeternae. Habitum est enim supra (*q*. 85, *a*. 2) quod peccatum non tollit totum bonum naturae.

Reply 2

The prudence of the flesh cannot be subject to the law of God, in regard to actions, since it inclines to acts contrary to the divine law. Yet, it is subject to the law of God in respect to receptivity because it deserves to suffer punishment according to the law of divine justice. Nonetheless, no man is so dominated by the prudence of the flesh that the whole good of his nature is corrupted. And, therefore, there remains in man an inclination to act according to the Eternal Law. For it was shown above (*q*. 85, *a*. 2) that sin does not remove the whole good of nature.

Comment

This Reply emphasizes a very important aspect of St. Thomas's view of human nature and of the effects of sin, Original and personal, on that nature. Man has a basic inclination to good and to acting according to reason. Sin impedes these inclinations, it darkens the understanding and weakens the will, but it does not destroy the good of human nature. With God's help man can overcome sin and do good.

Luther held that Original Sin totally destroyed man's goodness so that he remains evil even when God's Grace covers his sins. Calvin held that some, the "reprobate" were destined for Hell from all eternity and are totally corrupt. St. Thomas would have rejected this view with horror.

Hobbes saw man as essentially an aggressor, naturally the enemy of every other man, *Homo homini lupus*. The main purpose of law is to restrain man's aggressiveness by the power of the sword. As we have seen, St. Thomas's view is altogether different.

Thus, underlying the various jurisprudential theories is a profound disagreement about the nature of human beings.

OBJECTION 3

Praeterea, Augustinus dicit *De Lib. Arb.* i, 6 quod *lex aeterna est qua mali miseriam, boni vitam beatam merentur.* Sed homines jam beati vel jam damnati non sunt in statu merendi. Ergo non subsunt legi aeternae.

Objection 3

Further, Augustine says (*De Lib. Arb.* i, 6) that "the Eternal Law is that by which the wicked merit misery and the good a life of happiness." But men who are already in heaven or already damned cannot merit. Therefore, they are not under the Eternal Law.

REPLY 3

Ad tertium dicendum quod idem est per quod aliquid conservatur in fine et per quod movetur ad finem; sicut corpus grave gravitate quiescit in loco inferiori, per quam etiam ad locum ipsum movetur. Et sic dicendum est quod, sicut secundum legem aeternam aliqui merentur beatitudinem vel miseriam, ita per eamdem legem in beatitudine vel miseria conservantur. Et secundum hoc beati et damnati subsunt legi aeternae.

Reply 3

It is the same thing that keeps a thing in its goal and that moves it towards its goal. Thus, a heavy body rests in a lower place in virtue of gravity and by this same gravity the body is propelled to that very place. And so we must say that just as through the Eternal Law some merit happiness or misery, so also, through the same Eternal Law, they are maintained in happiness or misery. Thus, both the blessed (in heaven) and the damned are subject to the Eternal Law.

Comment

According to Aristotelian science, the elements of which all compound bodies were composed were earth, air, fire, and water. Each element had a proper place in the sublunary world. Fire held the highest place; below it came air, water, and earth, in that order. Each element, when displaced, tried to reach its proper place. The element earth and "mixed" bodies in which earth predominated all tried to reach the proper place for earth, namely the lowest possible place in the universe. Thus, in earth there was a force, gravity, which propelled it towards that proper place and kept it in that place when it came to rest as low as it could get. Thus, St. Thomas was able, in this example, drawn from contemporary science, to illustrate the principle he is using to show that the blessed and the damned are both subject to the Eternal Law, though in different ways.

ON THE CONTRARY

Sed contra est quod Augustinus dicit, *De Civ. Dei,* 19, 12 *Nullo modo aliquid legibus summi Creatoris ordinationique subtrahitur, a quo pax universitatis administratur.*

On the Contrary

Augustine says (*De Civ. Dei,* 19, 12), "In no way does anything escape the laws and governance of the most high Creator by whom the peace of the universe is administered."

CORPUS

Dicendum quod duplex est modus quo aliquid subditur legi aeternae, ut ex supra dictis patet (a. 5). Uno modo,

inquantum participatur lex aeterna per modum cognitionis.
Alio modo, per modum actionis et passionis, inquantum participatur per modum interioris principii motivi. Et hoc secundo modo subduntur legi aeternae irrationales creaturae,
ut dictum est (ibid.).

Sed quia rationalis natura cum eo quod est commune
omnibus creaturis habet aliquid sibi proprium inquantum est
rationalis, ideo secundum utrumque modum legi aeternae
subditur, quia et notionem legis aeternae aliquo modo habet,
ut supra dictum est (a. 2), et iterum unicuique rationali creaturae inest naturalis inclinatio ad id quod est consonum legi
aeternae. *Sumus enim innati ad habendum virtutes,* ut dicitur
in *Ethic* ii, 1.

Uterque tamen modus imperfectus quidem est et quodammodo corruptus in malis, in quibus et inclinatio naturalis
ad virtutem depravatur per habitum vitiosum, et iterum ipsa
naturalis cognitio boni in eis obtenebratur per passiones et
habitus peccatorum. In bonis autem uterque modus invenitur
perfectior, quia et supra cognitionem naturalem boni superadditur eis cognitio fidei et sapientiae; et supra naturalem
inclinationem ad bonum superadditur eis interius motivum
gratiae et virtutis.

Sic igitur boni perfecte subsunt legi aeternae, tanquam
semper secundum eam agentes; mali autem subsunt quidem
legi aeternae, imperfecte quidem quantum ad actiones ipsorum, prout imperfecte cognoscunt et imperfecte inclinantur
ad bonum. Sed quantum deficit ex parte actionis suppletur
ex parte passionis, prout scilicet intantum patiuntur quod lex
aeterna dictat de eis inquantum deficiunt facere quod legi
aeternae convenit. Unde Augustinus dicit in *De Lib. Arb.* i,
1, *Justos sub aeterna lege agere existimo;* et in *De Catech.
Rud.* xviii, dicit quod *Deus ex justa miseria animarum se
deserentium convenientissimis legibus inferiores partes creaturae suae novit ornare.*

Corpus

There are two ways in which something is subject to the Eternal
Law, as is clear from what has been said (a. 5). One way is by partic-

ipating in the Eternal Law by way of knowledge. A second way is by way of action and passive potency, that is, when a thing participates in the Eternal Law by possessing an internal moving principle. And, in this latter way, irrational creatures are subject to the Eternal Law, as has been said (ibid.).

But, since the rational nature, along with what is common to all creatures, has something that is proper to itself, inasmuch as it is rational, therefore, the rational creature is subject to the Eternal Law in both ways (mentioned above), for it has some idea of the Eternal Law, as was said above (*a.* 2), and, again, each rational nature has a natural inclination to what is in keeping with the Eternal Law, "We are born to be the possessors of the virtues" (*Ethic.* ii, 1).

However, each mode is imperfect and, in a way, is corrupted in evil people in whom both the natural inclination to virtue is perverted by vicious habit and, again, the natural knowledge of good is obscured in them by passions and sinful habits. In the good, however, each mode is found more perfectly, for, in addition to the natural knowledge of good, there is added in them the knowledge arising from faith and wisdom, and, in addition to the natural inclination to good, there is added in them the internal moving power of grace and virtue.

Thus, therefore, the good are perfectly subject to the Eternal Law, as always acting according to it, while evil people are indeed subject to the Eternal Law, imperfectly to be sure with regard to their actions, inasmuch as they imperfectly know and are imperfectly inclined to good. But their failures on the part of action are balanced by suffering inasmuch, as they suffer what the Eternal Law decrees for them inasmuch as they failed to act according to the Eternal Law. Thus, Augustine says (*De Lib. Arb.* i, 1), "I believe the just act in subjection to the Eternal Law" and (*De Catech. Rud.* xviii), "Out of the just misery of the souls that deserted him, God knew how to make appropriate laws for the ordering of the lower parts of his creation."

Comment

1. This *Corpus* well illustrates the secondary role of *auctoritates*, for every *auctoritas* in this *Corpus* could be omitted without destroying the smooth flow of the exposition.
2. The doctrinal point is that every creature is subject to the Eternal Law. The good are subject to it inasmuch as their knowledge and their actions are positively in accord with

it, while the evil are subject to it, inasmuch as the Eternal
Law provides just punishments equivalent to their sins.

3. The "wisdom" coupled with faith is not ordinary human
   wisdom but one of the gifts of the Holy Spirit. Also, the
   "virtue" coupled with grace is infused virtue, also a gift
   of God to the good.

QUESTION 94
DE LEGE NATURALI
CONCERNING NATURAL LAW

Deinde considerandum est de lege naturali; et circa hoc quaeruntur sex:

    1. quid sit lex naturalis;
    2. quae sint praecepta legis naturalis;
    3. utrum omnes actus virtutum sint de lege naturae;
    4. utrum lex naturalis sit una apud omnes;
    5. utrum sit mutabilis;
    6. utrum possit a mente hominis deleri.

Question 94

Next we must consider Natural Law, and with regard to this there are six points of inquiry.

    1. What is the Natural Law?
    2. What are the precepts of the Natural Law?
    3. Whether all acts of the virtues belong to the Natural Law?
    4. Whether Natural Law is the same for all people?
    5. Whether the Natural Law is changeable?
    6. Whether the Natural Law can be removed from the mind of a man?

ARTICLE 1
UTRUM LEX NATURALIS SIT HABITUS?
WHETHER THE NATURAL LAW
IS A HABIT?

Introductory Comment

At the beginning of this Question, the first point of inquiry was said to be, "What is the Natural Law?" As he now takes up the question he translates it into the more specific question, "Is the Natural Law a Habit?"

This question was raised at the beginning of the *Treatise* in the second objection of Question 90 where it is argued that law (in general) is a habit. In reply, St. Thomas argued that just as in the Speculative Intellect something is produced, e.g., definitions, so in the Practical Intellect something analogous is produced, namely the principles of the Natural Law. The Practical Intellect, by means of the habit of first principles, produces the principles themselves. They are then held in the Practical Intellect habitually. We know from experience that when we learn something we continue to keep it (habitually) even though we may rarely think of (consider) it. All this is congruent with the *Corpus* of this Article.

Thus St. Thomas, in answering the question, "Whether Natural Law is a habit?" has established that the Natural Law consists of principles and precepts habitually held in the Practical Intellect, thus answering the question as stated in the summary at the beginning of this Question. His conclusion here sets the question for the next Article, "What are the precepts of the Natural Law?"

OBJECTION 1

Videtur quod lex naturalis sit habitus, quia, ut Philosophus dicit in *Ethic.*, ii, 5, *tria sunt in anima, potentia, habitus, et passio*. Sed naturalis lex non est aliqua potentiarum animae nec aliqua passionum, ut patet enumerando per singula. Ergo lex naturalis est habitus.

Objection 1

It seems that the Natural Law is a habit, because, as the Philosopher says (*Ethic.*, ii, 5), "There are three things in the soul, power, habit, and passion." But the Natural Law is not any power of the soul nor is it one of the passions, as can be seen by going through them one by one. Therefore, the Natural Law is a habit.

REPLY 1

Ad primum ergo dicendum quod Philosophus intendit ibi investigare genus virtutis; et cum manifestum sit quod

virtus sit quoddam principium actus, illa tantum ponit quae
sunt principia humanorum actuum, scilicet potentias, habitus,
et passiones. Praeter haec autem tria sunt quaedam alia in
anima, sicut quidam actus, ut velle est in volente, et etiam
cognita sunt in cognoscente, et proprietates naturales animae
insunt ei, ut immortalitas et alia hujusmodi.

Reply 1

In that passage, the Philosopher intends to investigate the genus
of virtue. Since virtue is a principle of action, he mentions there are only
three things that are principles of human acts, namely, power, habit,
and passion. Besides these three, there are some other things in the soul,
namely, some acts, as willing is in the one willing and things known
are in the knower and the natural properties of the soul are in it, such
as immortality and the like.

Comment

Note that in handling this *auctoritas,* St. Thomas appeals to the
intent or purpose of Aristotle to explain why he seems, in this context,
to limit the things that are in the soul to just three. The powers of the
soul are primarily the intellect and the will. There are various habits in
the soul like the habit of first principles. The passions are numerous,
such as anger, hate, etc. St. Thomas argues that there are many other
things in the soul; hence the argument fails.

OBJECTION 2

Praeterea, Basilius dicit quod *conscientia,* sive synderesis, *est lex intellectus nostri;* quod non potest intelligi nisi
de lege naturali. Sed synderesis est habitus quidam, ut in
Primo habitum est (*q.* 72, *a.* 12). Ergo lex naturalis est
habitus.

Objection 2

Further, Basil says that "conscience or *synderesis* is the law of our
intellect." (The quotation appears in St. John Damascene, *De Fide Orthodoxa,* IV, 22 but there is a basis for it in St. Basil's *In Hexaem.,* 7).
This cannot be understood except as referring to the Natural Law. But

synderesis is a habit as was shown in the *First Part* (*q.* 72, *a.* 12). Therefore, the Natural Law is a habit.

REPLY 2

Ad secundum dicendum quod synderesis dicitur lex intellectus nostri inquantum est habitus continens praecepta legis naturalis, quae sunt prima principia operum humanorum.

Reply 2

Synderesis is said to be the law of our intellect inasmuch as it is a habit that contains the precepts of the Natural Law which are the first principles of human acts.

OBJECTION 3

Praeterea, lex naturalis semper in homine manet, ut infra patebit (*a.* 6). Sed non semper ratio hominis, ad quam lex pertinet, cogitat de naturali lege. Ergo lex naturalis non est actus, sed habitus.

Objection 3

Further, the Natural Law always remains in a man, as will be clear later (*a.* 6). But man's reason to which the Natural Law belongs does not constantly think about the Natural Law. Therefore, the Natural Law is not an act but a habit.

REPLY 3

Ad tertium dicendum quod ratio illa concludit quod lex naturalis habitualiter tenetur; et hoc concedimus.

Reply 3

This argument concludes that the Natural Law is habitually possessed, and this we concede.

ON THE CONTRARY

Sed contra est quod Augustinus dicit in *De Bono Con-*
jugali, XXI quod *habitus est quo aliquid agitur cum opus*
est. Sed naturalis lex non est hujusmodi: est enim in parvulis
et damnatis, qui per eam agere non possunt. Ergo lex naturalis non est habitus.

On the Contrary

St. Augustine says in *De Bono Conjugali,* XXI, that "a habit is
that by which something is done when necessary." But the Natural Law
is not this sort of thing, for it is in children and the damned who cannot
act through it.

ST. THOMAS'S COMMENT ON THE
ON THE CONTRARY

Ad id vero quod in contrarium objicitur, dicendum quod
eo quod habitualiter inest, quandoque aliquis uti non potest
propter aliquod impedimentum: sicut homo non potest uti
habitu scientiae propter somnum, et similiter puer non potest
uti habitu intellectus principiorum, vel etiam lege naturali,
quae ei habitualiter inest, propter defectum aetatis.

St. Thomas's Comment On the On the Contrary

However, with regard to what is objected to the contrary: Sometimes a person cannot use that which he habitually possesses because
of some impediment; for example, a person cannot use the habit of
science because of sleep. Likewise, a child, because of his age, cannot
use the habit of the understanding of the first principles or even the
Natural Law, both of which he habitually possesses.

CORPUS

Dicendum quod aliquid potest dici esse habitus dupliciter: uno modo proprie et essentialiter; et sic lex naturalis
non est habitus. Dictum est (*q.* 90, *a.* 1, Reply 2) enim supra,

quod lex naturalis est aliquid per rationem constitutum, sicut
etiam propositio est quoddam opus rationis. Non est autem
idem quod quis agit et quo quis agit: aliquis enim per habitum
grammaticae agit orationem congruam. Cum igitur habitus
sit quo quis agit, non potest esse quod lex aliqua sit habitus
proprie et essentialiter.

Alio modo potest dici habitus id quod habitu tenetur,
sicut dicitur Fides id quod fide tenetur. Et hoc modo, quia
praecepta legis naturalis quandoque considerantur in actu a
ratione, quandoque autem sunt in ea habitualiter tantum,
secundum hunc modum potest dici quod lex naturalis sit
habitus: sicut etiam principia indemonstrabilia in speculativis
non sunt ipsi habitus principiorum, sed sunt principia, quorum est habitus.

Corpus

Something can be called a habit in two ways. The first way is
properly and essentially, and in this way the Natural Law is not a
habit. For it was shown above (*q. 90, a.* 1, Reply 2) that the Natural
Law is something constituted through reason, just as a proposition
is a product of reason. For that which a person does and that by
which he does it are not the same thing. For, a person makes a
suitable speech through the habit of grammar. Since, therefore, a
habit is that by which someone acts, it cannot be that the Natural
Law is properly and essentially a habit.

In another way, that can be called a habit which the habit holds
just as Faith can be said to be that which is held by faith. Since the
principles of the Natural Law are sometimes actually considered by
reason and sometimes are in it only habitually, then according to this
second way of speaking, it can be said that the Natural Law is a
habit just as, in speculative matters, the indemonstrable principles
are not the habit of the principles but rather the principles which we
possess through the habit.

Comment

As is so often the case in St. Thomas, the *Corpus* and the
answers to objections are based on a key distinction between an
intellectual habit and that which the intellect knows and learns
through the habit. These things are not the habit, but they are habitually held in the intellect, once they have been acquired.

An intellectual habit is a perfection of the active power of the intellect. It, therefore, enables the reason to understand intelligibilities that the intellect is initially not ready to deal with.

Thus, a person is not ready to do mathematics without training and the acquisition of the ability to think mathematically. Once the active habit of thinking mathematically is acquired, he can then add to his mathematical knowledge. For example, in studying geometry, a person acquires the ability to do geometry, then through this acquired active power he can learn more and more theorems and possess them habitually without always thinking of (considering) them.

ARTICLE 2
UTRUM LEX NATURALIS CONTINEAT PLURA PRAECEPTA VEL UNUM TANTUM? WHETHER THE NATURAL LAW CONTAINS MANY PRECEPTS OR ONLY ONE?

OBJECTION 1

Videtur quod lex naturalis non contineat plura praecepta, sed unum tantum. Lex enim continetur in genere praecepti, ut supra habitum est (q. 92, a. 2). Si igitur essent multa praecepta legis naturalis sequeretur quod etiam essent multae leges naturales.

Objection 1

It seems that the Natural Law does not contain many precepts but one only. For, as stated above (q. 92, a. 2), the Natural Law is a kind of precept. If, therefore, there are many precepts of the Natural Law it would follow that there are many Natural Laws.

REPLY 1

Ad primum ergo dicendum quod omnia ista praecepta legis naturae inquantum referuntur ad unum primum praeceptum habent rationem unius legis naturalis.

Reply 1

All those precepts of the Natural Law, inasmuch as they are based on one first precept, have the formality of one Natural Law.

OBJECTION 2

Praeterea, lex naturalis consequitur hominis naturam. Sed humana natura est una secundum totum, licet sit multiplex secundum partes. Aut ergo est unum praeceptum tantum legis naturae propter unitatem totius, aut sunt multa secundum multitudinem partium naturae humanae; et sic oportebit quod etiam ea quae sunt de inclinatione concupiscibilis pertineant ad legem naturalem.

Objection 2

Further, the Natural Law is consequent on human nature. But human nature, viewed as a totality, is one, although it is multiple in its many parts. Therefore, either there is only one precept of the Natural Law because of the unity of the whole, or there are many precepts according to the parts of human nature. In this latter case, even things that refer to the inclination of the concupiscible faculty would belong to the Natural Law.

REPLY 2

Ad secundum dicendum quod omnes hujusmodi inclinationes quarumcumque partium naturae humanae, puta concupiscibilis et irascibilis, secundum quod regulantur ratione, pertinent ad legem naturalem, et reducuntur ad unum primum praeceptum, ut dictum est, et secundum hoc sunt multa praecepta legis naturae in seipsis, quae tamen communicant in una radice.

Reply 2

All such inclinations whatever of the parts of human nature, for example, of the concupiscible and irascible faculties, inasmuch as they are regulated by reason, belong to the Natural Law and are reduced to one first principle, as has been said in the *Corpus* of this Article; accordingly there are many precepts of the Natural Law in themselves, yet they all share in one root.

OBJECTION 3

Praeterea, lex est aliquid ad rationem pertinens, ut supra dictum est (*q.* 90, *a.* 1). Sed ratio in homine est una tantum. Ergo solum unum praeceptum est legis naturalis.

Objection 3

Law is something pertaining to reason, as was said above (*q.* 90, *a.* 1). But reason in man is one reason. Therefore, there is only one precept of the Natural Law.

REPLY 3

Ad tertium dicendum quod ratio, etsi in se una sit, tamen est ordinativa omnium quae ad homines spectant; et secundum hoc sub lege rationis continentur omnia ea quae ratione regulari possunt.

Reply 3

Reason, although one in itself, orders everything that pertains to men, and, therefore, the law of reason contains everything that can be regulated by reason.

ON THE CONTRARY

Sed contra est quia sic se habent praecepta legis naturalis in homine quantum ad operabilia sicut se habent prima principia in demonstrativis. Sed prima principia indemonstrabilia sunt plura. Ergo etiam praecepta legis naturae sunt plura.

On the Contrary

The first principles of the Natural Law are related to action in the same way as the first indemonstrable principles are related to demonstrations. But there are many first indemonstrable principles. Therefore, the precepts of the Natural Law are also many.

Comment

In *a.* 1 St. Thomas established that the Natural Law consists of principles and precepts habitually held in the Practical Intellect.

In this Article he asks about the inner structure of the Natural Law by posing the question, "Whether the Natural Law contains one precept only, or has many principles?"

The Replies to the Objections have shown 1) that the Natural Law is unified because all the precepts depend on one first principle and because all the precepts are ordered by reason; 2) that the multiplicity of precepts is due to the various inclinations and parts of human nature.

In the *Corpus* St. Thomas explains the source of unity in the Practical Reason and the first self-evident principles of the Natural Law.

The asserted self-evidence of moral principles creates a problem inasmuch as many people do not recognize this self-evidence. To deal with this problem, St. Thomas makes the distinction between self-evidence in itself and self-evidence to people.

St. Thomas then makes a survey of the inclinations natural to man, concluding with the inclination of man to act according to reason which brings the inclinations back to the unity in the Practical Reason.

To clarify the exposition, I arrange the *Corpus* of the Article in four Sections.

CORPUS [SECTION 1]

Dicendum quod, sicut supra dictum est (*q.* 91, *a.* 3), praecepta legis naturae hoc modo se habent ad rationem practicam sicut principia prima demonstrationum se habent ad rationem speculativam: utraque enim sunt quaedam principia per se nota.

Corpus [Section 1]

As was said above (*q*. 91, *a*. 3), the precepts of the Natural Law are related to Practical Reason, as the first principles of demonstration are related to the speculative reason, for, both are self-evident principles.

Comment

It will have been noticed that St. Thomas frequently uses the distinction between the Intellect (Reason) as Speculative and the Intellect (Reason) as Practical. This, of course, is not the modern distinction between theoretical and applied knowledge [299-309]. But before following up on this distinction, he first expands on his last remark and explains "self-evidence."

CORPUS [SECTION 2]

Dicitur autem aliquid per se notum dupliciter: uno modo secundum se, alio modo quoad nos. Secundum se quidem quaelibet propositio dicitur per se nota cujus praedicatum est de ratione subjecti: contingit tamen quod ignoranti definitionem subjecti talis propositio non erit per se nota, sicut ista propositio, 'Homo est rationale', est per se nota secundum sui naturam, quia qui dicit 'hominem' dicit 'rationale'; et tamen ignoranti quid sit homo, haec propositio non est per se nota. Et inde est quod, sicut dicit Boethius (*Hebdom.*, PL 64, 1311), *quaedam sunt dignitates vel propositiones per se notae communiter omnibus;* et hujusmodi sunt illae propositiones quarum termini sunt omnibus noti, ut 'Omne totum est majus sua parte' et 'Quae uni et eidem sunt aequalia sibi invicem sunt aequalia'.

Quaedam vero propositiones sunt per se notae solis sapientibus, qui terminos propositionum intelligunt quid significent; sicut intelligenti quod angelus non est corpus per se notum est quod non est circumscriptive in loco; quod non est manifestum rudibus, qui hoc non capiunt.

Corpus [Section 2]

Now, something can be said to be self-evident in two ways. First, in itself and secondly, with reference to us. Any proposition is said to be self-evident in itself, if the predicate is contained in the notion of the subject. It happens, however, that such a proposition will not be self-evident to one who does not know the definition of the subject. For example, this propostion, "Man is rational," is self-evident because of its nature, for he who says "man" says "rational." Yet, to one who does not know the definition of man, this proposition will not be self-evident. Hence it is that, as Boethius says (*Hebdom.,* PL 64, 1311), "Certain axioms or propositions are universally known to everyone." And of this sort are those propositions the terms of which are known to all, as "Every whole is greater than any one of its parts" and "Things equal to one and the same thing are equal to each other."

Some propositions, however, are known only to the wise who understand the meaning of the terms of the proposition, as to one who knows that an angel is not a body, it is self-evident that an angel is not circumscriptively in a place, but this is not manifest to the unlearned who cannot grasp it.

Comment

In Christian theology angels are pure spirits, individual and personal, but having no material parts. Hence, angels cannot exist in a definitively located and measured space, which would be to exist "circumscriptively." The distinction between propositions self-evident in themselves and propositions self-evident to different people is extremely important. Some require that self-evident propositions must be self-evident to everyone. St. Thomas does not interpret self-evidence in this limited fashion.

St. Thomas now elaborates on the distinction between the Speculative Intellect and the Practical Reason, as initiated in Section 1 of this *Corpus.*

CORPUS [SECTION 3]

In his autem quae in apprehensione hominum cadunt quidam ordo invenitur. Nam illud quod primo cadit sub apprehensione est ens, cujus intellectus includitur in omnibus quaecumque quis apprehendit. Et ideo primum principium indemonstrabile est quod non est simul affirmare et negare, quod fundatur supra rationem entis et non entis; et super hoc principio omnia alia fundantur, ut dicit Philosophus in IV *Meta.*

Sicut autem ens est primum quod cadit in apprehensione simpliciter, ita bonum est primum quod cadit in apprehensione practicae rationis, quae ordinatur ad opus. Omne enim agens agit propter finem, qui habet rationem boni. Et ideo primum principium in ratione practica est quod fundatur supra rationem boni quae est, bonum est quod omnia appetunt. Hoc est ergo primum praeceptum legis, quod 'bonum est faciendum et prosequendum, et malum vitandum'; et super hoc fundantur omnia alia praecepta legis naturae, ut scilicet omnia illa facienda vel vitanda pertineant ad praecepta legis naturae quae ratio pactica naturaliter apprehendit esse bona humana.

Corpus [Section 3]

In these things, however, which man comes to apprehend, a certain order is to be found. For, that which first comes into the understanding is "being" which is included in the understanding of everything whatever. And, therefore, the first indemonstrable principle is that one cannot simultaneously affirm and deny something; this principle which is founded on the notion of being and non-being, and on this principle all the others are based, as the Philosopher says (*Meta.* iv).

Now, just as being is the first thing that, without qualification, comes into man's apprehension, so good is the first thing that comes into the apprehension of the Practical Reason which is ordered to action, for every agent acts for an end under the aspect of good. And, therefore, the first principle of the Practical Reason is based on the notion of good which is that which all desire. Therefore, the first principle of the Natural Law is this, that good should be done and sought and evil is to be avoided. And on this principle are based all the other precepts of the law of nature so that all the things that Practical Reason apprehends as human goods belong to the law of nature.

Comment

In this Section St. Thomas briefly states two of his most important and most profound doctrines concerning the operations of the human intellect. The intellect in itself, operating simply as intellect, is a knowing faculty that apprehends things as beings, as things that *are*. This "is" is not the "is" of the logicians but the "is" of a Metaphysics of the real. Nor is it the common sense understanding that something is *there,* as a child might say that there are cookies in the cooky jar. It envelops the total reality of things, viewing all their concrete determinations as so many ways of existing, so many ways of being real. As the faculty of reality, the human intellect escapes the limitations of sense and matter and includes, as St. Thomas indicates later in this *Corpus,* an inclination to know the truth about God. A full understanding of what I am so briefly and inadequately saying here would require a complete study of Thomistic metaphysics.

But the intellect can operate also as a Practical Reason, that is, while retaining the intellectual grasp of being, it now, with the will, which is an intellectual appetite, grasps being as good. The good is desired and therefore has the quality of an end or a final cause, and so, in fact, is the first cause of all human activity; we always act for an end apprehended as good. Even when we act for what is objectively evil, we must somehow make ourselves see it as "good." So our rational life is governed by two distinct first principles, principles of being such as: "It is impossible simultaneously to affirm and deny the same thing" or, recasting this principle: "It is impossible for a thing to both be and not be under the same aspect." These principles of being are the fundamental principles of rational thought. There are principles of Practical Reason based on the understanding of the "good" such as, "Good is to be done and evil avoided." This is the first principle of the moral order. It is not a first principle in the sense that all other moral principles and precepts can be deduced from it, but in the sense that by stating the intrinsic attraction of the good it supplies the entire moral order with its obligatory nature [405-406].

Positivists tend to derive both moral and legal obligation from sovereign power or social pressure. John Austin derived legal obligation from fear of punishment by a lawgiver with physical power. H. L. A. Hart derived moral obligation from severe social pressure [*The Concept of Law,* pp. 79–88]. Hans Kelsen bases legal obligation on formal legal validity and physical power [*The Pure Theory of Law,* passim]. For them, sanctions are of the essence of law.

For St. Thomas, law needs a coercive force, not because of the nature or essence of law but because of the existence of non-observers, a fact that is outside the essence of law and only accidental to it (*q. 96, a. 5*).

Human goods are those goods to which human beings have natural inclinations. St. Thomas now makes a brief survey of human goods.

CORPUS [SECTION 4]

Quia vero bonum habet rationem finis, malum autem rationem contrarii, inde est quod omnia illa ad quae homo habet naturalem inclinationem ratio naturaliter apprehendit ut bona, et per consequens ut opere prosequenda, et contraria eorum ut mala et vitanda.

Secundum igitur ordinem inclinationum naturalium est ordo praeceptorum legis naturae. Inest enim primo inclinatio homini ad bonum secundum naturam in qua communicat cum omnibus substantiis, prout scilicet quaelibet substantia appetit conservationem sui esse secundum suam naturam; et secundum hanc inclinationem pertinent ad legem naturalem ea per quae vita hominis conservatur, et contrarium impeditur.

Secundo inest homini inclinatio ad aliqua magis specialia secundum naturam in qua communicat cum caeteris animalibus; et secundum hoc dicuntur ea esse de lege naturali quae natura omnia animalia docuit, ut est commixtio maris et feminae, et educatio liberorum, et similia.

Tertio modo inest homini inclinatio ad bonum secundum naturam rationis quae est sibi propria: sicut homo habet naturalem inclinationem ad hoc quod veritatem cognoscat de Deo, et ad hoc quod in societate vivat; et secundum hoc ad legem naturalem pertinent ea quae ad hujusmodi inclinationem spectant, utpote quod homo ignorantiam vitet, quod alios non offendat cum quibus debet conversari, et caetera hujusmodi quae ad hoc spectant.

Corpus [Section 4]

Now, since the good has the formality of the end and evil has the opposite formality, all those things to which man has a natural inclination are naturally apprehended by Practical Reason as good and, consequently, as to be actively pursued while their opposites are apprehended as evil and to be avoided.

Therefore, to the order of natural inclinations there corresponds the order of the precepts of the Natural Law. For, first of all, there is in man an inclination to the good according to the nature which he shares with all substances, namely, inasmuch as all substances desire the conservation of their own existence according to its nature, and in accord with this inclination, all those things by which the life of man is preserved and the opposite impeded belong to the Natural Law.

Secondly, there are in man certain special things according to the nature which he shares with the other animals, and, according to this, those things which nature teaches all animals are said to belong to the Natural Law such as intercourse between male and female, the education of children and the like.

In a third way, there is in man an inclination to good according to the nature of reason which is proper to him, as man has a natural inclination to know the truth about God, to live in society and, in accord with this inclination all those things which relate to it belong to the Natural Law, namely, that a man avoid ignorance and that he should not offend others with whom he ought to live and similar things which relate to this inclination.

Comment

This listing of human inclinations and human goods bears witness again to St. Thomas's view that human nature is basically good. One might, however, misinterpret this presentation as justifying a gratification of all human desires. All human inclinations are good in themselves but they must be regulated by the primary inclination, proper to man, to order all his acts according to reason, and this means according to the virtues which, in turn, enable a man to use all human goods correctly. Thus, to every inclination of man there corresponds some virtue [322–379].

ARTICLE 3
UTRUM OMNES ACTUS VIRTUTUM
SINT DE LEGE NATURAE?
WHETHER ALL THE ACTS OF THE VIRTUES
BELONG TO THE NATURAL LAW?

OBJECTION 1

Videtur quod non omnes actus virtutum sint de lege naturae, quia, ut supra dictum est (*q.* 90, *a.* 2), de ratione legis est ut ordinetur ad bonum commune. Sed quidam virtutum actus ordinantur ad bonum privatum alicujus, ut patet praecipue in actibus temperantiae. Non ergo omnes actus virtutum legi subduntur naturali.

Objection 1

It seems that not all the acts of the virtues belong to the Natural Law because, as it was said above (*q.* 90, *a.* 2), it is of the nature of the law that it be ordered to the Common Good. But certain acts of virtues are ordered to the private good of some individual, as is clear especially in the acts of temperance. Therefore, not all acts of the virtues are subject to the Natural Law.

REPLY 1

Ad primum ergo dicendum quod temperantia est circa concupiscentias naturales cibi et potus, et venereorum, quae quidem ordinantur ad bonum commune naturae, sicut et alia legalia ordinantur ad bonum commune morale.

Reply 1

Temperance is concerned with the natural desire for food, drink and sexual activity which are ordained to the natural Common Good, just as other legal matters are ordained to the common moral good.

OBJECTION 2

Praeterea, omnia peccata aliquibus virtuosis actibus opponuntur. Si igitur omnes actus virtutum sint de lege naturae, videtur ex consequenti quod omnia peccata sint contra naturam; quod tamen specialiter de quibusdam peccatis dicitur.

Objection 2

All sins are opposed to some acts of virtue. If, therefore, all acts of the virtues belong to the Natural law, it seems, consequently, that all sins are contrary to nature which nevertheless is said of only certain sins.

REPLY 2

Ad secundum dicendum quod natura hominis potest dici vel ila quae est propria hominis, et secundum hoc omnia peccata inquantum sunt contra rationem sunt etiam contra naturam, ut patet per Damascenum (*De Fide Orthodoxa,* ii, 30), vel illa quae est communis homini et aliis animalibus, et secundum hoc quaedam specialia peccata dicuntur esse contra naturam, sicut contra commixtionem maris et foeminae, quae est naturalis omnibus animalibus, est concubitus masculorum, quod specialiter dicitur vitium contra naturam.

Reply 2

The nature of man can be understood to be either the nature that is proper to man, and in this sense, all sins, inasmuch as they are contrary to reason, are also contrary to nature, as is clear from Damascene (*De Fide Orthodoxa,* ii, 30); or human nature can be understood of those things which are common to men and to the other animals and, in this sense, certain special sins are said to be contrary to nature, as sexual activity between males is contrary to the natural intercourse of male and female common to all animals. Such sins are said, in a special sense, to be contrary to nature.

OBJECTION 3

Praeterea, in his quae sunt secundum naturam omnes conveniunt. Sed in actibus virtutum non omnes conveniunt: aliquid enim est virtuosum uni quod est alteri vitiosum. Ergo non omnes actus virtutum sunt de lege naturae.

Objection 3

Further, in the things which are according to nature all agree. But with regard to the acts of virtue not all are alike, for what is virtuous in one man may be sinful in another. Therefore, not all acts of the virtues are prescribed by the Natural Law.

REPLY 3

Ad tertium dicendum quod ratio illa procedit de actibus secundum seipsos consideratos. Sic enim propter diversas hominum conditiones contingit quod aliqui actus sunt aliquibus virtuosis tanquam eis proportionati et convenientes, qui tamen sunt aliis vitiosi tanquam eis non proportionati.

Reply 3

That argument is based on considering acts simply in themselves. For, it happens that, because of the different conditions of people, some acts are virtuous in some, as being proportioned to and fitting for them, although these acts may be vicious in others as not being proportioned to them.

Comment

The point being made here can be illustrated as follows. Sexual intercourse is sinful for unmarried persons; but for married persons it is not only licit but virtuous. The difference arises from the different "conditions" of the persons.

ON THE CONTRARY

Sed contra est quod Damascenus dicit (*De Fide Ortho-doxa,* iii, 4) quod *virtutes sunt naturales.* Ergo et actus vir-tuosi subjacent legi naturae.

On the Contrary

Damascene says (*De Fide Orthodoxa.,* iii, 4) that "virtues are natural." Therefore, virtuous acts are also subject to the Natural Law.

CORPUS

Dicendum quod de actibus virtuosis dupliciter loqui pos-sumus: uno modo inquantum sunt virtuosi; alio modo in-quantum sunt tales actus in propriis speciebus considerati.

Si igitur loquamur de actibus virtutum inquantum sunt virtuosi, sic omnes actus virtuosi pertinent ad legem naturae. Dictum est (*a.* 2) quod ad legem naturae pertinet omne illud ad quod homo inclinatur secundum suam naturam. Inclinatur autem unumquodque naturaliter ad operationem sibi conven-ientem secundum suam formam, sicut ignis ad calefaciendum. Unde, cum anima rationalis sit propria forma hominis, na-turalis inclinatio inest cuilibet homini ad hoc quod agat se-cundum rationem; et hoc est agere secundum virtutem. Unde secundum hoc omnes actus virtutum sunt de lege naturali: dictat enim hoc naturaliter unicuique propria ratio ut virtuose agat.

Sed si loquamur de actibus virtuosis secundum seipsos, prout scilicet in propriis speciebus considerantur, sic non omnes actus virtuosi sunt de lege naturae. Multa enim se-cundum virtutem fiunt ad quae natura non primo inclinat; sed per rationis inquisitionem ea homines adinvenerunt quasi utilia ad bene vivendum.

Corpus

We can talk about virtues in two different ways. In one way, inasmuch as they are generically virtues; in another way, inasmuch as they are such and such acts, considered in their proper species.

If, therefore, we talk about virtuous acts inasmuch as they are virtuous acts, thus all virtuous acts belong to the Natural Law. For, it has been said (*a.* 2) that everything to which man has an inclination according to his nature belongs to the Natural Law. However, each thing is naturally inclined to the operation that is proper to it, because of its form, as, for example, fire is inclined to heating. Hence, since the rational soul is the form proper to man, every man has a natural inclination to act according to reason, and this is to act according to virtue. Hence, according to this, all acts of virtue are under the Natural Law. For each one's own reason orders him to act virtuously.

But if we talk about virtuous acts simply in themselves, namely as they are considered in their own proper species, so not all virtuous acts belong to the Natural Law. For many things are done in accordance with virtue to which nature does not at first incline men but have been discovered by the investigation of reason as helpful to man for living well.

Comment

We may clarify the distinctions made in this Article by the following illustration. If we consider human acts from the standpoint of their broad classification simply as virtuous acts (the genus of "virtue"), to judge a man justly and to establish a clinic for poor people are both acts of virtue. But if we look at them as specifically an act of judging justly and as establishing a clinic, the first act as such is likely ordered by the Natural Law, while establishing a clinic requires much study and development of knowledge, i.e., it is planned by human reason. The distinction is analogous to that made in *q.* 95, *a.* 2, *c.* between immediate conclusions from the Natural Law and determinations made by the human lawgiver.

St. Thomas's metaphysical analysis of finite substance includes the recognition of two intrinsic principles, namely, matter (the material cause) and form (the formal cause). The form, when united to matter, makes the substance be the *kind* of thing it is. The form, therefore, determines the kind of powers and inclination possessed by the specific substance. In man, the body, considered without the soul, is the matter; the soul is the form which determines the substance of man to be "rational animal." Hence, acting according to reason is specifically proper to man.

ARTICLE 4
UTRUM LEX NATURALIS SIT UNA APUD OMNES?
WHETHER THE NATURAL LAW IS THE SAME
FOR ALL PEOPLE?

OBJECTION 1

Videtur quod lex naturae non sit una apud omnes. Dicitur enim in *Decretis (Dist.* i), quod *jus naturale est quod in Lege et in Evangelio continetur.* Sed hoc non est commune omnibus, quia, ut dicitur Rom., x, 16, *non omnes obediunt Evangelio.* Ergo lex naturalis non est una apud omnes.

Objection 1

It seems that the Natural Law is not the same for all people. For it is said in the *Decretals (Dist.* i) that the Natural Law is what is contained in the Law and in the Gospel. But this is not common to all, for it is said (Rom. x, 16) that "not all obey the Gospel." Therefore, the Natural Law is not the same for all.

REPLY 1

Ad primum ergo dicendum quod verbum illud non est sic intelligendum quasi omnia quae in Lege et in Evangelio continentur sint de lege naturae, cum multa tradantur ibi supra naturam; sed ea quae sunt de lege naturae plenarie ibi traduntur. Unde cum dixisset Gratianus (*Decretum* I, I) quod *jus naturale est quod in Lege et in Evanelio continetur,* statim explicando subjunxit, *Quo quisque jubetur alii facere quod sibi vult fieri, et prohibetur alii facere quod sibi nolit fieri.*

Reply 1

That text is not to be understood as though everything that is contained in the Law and the Gospel belongs to the law of nature, since many things that are above nature are taught in them. Therefore, Gratian (*Decretum* I, I), after saying that "the Natural Law is what is fully contained in the Law and the Gospel," immediately adds as an explanation, "by which each one is ordered to do to others what he would have done to him and is forbidden to do to others what he would not want done to him."

Comment

The Law referred to here is the Law of the Old Testament, the Law of Moses.

OBJECTION 2

Praeterea, *quae sunt secundum legem, justa esse dicuntur,* ut dicitur in *Ethic* v, 3. Sed in eodem libro dicitur quod nihil est ita justum apud omnes quin apud aliquos diversificetur. Ergo etiam lex naturalis non est apud omnes eadem.

Objection 2

Further, "what is according to the law, is said to be just," as is said in *Ethic.* v, 3, but it is said in the same book that "nothing is so universally just that there are no differences among some people." Therefore, the Natural Law also is not the same for all.

REPLY 2

Ad secundum dicendum quod verbum Philosophi est intelligendum de his quae sunt naturaliter justa, non sicut principia communia, sed sicut quaedam conclusiones ex his derivatae (St. Thomas's Commentary on *Ethics* V, *Lectio* 12); quae ut in pluribus habent rectitudinem, et ut in paucioribus deficiunt.

Reply 2

That statement of the Philosopher is not to be understood of those things which are naturally just, not as common principles but as certain conclusions derived from the principles (St. Thomas's Commentary on *Ethics* V, *lect.* 12) which for the most part have rectitude but are in some instances defective.

OBJECTION 3

Praeterea, ad legem naturae pertinet id ad quod homo secundum naturam suam inclinatur, ut supra dictum est (*aa.* 2 and 3). Sed diversi homines naturaliter ad diversa inclinantur: alii quidem ad concupiscentiam voluptatum, alii ad desideria honorum, alii ad alia. Ergo non est una lex naturalis apud omnes.

Objection 3

Further, whatever man is inclined to by his nature belongs to the Natural Law, as was said above (*aa.* 2 and 3). But different men are naturally inclined to different things, as some are inclined to the desire for pleasure, some to the desire for honors, and other men to other things. Hence, the Natural Law is not the same for all.

REPLY 3

Ad tertium dicendum quod, sicut ratio in homine dominatur et imperat aliis potentiis, ita oportet quod omnes inclinationes naturales ad alias potentias pertinentes ordinentur secundum rationem. Unde hoc est apud omnes communiter receptum, ut secundum rationem dirigantur omnes hominum inclinationes.

Reply 3

As in man reason controls and commands the other powers, so all the natural inclinations belonging to the other powers should be ordered by reason. Hence, this is accepted by all men, that all the inclinations of man should be directed by reason.

ON THE CONTRARY

Sed contra est quod Isidorus dicit (*Etym.* v, 4), *Jus naturale est commune omni nationi.*

On the Contrary

Isidore says (*Etym.* v, 4), "The Natural Law is common to all nations."

CORPUS

Dicendum quod, sicut supra dictum est (*aa.* 2 and 3), ad legem naturae pertinent ea ad quae homo naturaliter inclinatur; inter quae homini proprium est ut inclinetur ad agendum secundum rationem. Ad rationem autem pertinet ex communibus ad propria procedere, ut patet ex *Phy.* i, I. Aliter tamen circa hoc se habet ratio speculativa et aliter practica: quia enim ratio speculativa praecipue negotiatur circa necessaria, quae impossibile est aliter se habere, absque aliquo defectu invenitur veritas in conclusionibus propriis sicut et in principiis communibus. Sed ratio practica negotiatur circa contingentia, in quibus sunt operationes humanae; et ideo, si in communibus sit aliqua necessitas, quanto magis ad propria descenditur tanto magis invenitur defectus.

Sic igitur in speculativis est eadem veritas apud omnes tam in principiis quam in conclusionibus, licet veritas non apud omnes cognoscatur in conclusionibus, sed solum in principiis, quae dicuntur 'communes conceptiones'. In operativis autem non est eadem veritas vel rectitudo practica apud omnes quantum ad propria, sed solum quantum ad communia, et apud quos est eadem rectitudo in propriis non est aequaliter omnibus nota.

Sic igitur patet quod quantum ad communia principia rationis, sive speculativae sive practicae, est eadem veritas seu rectitudo apud omnes, et aequaliter nota. Quantum vero ad proprias conclusiones rationis speculativae, est eadem veritas apud omnes, non tamen aequaliter omnibus nota: apud omnes enim verum est quod triangulus habet tres angulos aequales duobus rectis, quamvis hoc non sit omnibus notum. Sed quantum ad proprias conclusiones rationis practicae, nec est eadem veritas seu rectitudo apud omnes; nec etiam apud quos est eadem est aequaliter nota.

Apud omnes enim hoc rectum est et verum ut secundum rationem agatur. Ex hoc autem principio sequitur quasi conclusio propria, quod deposita sint reddenda, et hoc quidem ut in pluribus verum est; sed potest in aliquo casu contingere quod sit damnosum et per consequens irrationabile, si deposita reddantur, puta si aliquis petat ad impugnandam patriam. Et hoc tanto magis invenitur deficere, quanto magis ad particularia descenditur: puta si dicatur quod deposita sunt reddenda cum tali cautione vel tali modo. Quanto enim plures conditiones particulares apponuntur, tanto pluribus modis poterit deficere, ut non sit rectum vel in reddendo vel non reddendo.

Sic igitur dicendum est quod lex naturae, quantum ad prima principia communia, est eadem apud omnes et secundum rectitudinem et secundum notitiam. Sed quantum ad quaedam propria, quae sunt quasi conclusiones principiorum communium, est eadem apud omnes ut in pluribus et secundum rectitudinem et secundum notitiam. Sed ut in paucioribus potest deficere et quantum ad rectitudinem, propter aliqua particularia impedimenta—sicut etiam naturae generabiles et corruptibiles deficiunt ut in paucioribus propter impedimenta—et etiam quantum ad notitiam, et hoc propter hoc quod aliqui habent depravatam rationem ex passione, seu ex mala consuetudine, seu ex mala habitudine naturae; sicut apud Germanos olim latrocinium non reputabatur iniquum, cum tamen sit expresse contra legem naturae, ut refert Julius Caesar in lib. *De bello Gallico*.

Corpus

As stated above (*aa*. 2 and 3), those things to which man is naturally inclined pertain to the Natural Law, among which man is inclined to act according to reason; but it belongs to reason to proceed from what is common to what is particular, as is clear from *Phy*. i, I. But, Speculative Reason and Practical Reason differ in this regard. For the Speculative Reason deals especially with necessary things which cannot be otherwise, and without failure truth is found in its proper conclusions just as in universal principles. But Practical Reason deals with contingent things included in which are human operations. And, therefore, though there is some necessity in universal principles, the more we descend to details the greater the chance of error.

And so in speculative matters, truth is the same for all, both in the general principles and in the conclusions, although the truth in the conclusions is not known by all but only the principles which are called 'common conceptions'.

In operational matters, however, the truth or practical correctness is not the same for all with regard to particulars but only in regard to the universal principles, and the truth, with regard to details, is not equally known to all.

And so it is clear that, with regard to the general principles of reason, whether speculative or practical, there is the same truth or correctness for all, and these are equally known to all. However, with regard to the particular conclusions of Speculative Reason the truth is the same for all, though it is not equally known to all. For it is true for everyone that a triangle has three angles equal to two right angles, though this truth is not known to all. But, with reference to the particular conclusions of Practical Reason, neither is the truth the same for all nor is it equally known even to those for whom it is the same.

Now, all hold this to be correct and true that actions should conform to reason. From this principle, however, it follows as a sort of particular conclusion that deposits should be returned, and this indeed for the most part is true. But in a particular case it can happen that it would be harmful and, consequently, unreasonable to return a deposit if someone requested it in order to attack his country. And the more we add particular conditions, the more the principle is likely to fail, for example, if it is said that the entrusted goods must be returned with such and such a guarantee or in such and such a way. For, as we add more and more conditions, we increase the number of ways in which the principle may fail so that it would be right either to return or not to return the entrusted goods.

So therefore we must say that the law of nature with regard to its first common principles is the same for all, both as to correctness and as to knowledge. But with reference to certain particulars which are like conclusions from the common principles, the Natural Law is generally the same for all, both in correctness and in knowledge. But, in some few cases, it can fail because of some impediment— just as natures subject to generation and corruption can fail because of some impediment—and also in knowledge and this is because some people have depraved understanding due to passion or a bad custom or a bad natural disposition. Thus, according to Julius Caesar's report in his *Gallic War,* among the Germans in past time, thievery, though contrary to the Natural Law, was not regarded as wrong.

Comment

1. *Common conceptions* are those general principles or axioms that are used in all disciplines and are self-evident and indemonstrable. Such principles are the principle of contradiction, "It is impossible to affirm and deny the same thing under the same aspect at the same time." This logical form is the same as the metaphysical form, "A thing cannot both exist and not exist at the same time under the same aspect." In St. Thomas's philosophy the logical version is true because the metaphysical version is true. This is because, for St. Thomas, reality controls knowledge, not the reverse as in Kantianism. Another example, "If two things are equal to a third thing then they are equal to each other."

2. *Right Reason:* St. Thomas's reference to things that can corrupt the right use of reason, such as violent anger, sexual infatuation, corrupt customs of society, and so forth makes it clear that when he talks of Practical Reason he is usually assuming that he is talking about right reason, that is, reason operating according to its own nature without any corrupting influences.

3. *Speculative Reason/Practical Reason:* This *Corpus* shows the great importance of St. Thomas's (and Aristotle's) distinction between two different modes of human thinking. We have one intellect, but we can use it simply to know and understand (Speculative Reason) or we can use it to make decisions about our actions, human acts as such (Practical Reason).

"Speculative" is not used here in the modern sense. Rather it simply means the use of the intellect in order to understand and reason about the truth of things. This use results in new knowledge. Speculative Reason gives rise to the sciences, mathematics, and other intellectual disciplines. The work of Speculative Reason is governed by certain principles which are self-evident and cannot be demonstrated. As soon as they are understood, they are seen to be necessarily true. Thus, the principle of contradiction.

The Practical Reason concerns human acts and, by an interplay of intellect and will, terminates at a decision with regard to action. Practical Reason has its own first governing principles. The first principle of the Practical Reason is, "Good is to be done and evil avoided." This is the first principle of the Natural Law and, therefore, of the moral order. It is not a principle from which any particular decision can be deduced. It is a formal principle which establishes the "ought" of the moral order.

Rationalistic interpreters of Natural Law tried to deduce the moral order from a speculative knowledge of man. St. Thomas doesn't do this. He constantly talks about the natural inclination (the appetency) of man and its control by Practical Reason. He is not open to Hume's argument that the "ought" cannot be derived from the "is."

4. *Self-evidence:* St. Thomas makes an important distinction between intrinsic self-evidence and self-evidence with regard to people. Many things, says St. Thomas, are self-evident in themselves but are recognized as such only by the wise and learned.

5. *A Modern Problem:* Some anthropologists, Ethical Relativists, and others argue that the precepts of the Natural Law are not known to all. They cite varying as well as fully divergent customs of many tribes and societies.

If we apply the careful distinction St. Thomas makes in this Article, all these objections can be accommodated without destroying the basic universality of human Practical Reason.

In all societies there is some general sense of justice. But in many particular cases, particular rules and decisions can be found which are incompatible with that general sense. A tribe may particularize the precept, "Harm no man" to apply to fellow tribesmen but not to the people of the tribe across the river. The particularization of them as enemies impedes the general principle.

Thomas Jefferson was a man of strong convictions about liberty, rights, and justice, yet he was a slaveholder. In a way, he justified slavery because of the alleged intellectual and moral incapacity of Black people.

St. Thomas allows for the fact of evil social customs, passions, and other human evils.

In every society there is a recognition that human inclinations must be controlled in some way and to some extent.

ARTICLE 5
UTRUM LEX NATURAE MUTARI POSSIT?
WHETHER THE LAW OF NATURE
CAN BE CHANGED?

OBJECTION 1

Videtur quod lex naturae mutari possit; quia super illud Ecclus., xvii, 9, *Addidit illis disciplinam et legem vitae,* dicit *Glossa ordin., Legem litterae, quantum ad correctionem legis naturalis, scribi voluit.* Sed illud quod corrigitur mutatur. Ergo lex naturalis potest mutari.

Objection 1

It seems that the law of nature can be changed because a gloss on the text of Ecclus. xvii, 9, "He gave them instructions and the Law of Life," says, "He wished the law of the letter to be written in order to correct the law of nature." But what is corrected is changed. Therefore, the Natural Law can be changed.

REPLY 1

Ad primum ergo dicendum quod lex scripta dicitur esse data ad correctionem legis naturalis, vel quia per legem scriptam suppletum est quod legi naturae deerat, vel quia lex naturae in aliquorum cordibus quantum ad aliqua corrupta erat, intantum ut existimarent esse bona quae naturaliter sunt mala; et talis corruptio correctione indigebat.

Reply 1

The written law is said to be given in order to correct the Natural Law, either because the written law supplied something that the Natural Law lacked, or because the Natural Law had been corrupted in the hearts of some people so that they thought some naturally evil things were good, a corruption that needed correction.

OBJECTION 2

Praeterea, contra legem naturalem est occisio innocentis, et etiam adulterium et furtum. Sed ista inveniuntur esse mutata a Deo, puta cum Deus praecepit Abrahae quod occideret filium innocentem, ut habetur Gen. xxii, 2; et cum praecepit Judaeis ut mutuata Aegyptiorum vasa subriperent, ut habetur Exod. xii, 35; et cum praecepit Osee ut uxorem fornicariam acciperet, ut habetur Hosea i, 2. Ergo lex naturalis potest mutari.

Objection 2

Further, the murder of the innocent as well as adultery and theft are against the Natural Law. But these things are found to have been changed by God, as, for example, when God ordered Abraham to kill his innocent son, as is related in Gen. xxii, 2, and, when God ordered the Jews to borrow and steal the vessels of the Egyptians (Exod. xii, 35), and when He commanded Osee to take a wife of fornication, as stated in Hosea i, 2. Therefore, the Natural Law can be changed.

REPLY 2

Ad secundum dicendum quod naturali morte moriuntur omnes communiter, tam nocentes quam innocentes; quae quidem naturalis mors divina potestate inducitur propter peccatum originale, secundum illud King ii, 6, *Dominus mortificat et vivificat.* Et ideo absque aliqua injustitia secundum mandatum Dei potest infligi mors cuicumque homini vel nocenti vel innocenti. Similiter etiam adulterium est concubitus cum uxore aliena, quae quidem est ei deputata secundum legem Dei divinitus traditam: unde ad quamcumque mulierem aliquis accedat ex mandato divino non est adulterium nec fornicatio. Et eadem ratio est de furto, quod est acceptio rei alienae: quidquid enim accipit aliquid ex mandato Dei, qui est dominus universorum, non accipit absque voluntate domini; quod est furari. Nec solum in rebus humanis quidquid a

Deo mandatur hoc ipso est debitum, sed etiam in rebus naturalibus quidquid a Deo fit, est naturale quodammodo, ut
in *Primo* (*q.* 105, *a.* 6, Reply) dictum est.

Reply 2

All people, both guilty and innocent, die a natural death, and
this natural death is brought about by Divine power because of
original sin, according to Kings ii, 6, "The Lord kills and brings to
life." Consequently, at the command of God death can be inflicted
on any man, whether guilty or innocent, without any injustice whatever. Likewise, adultery is having intercourse with another man's wife
who is allotted to him by the law given by God. Consequently,
whoever has intercourse with any woman at the command of God
commits neither adultery nor fornication. And the same reasoning
applies to theft, which is the taking of another's property. For, whatever is taken at the command of God, who is the master of all things,
is not taken against the will of the owner which would be theft. Nor
is it only in human affairs that whatever is commanded by God is,
by this very fact, right, but also in natural things whatever is done
by God is, in some way, natural, as was shown in the *First Part* (*q.*
105, *a.* 6, Reply 1).

OBJECTION 3

Praeterea, Isidorus dicit (*Etym.,* v, 4) quod *communis
omnium possessio et una libertas est de jure naturali.* Sed
haec videmus esse mutata per leges humanas. Ergo videtur
quod lex naturalis sit mutabilis.

Objection 3

Further, Isidore says (*Etym.,* v, 4) that "the common possession
of all things and universal liberty are from the Natural Law," but we
see that these things are changed by human law. Therefore, the Natural Law is changeable.

REPLY 3

Ad tertium dicendum quod aliquid dicitur esse de jure naturali dupliciter: uno modo, quia ad hoc natura inclinat, sicut non esse injuriam alteri faciendam; alio modo, quia natura non inducit contrarium, sicut possemus dicere quod hominem esse nudum est de jure naturali, quia natura non dedit ei vestitum, sed ars adinvenit. Et hoc modo communis onium possessio et una libertas dicitur esse de jure naturali, quia scilicet distinctio possessionum et servitus non sunt inductae a natura, sed per hominum rationem ad utilitatem humanae vitae; et sic etiam in hoc lex naturae non est mutata nisi per additionem.

Reply 3

We speak of things being from the Natural Law in two different ways. The first way is because nature inclines us to something, such as that injury should not be done to another. In the second way, because nature has not provided the contrary, as we might say that for man to be nude is from the Natural Law because nature had not given him clothes, but they were devised by art. In this way, the common possession of all things and universal liberty may be said to belong to the Natural Law, since nature has not provided for the distinction of ownership and slavery, but men have brought these in for their usefulness in human life. Therefore, in this respect the Natural Law has not been changed except by addition.

Comment

One is surprised to find St. Thomas saying that slavery was devised for usefulness in human life. Aristotle said that some people are naturally born slaves, and St. Thomas repeats this idea. There is much controversy about this, but it can be thought of as follows. Some people are mentally retarded or otherwise severely handicapped. How are they to be taken care of? There were no institutions or organizations in ancient Greece or in medieval society that took care of them; hence, they could be attached to someone whom they would serve in some simple way and who would take care of them. Today we recognize that such people cannot handle their own affairs and can never be completely independent. Aristotle's slavery might be called a benign state of dependence.

ON THE CONTRARY

Sed contra est quod dicitur in *Decretis* (*Dist.* v), *Naturale jus ab exordio rationalis creaturae coepit; nec variantur tempore, sed immutabile permanet.*

On the Contrary

It is stated in the *Decretals* (*Dist.* v) that "the Natural Law began with the creation of rational creatures. It does not vary with time but remains unchangeable."

CORPUS

Dicendum quod lex naturalis potest intelligi mutari dupliciter. Uno modo, per hoc quod aliquid ei addatur; et sic nihil prohibet legem naturalem mutari: multa enim supra legem naturalem superaddita sunt ad humanam vitam utilia, tam per legem divinam quam etiam per leges humanas.

Alio modo potest intelligi mutatio legis naturalis per modum subtractionis, ut scilicet aliquid desinat esse de lege naturali quod prius fuit secundum legem naturalem; et sic quantum ad prima principia legis naturae, lex naturae est omnino immutabilis. Quantum autem ad secunda praecepta, quae diximus (*a*. 4) esse quasi quasdam proprias conclusiones propinquas primis principiis, sic lex naturalis non immutatur quin ut in pluribus sit rectum semper quod lex naturalis habet; potest tamen mutari et in aliquo particulari et in paucioribus, propter aliquas speciales causas impedientes obervantiam talium praeceptorum, ut supra dictum est (*a*. 4).

Corpus

The Natural Law can be understood to change in two different ways. In the first way, inasmuch as something is added to the Natural Law, and in this sense, nothing prevents Natural Law from changing, for we see that many things have been added to the Natural Law that are useful for human life, and these have been added both by Divine Law and also by human law.

Secondly, it is possible to understand the change in the Natural Law as a subtraction, that is, that something ceases to belong to the Natural Law which was formerly according to the Natural Law, and, in this sense, with regard to the first principles of the Natural Law, the Natural Law is altogether unchangeable. But with regard to the secondary principles which we have said (*a.* 4) are like detailed conclusions drawn proximately from the first principles, in this sense, the Natural Law is not changed, for, what the Natural Law orders is always right in most cases, yet, it can be changed, in some particular case, which infrequently happens, because of certain obstacles in the carrying out of such precepts of the Natural Law, as was stated above (*a.* 4).

Comment

St. Thomas distinguishes two levels of Natural Law principles, namely that of primary general principles and that of secondary particular principles. The primary principles, which are abstract and very general, cannot be changed, principles like, "Good is to be done, evil avoided" or, "Give every man his due" or "Harm no man." Hardly anyone would reject these principles in the abstract.

The secondary particular principles are quasi-conclusions from the primary principles. These principles, St. Thomas says, can, in some few cases, be changed because of "impediment" or added details. He uses the example of a deposit, goods entrusted to the keeping of someone, which should be returned on demand. But if the owner plans to use the goods to attack his own country, the requirement of returning the deposit fails.

There is a third set of principles, not mentioned by St. Thomas here but stressed by subsequent writers who called them "tertiary" principles. These are principles which are a combination of secondary Natural Law principles with some contingent but long-standing matters. Various particularized principles of justice attaching to a particular economic system could exemplify the tertiary principles. The varying ethical assessment of usury is a common example.

St. Thomas recognizes some of this third type when he speaks of the fact that increasingly detailed additions to a case can change the application of the principle (*a.* 2) and also when he speaks of "determinations" of the Natural Law by the human lawgiver (*q. 95, a. 2*).

ARTICLE 6
UTRUM LEX NATURALIS POSSIT A CORDE HOMINIS ABOLERI?
WHETHER THE NATURAL LAW CAN BE REMOVED FROM THE HEART OF MAN?

OBJECTION 1

Videtur quod lex naturae possit a corde hominis aboleri, quia Rom. ii, 14 super illud, *Cum gentes, quae legem non habent,* etc., dicit *Glossa quod in interiori homini per gratiam innovato lex justitiae inscribitur, quam deleverat culpa.* Sed lex justitiae est lex naturae. Ergo lex naturae potest deleri.

Objection 1

It seems that the Natural Law can be removed from the heart of man, because a Gloss on the text of Rom. ii, 14, "When the Gentiles who do not have the Law, etc.," says, "The law of justice which sin had abolished is inscribed in the interior of man, once he is restored by grace." But the law of justice is the Natural Law. Therefore, the Natural Law can be abolished.

REPLY 1

Ad primum ergo dicendum quod culpa delet legem naturae in particulari, non autem in universali; nisi forte quantum ad secundaria praecepta legis naturae, eo modo quo dictum est in corp.

Reply 1

Sin destroys the Natural Law in particular matters, not, however, in general, unless perhaps in regard to the secondary precepts as is described in the *Corpus* of this Article.

OBJECTION 2

Praeterea, lex gratiae est efficacior quam lex naturae. Sed lex gratiae deletur per culpam. Ergo multo magis lex naturae potest deleri.

Objection 2

Further, the law of grace is more effective than the Natural Law, but the law of grace is removed by sin, therefore much more can the Natural Law be removed.

REPLY 2

Ad secundum dicendum quod gratia, etsi sit efficacior quam natura, tamen natura essentialior est homini, et ideo magis permanens.

Reply 2

Although grace is more effective than nature, yet nature is more essential to man and, therefore, more permanent.

Comment

The "law of grace" is the Divine Law of the New Testament as revealed in the life and teachings of Christ.

OBJECTION 3

Praeterea, illud quod lege statuitur inducitur quasi justum. Sed multa sunt ab hominibus statuta contra legem naturae. Ergo lex naturae potest a cordibus hominum aboleri.

Objection 3

Further, that which is established by law is brought in as being just. But many things are established by men which are contrary to the law of nature. Therefore, the Natural Law can be removed from the hearts of men.

REPLY 3

Ad tertium dicendum quod ratio illa procedit de secundis praeceptis legis naturae, contra quae aliqui legislatores statuta aliqua fecerunt quae sunt iniqua.

Reply 3

That argument refers to the secondary precepts of the Natural Law against which some legislators have made some statutes which are wicked.

ON THE CONTRARY

Sed contra est quod Augustinus dicit in *Conf.* ii., *Lex tua scripta est in cordibus hominum, quam nec ulla quidem delet iniquitas.* Sed lex scripta in cordibus hominum est lex naturalis. Ergo lex naturalis deleri non potest.

On the Contrary

Augustine says (*Conf.* ii) that "your law is written in the hearts of men, which no iniquity can destroy." But the law written in the hearts of men is the Natural Law. Therefore, the Natural Law cannot be destroyed.

CORPUS

Dicendum quod, sicut supra dictum est (*aa.* 4 and 5), ad legem naturalem pertinent, primo quidem quaedam praecepta communissima, quae sunt omnibus nota; secundario autem quaedam secundaria praecepta magis propria, quae sunt quasi conclusiones propinquae principiis.

Quantum ergo ad illa principia communia, lex naturalis nullo modo potest a cordibus hominum deleri in universali; deletur tamen in particulari operabili, secundum quod ratio impeditur applicare commune principium ad particulare operabile, propter concupiscentiam vel aliquam aliam passionem, ut supra dictum est (*q.* 77, *a.* 2).

Quantum vero ad alia praecepta secundaria, potest lex naturalis deleri de cordibus hominum, vel propter malas persuasiones—eo modo quo etiam in speculativis errores contingunt circa conclusiones necessarias—vel etiam propter pravas consuetudines et habitus corruptos, sicut apud quosdam non reputabantur latrocinia peccata, vel etiam vitia contra naturam, ut etiam Apostolus dicit, Rom. i.

Corpus

As was stated above (*aa.* 4, 5), first of all, certain very universal precepts which are known to all belong to the Natural Law. Secondly, there are secondary precepts, more detailed, which are, as it were, conclusions following closely from the first principles.

Therefore, as regards those common principles, the Natural Law can in no way be abolished from the hearts of men in general; but it is abolished in some particular actions insofar as reason is prevented from applying the general principles to the particular action, because of concupiscence or some other passion, as was stated above (*q.* 77, *a.* 2).

However, as for the other secondary precepts, the Natural Law can be abolished from the hearts of men either because of evil passions—in the same way as in speculative science some errors occur in necessary conclusions—or because of depraved customs or corrupt habits, as among some peoples thefts were not considered to be sins, or even because of vices against nature such as St. Paul mentions (Rom. i).

Comment

The very general principle, such as, "Harm no person," when considered in abstraction from any particular case or application, is clearly known to everyone. But, if we apply it to some particular, more detailed case, especially, as St. Thomas says, when there is a contrary vicious custom, it can be removed from the conscience of men. Thus, "Kill no prisoners of war" is not even thought of in some primitive tribes. Thus the Aztecs regularly and ritually killed prisoners of war by the hundreds.

Later moral theologians added another class of principles, called tertiary principles of the Natural Law, which were quite far removed from the first principle. These principles often depended on some de facto situation which can change. Thus, the old prohibition against lending at interest (usury) was dependent on the economic system which changed over the centuries.

The reference to theft is based on a discussion of the customs of the Germanic tribes in Julius Caesar's *De Bello Gallico*.

QUESTIONS 95, 96, AND 97
DE LEGE HUMANA
CONCERNING HUMAN LAW

Deinde considerandum est de lege humana, et

primo quidem, de ipsa lege secundum se;
secundo, de potestate ejus;
tertio, de ejus mutabilitate.

Concerning Human Law

Now we must consider human law,

first, in itself;
secondly, its power; and,
thirdly its mutability.

QUESTION 95
DE LEGE HUMANA SECUNDUM SE
CONCERNING HUMAN LAW IN ITSELF

Circa primum quaeruntur quatuor:

1. de utilitate ipsius;
2. de origine ejus;
3. de qualitate ipsius;
4. de divisione ejusdem.

Question 95

Here there are four points of inquiry:

first, the utility of human law;
secondly, its origin;
thirdly; its qualities;
fourthly, its divisions.

Introductory Comment

From the standpoint of modern jurisprudence, which takes positive or human law for its immediate subject matter (i.e., its material object), these three questions, together with *q.* 90, are most important and relevant, since they deal directly with positive human law. As one reads these questions, it should be noted that the exposition is, for the most part, experiential and philosophical, although there are references to the larger metaphysical and theological framework previously established in the *Treatise*. There are also *auctoritates* from the Bible and from theologians, but these are generally confirmatory, illustrative, or merely decorative.

ARTICLE 1
UTRUM FUERIT UTILE ALIQUAS LEGES PONI AB HOMINIBUS?
WHETHER IT WAS USEFUL FOR SOME LAWS TO BE MADE BY MEN?

OBJECTION 1

Videtur quod non fuerit utile aliquas leges poni ab hominibus. Intentio enim cujuslibet legis est ut per eam homines fiant boni, sicut supra dictum est (*q.* 92, *a.* 1). Sed homines magis inducuntur ad bonum voluntarii per monitiones quam coacti per leges. Ergo non fuit necessarium leges ponere.

Objection 1

It seems that it was not useful that some laws be made by men. For it is the intention of every law that through it men be made good, as was said above (*q.* 92, *a.* 1). But men are more easily brought to goodness voluntarily through admonitions than by being forced through laws. Therefore, it was not necessary to make laws.

REPLY 1

Ad primum ergo dicendum quod, homines bene dispositi melius inducuntur ad virtutem monitionibus voluntarii quam coactione; sed quidam male dispositi non ducuntur ad virtutem nisi cogantur.

Reply 1

Well-disposed men are willingly led to virtue better by admonitions than by compulsion, but some men who are evilly disposed are not led to virtue unless they are compelled.

OBJECTION 2

Praeterea, sicut dicit Philosophus in *Ethic.* v, 4, *ad judicem confugiunt homines sicut ad justum animatum.* Sed justitia animata est melior quam inanimata quae legibus continetur. Ergo melius fuisset ut executio justitiae committeretur arbitrio judicum quam quod super hoc lex aliqua conderetur.

Objection 2

Further, as the Philosopher says (*Ethic.* v, 4) "men have recourse to a judge as to animate justice." But animate justice is better than inanimate justice which is contained in laws. Therefore, it would have been better to leave the execution of justice to the decision of judges rather than to enact laws in addition.

REPLY 2

Ad secundum dicendum quod, sicut Philosophus dicit, *Rhet*. i, 1, *melius est omnia ordinari lege quam dimittere judicum arbitrio;* et hoc propter tria. Primo quidem, quia facilius est invenire paucos sapientes qui sufficiant ad rectas leges ponendas, quam multos qui requirerentur ad recte judicandum de singulis. Secundo, quia illi qui leges ponunt ex multo tempore considerant quid lege ferendum sit; sed judicia de singularibus factis fiunt ex casibus subito exortis. Facilius autem ex multis consideratis potest homo videre quid rectum sit, quam solum ex aliquo uno facto. Tertio, quia legislatores judicant in universali et de futuris; sed homines judiciis praesidentes judicant de praesentibus, ad quae afficiuntur amore vel odio aut aliqua cupiditate; et sic eorum depravatur judicium.

Quia ergo justitia animata judicis non invenitur in multis, et quia flexibilis est, ideo necessarium fuit, in quibuscumque est possibile, legem determinare quid judicandum sit, et paucissima arbitrio hominum committere.

Reply 2

As the Philosopher says (*Rhet*. i, 1) "It is better that all things be regulated by law rather than be left to the discretion of judges" and this for three reasons.

First, because it is easier to find a few wise men competent to make right laws than to find the many that would be necessary to judge aright in each single case.

Secondly, those who make laws consider for a long time what should be made into law, whereas judgment concerning individual facts must be made in cases which are suddenly presented. However, it is easier for a man to see what is right from many considerations rather than solely from one single fact.

Thirdly, because lawgivers judge in general and about future events, whereas those who sit in judgment judge of present matters toward which they are affected by love or hatred or some greed, and so their judgment is perverted.

Since, therefore, the animate justice of a judge is not found in many and, since it is changeable, therefore, it was necessary, wherever possible, for the law to determine what decisions are to be made and to leave very few to the judgment of men.

Comment

It's clear that St. Thomas holds for the rule of law rather than a rule of men. Yet, he realizes that some things must be left to the discretion of judges. It will be remembered that Lon Fuller's King Rex tried to administer justice on a case-by-case basis (*The Morality of Law*, pp. 34–35). Here, too, St. Thomas sees that there must be laws to guide judicial decisions.

The first argument advanced by St. Thomas, namely, that wise men being always in short supply, it is better to have them make general rules rather than to leave all decisions to the many lesser men who would be the judges, may seem dubious in today's democracies.

OBJECTION 3

Praeterea, lex omnis directiva est actuum humanorum, ut ex supra dictis patet (*q*. 90, *aa*. 1 and 2). Sed cum humani actus consistant in singularibus, quae sunt infinita, non possunt ea quae ad directionem humanorum actuum pertinent sufficienter considerari, nisi ab aliquo sapiente qui inspiciat singula. Ergo melius fuisset arbitrio sapientum dirigi actus humanos quam aliqua lege posita. Ergo non fuit necessarium leges humanas ponere.

Objection 3

Every law is directive of human acts, as is clear from what was said above (*q*. 90, *aa*. 1 and 2). But, since human acts deal with singulars, what pertains to human acts cannot be adequately considered except by some wise man who looks into each singular case. Therefore, it would have been better to have human acts directed by the judgment of wise men rather than by a positive law. Therefore, it was not necessary to make laws.

REPLY 3

Ad tertium dicendum quod quaedam singularia, quae
non possunt lege comprehendi, necesse est committere judi-
cibus, ut ibidem Philosophus dicit *Rhet.* i, i, puta, de eo quod
est factum esse vel non esse, et de aliis hujusmodi.

Reply 3

Certain singulars which cannot be covered by law must be left to
the judges, as the Philosopher says (*Rhet.*, i, i), such as whether something happened or not and similar matters.

ON THE CONTRARY

Sed contra est quod Isidorus dicit *Etym.* v, 20, *Factae
sunt leges, ut earum metu humana coerceatur audacia, tu-
taque sit inter improbos innocentia, et in ipsis improbis for-
midato supplicio refrenetur nocendi facultas.* Sed haec sunt
necessaria maxime humano generi. Ergo necessarium fuit
ponere leges humanas.

On the Contrary

Isidore says (*Etym.* v, 20) "Laws were made that, through fear
thereof, human audacity might be repressed, and that innocence might
be safe in the midst of the wicked, and that the wicked themselves might,
by fear of punishment, be restrained from doing harm." But these are
extremely necessary for the human race. Therefore, it was necessary to
make laws.

CORPUS

Dicendum quod, sicut ex supra dictis patet (*q.* 93, *a.*
1 and *q.* 94, *a.* 3), homini naturaliter inest quaedam aptitudo
ad virtutem; sed ipsa virtutis perfectio necesse est quod homini adveniat per aliquam disciplinam. Sicut etiam videmus
quod per aliquam industriam subvenitur homini in suis ne-
cessitatibus, puta, in cibo et vestitu, quorum initia quaedam

habet a natura, scilicet rationem et manus, non autem ipsum complementum, sicut caetera animalia quibus natura dedit sufficienter tegumentum et cibum. Ad hanc autem disciplinam non de facili invenitur homo sibi sufficiens, quia perfectio virtutis praecipue consistit in retrahendo hominem ab indebitis delectationibus, ad quas praecipue homines sunt proni, et maxime juvenes, circa quos est efficacior disciplina. Et ideo oportet quod hujusmodi disciplinam, per quam ad virtutem pervenitur, homines ab alio sortiantur.

Et quidem quantum ad illos juvenes qui sunt proni ad actus virtutum ex bona dispositione naturae vel consuetudine, vel magis ex divino munere, sufficit disciplina paterna quae est per monitiones. Sed quia inveniuntur quidam protervi et ad vitia proni, qui verbis de facili moveri non possunt, necessarium fuit quod per vim vel metum cohiberentur a malo, ut saltem sic malefacere desistentes et aliis quietam vitam redderent, et ipsi tandem per hujusmodi assuetudinem ad hoc perducerentur quod voluntarie facerent quae prius metu implebant, et sic fierent virtuosi. Hujusmodi autem disciplina cogens metu poenae est disciplina legum.

Unde necessarium fuit ad pacem hominum et virtutem, quod leges ponerentur, quia, sicut Philosophus dicit in *Pol.* i, 4, *sicut homo si sit perfectus virtute est optimum animalium, sic si sit separatus a lege et justitia est pessimum omnium,* quia homo habet arma rationis ad expellendas concupiscentias et saevitias, quae non habent alia animalia.

Corpus

As is clear from what was said above (*q.* 93, *a.* 1 and *q.* 94, *a.* 3), human beings have a certain natural aptitude for virtue, but they must reach the perfection of virtue by some sort of training.

Likewise, we also observe that human beings are helped in their necessities by industry, for example, in matters of food and clothing. In these matters human beings have, by nature, certain beginnings, namely, reason and hands, but not the full complement, unlike the other animals to which nature has given a sufficiency of covering and food.

Now, it is difficult to see how a man could adequately provide this training for himself, since the perfection of virtue consists largely in withdrawal from undue pleasures to which human beings are principally inclined and especially the young for whom training is more effective. Therefore, it is necessary for a man to receive from another this sort of training which leads to virtue.

And indeed for those young people who are inclined to acts of virtue by a good, natural disposition or by habit or rather by the grace of God, paternal training which consists in admonition suffices. But, since some who are found to be wanton and inclined to vice are not easily moved by words, it was necessary to restrain them from evil by force or fear so that thus they would desist from evil-doing and leave others in peace and that they themselves, through becoming accustomed to virtuous acts, might finally come to do voluntarily what they previously did through fear of punishment and thus become virtuous.

Now this kind of training which compels by fear of punishment is the training through laws. Hence, it was necessary for peace among men and for virtue that laws be made, because, as the Philosopher says (*Polit.*, i, 4), "Just as man is the best of animals, if he be perfect in virtue, so he is the worst of animals if he be without law or justice," for man can use reason to satisfy his passions and his aggressiveness, which the other animals the weapons of do not have.

Comment

In the extended Reply 2, St. Thomas develops what may be called the juristic reasons why there should be human laws and not merely judges.

In the *Corpus* he concentrates on the training or educative function of law. This is in keeping with St. Thomas's primary interest in law as one of the factors influencing human conduct and character. The training function of law is particularly important for those who must be restrained by fear. The law not only restrains their violence and so maintains the peace and order of the Common Good, but also leads them to a better state of mind by accustoming them to doing virtuous acts.

When St. Thomas speaks of accustoming people to doing the acts of virtue as producing in them the virtue itself, I think we can safely say that he is not thinking of producing a mechanical habit, a sort of "programming," but rather also a growing realization that what one is forced to do is really good and desirable.

This Article might be regarded as an extension of *q.* 92, *a.* 1.

ARTICLE 2
UTRUM OMNIS LEX HUMANITUS POSITA
A LEGE NATURALI DERIVETUR?
WHETHER EVERY LAW MADE BY MAN IS
DERIVED FROM THE NATURAL LAW?

OBJECTION 1

Videtur quod non omnis lex humanitus posita a lege naturali derivetur. Dicit enim Philosophus, in *Ethic.* v, 7, quod *justum legale est quod principio quidem nihil differt utrum sic vel aliter fiat.* Sed in his quae oriuntur ex lege naturali differt utrum sic vel aliter fiat. Ergo ea quae sunt legibus humanis statuta non omnia derivantur a lege naturae.

Objection 1

It seems that not every law made by man is derived from the Natural Law. For the Philosopher says (*Ethic.* v, 7): "The legal just is that which originally is indifferent as to whether it is done in this way or that." But what is derived from the Natural Law is not indifferent in that way. Therefore, not all human laws are derived from the Natural Law.

REPLY 1

Ad primum ergo dicendum quod Philosophus loquitur de illis quae sunt lege posita per determinationem vel specificationem quandam praeceptorum legis naturae.

Reply 1

The Philosopher is speaking about those things which are established by law by way of a determination or a specification of the precepts of the Natural Law.

Comment
See the *Corpus* of this article for a complete explanation.

OBJECTION 2

Praeterea, jus positivum dividitur contra jus naturale, ut patet per Isidorum (*Etym.*, v, 4) et per Philosophum (*Ethic*, v, 7). Sed ea quae derivantur a principiis communibus legis naturae sicut conclusiones pertinent ad legem naturae, ut supra dictum est. Ergo ea quae sunt de lege humana, non derivantur a lege naturae.

Objection 2

Further, Positive Law is distinguished from Natural Law according to Isidore (*Etym.*, v, 4) and the Philosopher (*Ethic.* v, 7). But those things which are derived from the common principles of the Natural Law by way of conclusions belong to the Natural Law as was stated above (*q.* 94, *a.* 4). Therefore, those things that are established by human law are not derived from the law of nature.

REPLY 2

Ad secundum dicendum quod ratio illa procedit de his quae derivantur a lege naturae tanquam conclusiones.

Reply 2

That argument concerns those things that are derived from the Natural Law by way of conclusions.

Comment

See the *Corpus* of this article for a full explanation.

OBJECTION 3

Praeterea, lex naturae est eadem apud omnes: dicit enim Philosophus, in V *Ethic.* v, 7, quod *naturale jus est quod ubique habet eandem potentiam*. Si igitur leges humanae a naturali lege derivarentur, sequeretur quod etiam ipsae essent eadem apud omnes, quod patet esse falsum.

Objection 3

Further, the law of nature is the same among all people. For the Philosopher says (*Ethic.* v, 7): "The natural just is that which everywhere has the same force." If, then, human laws were derived from the Natural Law, it would follow that they also would be the same among all peoples, which is clearly false.

REPLY 3

Ad tertium dicendum quod principia communia legis naturae non eodem modo applicari possunt omnibus propter multam varietatem rerum humanarum; et ex hoc provenit diversitas legis positivae apud diversos.

Reply 3

The general principles of the Natural Law cannot be applied to all people in the same way because of the great diversity of human affairs, and hence arises the diversity of Positive Law among different peoples.

OBJECTION 4

Praeterea, eorum quae a lege naturali derivantur potest aliqua ratio assignari. Sed non omnium quae a majoribus lege statuta sunt ratio reddi potest, ut jurisperitus dicit (*Digest,* I, III, 20). Ergo non omnes leges humanae derivantur a lege naturali.

Objection 4

It is possible to give a reason for the things that are derived from the Natural Law, but "it is not possible to give a reason for all the things that have been established as law by the elders," as the Jurist says (*Digest* I, III, 20). Therefore, not all human laws are derived from the Natural Law.

REPLY 4

Ad quartum dicendum quod verbum illud Jurisperiti intelligendum est in his quae introducta sunt a majoribus circa particulares determinationes legis naturalis; ad quas quidem determinationes se habet expertorum et prudentum judicium sicut ad quaedam principia, inquantum scilicet statim vident quid congruentius sit particulariter determinandum. Unde Philosophus dicit in *Ethic.* vi, 11 quod *in talibus oportet attendere judicium expertorum et seniorum vel prudentum indemonstrabilibus enuntiationibus et opinionibus, non minus quam demonstrationibus.*

Reply 4

That statement of the Jurist is to be understood as referring to things introduced by predecessors as particular determinations of the Natural Law. The judgment of learned and prudent men is based on their determination as on certain principles, insofar as they immediately see what is the better thing to decide in particular cases. Hence, the Philosopher says (*Ethic.* vi, 11) that in such matters, "we should pay as much attention to the indemonstrable statements and opinions of experienced and older men or prudent men as we do to their demonstrations."

Comment

St. Thomas is here referring to the prudential judgments of wise, experienced, and prudent men, that is, men who have developed the virtue of prudence to a high degree. Their prudential judgments are as important as their demonstrations [361–378].

ON THE CONTRARY

Sed contra est quod Tullius dicit in sua *Rhet.* ii, *Res a natura profectas et a consuetudine probatas legum metus et religio sanxit.*

On the Contrary

Tully says (*Rhet.,* ii): "Things arising from nature and approved by custom are sanctioned by fear of and reverence for laws."

CORPUS

Dicendum quod, sicut Augustinus dicit in I *De Lib. Arb.*, I, 5, *non videtur esse lex quae justa non fuerit:* unde inquantum habet de justitia intantum habet de virtute legis. In rebus autem humanis dicitur esse aliquid justum ex eo quod est rectum secundum regulam rationis. Rationis autem prima regula est lex naturae, ut ex supra dictis patet (*q.* 91, *a.* 1, Reply 2).

Unde omnis lex humanitus posita intantum habet de ratione legis inquantum a lege naturae derivatur. Si vero in aliquo a lege naturali discordet, jam non erit lex, sed legis corruptio.

Sed sciendum est quod a lege naturali dupliciter potest aliquid derivari: uno modo sicut conclusiones ex principiis, alio modo sicut determinationes quaedam aliquorum communium. Primus quidem modus similis est ei quo in scientiis ex principiis conclusiones demonstrativae producuntur. Secundo vero modo simile est quod in artibus formae communes determinantur ad aliquid speciale: sicut artifex formam communem domus necesse est quod determinet ad hanc vel illam domus figuram.

Derivantur ergo quaedam a principiis communibus legis naturae per modum conclusionum: sicut hoc quod est 'non esse occidendum', ut conclusio quaedam derivari potest ab eo quod est 'nulli esse faciendum malum'; quaedam vero per modum determinationis, sicut lex naturae habet quod ille qui peccat puniatur; sed quod tali poena vel tali puniatur, hoc est quaedam determinatio legis naturae.

Utraque igitur inveniuntur in lege humana posita. Sed ea quae sunt primi modi continentur in lege humana, non tanquam sint solum lege posita, sed habent etiam aliquid vigoris ex lege naturali. Sed ea quae sunt secundi modi, ex sola lege humana vigorem habent.

Corpus

As Augustine says (*De Lib. Arb.* i, 5): "That which is not just seems to be no law at all." Hence a law has as much force as it has justice. Now, in human affairs, a thing is said to be just from the fact that it is right according to the rule of reason. Now the first rule of reason is the law of nature, as is clear from what has been said above (*q.* 91, *a.* 2, reply 2).

Hence every human positive law has the nature of law to the extent that it is derived from the Natural Law. If, however, in some point it conflicts with the law of nature it will no longer be law but rather a perversion of law. [This paragraph should be compared with *q.* 96, *a.* 4, *c.*]

However, it should be noted that there are two ways in which something can be derived from the Natural Law. The first way is as conclusions are derived from principles. The second way is through determination of certain generalities. The first resembles the way by which in the sciences conclusions are produced from principles by demonstration. The second is similar to the way in the arts general forms are determined to particularities just as the craftsman has to determine the general form of a house to some particular shape.

Therefore, some things are derived from the Natural Law by way of conclusion; thus the precept, "One should not kill" can be derived as a conclusion from the principle, "Do harm to no person." Other things, however, are derived by way of determination; thus, the Natural Law has it that he who does wrong should be punished, but whether he is punished in this or that way is a determination of the Natural Law.

Consequently, both are found in human Positive Law. But those things that are contained in human law, not as arising exclusively therefrom, have some force from the Natural Law as well. But those that are derived from the Natural Law in the second way have force exclusively from human laws.

Comment

This is one of the most important articles in St. Thomas's treatment of the Natural Law. Positivists sometimes say that Natural Law thinkers want to transpose the Natural Law, exactly and wholly, into the systems of Positive Law. According to St. Thomas, the Natural Law provides only general principles and general precepts which cannot possibly dictate all the detailed determinations necessary for the Common Good of any given society.

If we compare a rural village in twelfth-century France with New York City, it is clear that traffic laws would be quite different in the two cases. In fact, the rural village might need no traffic law.

In the case of New York, it is clear that Natural Law requires that some measures be taken to regulate traffic so as to protect the lives, property, and mobility of the citizens, but the determination of the particular measures rests with the human lawgiver(s), e.g., traffic lights or traffic officers, one-way streets, no left turns, speed limits, etc. Thus, these measures are derived from the Natural Law by way of determination, but the determination itself derives directly from the human lawgiver. Thus, an enormous range of decisions is a matter for human Positive Law. Without the intervention of the human lawgiver no rule concerning one-way streets would exist.

Still, all human law is, in a general sense, dependent upon the Natural Law, since all positive determination must be just in order to be a law. Thus, if traffic is reduced by allowing only white people to drive cars in the city, the regulation would be unjust and thus fail precisely as law.

ARTICLE 3
UTRUM ISIDORUS CONVENIENTER QUALITATEM LEGIS POSITIVAE DESCRIBAT?
WHETHER ISIDORE APPROPRIATELY DESCRIBED THE QUALITY OF POSITIVE LAW?

Introductory Comment

This is an unusual Article. The objections are not directly against St. Thomas but, rather, first of all, against Isidore's listing of the qualities human or Positive Law should have. Hence, indirectly, they tell against St. Thomas's approval and defense of Isidore's list. What St. Thomas does is to order and organize a list that, in Isidore, seems rather haphazard.

All the Objections in this Article are based on an alleged redundancy in Isidore's list, and the alleged superfluous character of some of the terms. No further comment on them seems necessary. In the *Sed Contra,* St. Thomas simply cites the authority of Isidore as an *auctor.* Moreover, since, in the *Corpus,* St. Thomas attempted to show that each term contributes something that the others do not, there are no answers to the individual objections.

OBJECTION 1

Videtur quod Isidorus inconvenienter qualitatem legis positivae describat, dicens, *Etymol.* v, 21, *Erit lex honesta, justa, possibilis, secundum naturam, secundum consuetudinem patriae, loco temporique conveniens, necessaria, utilis, manifesta quoque, ne aliquid per obscuritatem in captione contineat, nullo privato commodo, sed pro communi utilitate civium scripta.* Supra enim, cap. 2, in tribus conditionibus qualitatem legis explicaverat, dicens, *Lex erit omne quod ratione constiterit, dumtaxat quod religioni congruat, quod disciplinae conveniat, quod saluti proficiat.* Ergo superflue postmodum conditiones legis multiplicat.

Objection 1

It seems that Isidore did not appropriately describe the quality of Positive Law, when he says (*Etym.* v, 21): Law shall be virtuous, just, possible with regard to nature and with regard to the custom of the country, appropriate to time and place, necessary, useful, also clearly expressed lest its obscurity lead to some misunderstanding, framed not for any private benefit but for the common benefit of the citizens. For he had previously (*Cap.* 2) explained the quality of law in three requirements, saying: "Law shall be anything based on reason provided it conforms to religion, fosters order and promotes the common good." Therefore it was superfluous later to multiply the requirements of law.

Comment

There is no reply since the problem is adequately addressed in the *Corpus.*

OBJECTION 2

Praeterea, justitia est pars honestatis, ut Tullius dicit, in *De Offic.* I, 7. Ergo postquam dixerat 'honesta' superflue additur 'justa.'

Objection 2

Further, justice is a part of virtue, as Tully says (*De Offic.* I, 7). Therefore, it was superfluous to add "just" to "honest."

Comment

Again there is no reply, since the problem is adequately dealt with in the *Corpus*.

OBJECTION 3

Praeterea, lex scripta, secundum Isidorum (*Etym.* ii, 10) contra consuetudinem dividitur. Non ergo debuit in definitione legis poni quod esset secundum consuetudinem patriae.

Objection 3

Further, according to Isidore (*Etym.*, ii, 10) written law is distinguished from custom; therefore it should not have been put in the definition of law that it be "according to the custom of the country."

Comment
Again, there is no reply.

OBJECTION 4

Praeterea, necessarium dupliciter dicitur: scilicet id quod est necessarium simpliciter, quod impossibile est aliter se habere, et hujusmodi necessarium non subjacet humano judicio; unde talis necessitas ad legem humanam non pertinet. Est etiam aliquid necessarium propter finem; et talis necessitas idem est quod utilitas. Ergo superflue utrumque ponitur, 'necessaria' et 'utilis.'

Objection 4

Further, a thing can be necessary in one of two ways. It may be necessary *simpliciter,* that is, because it cannot be otherwise, and this sort of necessity is not subject to human judgment and so such necessity has nothing to do with human law. A thing may be necessary for an end, and this kind of necessity is the same as usefulness. Therefore, it was superfluous to say both "necessary" and "useful."

Comment
Again, there is no reply.

ON THE CONTRARY

Sed contra est auctoritas ipsius Isidori, cit. in obj. I.

On the Contrary

The *auctoritas* from Isidore himself is quoted in the first Objection.

Introductory Comment to the *Corpus*

The *Corpus* falls into two clearly distinguishable parts. In the first Section, St. Thomas sets up Isidore's three major requirements as the general categories for all the more detailed qualities and derives these three general requirements from the very nature of law itself, thus giving the entire list a rational foundation.

In the second Section, he explains how all the other detailed requirements of Isidore's list can be reduced to the three general categories and yet can be distinguished among themselves.

CORPUS [SECTION 1]

Dicendum quod uniuscujusque rei quae est propter finem, necesse est quod forma determinetur secundum proportionem ad finem: sicut forma serrae talis est, qualis convenit sectioni, ut patet in *Phy.*, ii, 9. Quaelibet etiam res recta et mensurata oportet quod habeat formam proportionatam suae regulae et mensurae. Lex autem humana utrumque habet, quia et est aliquid ordinatum ad finem, et est quaedam regula vel mensura regulata vel mensurata quadam superiori mensura; quae quidem est duplex, scilicet divina lex et lex naturae, ut ex supra dictis patet (*a.* 2: *q.* 92, *a.* 3).

Finis autem humanae legis est utilitas hominum, sicut etiam Jurisperitus dicit (*Digest,* I, III, 5). Et ideo Isidorus in conditione legis primo quidem tria posuit: scilicet quod religioni congruat, inquantum scilicet est proportionata legi divinae; quod disciplinae conveniat, inquantum est proportionata legi naturae; quod saluti proficiat, inquantum est proportionata utilitati humanae.

Corpus [Section 1]

The form of anything that is made for an end must be such as is proportionate to that end, as the form of a saw is appropriate for cutting, as is clear from *Phy.*, ii, 9. Also, whatever is ruled and measured must have a form proportionate to its rule and measure. Now, both of these requirements hold for human law which is something ordained to an end and is a rule and a measure ruled and measured by a superior rule and measure. This superior rule and measure is twofold, namely, the Divine Law and the Natural law, as is clear from what was said above (*a.* 2 and *q.* 92, *a.* 3). Now, human law is ordered to the good of human beings, as also the jurisprudent says (*Digest* I, III, 5). And, therefore, Isidore, in laying down the requirements of human law first lays down three, namely that it agree with religion, inasmuch as it is proportionate to the Divine Law, that it fosters training, inasmuch as it is proportionate to the Natural Law, and that it promotes the Common Good inasmuch as it is proportionate to human benefit.

CORPUS [SECTION 2]

Et ad haec tria omnes aliae conditiones quas postea ponit reducuntur. Nam quod dicitur 'honesta' refertur ad hoc quod 'religioni congruat'; quod autem subditur, 'justa, possibilis, secundum naturam, secundum consuetudinem patriae, loco temporique conveniens', reducitur ad hoc quod 'conveniat disciplinae'. Attenditur enim humana disciplina, primum quidem quantum ad ordinem rationis, qui importatur in hoc quod dicitur 'justa'. Secundo, quantum ad facultatem agentium: debet enim esse disciplina conveniens unicuique secundum suam possibilitatem, observata etiam possibilitate naturae—non enim eadem sunt imponenda pueris quae imponuntur viris perfectis—et secundum humanam conditionem: non enim potest homo solus in societate vivere, aliis morem non gerens. Tertio, quantum ad debitas circumstantias dicit, 'loco temporique conveniens'. Quod vero subditur, 'necessaria, utilis', etc., refertur ad hoc quod expediat saluti: ut necessitas referatur ad remotionem malorum, utilitas ad consecutionem bonorum, manifestatio vero ad cavendum nocumentum, quod ex ipsa lege posset provenire. Et quia, sicut supra dictum est (*q.* 90, *a.* 2), lex ordinatur ad bonum commune, hoc ipsum in ultima parte determinationis ostenditur.

Et per hoc patet responsio ad objecta.

Corpus [Section 2]

And to these three, all the other requirements which he adds further on, are reducible. For, when he says "virtuous" he means that law should conform to religion. When he goes on to say, "just, possible to nature, in accordance with the custom of the country, adapted to time and place," all these can be reduced to the requirement that it foster training. For human training is covered in saying first, with reference to the ordination of reason, which is implied in saying that law should be just. Secondly, with reference to the ability of the agents, taking into account each one's natural powers—for one does not require the same thing from children as from adults—and according to human conditions, for a man cannot live alone in society, taking no account of others. Thirdly, with reference to relevant circumstances, he says, "adapted to place and time." When he adds, "necessary, useful, etc.," he refers to what promotes the Common Good, "necessary" refers to the removal of evils, "useful to the acquisition of goods, clarity of expression" refers to preventing harm that could come from the law itself. And since, as is stated above (*q.* 90, *a.* 2), law is ordered to the Common Good, this very aspect is shown in the last part of his description. And from all this, the answer to the Objections is obvious.

Comment

This would seem to be an appropriate place to present an illuminating comparison.

Lon Fuller, in the Second Chapter of his *The Morality of Law*, sets forth eight principles of legality which he also calls "inner morality of the law" or the principles that make law possible. Now Fuller himself connects these principles with St. Thomas's *Treatise*:

> In the reorientation that seems to be taking place, one hopes that there will develop a little more tolerance for, and interest in, the great tradition embodied in the literature of natural law. One will find in this literature much foolishness and much that is unacceptable to modern intellectual tastes; one will also find in it practical wisdom applied to problems that may broadly be called those of social architecture. St. Thomas Aquinas stands for many as a kind of symbol of all that is dogmatic and theological in the tradition of natural law. Yet as one writer has recently pointed out, Aquinas in some measure recognized and dealt with all eight of the principles of

legality discussed in my second chapter. I know of no writer
in the positivist vein who has concerned himself in more than
a perfunctory way with the general problem of achieving and
maintaining legality. [*Op. cit.*, pp. 241–242.]

I now list Fuller's eight principles, indicating at least most of the relevant
loci in the *Treatise*:

1. The Generality of Law
   q. 96, *a.* 1
   q. 90, *a.* 1, *c* ("rule and measure")
2. Promulgation
   q. 90, *a.* 4
   The present Article
3. Retroactive Laws
   St. Thomas does not speak of retroactive laws as such,
   but his constant insistence that laws are directive of human
   acts (*q.* 90, *a.* 1, *c.*; *g.* 96, *a.* 5, *c.*) implies a rejection of
   retroactive laws.
4. The Clarity of Laws
   In the present Article
   St. Thomas's argument for the requirement of promulgation
   (*q.* 90, *a.* 4, *c.*) would also support the desideratum of
   clarity.
5. Contradictions in the Law
   St. Thomas does not speak directly to this problem. However, his insistence on the directive function of law would
   implicitly condemn internal contradictions in law.
6. Laws Requiring the Impossible
   In this Article, Isidore and St. Thomas agree that laws
   must be "possible according to nature and according to
   the custom of the country." Also, from a different point
   of view ("moral" possibility) in *q.* 96, *a.* 2, *c.*
7. The Constancy of Law Through Time
   St. Thomas devotes two Articles to the question of change
   in law, using arguments very similar to those used by Fuller.
   [See *q.* 97, *aa.* 1 and 2.]
8. Congruence Between Official Action and Declared Rule
   St. Thomas does not address this problem. He clearly implies that judges should judge according to the laws (*q.* 95,

a. 1, Reply 2). It is clear from *q.* 96, *a.* 5, *c.*, that the coercive power of the law is to be used to make the recalcitrant obey the law.

It is remarkable that a Catholic Bishop of the seventh century and a thirteenth-century Dominican friar and a twentieth-century Harvard Professor should agree so closely on the qualities of law/the principles of legality.

ARTICLE 4
UTRUM ISIDORUS CONVENIENTER PONAT DIVISIONEM HUMANARUM LEGUM? WHETHER ISIDORE'S DIVISION OF HUMAN LAWS IS APPROPRIATE?

Introductory Comment

The underlying problem of this Article concerns the methodology of classifying positive laws. St. Thomas works with Isidore's division of Roman laws. Isidore was a respected *auctor* whose *Etymologies* provided a source of information about classical Roman culture for which the medieval scholars had no other similar source. As he usually does (compare Article 3), St. Thomas gives a rational organization to Isidore's divisions.

In classifying, a principle is needed which is both complete and consistent. For example, we classify the books of a library according to subject matter since such a principle will cover *all* the books. We cannot classify the books as either mathematical or poetic since this would leave many books out and so would be incomplete. We cannot classify books *simultaneously* according to authors and the color of their bindings. Such a principle would be inconsistent.

In the first part of the *Corpus* of the Article, St. Thomas sets up his principle of classification. He proposes to classify laws according to what belongs to law *per se*, that is, according to its essence or nature as defined in *q.* 90, *a.* 4, *c.*

He illustrates this procedure by explaining the *per se* division of the genus "animal." According to Aristotle, all animals (whether human or brute) have a formal intrinsic principle which he called the "soul" (*anima*) which made each animal to be the kind of animal it is. Now, there are two kinds of souls (*animae*), rational and irrational, and so to divide "animal" into two species, rational animals (human beings) and irrational animals (brute animals), is a *per se* division. St. Thomas contrasts this with a division according to "white" and "black" which is a characteristic wholly accidental to animality.

St. Thomas, then, relates each of Isidore's divisions to something that pertains *per se* and properly to law as such. I have divided the *Corpus* into Sections to highlight each division.

In Section 1, St. Thomas uses the necessary dependence of Positive Law on Natural Law to establish Isidore's division.

Now, the essence or nature of law is set forth in the definition given in *q*. 90, *a*. 4, *c*., Section 2. This definition is itself based on the doctrine of the Four Causes [183–210]. Hence, in each subsequent Section one of the causes is basic. In each cause I have indicated the relevant cause.

OBJECTION 1

Videtur quod inconvenienter Isidorus divisionem legum humanarum ponat, sive juris humani. Sub hoc enim jure comprehendit jus gentium, quod ideo sic nominatur, ut ipse dicit (*Etym.* v, 4), quia *eo omnes fere gentes utuntur.* Sed, sicut ipse dicit, ibid., *jus naturale est quod est commune omnium nationum.* Ergo jus gentium non continetur sub jure positivo humano, sed magis sub jure naturali.

Objection 1

It would seem that Isidore inappropriately divided human statutes or human law. For under this head he included the Law of Nations, which, as he says (*Etym.*, v, 4), is so called, "because almost all nations use it." But, as he himself says (*ibid.*), "It is the Natural Law that is common to all nations." Therefore, the Law of Nations is not contained under positive human law but rather under the Natural law.

REPLY 1

Ad primum ergo dicendum quod jus gentium est quidem aliquo modo naturale homini, secundum quod est rationalis,

inquantum derivatur a lege naturali per modum conclusionis,
quae non est multum remota a principiis, unde de facili in hujusmodi homines consenserunt; distinguitur tamen a lege naturali, maxime ab eo quod est omnibus animalibus commune.

Reply 1

The Law of Nations is indeed in some way natural to man inasmuch
as it is rational, since it is derived from the Natural Law by way of a
conclusion, which is not very far from the principles. Hence, in such
matters men easily agree. But nonetheless, it is distinguished from the
Natural Law, especially from that part that is common to all animals.

Comment

In ancient Rome only Roman citizens had access to the civil law
of Rome. As Rome began to incorporate other peoples (*gentes*) into its
empire, problems arose with regard to the legal status of those who were
not Roman citizens. To solve these problems, Rome set up special judges
(*praetores*) to deal with legal cases involving non-Romans. The Roman
jurists did not apply the rules and procedures of the Roman civil law
to these cases but developed a set of general principles of justice which
they believed were accepted by all people as just and reasonable. This
set of principles constituted the *Jus Gentium*—the Law of Nations. The
Roman jurists, who were generally Stoic philosophers and Natural Law
thinkers, recognized the close relationship between the *Jus Gentium* and
the Natural Law. Some even identified them.

Modern readers often think the *Jus Gentium* refers to International
Law, the body of legal principles established by custom, covenant and
treaties to govern the legal relations between sovereign states. This was
not the ancient meaning of the term, as explained above. St. Thomas
uses the term in the same sense as the Roman jurists did.

The last part of the Reply, "especially with regard to the part that is
common to all animals" refers to the list of human inclinations set forth
in *q*. 94, *a*. 2. The inclinations common to all animals include the desire
for food, drink, sex, etc. The *Jus Gentium* had little to do with such matters since it was mainly concerned with justice and especially with commercial and business transactions, as is stated in this same Reply.

OBJECTION 2

Praeterea, ea quae habent eandem vim non videntur
formaliter differre, sed solum materialiter. Sed leges, plebiscita, senatusconsulta, et alia hujusmodi, quae ponit ibid.,

omnia habent eandem vim. Ergo videtur quod non differant nisi materialiter. Sed talis distinctio in arte non est curanda, cum possit esse in infinitum. Ergo inconvenienter hujusmodi divisio humanarum legum introducitur.

Objection 2

Further, those things that have the same force do not seem to differ formally but only materially. But statutes, decrees of the community, decrees of the Senate and the like which he mentions (*ibid.*, 9), all have the same force. Therefore they only differ materially. But art takes no notice of such a distinction, since it could go on to infinity. Therefore this distinction was inappropirately introduced into the division of human law.

[There is no Reply since the answer is evident from Section 4 of the *Corpus.*]

Comment

Things differ formally (*formaliter*) when they differ in kind, as a man differs from a tree. Things differ materially (*materialiter*) when they differ only in number, as one man differs from another. Material diversity can be extended, man from man from man . . . to infinity.

OBJECTION 3

Praeterea sicut in civitate sunt principes, sacerdotes et milites, ita etiam sunt et alia hominum officia. Ergo videtur quod, sicut ponitur quoddam jus militare et jus publicum quod consistit in sacerdotibus et magistratibus, ita etiam debeant poni alia jura ad alia officia civitatis pertinentia.

Objection 3

Further, just as there are in the state, princes, priests, and soldiers, so there are also other functionaries. Therefore, it seems that just as he identified a military law and a public law that applied to priests and magistrates, so he should have identified other laws for the other functionaries in the state.

[Again, there is no Reply since the answer is evident from the *Corpus.*]

OBJECTION 4

Praeterea, ea quae sunt per accidens sunt praetermit-
tenda. Sed accidit legi ut ab hoc vel ab alio homine feratur.
Ergo inconvenienter ponitur divisio legum humanarum ex
nominibus legislatorum, ut scilicet quaedam dicatur *Cornelia,*
quaedam *Falcidia,* etc.

Objection 4

Further, what is accidental should be ignored. But it is accidental
to law that it be framed by this or that man. Therefore, it is inappropriate
to divide laws according to the name of the lawgiver, so that one is
called the Cornelian Law, another the Falcidian Law, and so forth.

[Again, there is no Reply since the answer is evident from Section
5 of the *Corpus.*]

ON THE CONTRARY

In contrarium auctoritas Isidori sufficiat.

On the Contrary

The *auctoritas* from Isidore (*Etym.* v, 4) is sufficient.

CORPUS [SECTION 1:
THE METHODOLOGY OF CLASSIFICATION]

Dicendum quod unumquodque potest per se dividi secundum id quod in ejus ratione continetur: sicut in ratione
animalis continetur anima, quae est rationalis vel irrationalis;
et ideo animal proprie et per se dividitur secundum rationale
et irrationale, non autem secundum album et nigrum, quae
sunt omnino praeter rationem ejus. Sunt autem multa de
ratione legis humanae secundum quorum quodlibet lex humana proprie et per se dividi potest.

Corpus [Section 1:
The Methodology of Classification]

Each thing can be divided per se according to what is contained
in its essential notion, just as, in the essential notion of animal, there

is contained "soul," either rational or nonrational, and so "animal," properly and *per se,* is divided according to rational or nonrational, not, however, according to white or black which are altogether outside its essential notion. However, there are many things contained in the essential notion of human law, according to each one of which law can properly and per se be divided.

CORPUS [SECTION 2:
DIVISION BASED ON DERIVATION FROM THE
NATURAL LAW; SEE Q. 95, A. 2]

Est enim primo de ratione legis humanae quod sit derivata a lege naturae, ut ex dictis patet, et secundum hoc dividitur jus positivum in jus gentium et jus civile, secundum duos modos quibus aliquid derivatur a lege naturae, ut supra dictum est (ibid). Nam ad jus gentium pertinent ea quae derivantur ex lege naturae sicut conclusiones ex principiis: ut justae emptiones, venditiones et alia hujusmodi, sine quibus homines ad invicem convivere non possunt; quod est de lege naturae, quia homo est naturaliter animal sociabile, ut probatur in I *Pol.* Quae vero derivantur a lege naturae per modum particularis determinationis pertinent ad jus civile, secundum quod quaelibet civitas aliquid sibi accommodum determinat.

Corpus [Section 2:
Division Based on Derivation from the Natural Law;
see q. 95, a. 2]

For the first thing in the essential notion of human law is that it is derived from the Natural Law as is clear from what has previously been said (*a.* 2) and in this respect human law is divided into the Law of Nations and Civil Law according to the two ways in which things can be derived from the Natural Law (*ibid.*). For those things belong to the Law of Nations which are derived from the Natural Law as conclusions from principles, such as just buying and selling and the like without which men cannot live together, which is from the Natural Law because man is by nature a social animal as is proved in *Polit.* i, 1. But those things that are derived from the Natural Law by way of particular determination belong to the Civil Law according as each state determines something appropriate for itself.

CORPUS [SECTION 3:
DIVISION BASED ON ORDINATION TO THE
COMMON GOOD: THE FINAL CAUSE OF LAW]

Secundo est de ratione legis humanae quod ordinetur ad bonum commune civitatis; et secundum hoc lex humana dividi potest secundum diversitatem eorum qui specialiter dant operam ad bonum commune; sicut sacerdotes pro populo Deum orantes, principes populum gubernantes, et milites pro salute populi pugnantes: et ideo istis hominibus specialia quaedam jura aptantur.

Corpus [Section 3:
Division Based on Ordination to the Common Good:
The Final Cause of Law]

Secondly, it belongs to the essential notion of human law that it be ordered to the Common Good of the state, and, in this respect, human law can be divided according to the diversity of those who work in a special way for the Common Good, as priests who pray for the people, rulers who govern the people, and soldiers who fight for the safety of the people, and, so special laws are adopted for such persons.

CORPUS [SECTION 4:
DIVISION BASED ON TYPE OF GOVERNMENT:
THE EFFICIENT CAUSE OF LAW]

Tertio, est de ratione legis humanae ut instituatur a gubernante communitatem civitatis, sicut supra dictum est; et secundum hoc distinguuntur leges humanae secundum diversa regimina civitatum. Quorum unum, secundum Philosophum in III *Polit.*, est regnum, quando scilicet civitas gubernatur ab uno; et secundum hoc accipiuntur constitutiones principum. Aliud vero regimen est aristocratia, id est principatus optimorum vel optimatum; et secundum hoc sumuntur responsa prudentum, et etiam senatusconsulta. Aliud regimen est oligarchia, id est principatus paucorum divitum et potentum; et secundum hoc sumitur jus praetorium, quod etiam honorarium dicitur. Aliud autem regimen est populi, quod nominatur democratia; et secundum hoc sumuntur plebiscita. Aliud autem est tyrannicum, quod est omnino corruptum: unde ex hoc non sumitur aliqua lex. Est etiam aliquod regimen ex istis commixtum, quod est optimum; et secundum hoc sumitur lex *quam majores natu simul cum plebibus sanxerunt,* ut Isidorus dicit.

Corpus [Section 4:
Division Based on Type of Government:
The Efficient Cause of Law]

Thirdly, it belongs to the essential notion of human law that it be established by the one who governs the community of the state as shown above (*a.* 90, *a.* 3). In this respect laws are divided according to the different forms of government of states. One form, according to the Philosopher (*Polit.* iii, 10) is monarchy, that is, when the state is governed by one person. In this case there are royal ordinances.

Another form of government is aristocracy, that is, rule by the best men or men of the highest rank, and, in this case, there are prudential legal opinions or decrees of the Senate. Another form is oligarchy, that is, the rule of a few rich and powerful men, and, in this respect, there are Praetorian laws, also called honorary laws. Another form is that of the people, which is called democracy. There are decrees of the people. Another form is tyranny which is totally corrupt and therefore has no law. There is also a form which is a mixture of all these forms and this is the best form of government. In this form there are laws sanctioned by the Lords and the Commons, as Isidore says (*loc. cit.*)

Comment

Both Aristotle and St. Thomas hold that the mixed form of government (combining monarchy, aristocracy, and democracy) is the best form of government. It combines the advantages of the three good forms of government and, in effect, sets up what today we call a system of checks and balances. The Federal Government of the United States is an example of the mixed regime.

CORPUS [SECTION 5:
DIVISION BASED ON TYPES OF ACTS REGULATED:
THE MATERIAL CAUSE OF LAW]

Quarto vero, de ratione legis humanae est quod sit directiva humanorum actuum; et secundum hoc secundum diversa de quibus leges feruntur distinguuntur leges, quae interdum ab auctoribus nominantur; sicut distinguitur lex Julia de adulteriis, lex Cornelia de sicariis, et sic de aliis, non propter auctores, sed propter res de quibus sunt.

Corpus [Section 5:
Division Based on Types of Acts Regulated:
The Material Cause of Law]

Fourthly, it belongs to the essence of law that it be a rule of human acts, and, in this respect, laws are distinguished according to the different kinds of acts with which laws deal and which are sometimes named for their authors. In this way there are the *Lex Julia* concerning adultery, the *Lex Cornelia* concerning assassins, and so on, distinguished not by their authors but by the matter with which they deal.

Comment

Thus, St. Thomas gives us a neat classification of positive (human) laws. We might apply these divisions to our own laws, at least in a general way. Thus, corresponding to Section 3, we have a civil code and a military code; Section 4, we have Federal laws and State laws, a mixed form of government, with democratic laws; Section 5, The Material Cause, we have laws against assault and murder, against fraud, against robbery, etc.

QUESTION 96
DE POTESTATE LEGIS HUMANAE
OF THE POWER OF HUMAN LAW

Deinde considerandum est de potestate legis humanae, et circa hoc quaeruntur sex:

1. utrum humana lex debeat poni in communi;
2. utrum lex humana debeat omnia vitia cohibere;
3. utrum omnium virtutum actus habeat ordinare;
4. utrum imponat homini necessitatem quantum ad forum conscientiae;
5. utrum omnes homines legi humanae subdantur;
6. utrum his qui sunt sub lege liceat agere praeter verba legis.

Question 96

Next we must consider the power of human law, and, in this matter, there are six points of inquiry:

1. Whether human law should be general?
2. Whether human law ought to suppress all vices?
3. Whether it is competent to order acts of all the virtues?
4. Whether it imposes on man an obligation in conscience?
5. Whether all men are subject to human law?
6. Whether those who are subject to the law may act contrary to the letter of the law?

ARTICLE 1
UTRUM LEX HUMANA DEBEAT PONI IN COMMUNI MAGIS QUAM IN PARTICULARI?
WHETHER HUMAN LAW SHOULD BE FRAMED IN GENERAL OR FOR INDIVIDUAL CASES?

Introductory Comment

The problem St. Thomas deals with in this Article is that of the generality of law. Is law always a general rule applicable to many cases of a certain kind and addressed to a certain class of people or can a law be made for an individual case or act?

Lon Fuller lays down the requirement of generality as one of his principles of legality or of the inner morality of law (*The Morality of Law*, p. 47). His argument is simple. There must be rules and rules are general.

In *q.* 90, *a.* 1, St. Thomas explains that law is a "rule and measure of human acts." Both as a rule and as a measure, law must be general, dealing with a specific kind of human act and addressed to a certain class of people. Thus, there are laws forbidding all acts of theft as well as laws addressed to soldiers which are different from laws addressed to merchants (*q.* 91, *a.* 6, *c.*). Of course, in both cases, the laws must serve the Common Good (*q.* 90, *a.* 1).

H. L. A. Hart also says that laws must be general in two ways (*The Concept of Law*, p. 21). He lists the question of rules as one of the persistent questions of jurisprudence. For St. Thomas, determining the nature of a rule in general or that kind of rule that is a law was no real problem.

A rule is a general directive for action. If I tell my servant to close the window, I am giving him a command that applies to a singular act, not laying down a rule of action. If, however, I tell the cook to serve breakfast every day at 7:00 A.M., I am indeed giving him a rule that applies to a succession of similar acts.

St. Thomas argues that a measure (a standard) must be general. Otherwise, we would need a different measure for every act. This would make measure useless.

Laws, of course, apply to individual cases, and this must be done by judges (*q.* 95, *a.* 1).

OBJECTION 1

Videtur quod lex humana non debeat poni in communi, sed magis in particulari. Dicit enim Philosophus, in *Ethic.* v, 7, quod *legalia sunt quaecumque in singularibus legem ponunt, et etiam sententialia,* quae sunt etiam singularia, quia de singularibus actibus sententiae feruntur. Ergo lex non solum ponitur in communi, sed etiam in singulari.

Objection 1

It seems that human law should not be framed in general but rather for the particular case. For the Philosopher says (*Ethic.* v, 7) that "the legal just is whatever makes law for singular cases," and also [he includes] judicial decisions since they pass judgment on individual acts. Therefore, law is made not only in general but also for the individual act.

REPLY 1

Ad primum ergo dicendum quod Philosophus ponit tres partes justi legalis, quod est jus positivum (*Ethic.* v, 7). Sunt enim quaedam quae simpliciter in communi ponuntur, et haec sunt leges communes; et quantum ad hujusmodi dicit quod *legale est quod ex principio quidem nihil differt sic vel aliter; quando autem ponitur, differt,* puta quod *captivi statuto pretio redimantur.* Quaedam vero sunt quae sunt communia quantum ad aliquid et singularia quantum ad aliquid: et hujusmodi dicuntur 'privilegia', quasi 'leges privatae', quia respiciunt singulares personas, et tamen potestas eorum extenditur ad multa negotia; et quantum ad hoc subdit, *adhuc quaecumque in singularibus legem ponunt.* Dicuntur etiam quaedam legalia, non quia sint leges, sed propter applicationem legum communium ad aliqua particularia facta, sicut sunt 'sententiae', quae pro jure habentur: et quantum ad hoc subdit, *et sententialia.*

Reply 1

Aristotle divides the legal just, which is the positive law, into three divisions (*Ethic.* v, 7). For there are some which are completely general, and these are the general laws, and with reference to these, he says (*Ethic.* v, 7), that the legal just is that which initially is indifferent to being in this or in that way, but which, after the law is made, is no longer indifferent, for example, that captives are to be ransomed for an established amount.

But there are some which are general in one respect and singular in another respect. And such are called "privileges," as it were "private laws" for they refer to individual persons, yet their power extends to many affairs. With regard to these, he adds, "and whatever makes law for individuals."

And there are some things that are considered to have legal force, not because they are laws but because they apply common laws to some individual facts. And such are "judgments" (*sententiae*) which are considered law, and with regard to these, he adds, "and judicial decisions" (*sententialia*).

OBJECTION 2

Praeterea, lex est directiva humanorum actuum, ut supra dictum est (*q*. 90, *a*. 1, *c*). Sed humani actus in singularibus consistunt. Ergo lex humana non debet in universali ferri, sed magis in singulari.

Objection 2

Further, law is directive of human acts, as was shown above (*q*. 90, *a*. 1, *c*.). But human acts have to do with singular matters. Therefore, human law ought not be universal but rather for singular matters.

REPLY 2

Ad secundum dicendum quod illud quod est directivum oportet esse plurium directivum. Unde in *Meta*. x, 4, Philosophus dicit quod *omnia quae sunt unius generis mensurantur aliquo uno, quod est primum in genere illo*. Si enim essent tot regulae vel mensurae quot sunt mensurata vel regulata, cessaret utique utilitas regulae vel mensurae, quae est ut ex uno multa possint cognosci; et ita nulla esset utilitas legis si non se extenderet nisi ad unum singularem actum. Ad singulares enim actus dirigendos dantur singularia praecepta prudentum; sed lex est praeceptum commune, ut supra dictum est (*q*. 92, *a*. 2, *obj*. 2).

Reply 2

That which directs must direct many things. Hence, the Philosopher said (*Meta*. x, 4) that "everything in one genus is measured by one thing that is first in that genus." For, if there were as many rules and measures as there are things measured and ruled, rules and measures would indeed cease to be useful, for their usefulness consists in making it possible to know many things from one thing. And so law would be of no use, if it extended only to one single act. For the direction of individual acts, there is the singular precept of prudent men, but law is a general precept, as was said above (*q.* 92, *a.* 2, *obj.* 2).

Comment

For the prudential judgment referred to in this Reply and its relation to individual cases, see [362–374].

OBJECTION 3

Praeterea, lex est regula et mensura humanorum actuum, ut supra dictum est (*q.* 90, *a.* 1, *c.*). Sed *mensura debet esse certissima,* ut dicitur in *Meta.* x, 9. Cum ergo in actibus humanis non possit esse aliquod universale ita certum quin in particularibus deficiat, videtur quod necesse sit leges non in universali, sed in singularibus poni.

Objection 3

Further, law is a rule and measure of human acts, as was said above (*q.* 90, *a.* 1, *c.*). But "a measure must be most certain," as is said in *Meta.* x, 9. But in human acts, there is no general rule so certain that it does not fail in some particular cases. Hence, law ought not be framed in general but rather for individual cases.

REPLY 3

Ad tertium dicendum quod *non est eadem certitudo quaerenda in omnibus,* ut in *Ethic.* i, 3. dicitur. Unde in rebus contingentibus, sicut sunt naturalia et res humanae, sufficit talis certitudo ut aliquid sit verum ut in pluribus, licet interdum deficiat ut in paucioribus.

Reply 3

We must not seek the same degree of certitude in everything, as is said in *Ethic.* i, 3. Consequently, in contingent matters such as the things of nature and human affairs we have certitude that is true for the most part, though sometimes fails in a few cases.

Comment

Absolute certitude can be had only in necessary matters, as in mathematics and in metaphysics. In contingent affairs, principles and rules can be certain only in general and not absolutely. This is common Aristotelian and Thomistic doctrine and is quite evident, since in contingent matters there are many modifying factors. This is another reason why there must be judicial discretion in applying general statutes and principles. Thus, valid wills should be enforced by the Courts, but not when the testee has murdered the testator in order to inherit.

ON THE CONTRARY

Sed contra est quod Jurisperitus dicit (*Pandect Justim., Lib.* ii, *Tit.* iii, *art.* ii, *De Legibus,* etc.) quod *jura constitui oportet in his quae saepius accidunt; ex his autem quae forte uno casu accidere possunt, jura non constituuntur.*

On the Contrary

The Jurist says (*Pandect Justim., Lib.* ii, *Tit.* iii, *art.* ii, *De Legibus,* etc.) that "laws should be made to deal with what frequently happens, but for things that might possibly happen in some one case, laws are not framed."

CORPUS

Dicendum quod quia unumquodque quod est propter finem necesse est quod sit fini proportionatum. Finis autem legis est bonum commune, quia, ut Isidorus dicit (*Etym.* v, 21), *nullo privato commodo, sed pro communi utilitate civium lex debet esse conscripta.* Unde oportet leges humanas esse proportionatas ad bonum commune. Bonum autem commune constat ex multis; et ideo oportet quod lex ad multa respiciat, et secundum personas et secundum negotia et secundum tempora. Constituitur enim communitas civitatis ex

multis personis, et ejus bonum per multiplices actiones pro-
curatur; nec ad hoc instituitur quod aliquo tempore modico
duret, sed quod omni tempore perseveret per civium successionem, ut Augustinus dicit in *De Civ. Dei,* ii, 21, xxii, 6.

Corpus

Whatever is ordered to an end must necessarily be proportioned
to that end. The end, however, of law is the common good, for, as
Isidore says (*Etym.* v, 21) that "law ought to be framed, not for any
private good but for the common benefit of the citizens." Hence, human
laws should be proportioned to the Common Good.

Now the common good consists of many things. Therefore law
should relate to many, with respect to persons and affairs and time.

For the community of the state is made up of many persons, and
its good is achieved through many actions; nor is it established for some
short period of time but to endure for all time through the sucession of
its citizens, as Augustine says (*De Civ. Dei,* ii, 21, xxii, 6).

Comment

One may be suprised to find St. Thomas adding time to this discussion. The distinction running through this discussion is between a
singular directive (command) to an individual for a single act and, on
the other hand, a general directive (a rule) to many individuals covering
many acts. In the first case, a single act would take place at a definite
time and cease. In the second case, the acts are successive and so over
a period of time. This consideration completes the understanding of the
basic distinction.

ARTICLE 2
UTRUM AD LEGEM HUMANAM PERTINEAT OMNIA VITIA COHIBERE?
WHETHER IT BELONGS TO HUMAN LAW TO REPRESS ALL VICES?

Introductory Comment

This Article together with Article 3 demonstrates that, although human law is derived in some way from the Natural Law (*q. 95, a. 2*), it is

not merely a transcript of Natural Law. Many factors limit and determine human law. Among these factors are the condition of the citizen, the customs of the country, the Common Good and, especially, the things, like peace and order, that are necessary for the existence of society. Some have criticized Natural Law theorists for wishing to transcribe the Natural Law completely and exactly into human law. This criticism is certainly invalid as against St. Thomas who places a great deal of creative responsibility on the human lawgiver. [See especially, *q. 95, a. 2.*]

OBJECTION 1

Videtur quod ad legem humanam pertineat omnia vitia cohibere. Dicit enim Isidorus (*Etym.* v, 20) quod *leges sunt factae ut earum metu coerceatur audacia.* Non autem sufficienter coerceretur nisi quaelibet mala cohiberentur per legem. Ergo lex humana debet quaelibet mala cohibere.

Objection 1

It seems that it belongs to human law to repress all vice. For Isidore says (*Etym.* v, 20) that "laws are made that, through fear of them, man's audacity may be restrained." However, it would not be sufficiently restrained unless all evils were suppressed by law. Therefore, human law ought to suppress all evils.

REPLY 1

Ad primum ergo dicendum quod audacia pertinere videtur ad invasionem aliorum: unde praecipue pertinet ad illa peccata quibus injuria proximis irrogatur, quae lege humana prohibentur, ut dictum est in corpore articuli.

Reply 1

Audacity seems to refer to attacks on others. Hence, it especially refers to those sins by which injury is done to one's neighbors and which are prohibited by human law, as is said in the *Corpus* of this Article.

OBJECTION 2

Praeterea, intentio legislatoris est cives facere virtuosos. Sed non potest aliquis esse virtuosus nisi ab omnibus vitiis compescatur. Ergo ad legem humanam pertinet omnia vitia compescere.

Objection 2

Further, the intention of the legislator is to make the citizen virtuous. But one cannot be virtuous unless he is restrained from all vices. Therefore, it belongs to human law to curb all vices.

REPLY 2

Ad secundum dicendum quod lex humana intendit homines inducere ad virtutem, non subito sed gradatim; et ideo non statim multitudini imperfectorum imponit ea quae sunt jam virtuosorum, ut scilicet ab omnibus malis abstineant; alioquin imperfecti hujusmodi praecepta ferre non valentes in deteriora mala prorumperent; sicut dicitur Prov. xxx, 33, *Qui nimis emungit, elicit sanguinem;* et Matt. ix, 17 quod *si vinum novum,* idest praecepta perfectae vitae, *mittatur in utres veteres,* idest in homines imperfectos, *utres rumpuntur, et vinum effunditur,* idest praecepta contemnuntur, et homines ex contemptu ad pejora mala prorumpunt.

Reply 2

Human law intends to bring men to virtue, not suddenly but gradually, and so, it does not impose immediately upon the multitude of imperfect men those things which the virtuous already possess, namely, that they abstain from all evils, otherwise these imperfect men, being unable to bear such precepts, would break forth into worse evils, as is said in (Prov. xxx, 33), "He who blows his nose too violently, brings forth blood," and in (Matt. ix, 17), "If wine is put in old skins," i.e., if the precepts of a perfect life are imposed on imperfect men, "the skins would break, and the wine would flow out," i.e., the precepts would be contemned and men would break out into worse evils.

OBJECTION 3

Praetera, lex humana a lege naturali derivatur, ut supra dictum est (*q.* 95, *a.* 2). Sed omnia vitia repugnant legi naturae. Ergo lex humana omnia vitia debet cohibere.

Objection 3

Further, human law is derived from the Natural Law, as was said above (*q.* 95, *a.* 2). But all vices are contrary to the Natural Law. Therefore, human law should repress all vices.

REPLY 3

Ad tertium dicendum quod lex naturalis est quaedam participatio legis aeternae in nobis; lex autem humana deficit a lege aeterna. Dicit enim Augustinus (*De Lib. Arb.,* i, v; ii), *Lex ista, quae regendis civitatibus fertur, multa concedit, atque impunita relinquit quae per divinam Providentiam vindicantur; neque enim quia non omnia facit, ideo quae facit improbanda sunt.* Unde etiam lex humana non omnia potest prohibere quae prohibet lex naturae.

Reply 3

The Natural Law is a participation in us of the Eternal Law, but human law falls short of the Eternal Law. For Augustine says (*De Lib. Arb.,* i, v; ii), "The law that is for the governance of states allows and leaves unpunished many things that are punished through Divine Providence, nor should this law be blamed for not doing everything." Hence, also, human law cannot prohibit everything that is prohibited by the Natural Law.

ON THE CONTRARY

Sed contra est quod dicitur in *De Lib. Arb.* i, 5, *Videtur mihi legem istam quae populo regendo scribitur, recte ista permittere, et divinam Providentiam vindicare.* Sed divina

Providentia non vindicat nisi vitia. Ergo recte lex humana permittit aliqua vitia, non cohibendo ipsa.

On the Contrary

It is said in *De Lib. Arb.*, (i, 5): "It seems to me that the law that is made for governing the people rightly permits these things, and Divine Providence rightly punishes them." But Divine Providence punishes nothing but vice. Therefore, human law rightly permits certain vices by not condemning them.

CORPUS

Dicendum quod, sicut jam dictum est (*q.* 90, *a.* 1, *c.*), lex ponitur ut quaedam regula vel mensura humanorum actuum. Mensura autem *debet esse homogenea mensurato,* ut dicitur in *Meta.* ix; diversa enim diversis mensurantur. Unde oportet quod etiam leges imponantur hominibus secundum eorum conditionem, quia, ut Isidorus dicit (*Etym.* v, 21), *lex debet esse possibilis, et secundum naturam et secundum consuetudinem patriae.*

Potestas autem sive facultas operandi ex interiori habitu seu dispositione procedit: non enim idem est possibile ei qui non habet habitum virtutis et virtuoso; sicut etiam non est idem possibile puero et viro perfecto: et propter hoc non ponitur eadem lex pueris quae ponitur adultis; multa enim pueris permittuntur quae in adultis lege puniuntur, vel etiam vituperantur. Et similiter multa sunt permittenda hominibus non perfectis virtute quae non essent toleranda in hominibus virtuosis.

Lex autem humana ponitur multitudini hominum, in qua major pars est hominum non perfectorum virtute. Et ideo lege humana non prohibentur omnia vitia a quibus virtuosi abstinent, sed solum graviora a quibus possibile est majorem partem multitudinis abstinere, et praecipue quae sunt in nocumentum aliorum, sine quorum prohibitione societas humana conservari non posset: sicut prohibentur lege humana homicidia, furta, et hujusmodi.

Corpus

As has already been said (*q.* 90, *a.* 1, *c.*), law is framed as a rule or measure of human acts. Now, a measure ought to be homogeneous with that which it measures, as is said in *Meta.* ix. For different things are measured by different measures. Hence, laws also should be imposed on men according to their condition, for, as Isidore says (*Etym.* v, 21), "Law ought to be possible both in respect to nature and in respect to the customs of the country."

Now, the power or faculty of acting comes from an internal habit or disposition, for the same thing is not possible for him who lacks the habit of virtue as for the virtuous man, thus, also, the same thing is not possible for children as for a grown man. Hence, because of this, the same law is not framed for children as for adults. For many things are permitted to children which in adults are punished by law or also are blamed. Likewise, many things must be permitted to men lacking perfection, which would be intolerable in virtuous men.

Now, human law is framed for the whole community of men in which most men are not perfect in virtue. And therefore human law does not prohibit all vices from which the virtuous abstain but only the more serious ones from which it is possible for the majority to abstain and especially those which are harmful to others and which, if not prohibited, would make the preservation of human society impossible: Thus human law prohibits murders, thefts and the like.

ARTICLE 3
UTRUM LEX HUMANA PRAECIPIAT ACTUS OMNIUM VIRTUTUM?
WHETHER HUMAN LAW COMMANDS THE ACTS OF ALL THE VIRTUES?

OBJECTION 1

Videtur quod lex humana non praecipiat actus omnium virtutum. Actibus enim virtutum opponuntur actus vitiosi. Sed lex humana non prohibet omnia vitia, ut dictum est (*a.* 2). Ergo etiam non praecipit actus omnium virtutum.

Objection 1

It seems that human law does not command the acts of all the virtues. For acts of the virtues are the opposite of acts of vices. But human law, as has been said (*a.* 2), does not forbid the acts of all the vices. Therefore, human law does not command the acts of all the virtues.

REPLY 1

Ad primum ergo dicendum quod lex humana non prohibet omnes actus vitiosos secundum obligationem praecepti, sicut nec praecipit omnes actus virtuosos; prohibet tamen aliquos actus singulorum vitiorum, sicut etiam praecipit quosdam actus singularum virtutum.

Reply 1

Human law does not prohibit the acts of all the vices under the obligation of a precept, just as it does not command all the acts of the virtues. For it forbids certain acts of the individual vices just as it also commands certain acts of individual virtues.

OBJECTION 2

Praeterea, actus virtutis a virtute procedit. Sed virtus est finis legis; et ita quod est ex virtute sub praecepto legis cadere non potest. Ergo lex humana non praecipit actus omnium virtutum.

Objection 2

Further, the acts of virtue come from the virtue, but virtue is the end of the law, and so that which comes from virtue cannot come under the precept of a law. Therefore, human law does not order the acts of all the virtues.

REPLY 2

Ad secundum dicendum quod aliquis actus dicitur esse virtutis dupliciter. Uno modo, ex eo quod homo operatur

virtuosa, sicut actus virtutis justitiae est facere recta, et actus
fortitudinis facere fortia, et sic lex praecipit aliquos actus
virtutum. Alio modo dicitur actus virtutis, quia aliquis operatur virtuosa eo modo quo virtuosus operatur; et talis actus
semper procedit a virtute, nec cadit sub praecepto legis sed
est finis ad quem legislator ducere intendit.

Reply 2

An act is said to be an act of virtue in two senses. In one sense,
that a man does what is virtuous, as the act of the virtue of justice is
to do what is right, and the act of fortitude is to do what is brave, and,
in this sense, law commands certain acts of the virtues. In another sense
an act is said to be an act of virtue, if it is done in the way a virtuous
man does it. And in this sense, acts always come from virtue and do
not come under the precept of law, but virtue is rather the end which
the legislator intends.

Comment

This reply may seem cryptic to a modern reader.

St. Thomas is distinguishing the external act of a virtue from the
internal virtue itself. For example, to pay one's just debts is an act of
justice, even though a person may be performing the act of paying his
debts only because of fear of a penalty, not from an internal disposition
to do justice, that is, not from the internal virtue itself. Thus, the external
acts of virtue come under the competence of human law, but the internal
just disposition does not. The law can order a man to tip his hat when
the Queen is passing by; it cannot order him to love her in his heart.

However, St. Thomas adds what he argued for in Article 1, namely,
that every lawgiver intends to lead men (indirectly) to true virtue.

OBJECTION 3

Praeterea, lex humana ordinatur ad bonum commune,
ut dictum est. Sed quidam actus virtutum non ordinantur ad
bonum commune, sed ad bonum privatum. Ergo lex non
praecipit actus omnium virtutum.

Objection 3

Further, human law is ordered to the Common Good, as has been
said (*q.* 90, *a.* 2), but some acts of virtue are not ordered to the Common

Good but to a private good. Therefore, law does not command the acts of all the virtues.

REPLY 3

Ad tertium dicendum quod non est aliqua virtus cujus actus non sint ordinabiles ad bonum commune, ut dictum est, vel mediate vel immediate.

Reply 3

There is no virtue whose acts cannot be ordered to the Common Good, either immediately or mediately, as has been said (*Corpus* of this article).

ON THE CONTRARY

Sed contra est quod Philosophus dicit in *Ethic.* v, 1, quod *praecipit lex et fortis opera facere, et quae temperati, et quae mansueti; similiter autem secundum alias virtutes et malitias, haec quidem jubens, haec autem prohibens.*

On the Contrary

The Philosopher says (*Ethic.* v, 1), "the law commands that the acts of a brave man be performed, and those of a temperate man and of a gentle man, and likewise for the other virtues and vices, ordering the first and forbidding the second."

Comment

St. Thomas quotes the Aristotelian text in an abbreviated form. In order to clarify the text and to emphasize its main point, I present the full text from *Ethic.* v, 7, 14.

> And the law prescribes certain conduct; the conduct of a brave man, for example not to desert one's post, not to run away, not to throw down one's arms; that of a temperate man, for example not to commit adultery or outrage; that of a gentle man, for example not to strike, not to speak evil; and so with

actions exemplifying the rest of the virtues and vices, com-
manding these and forbidding those—rightly if the law has
been rightly enacted, not so well if it has been made at
random.

CORPUS

Dicendum quod species virtutum distinguuntur secun-
dum objecta, ut ex supra dictis patet (*q*. 59, *a*. 2; *q*. 60, *a*.
1). Omnia autem objecta virtutum referri possunt vel ad bonum privatum alicujus personae vel ad bonum commune multitudinis: sicut ea quae sunt fortitudinis potest aliquis exequi
vel propter conservationem civitatis vel ad conservandum jus
amici sui; et simile est in aliis.

Lex autem, ut dictum est (*q*. 90, *a*. 2), ordinatur ad
bonum commune; et ideo nulla virtus est de cujus actibus lex
praecipere non possit. Non tamen de omnibus actibus omnium virtutum lex humana praecipit, sed solum de illis qui
ordinabiles sunt ad bonum commune, vel immediate, sicut
cum aliqua directe propter bonum commune fiunt, vel mediate, sicut cum aliqua ordinantur a legislatore pertinentia ad
bonam disciplinam, per quam cives informantur, ut commune
bonum justitiae et pacis conservent.

Corpus

Virtues are specifically distinguished according to their objects, as
is clear from what has been said above (*q*. 59, *a*. 2; *q*. 60, *a*. 1). Now,
all the objects of the virtues can be referred to the private good of some
individual or to the Common Good of the community. Thus, one can
perform the acts of fortitude either to preserve the state or to uphold
the right of a friend, and so on in the other virtues.

Now, law, as has been said (*q*. 90, *a*. 2), is ordered to the Common
Good, and, therefore, there is no virtue whose acts the law cannot
command. But human law does not command all the acts of all the
virtues but only those which can be ordered to the Common Good,
either immediately, as when some things are done directly for the Common Good, or indirectly, as when the legislators order the citizens to
do something for good order, thus training them in upholding the Common Good of justice and peace.

Comment

Two important points are made in this Article. First, there is the distinction between the act of a virtue and the virtue itself, which is an internal acquired disposition to do the act. Human law can only order the external act (e.g., pay taxes) but not that the act be performed with a virtuous disposition, that is, a recognition that it is just and right to pay taxes. A person may pay taxes simply out of fear, while hating to do so.

Secondly, it makes clear that while under certain circumstances the acts of any virtue can come under the precept of human law, such acts must be ordered to the Common Good. The law cannot simply order virtuous acts because they are virtuous but only if they can be ordered to the Common Good. Human law cannot order sobriety for its own sake, but it can order sobriety while driving or while acting in public.

ARTICLE 4
UTRUM LEX HUMANA IMPONAT HOMINI NECESSITATEM IN FORO CONSCIENTIAE?
WHETHER HUMAN LAW BINDS MAN IN CONSCIENCE?

OBJECTION 1

Videtur quod lex humana non imponat homini necessitatem in foro conscientiae. Inferior enim potestas non potest imponere legem in judicio superioris potestatis. Sed potestas humana, quae fert legem humanam, est infra potestatem divinam. Ergo lex humana non potest imponere legem quantum ad judicium divinum, quod est judicium conscientiae.

Objection 1

It seems that human law does not impose an obligation in conscience on man. For an inferior power cannot impose a law in a court of a higher power. But the court of divine power is superior to human jurisdiction. Therefore, human law cannot impose an obligation in the court of divine power which is the court of conscience.

REPLY 1

Ad primum ergo dicendum quod, sicut Apostolus dicit, Rom., xiii, 1, *omnis potestas* humana *a Deo est;* et ideo, *qui potestati resistit* in his quae ad potestatis ordinem pertinent, *Dei ordinationi resistit;* et secundum hoc efficitur reus quantum ad conscientiam.

Reply 1

The Apostle says (Rom. xiii, 1), "All human authority is from God" and therefore "he who resists authority" in these things that belong to authority, "resists the ordination of God," and therefore he is guilty in conscience.

OBJECTION 2

Praeterea, judicium conscientiae maxime dependet ex divinis mandatis. Sed quandoque divina mandata evacuantur per leges humanas, secundum illud Matt. xv, 6, *Irritum fecistis mandatum Dei propter traditiones vestras.* Ergo lex humana non imponit homini necessitatem quantum ad conscientiam.

Objection 2

The judgment of conscience depends especially on divine commandments. But, sometimes divine commandments are rendered void by human laws, according to Matt. xv, 6, "You have made God's command void because of your traditions." Therefore, human law does not impose on man an obligation in conscience.

REPLY 2

Ad secundum dicendum quod ratio illa procedit de legibus humanis quae ordinantur contra Dei mandatum; et ad hoc ordo potestatis non se extendit: unde in talibus legi humanae non est parendum.

Reply 2

This argument concerns human laws which run contrary to the law of God and to such laws the jurisdiction of authority does not extend. Therefore, in such matters human law is not to be obeyed.

OBJECTION 3

Praeterea, leges humanae frequenter ingerunt calumniam et injuriam hominibus, secundum illud Isa. x, 1, ff., *Vae qui condunt leges iniquas, et scribentes, injustitias scripserunt, ut opprimerent in judicio pauperes, et vim facerent causae humilium populi mei!* Sed licitum est unicuique oppressionem et violentiam evitare. Ergo leges humanae non imponunt necessitatem homini quantum ad conscientiam.

Objection 3

Further, human laws often cause calumny and injury for men, according to Isa., x, 1, ff., "Woe to them that make wicked laws, and when they write, write injustice, so that they oppress the poor in judgment and do violence to the cause of the humble ones of my people." But it is lawful for anyone to avoid oppression and violence. Therefore, human laws do not bind men in conscience.

REPLY 3

Ad tertium dicendum quod ratio illa procedit de lege quae infert gravamen injustum subditis, ad quod etiam ordo potestatis divinitus concessus non se extendit: unde nec in talibus homo obligatur ut obediat legi, si sine scandalo vel majori detrimento resistere possit.

Reply 3

That argument concerns a law which imposes an unjust burden on its subjects. To such a law the order of power divinely conferred does not extend. Hence, in such matters, man is not bound to obey the law, if it can be resisted without scandal or greater harm.

ON THE CONTRARY

Sed contra est quod dicitur I Pet. ii, 19, *Haec est gratia, si propter conscientiam sustineat quis tristitias, patiens injuste.*

On the Contrary

It is written (I Pet., ii, 19): "This is a grace that a person, for conscience's sake, endure sorrows, suffering unjustly."

Introductory Comment to the Corpus

I have divided the *Corpus* into five Sections. Section 1 states the general principle of authority; Section 2 describes the ways in which laws can be just; Section 3 describes the ways in which laws can be unjust; Section 4 deals with the evaluation of unjust human laws; Section 5 deals with the special case of laws against "God's Good."

CORPUS [SECTION 1: THE GENERAL PRINCIPLE OF LEGAL AUTHORITY]

Dicendum quod leges positae humanitus vel sunt justae vel injustae. Si quidem justae sint, habent vim obligandi in foro conscientiae a lege aeterna a qua derivantur, secundum illud Prov., *Per me reges regnant, et legum conditores justa decernunt.*

Corpus [Section 1: The General Principle of Legal Authority]

Positive human laws are either just or unjust. If they are just, they have the power of binding in conscience, a power which comes from the Eternal Law from which they are derived, in accordance with Prov., viii, 5, "Through me kings rule and the framers of laws decree what is just."

Comment

It must be remembered that the derivation of human law from the Eternal Law is by way of creative causality (see q. 91, aa. 1, 2, 3); it in no way contradicts the position that the immediate authority to make human law lies with the people of a given society.

CORPUS [SECTION 2: THE WAYS IN WHICH LAWS MAY BE JUST]

Dicuntur autem leges justae:

1. et ex fine, quando scilicet ordinantur ad bonum commune;
2. et ex auctore, quando scilicet lex lata non excedit potestatem ferentis;
3. et ex forma, quando scilicet secundum aequalitatem proportionis imponuntur subditis onera in ordine ad bonum commune. Cum enim unus homo sit pars multitudinis, quilibet homo hoc ipsum quod est, et quod habet, est multitudinis, sicut et quaelibet pars id quod est est totius; unde et natura aliquod detrimentum infert parti ut salvet totum. Et secundum hoc leges hujusmodi onera proportionabiliter inferentes, justae sunt, et obligant in foro conscientiae, et sunt leges legales.

Corpus [Section 2: The Ways in Which Laws May be Just]

Now, laws are said to be just:

1. from the end, namely when they are ordered to the Common Good;
2. from the lawgiver, namely when the law passed does not exceed the lawgiver's authority;
3. from the form, namely when burdens are imposed on the subjects according to proportionate equality for the Common Good. For since one man is part of the community, whatever any man is and has belongs to the community just as what any part is belongs to the whole; hence nature also imposes some loss on the part in order to preserve the whole. And, according to this, laws of this kind, imposing burdens proportionately, are just and oblige in conscience and are legal laws.

CORPUS [SECTION 3: THE WAYS IN WHICH LAWS MAY BE UNJUST]

Injustae autem sunt leges dupliciter:

1. Uno modo per contrarietatem ad bonum humanum e contrario praedictis:

a. vel ex fine, sicut cum aliquis praesidens leges imponit onerosas subditis, non pertinentes ad utilitatem communem, sed magis ad propriam cupiditatem vel gloriam;

b. vel etiam ex auctore, sicut cum aliquis legem fert ultra sibi commissam potestatem;

c. vel etiam ex forma, puta, cum inaequaliter onera multitudini dispensantur, etiamsi ordinentur ad bonum commune.

Corpus [Section 3: Ways in Which Laws May be Unjust]

However, laws can be unjust in two ways, one way, by being contrary to human good through being opposed to what has just been mentioned:

a. either from the end as when some authority imposes burdens on the subjects that do not pertain to the common utility but rather to his own greed or glory;

b. or from the lawgiver, as when someone makes a law that is beyond the authority granted to him;

c. or from the form, as when burdens are unequally distributed in the community, even though they pertain to the Common Good.

Comment

It should be noted that sometimes laws made for the Common Good can be unjust. An example might be a tax for the support of public education (hence, for the Common Good) but levied disproportionately on the poor (hence, unjust).

CORPUS [SECTION 4: EVALUATION OF UNJUST HUMAN LAWS]

Et hujusmodi magis sunt violentiae quam leges, quia, sicut Augustinus dicit (*De Lib. Arb.,* i, 5), *lex esse non videtur quae justa non fuerit.* Unde tales leges non obligant in foro conscientiae, nisi forte propter vitandum scandalum vel turbationem; propter quod etiam homo juri suo debet cedere, secundum illud Matt. v, 40, *Qui angariaverit te mille passus, vade cum eo alia duo; et qui abstulerit tibi tunicam, da ei et pallium.*

Corpus [Section 4: Evaluation of Unjust Human Laws]

And laws of this sort (i.e., unjust laws as described in Section 3) are acts of violence rather than laws, as Augustine says (*De Lib. Arb., i, 5*), "A law that is unjust seems not to be a law." Such laws do not bind in conscience, except perhaps in order to avoid scandal or disturbances. And for this reason a person may even give up his own right, according to Matt., v, 40, "If a man forces you to go one mile, go an additional two with him; if a man takes away your coat give him your cloak also."

CORPUS [SECTION 5: LAWS AGAINST "GOD'S GOOD"]

Alio modo leges possunt esse injustae per contrarietatem ad bonum divinum, sicut leges tyrannorum inducentes ad idololatriam, vel ad quodcumque aliud quod sit contra legem divinam; et tales leges nullo modo licet observare, quia, ut dicitur in Acta, v, 29, *Deo oportet obedire magis quam hominibus.*

Corpus [Section 5: Laws Against "God's Good"]

In the second way, laws can be unjust by being contrary to the Divine Good, such as the laws of tyrants inducing to idolatry or to anything else that is contrary to the Divine Law, because, as is said in Acts, v, 29, "We ought to obey God rather than men."

Comment

1. It should be noted that in regard to the unjust laws described in Section 3, even though they do not bind in conscience *per se,* yet, *per accidens,* a person might be obliged to yield his right and go along with the law, if disobeying it would, for example, cause a bloody revolution with no hope of success, or if a dissenter might be imprisoned to the great distress of his family.

2. Note that in the case of laws against the Divine Law described in Section 4, there *is no way* in which such laws may be obeyed.

3. This Article is of supreme importance since it sets forth the sharpest opposition between Natural Law thinkers like St. Thomas and all varieties of Positivists, Relativists, Pragmatists, etc.: "An unjust law is not a law."

Jurists usually begin the history of this debate by quoting a speech of Antigone, from the play named for her, written by the great Greek dramatist Sophocles (496?–406 B.C.). In the play, Antigone faces the tyrant Creon, admits that she knowingly disobeyed his law, and accepts death for it. In her defense Antigone appeals to Eternal Justice. These are her words:

> For me it was not Zeus who made that order. Nor did that Justice who lives with the gods below mark out such laws to hold among mankind. Nor did I think your orders were so strong that you, a mortal man, could over-run the gods' unwritten and unfailing laws. Not now, nor yesterday's, they always live, and no one knows their origin in time. So not through fear of any man's proud spirit would I be likely to neglect these laws . . . I knew that I must die; how could I not? . . .

Plato explored the meaning of justice in the *Republic* and elsewhere and set it up as an eternal and demanding norm in opposition to the Sophists and tyrants of his day. In the *Republic* he faced Socrates with the antagonist, Thrasymachus (Chap. III (I. 336 B–347 E): "What I say is that 'just' or 'right' means nothing but what is to the interest of the stronger party." Aristotle, in the classic Fifth Book of the *Nicomachean Ethics,* presented a profound analysis of natural justice. St. Thomas absorbed that analysis into his own thought, as the *Treatise* constantly attests.

The tradition moved on through Cicero and the great Roman jurists, Augustine, the Scholastics, the Salamancan Dominicans of the sixteenth century, the great Jesuit jurist Francisco Suarez, to Locke, Blackstone, and the Founding Fathers, to the Declaration of Independence which asserts that human rights were "unalienable" prior to governments that should guard them but could not create them.

And, in an effort to exorcise the devils of Naziism, the Germans wrote as the First Article of their new Basic Law this echo of our own Declaration:

Article 1 (Protection of human dignity)
(1) The dignity of man shall be inviolable. To respect and protect it shall be the duty of all state authority.
(2) The German people therefore acknowledge inviolable and inalienable human rights as the basis of every community, of peace and of justice in the world.
(3) The following basic rights shall bind the legislature, the executive and the judiciary as directly enforceable law.

And, today, at a crucial moment in the Civil Rights movement, Martin Luther King, in his Letter from a Birmingham Jail to his fellow clergymen, wrote these words that are almost a quotation from St. Thomas:

There are *just* laws and there are *unjust* laws. I would be the first to advocate obeying just laws. One has not only a legal but moral responsibility to obey just laws. Conversely, one has a moral responsibility to disobey unjust laws. I would agree with Saint Augustine that "An unjust law is no law at all."
    Now what is the difference between the two? How does one determine when a law is just or unjust? A just law is a man-made code that squares with the moral law or the law of God. An unjust law is a code that is out of harmony with the moral law. To put it in the terms of Saint Thomas Aquinas, an unjust law is a human law that is not rooted in eternal and natural law. Any law that uplifts human personality is just. Any law that degrades human personality is unjust. All segregation statutes are unjust because segregation distorts the soul and damages the personality.

4. For a discussion of the alleged inconsistency or contradiction in saying "An unjust law is not a law," see [142–146].

ARTICLE 5
UTRUM OMNES SUBJICIANTUR LEGI?
WHETHER EVERYONE IS SUBJECT TO THE LAW?

OBJECTION 1

Videtur quod non omnes legi subjiciantur. Illi enim soli subjiciuntur legi quibus lex ponitur. Sed Apostolus dicit, I

Tim. i, 9, quod *justo non est lex posita.* Ergo justi non subjiciuntur legi humanae.

Objection 1

It seems that not everyone is subject to law. For only those are subject to the law for whom the law is framed. But the Apostle says (I Tim. i, 9), "There is no law for the just man." Therefore the just are not subject to human law.

REPLY 1

Ad primum ergo dicendum quod ratio illa procedit de subjectione quae est per modum coactionis. Sic enim *justis non est lex posita,* quia *ipsi sibi sunt lex, dum ostendunt opus legis scriptum in cordibus suis,* sicut Apostolus dicit (Rom. ii, 14, 15). Unde in eos non habet lex vim coactivam, sicut habet in injustos.

Reply 1

That argument is based on the coercive character of law. For in this regard no law is framed for the just, because "they are a law unto themselves as they display the work of the law written in their hearts," as the Apostle says (Rom. ii, 14, 15). Hence the law does not have coercive force for those, as it has for the unjust.

OBJECTION 2

Praeterea, Urbanus II papa dicit, et habetur in *Decretis* (*Decret. caus.* xix, *qu.* 2), *Qui lege privata ducitur, nulla ratio exigit ut publica constringatur.* Lege autem privata Spiritus sancti ducuntur omnes viri spirituales, qui sunt filii Dei, secundum illud Rom. viii, 14, *Qui Spiritu Dei aguntur, hi filii Dei sunt.* Ergo non omnes homines legi humanae subjiciuntur.

Objection 2

Further, Pope Urban II says, as is stated in the *Decretals* (*Decret. caus.* xix, *qu.* 2), "No reason demands that one who is guided by a private law should be subject to public law." But the private law of the Holy Spirit guides all spiritual men who are sons of God, according to Rom., viii, 14, "Those who are led by the Spirit of God are sons of God." Therefore, not all men are subject to human law.

REPLY 2

Ad secundum dicendum quod lex Spiritus sancti est superior omni lege humanitus posita; et ideo viri spirituales secundum hoc quod lege Spiritus sancti ducuntur non subduntur legi quantum ad ea quae repugnant ductioni Spiritus sancti. Sed tamen hoc ipsum est de ductu Spiritus sancti quod homines spirituales legibus humanis subdantur, secundum illud I Pet. ii, 1, *Subjecti estote omni humanae creaturae propter Deum.*

Reply 2

The law of the Holy Spirit is superior to every law humanly established. And therefore, spiritual men are not subject to the law with reference to those things which are opposed to the direction of the Holy Spirit, but that spiritual men should be subject to human laws is itself part of the direction of the Holy Spirit (according to I Pet. ii, 1), "Be subject to every human creature for God's sake."

OBJECTION 3

Praeterea, Jurisperitus dicit (*Pandect. Justin,* i ff., *Tit.* 3; *De Leg. et Senat.*), quod *princeps legibus solutus est.* Qui autem est solutus a lege, non subditur legi. Ergo non omnes subjecti sunt legi.

Objection 3

Further, the Jurisprudent says (*Pandect. Justin,* i ff., *Tit.* 3; *De Leg. et Senat.*), "The prince is released from the laws." But he who is released from the law is not subject to the law. Therefore, not everyone is subject to the law.

REPLY 3

Ad tertium dicendum quod princeps dicitur esse solutus
a lege quantum ad vim coactivam legis, nullus enim proprie
cogitur a seipso; lex autem non habet vim coactivam nisi ex
principis potestate. Sic igitur princeps dicitur esse solutus a
lege, quia nullus in ipsum potest judicium condemnationis
ferre, si contra legem agat. Unde super illud Psalm. l, 6, *Tibi
soli peccavi, etc.*, dicit glossa quod *rex non habet hominem
qui sua facta dijudicet.*

Sed quantum ad vim directivam legis princeps subditur
legi propria voluntate, secundum quod dicitur, *Extra de Con-
stitutionibus, Quod quisque juris in alterum statuit, ipse eodem jure uti debet.* Et sapientis dicit auctoritas (Dionysius
Cato, *Dist. de Moribus*), *Patere legem quam ipse tuleris.*
Improperatur etiam his a Domino *qui dicunt et non faciunt,*
et qui *aliis onera gravia imponunt, et ipsi nec digito volunt
ea movere,* ut dicitur Matt. xxiii, 3.

Unde quantum ad Dei judicium, princeps non est solutus
a lege quantum ad vim directivam ejus, sed debet voluntarius,
non coactus, legem implere. Est etiam princeps supra legem
inquantum, si expediens fuerit, potest legem mutare, et in ea
dispensare pro loco et tempore.

Reply 3

The prince is said to be freed from the law with reference to the
coercive force of the law, for no one, properly speaking, can be forced
by himself. Thus, therefore, the prince is said to be free from the law
because no one can make condemnatory judgment against him, for law
has its coercive force only from the power of the prince, if he acts contrary
to the law. Hence in Ps. l, 6, "Against you alone have I sinned," a gloss
says, "There is no man who can judge the acts of the King."

But with reference to the directive force of the law, the King is
subject to it by his own will, according to the statement (*Extra, De
Constit, cap., Cum omnes*), "Whoever subjects another to a law should
observe the same law himself." And the *auctoritas* of a wise man (Dionysius Cato, *Dist. de Moribus*) says, "Obey the law that you yourself
have made." Moreover, the Lord reproaches those who say but do not

do, and those who "impose heavy burdens on others, and themselves lift not a finger to remove them," as is said in Matt. xxiii, 3.

Hence, as regards the judgment of God, the prince is not free from the law in reference to its directive force and ought voluntarily, and not through being forced, fulfill the law. And also the prince is above the law in the sense that, if it is expedient, he can change it or dispense from it according to place and time.

ON THE CONTRARY

Sed contra est quod Apostolus dicit, Rom. xiii, 1, *Omnis anima potestatibus sublimioribus subdita sit.* Sed non videtur esse subditus potestati qui non subjicitur legi quam fert potestas. Ergo omnes homines debent esse legi subjecti.

On the Contrary

The Apostle says (Rom. xiii, 1), "Let every soul be subject to the higher powers." But a person does not seem to be subject to a power, if he does not obey the law made by that power. Therefore, all men ought to be subject to law.

CORPUS

Dicendum quod, sicut ex supra dictis patet, lex de sui ratione duo habet: primo quidem, quod est regula humanorum actuum; secundo, quod habet vim coactivam. Dupliciter ergo aliquis homo potest esse legi subjectus.

Uno modo, sicut regulatum regulae; et hoc modo omnes illi qui subduntur potestati subduntur legi quam fert potestas. Quod autem aliquis potestati non subdatur potest contingere dupliciter. Uno modo, quia est simpliciter absolutus ab ejus subjectione—unde illi qui sunt de una civitate vel regno non subduntur legibus principis alterius civitatis vel regni, sicut nec ejus dominio. Alio modo, secundum quod regitur superiori lege: puta si aliquis subjectus sit proconsuli regulari debet ejus mandato, non tamen in his quae dispensantur ei ab imperatore, quantum enim ad illa non adstringitur mandato inferioris, cum superiori mandato dirigatur. Et secundum hoc contingit quod aliquis simpliciter subjectus legi secundum aliqua legi non adstringitur secundum quae regitur superiori lege. Alio vero modo dicitur aliquis subjectus legi sicut coactum cogenti; et hoc modo homines virtuosi et justi non subduntur legi, sed soli mali. Quod enim est coactum et violentum, est contrarium voluntati. Voluntas autem bonorum consonat legi, a qua malorum voluntas discordat; et ideo secundum hoc boni non sunt sub lege, sed solum mali.

Corpus

As is clear from what has been said above (*q., 90, aa.* 1 and 2; *a.* 3 Reply 2), the idea of law contains two things, first, that it is a rule of human acts, and, second, that it has coercive force. Therefore, a person can be said to be subject to law in two different ways.

In one way, as guided by a rule. In this way, all who are subject to an authority are subject to the law that authority makes. However, it can happen in two ways that a person is not subject to an authority. In one way, because he is simply free from subjection to that authority, hence, those who belong to one state or kingdom are not subject to the laws of a prince of some other state or kingdom just as they are subject to his control. In another way, if he is subject to a higher law, for example, if someone is subject to a proconsul, he should be ruled by his order, not, however, in those matters in which he has been dispensed by the emperor, for in such matters he is not bound by the order of an inferior power, since he is being guided by a higher command.

In another way a person can be said to be subject to law as the coerced is subject to the coercer. And in this way the virtuous and just are not subject to the law but only the wicked. For coercion and violence are contrary to the will, and the will of the good is in accord with the law, whereas the will of the wicked is contrary to it. And in this way the good are not subject to the law, but only the wicked.

Comment

Despite the opening sentence of the *Corpus* of this article, the coercive force of law (sanctions) is not part of the essence of law. *Ratio* ("notion", "understanding") is broader than *essentia* ("essence"). The law is essentially a "rule and measure of human acts" (*q.* 90, *a.* 1, *c.*). The necessity for law to have coercive power does not arise from the essence of law but from the state of fallen man, which is accidental to the essence of law. Lon Fuller wrote (*The Morality of Law,* p. 108):

> The notion that its authorization to use physical force can serve to identify law and to distinguish it from other social phenomena is a very common one in modern writings. In my opinion it has done great harm to clarity of thought about the functions performed by law. It will be well to ask how this identification came about.
>
> In the first place, given the facts of human nature, it is perfectly obvious that a system of legal rules may lose its efficacy if it permits itself to be challenged by lawless violence. Sometimes violence can only be restrained by violence. Hence it is quite predictable that there must normally be in society some mechanism ready to apply force in support of law in case it is needed. But this in no sense justifies treating the use or potential use of force as the identifying characteristic of law. Modern science depends heavily upon the use of measuring and testing apparatus; without such apparatus it could not have achieved what it has. But no one would conclude on this account that science should be defined as the use of apparatus for measuring and testing. So it is with law. What law must foreseeably do to achieve its aims is something quite different from law itself.

St. Thomas's distinction between law as a directive rule of human acts and the law's coercive power (as Fuller says, to make law efficacious in view of "lawless violence") restores the "clarity of thought" which was lost through making coercive force or sanctions part of the essence of law.

There has been a vigorous debate as to whether the sovereign legislator's power is above (free from) the law. In the Imperial Law of Rome, the emperor was above the law (although this was sometimes a sore point between some emperors and some of the great jurists). In England, the debate frequently had a practical effect, as when the Lords Spiritual and Temporal forced King John to sign the Magna Charta. The revival of the theory of the Divine Right of Kings in the Renaissance revived the debate, exemplified in the struggle between James I of England and Justice Coke. In theory, the Austin sovereign "habitually obeyed no one" and so was above the law.

St. Thomas uses his distinction between the directive and the coercive function of law. The lawgiver, whoever he be, is bound to follow the directive force of his own legislation, and, for this, he is responsible to God. But, St. Thomas says, "the lawgiver is not subject to the coercive power of the law." This position, I think, presupposes that the lawgiver and the judge are the same person. The situation is quite different when the government is a "mixed" type and especially when there is the triple division of powers. In this case, the relationship (e.g., "immunities") between the legislators, the chief executive, and the Courts is a matter to be resolved by positive Constitutional law.

It should be remembered that St. Thomas's criterion for a good government is its ordination not to privilege or private gain but to the Common Good. If a lawgiver makes laws for the Common Good, clearly he is obliged to obey them (unless, in some special case, there is an excusing cause). In the *Regimine Principum,* St. Thomas asserts that the good monarch who rules for the Common Good of the people will be rewarded in Heaven while the tyrant, who ignores the human Good, will be damned to Hell.

ARTICLE 6
UTRUM EI QUI SUBDITUR LEGI LICEAT PRAETER VERBA LEGIS AGERE?
WHETHER HE WHO IS SUBJECT TO A LAW MAY ACT AGAINST THE LETTER OF THE LAW?

OBJECTION 1

Videtur quod non liceat ei qui subditur legi, praeter verba legis agere. Dicit enim Augustinus (*De Vera Relig.* xxxi), *In temporalibus legibus quamvis homines judicent de his cum eas instituunt, tamen quando sunt institutae et firmatae non licebit de ipsis judicare, sed secundum ipsas.* Sed si aliquis praetermittat verba legis, dicens se intentionem legislatoris serare, videtur judicare de lege. Ergo non licet ei qui

subditur legi praetermittere verba legis, ut intentionem legislatoris servet.

Objection 1

It seems that he who is subject to a law may not act against the
letter of the law. For Augustine says (*De Vera Relig.* xxxi), "In temporal
laws, although men judge them when they make them, once they are
made and framed, it will not be licit to judge them but only according
to them." But, if someone acts against the letter of the law, saying that
he is preserving the intention of the lawgiver, he seems to be judging
about the law. Therefore, it is not licit for him who is subject to a law
to act against the letter of the law in order to preserve the intention of
the lawgiver.

REPLY 1

Ad primum ergo dicendum quod ille qui in casu necessitatis agit praeter verba legis non judicat de ipsa lege, sed
judicat de casu singulari, in quo videt verba legis observanda
non esse.

Reply 1

He who in a case of necessity acts against the letter of the law,
does not judge concerning the law itself but concerning an individual
case in which he sees that the letter of the law is not to be followed.

OBJECTION 2

Praeterea, ad eum solum pertinet leges interpretari cujus
et condere leges. Sed omnium subditorum legi non est leges
condere. Ergo eorum non est interpretari legislatoris intentionem, sed semper secundum verba legis agere debent.

Objection 2

Further, the interpretation of laws belongs solely to him who can
make laws. But all who are subject to laws cannot make laws. Therefore,

they may not interpret the intention of the lawgiver but should always act according to the letter of the law.

REPLY 2

Ad secundum dicendum quod ille qui sequitur intentionem legislatoris non interpretatur legem simpliciter, sed in casu in quo manifestum est per evidentiam nocumenti legislatorem aliud intendisse. Si enim dubium sit, debet vel secundum verba legis agere, vel superiorem consulere.

Reply 2

He who follows the intention of the lawgiver does not interpret the law completely but only in a case in which it is manifest through evident harm that the lawgiver intended otherwise. For if the matter is doubtful, he ought either to act according to the letter of the law or to consult a superior authority.

Comment

St. Thomas requires clear evidence of impending harm in order to justify acting against the letter of the law. Otherwise laws could be so weakened as to fail in their primary intent.

OBJECTION 3

Praeterea, omnis sapiens intentionem suam verbis novit explicare. Sed illi qui leges condiderunt, reputari debent sapientes; dicit enim sapientia, Prov. viii, 1, *Per me reges regnant, et legum conditores justa decernunt.* Ergo de intentione legislatoris non est judicandum nisi per verba legis.

Objection 3

Further, every wise man knows how to express his intention in words. But lawgivers must be regarded as wise, for Wisdom says (Prov. viii, 1), "Through me kings rule and lawmakers make just decrees." Therefore, no judgment should be made about a law except according to its letter.

REPLY 3

Ad tertium dicendum quod nullius hominis sapientia tanta est ut possit omnes singulares casus excogitare; et ideo non potest sufficienter per verba sua exprimere ea quae conveniunt ad finem intentum. Et si posset legislator omnes casus considerare, non oporteret ut omnes exprimeret propter confusionem vitandam; sed legem ferre deberet secundum ea quae in pluribus accidunt.

Reply 3

No man is so wise that he can take into account every single case, and, therefore, he cannot sufficiently express in words everything that is conducive to the end he intends. And, if the lawgiver were able to consider every case, in order to avoid confusion he ought not express them all, but he should frame the law according to what generally happens.

ON THE CONTRARY

Sed contra est quod Hilarius dicit in IV *De Trinit.*, circa med., *Intelligentia dictorum ex causis est assumenda dicendi; quia non sermoni res, sed rei debet esse sermo subjectus.* Ergo magis est attendendum ad causam quae movit legislatorem quam ad ipsa verba legis.

On the Contrary

Hilary says (*De. Trin.*, IV), "The meaning of what is said must be gathered from the reason for saying it, for things are not subject to speech but speech to things." Therefore, we should pay attention to the motive of the lawgiver more than to the words of law themselves.

CORPUS

Dicendum quod, sicut supra dictum est (*a.* 4; *q.* 90, *a.* 2), omnis lex ordinatur ad communem hominum salutem, et intantum obtinet vim et rationem legis; secundum vero quod ab hoc deficit virtutem obligandi non habet. Unde Jurisperitus dicit (*Pandect. Justin. Lib.* 1 ff. *Tit.* 3; *De Lege et Senat*) quod *nulla ratio juris aut aequitatis benignitas patitur ut quae salubriter pro salute hominum introducuntur, ea nos duriori interpretatione contra ipsorum commodum perducamus ad severitatem.*

Contingit autem multoties quod aliquid observari communi saluti est utile ut in pluribus, tamen in aliquibus casibus est maxime nocivum.

Quia igitur legislator non potest omnes singulares casus intueri, proponit legem secundum ea quae in pluribus accidunt, ferens intentionem suam ad communem utilitatem. Unde si emergat casus in quo observatio talis legis sit damnosa communi saluti non est observanda: sicut si in civitate obsessa statuatur lex quod portae civitatis maneant clausae, hoc est utile communi saluti ut in pluribus; si tamen contingat casus quod hostes insequantur aliquos cives per quos civitas conservatur, damnosissimum esset civitati nisi eis portae aperirentur. Et ideo in tali casu essent portae aperiendae contra verba legis, ut servaretur utilitas communis quam legislator intendit.

Sed tamen hoc est considerandum, quod si observatio legis secundum verba non habeat subitum periculum cui oporteat statim occurri, non pertinet ad quemlibet ut interpretetur quid sit utile civitati, et quid inutile civitati; sed hoc solum pertinet ad principes, qui propter hujusmodi casus habent auctoritatem in legibus dispensandi. Si vero sit subitum periculum, non patiens tantam moram ut ad superiorem recurri possit, ipsa necessitas dispensationem habet annexam, quia necessitas non subditur legi.

Corpus

As stated above (*a.* 4; *q.* 90, *a.* 2), every law is ordered to the common well-being of men, and, inasmuch as it does so, it has therefore the force and nature of law, and, insofar as a law fails in this respect, it loses the power to obligate. Wherefore, the Jurist says (*Pandect. Justin. Lib.* 1 ff. *Tit.* 3; *De Lege et Senat.*), "that no reason of law nor any favor of justice allows the suitable measures that have been enacted for the welfare of the people to be more harshly interpreted by us against the welfare of the people themselves and leading to severity."

However, it happens many times that the observance of something is useful for the common welfare in most cases, yet in some cases is extremely harmful.

Therefore, since the lawgiver cannot have in view all the individual cases, he frames the law according to what usually happens, by directing his intention to the common utility. Hence, in a case in which the observance of such a law would be injurious to the common welfare, the law is not to be observed. If, for example, in a besieged city, a law has been made that the gates should remain closed, this is useful for the common welfare in most cases. Yet, if it should happen that enemies were pursuing some citizens through whom the city is preserved, it would be disastrous if the gates were not opened to the citizens. In such a case, the gates should be opened in violation of the letter of the law in order to serve the common utility which the lawgiver intended.

Nonetheless, this is to be considered, that if the observance of the letter of the law does not present a sudden danger which must be faced at once, it does not belong to just anyone to interpret what is useful to the state and what is not, but this belongs solely to the rulers who, because of such cases, have the authority to dispense from the laws. If, however, there is a sudden danger which will not allow such a delay as would permit recourse to the rulers, the very necessity itself brings a dispensation from the law, for necessity knows no law.

Comment

The problem dealt with in this Article should not be confused with that discussed in *q*. 96, *a*. 4. Here the law in question is a just law that generally serves the Common Good; in *q*. 96, *a*. 4 the law involved was an unjust law. The problems are quite different.

St. Thomas carefully strikes a balance between permitting an individual citizen to make the decision that a law is to be disobeyed and obeying the authority of the rulers.

The case cited by St. Thomas would have been very familiar to people in the thirteenth century because of the frequent wars between the cities in Italy. We might think of a person violating the law of trespass to stop a murder or a person violating the traffic laws to get a dying man to an emergency ward.

QUESTION 97
DE MUTATIONE LEGUM
CONCERNING CHANGE OF LAWS

Deinde considerandum est de mutatione legum, et circa hoc quaeruntur quatuor:

1. utrum lex humana sit mutabilis;
2. utrum semper debeat mutari quando aliquid melius occurrerit;
3. utrum per consuetudinem aboleatur, et utrum consuetudo obtineat vim legis;
4. utrum usus legis humanae per dispensationem rectorum immutari debeat.

Question 97

We now must consider change in law and here there are four points of inquiry:

1. Whether human law can be changed?
2. Should it always be changed whenever anything better is found?
3. Whether law is abolished by custom, and whether custom has the force of law?
4. Whether the application of law should be changed by dispensation of the governing authorities?

Introductory Comment for Articles 1 and 2

It is important to note the difference between Article 1 and Article 2. Article 1 deals with the possibility of changing human law. *Can* human law be changed? The conclusion is that human law can be changed. But now the Second Article asks whether it *should* be changed, and, if so, under what circumstances or according to what principles.

St. Thomas displays a prudent and balanced flexibility with regard to Positive Law. His discussion should be compared with modern presentations like that of Lon Fuller under the rubric of "The Constance of Law" through time (*The Morality of Law,* pp. 79–86).

Some people think that the Natural Law, as conceived by its proponents, is a rigid, *a priori,* and complete set of precepts and that Natural Law thinkers want to impose this set on civil law thus making it also rigid and unchangeable. Obviously, this is not St. Thomas's view.

Bentham was convinced that the Criminal Law and the penal system of England should be radically reformed. He thought that a major obstacle to this reform was Blackstone's rigid Natural Law theory. This, in part, explains Bentham's almost violent opposition to Natural Law.

ARTICLE 1
UTRUM LEX HUMANA DEBEAT MUTARI ALIQUO MODO?
WHETHER HUMAN LAW SHOULD BE CHANGED IN ANY WAY?

OBJECTION 1

Ad Primum sic proceditur: I. Videtur quod lex humana nullo modo debeat mutari. Lex enim humana derivatur a lege naturali, ut supra dictum est (*q. 95, a. 2*). Sed lex naturalis immobilis permanet. Ergo et lex humana debet immobilis permanere.

Objection 1

It seems that human law should not be changed in any way whatever. For human law is derived from the Natural Law, as was stated above (*q. 95, a. 2*). But Natural Law remains unchangeable. Therefore, human law should also remain unchangeable.

REPLY 1

Ad primum ergo dicendum quod naturalis lex est participatio quaedam legis aeternae, ut supra dictum est (*q. 95, a. 1*), et ideo immobilis perseverat; quod habet ex immobilitate et perfectione divinae rationis instituentis naturam. Sed ratio humana mutabilis est et imperfecta, et ideo ejus lex mutabilis est. Et praeterea lex naturalis continet quaedam universalia praecepta quae semper manent; lex vero posita ab homine continet praecepta quaedam particularia, secundum diversos casus qui emergunt.

Reply 1

The Natural Law is a certain participation in the Eternal Law as was stated above (*q.* 95, *a.* 1) and therefore it remains unchangeable. This it has from the unchangeableness and perfection of the Divine Reason, the author of nature. But human reason is changeable and imperfect and so its law is changeable. And besides, the Natural Law contains certain universal precepts which endure forever, while law made by man contains certain particular precepts according to the different situations which arise.

Comment

The Objection turns on the fact that human law is derived from the Natural Law which is unchangeable. One should read this Objection and the corresponding Reply in the light of *q.* 93, *a.* 2 wherein St. Thomas distinguishes two ways in which human law derives from Natural Law. The first way is a sort of reasoning process from the general principles or precepts of the Natural Law. These are immutable. Thus from the general precept, "Harm no person," we can derive the special principle, "Do not torture people." But the Natural Law provides only universal precepts and only these are unchangeable. The Natural Law leaves many particular matters indeterminate. These must be determined by the human lawgiver. These determinations must, of course, conform to the general requirements of the Natural Law (e.g., the requirements of justice). Thus, when automobiles first appeared in the streets of London, the city's speed limit was set at 15 miles per hour. This speed limit has been changed from time to time and varies from place to place. Yet back of it is the general Natural Law precept, "Harm no person." Of course, like all laws, the traffic laws must be just. For example, if a law to reduce traffic in the city forbade black people to drive cars in the city were passed, it would be unjust.

OBJECTION 2

Praeterea, sicut Philosophus dicit in *Ethic.* v, 5, *mensura maxime debet esse permanens.* Sed lex humana est mensura humanorum actuum, ut supra dictum est. Ergo debet immobiliter permanere.

Objection 2

Further, as the Philosopher says (*Ethic.* v, 5), "a measure should be permanent." But human law is the measure of human acts, as was stated above (*q.* 90, *aa.* 1 and 2). Therefore, it should remain unchanged.

REPLY 2

Ad secundum dicendum quod mensura debet esse permanens quantum est possibile. Sed in rebus mutabilibus non potest esse aliquid omnino immutabiliter permanens, et ideo lex humana non potest esse omnino immutabilis.

Reply 2

A measure ought to be as permanent as possible. But in changeable things, it is not possible for something to be altogether unchangeable. Therefore, human law cannot be altogether unchangeable.

OBJECTION 3

Praeterea, de ratione legis est quod sit justa et recta, ut supra dictum est (*q.* 95, *a.* 2). Sed illud quod semel est rectum semper est rectum. Ergo illud quod est semel lex semper debet esse lex.

Objection 3

Further, it is of the essence of law that it be just and right, as stated above (*q.* 95, *a.* 2). But what is right once is always right. Therefore, what is law once should always be law.

REPLY 3

Ad tertium dicendum quod rectum in rebus corporalibus dicitur absolute; et ideo semper quantum est de se manet rectum. Sed rectitudo legis dicitur in ordine ad utilitatem communem, cui non semper proportionatur una eademque res, sicut supra dictum est [in the *Corpus* of this Article], et ideo talis rectitudo mutatur.

Reply 3

In corporeal things right is predicated absolutely and, therefore, as far as concerns itself, remains always right. But right is predicated of law with reference to the common utility, as stated above (in the *Corpus* of this Article) to which one and the same thing is not always adapted. Therefore, this sort of rectitude is subject to change.

ON THE CONTRARY

Sed contra est quod Augustinus dicit (*De Lib. Arb.* i, 6), lex temporalis, quamvis justa sit, commutari tamen per tempora juste potest.

On the Contrary

Augustine says (*De Lib. Arb.* i, 6) "A law, though it be just, may justly be changed in the course of time."

Introductory Comment to the Corpus

This Article falls neatly into three Sections. The first Section states two different bases for possible changes in human laws, derived from the nature of law as a dictate of reason directing human acts.

In the second Section St. Thomas develops the reasons for change on the part of human reason itself. Here, he distinguishes between the speculative sciences and practical arrangements. The progress in speculative sciences is based on Aristotle's account of the progress of philosophical thought from the early Naturalists to Aristotle's own day.

In the third Section St. Thomas deals with the changes necessitated by the changing conditions of the men whose acts are regulated by law.

CORPUS [SECTION 1]

Dicendum quod, sicut supra dictum est (*q.* 90, *aa.* 1 and 4), lex humana est quoddam dictamen rationis quo diriguntur humani actus, et secundum hoc duplex causa potest esse quod lex humana juste mutetur: una quidem ex parte rationis; alia vero ex parte hominum quorum actus lege regulantur.

Corpus [Section 1]

As was said above (*q*. 90, *aa*. 1 and 4), human law is a dictate of reason by which human acts are directed, and, in accordance with this, there can be two causes for changing human law, the one on the part of reason, the other on the part of men whose acts are regulated by law.

CORPUS [SECTION 2]

Ex parte quidem rationis, quid humanae rationi naturale esse videtur ut gradatim ab imperfecto ad perfectum perveniat. Unde videmus in scientiis speculativis, quod qui primo philosophati sunt quaedam imperfecta tradiderunt, quae postmodum per posteriores sunt tradita magis perfecte. Ita etiam et in operabilibus: nam primi qui intenderunt invenire aliquid utile communitati hominum, non valentes omnia ex seipsis considerare, instituerunt quaedam imperfecta in multis deficientia, quae posteriores mutaverunt, instituentes aliqua quae in paucioribus deficere possunt a communi utilitate.

Corpus [Section 2]

On the part of reason, since it seems natural for human reason to progress gradually from an imperfect state to one of perfection. Hence, in the speculative sciences, we see that the teaching of the early philosophers was imperfect and was improved by those who succeeded them. We see the same thing in practical matters, for those who first tried to find something useful to the human community, not being able of themselves to consider everything, established certain imperfect institutions which were defective in many ways, and their successors improved them so they would fail the Common Good in fewer ways.

CORPUS [SECTION 3]

Ex parte vero hominum, quorum actus lege regulantur, lex recte mutari potest propter mutationem conditionum hominum, quibus secundum diversas eorum conditiones diversa expediunt, sicut Augustinus ponit exemplum in I *De lib. arb.* i, 6, quod *si populus sit bene moderatus et gravis, communisque utilitatis diligentissimus custos, recte lex fertur qua tali populo liceat creare sibi magistratus, per quos respublica administretur. Porro si paulatim idem populus depravatus habeat venale suffragium, et regimen flagitiosis sceleratisque committat, recte adimitur populo talis potestas dandi honores, et ad paucorum bonorum redit arbitrium.*

Corpus [Section 3]

With respect to men, whose acts are regulated by law, law can rightly be changed on account of change in the condition of men to whom different things are useful according to these different conditions. St. Augustine gives an example in *De. Lib. Arb.*, i, 6.: "If a people is moderate and serious, and most careful in taking care of the common good, it is right to pass a law allowing such a people to choose their own magistrates for the governance of the community. If, however, that people should gradually become so corrupt as to sell their votes and select scoundrels and criminals to govern the commonwealth, then the right of choosing those public officials is rightly taken from them and entrusted to a few good men."

ARTICLE 2
UTRUM LEX HUMANA SEMPER SIT MUTANDA QUANDO OCCURRIT ALIQUID MELIUS? WHETHER HUMAN LAW SHOULD ALWAYS BE CHANGED WHEN SOMETHING BETTER PRESENTS ITSELF?

Introductory Comment

In Article 1, St. Thomas established that human laws can be changed and explained the twofold basis for change. In this Article he examines the factors that govern the *actual* decision to change a law. A prudential judgment is necessary which balances the harm done by changing a law with the "benefit to the Common Good" derived from the change.

OBJECTION 1

Ad secundum sic proceditur: Videtur quod semper lex humana, quando aliquid melius occurrit, sit mutanda. Leges enim humanae sunt adinventae per rationem humanam, sicut etiam aliae artes. Sed aliis in artibus mutatur id quod prius tenebatur, si aliquid melius occurrat. Ergo idem est etiam faciendum in legibus humanis.

Objection 1

It seems that human law should always be changed whenever something better presents itself. For human laws are devised by human reason just as other arts are. But in the other arts, tenets previously held are changed when something better presents itself. Therefore, the same thing should also be done in human laws.

REPLY 1

Ad primum ergo dicendum quod ea quae sunt artis habent efficaciam ex sola ratione; et ideo, ubicumque melioratio occurrit, est mutandum quod prius tenebatur. Sed leges habent maximam virtutem ex consuetudine, ut Philosophus dicit in II *Polit.* ii, 5, et ideo non sunt de facili mutandae.

Reply 1

The other arts derive their efficacy from reason alone, and so previously held rules of art should be changed whenever an improvement presents itself. But laws obtain a very great force from custom, as the Philosopher says (*Polit.,* ii, 5) and therefore should not be easily changed.

Comment

It should be noted that *artes* (the arts) include not only what we call fine arts today but also crafts like woodworking and practical skills like the ability to draft laws.

The Objection thus proceeds on a comparison of the art of making laws with other arts. St. Thomas points out that the comparison fails because there is a special relevant factor in the case of law that is not present in the other arts, namely the force of custom, the custom of obeying established laws. The nature of this factor is explained in the *Corpus*.

OBJECTION 2

Praeterea, ex his quae praeterita sunt providere possumus de futuris. Sed, nisi leges humanae mutatae fuissent supervenientibus melioribus adinventionibus, multa inconvenientia sequerentur, eo quod leges antiquae inveniuntur multas ruditates continere. Ergo videtur quod leges sint mutandae quotiescumque aliquid melius occurrit statuendum.

Objection 2

Further, from the lessons of the past we are able to provide for the future. But, unless human laws had been changed as improvements were discovered, many difficulties would have ensued, since ancient laws are found to contain many crudities. Therefore, it seems that laws should be changed, whenever any better legislation presents itself.

REPLY 2

Ad secundum dicendum quod ratio illa concludit quod leges sunt mutandae, non tamen pro quacumque melioratione, sed pro magna utilitate vel necessitate, ut dictum est in corp. art.

Reply 2

That argument concludes that laws should be changed, not, however, for the sake of any improvement whatever but only for great utility or necessity, as is said in the *Corpus* of this Article.

OBJECTION 3

Praeterea, leges humanae circa actus singulares hominum statuuntur. In singularibus autem perfectam cognitionem adipisci non possumus nisi per experientiam, quae tempore indiget, ut dicitur in II *Ethic.*, ii, 1. Ergo videtur quod per successionem temporis possit aliquid melius occurrere statuendum.

Objection 3

Human laws are enacted concerning individual human acts. But of individual things we cannot achieve perfect knowledge except through experience which requires time, as is said in *Ethic.*, ii, 1. Therefore, it seems that, with the passage of time, some better legislation would present itself.

REPLY 3

Et similiter dicendum est ad tertium.

Reply 3

The same answer as in Reply 2 should be used here.

ON THE CONTRARY

Sed contra est quod dicitur in *Decretis*, (*Decretal*, ixx, 5), *Ridiculum est et satis abominabile dedecus ut traditiones, quas antiquitus a patribus suscepimus, infringi patiamur.*

On the Contrary

It is said in the *Decretals* (*Decretal* xii, 5) that it is absurd and a disgraceful shame if we should permit the traditions which we have received from our fathers of old to be violated.

Comment

This *sed contra* well illustrates the fact that the *sed contra* does not always present St. Thomas's nuanced position. It does, however, serve as a counterpoise to the positions taken in the objections.

CORPUS

Dicendum quod, sicut dictum est (*a.* 1), lex humana in tantum recte mutatur inquantum per ejus mutationem communi utilitati providetur. Habet autem ipsa legis mutatio, quantum in se est, detrimentum quoddam communis salutis, quia ad observantiam legum plurimum valet consuetudo, intantum quod ea quae contra communem consuetudinem fiunt, etiamsi sint leviora de se, graviora videntur. Unde, quando mutatur lex diminuitur vis constrictiva legis, inquantum tollitur consuetudo. Et ideo nunquam debet mutari lex humana, nisi ex alia parte tantum recompensetur communi saluti quantum ex ista parte derogatur.

Quod quidem contingit vel ex hoc quod aliqua maxima et evidentissima utilitas ex novo statuto provenit; vel ex eo quod est maxima necessitas, vel ex eo quod lex consueta aut manifestam iniquitatem continet, aut ejus observatio est plurimum nociva. Unde dicitur a jurisperito Ulpiano (*Pandect. Justin. lib.* i, ff, *tit.* 4, *De Constii. Princip.*), quod *in rebus novis constituendis evidens debet esse utilitas, ut recedatur ab eo jure quod diu aequum visum est.*

Corpus

As was said (*a.* 1), human law is rightly changed insofar as the Common Good is thereby promoted. However, a change in law, simply in itself, is somewhat detrimental to the common welfare inasmuch as the observance of law is greatly supported by custom, since what is done against a common custom, even though trivial of itself, is looked upon as quite serious. Hence, when law is changed, the binding power of law is diminished inasmuch as the custom is abolished. Hence, human law should not be changed unless the damage done thereby to the common welfare is compensated for by some other benefit.

And this happens when some very great and most evident benefit comes from the new law, or when there is the greatest necessity or when either the customary law clearly contains injustice or when its observation is extremely harmful. Wherefore, the jurist Ulpian said (*Pandect. Justin. lib.* i, ff, *tit.* 4, *De Constii. Princip.*) that in establishing new laws, there must be evidence of the benefit to be derived before departing from a law long held to be just.

Comment

In Article 1 St. Thomas established that human laws can be changed. In this Article he first asserts that change in itself is detrimental to the observance of law, since, when people have become accustomed to observing a law, a change removes one of the powerful aids to observance, namely, the custom of obeying it. Hence, change in the law requires a serious reason. St. Thomas lists a number of valid reasons for change in law.

1. A very great counterbalancing benefit;
2. When the law is unjust;
3. When the observance of the law is extremely harmful. And these situations must be clear and evident.

ARTICLE 3
UTRUM CONSUETUDO POSSIT OBTINERE VIM LEGIS?
WHETHER CUSTOM CAN OBTAIN THE FORCE OF LAW?

OBJECTION 1

Ad tertium sic proceditur: I. Videtur quod consuetudo non possit obtinere vim legis, nec legem amovere. Lex enim humana derivatur a lege naturae et a lege divina, ut ex supra dictis (*q.* 93, *a.* 3; *q.* 95, *a.* 2) patet. Sed consuetudo hominum non potest mutare legem naturae nec legem divinam. Ergo etiam nec legem humanam immutare potest.

Objection 1

It seems that custom cannot obtain the force of law or remove a law. For human law is derived from the Law of Nature and from the Divine Law, as is clear from what has been said above (*q.* 93, *a.* 3; *q.* 95, *a.* 2). But the custom of men cannot change the Law of Nature nor the Divine Law. Therefore, neither can it change human law.

REPLY 1

Ad primum ergo dicendum quod lex naturalis et divina procedit a voluntate divina, ut dictum est [in the *Corpus* of this Article], unde non potest mutari per consuetudinem procedentem a voluntate hominis, sed solum per auctoritatem divinam mutari posset; et inde est quod nulla consuetudo vim legis obtinere potest contra legem divinam vel legem naturalem. Dicit enim Isidorus in *Synon.*, ii, 16, *Usus auctoritati cedat; pravum usum lex et ratio vincat.*

Reply 1

The Natural and Divine Laws come from the will of God, as stated above (in the *Corpus* of this Article). Therefore they cannot be changed by a custom coming from the will of man, but only by Divine authority. Hence it is that no custom can obtain the force of law against Natural or Divine Law. For Isidore says (*Synon.*, ii, 16), "Let usage yield to authority; a wicked custom is overcome by law and reason."

Comment

The Reply explicitly says that the Natural Law and the Divine Law cannot be changed by custom which arises from human actions. Read in the light of the *Corpus,* it implies that human law can be changed when it depends on the will of man (*q.* 92, *a.* 3, *c.*) and the change is not against either the Natural or the Divine Law. (St. Thomas is here using "Divine Law" for the "Eternal Law.")

OBJECTION 2

Praeterea, ex multis malis non potest fieri unum bonum. Sed ille qui incipit primo contra legem agere male facit. Ergo multiplicatis similibus actibus non efficietur aliquod bonum. Lex autem est quoddam bonum, cum sit regula humanorum actuum. Ergo per consuetudinem non potest removeri lex ut ipsa consuetudo vim legis obtineat.

Objection 2

Further, many evils cannot produce one good. But he who first begins to act against the law, does evil. Therefore, the multiplication of such acts cannot produce anything good. But the law is something good since it is the rule of human acts. Therefore, custom cannot abolish a law so that the custom itself obtains the force of law.

REPLY 2

Ad secundum dicendum quod, sicut supra dictum est (*q. 96, a.* 6), leges humanae in aliquibus casibus deficiunt. Unde possibile est quandoque praeter legem agere, in casu scilicet in quo deficit lex; et tamen actus non erit malus. Et cum tales casus multiplicantur propter aliquam mutationem hominum, tunc manifestatur per consuetudinem quod lex ulterius non est utilis; sicut etiam manifestaretur si lex contraria verbo promulgaretur. Si autem adhuc maneat ratio eadem propter quam prima lex utilis erat, non consuetudo legem sed lex consuetudinem vincit; nisi forte propter hoc solum inutilis lex videatur, quoniam "non est possibilis secundum consuetudinem patriae," quae erat una de conditionibus legis (*q.* 95, *a.* 3). Difficile enim est consuetudinem multitudinis removere.

Reply 2

As stated above (*q. 96, a.* 6), human laws in some cases fail. Hence, it is possible to act against the law—namely in a case where the law fails, without, however, doing an evil act. When such cases are multiplied, because of some change in people, it becomes clear through custom that the law is no longer useful, just as the same thing would be made clear if a contrary law were verbally promulgated. But, if the same reason still remains for which the first law was useful, custom does not abolish the law, but the law overthrows the custom, unless, perhaps, the law should appear useless for this reason alone that "it is not possible according to the custom of the country," which was one of the conditions for law (*q.* 95, *a.* 3). For it is difficult to remove the custom of a people.

Comment

The Reply sets forth a very nuanced relationship between custom and law. Of course, in the Middle Ages custom played a much greater role in the life of the people than it does today. When Henry Bracton (d. 1268) wrote his famous handbook for the guidance of the new judges in the King's Courts in England, he entitled it *De Legibus et Consue-tudinibus Angliae* (*Concerning the Laws and Customs of England*).

OBJECTION 3

Praeterea, ferre leges pertinet ad publicas personas, ad quas pertinet regere communitatem: unde privatae personae legem facere non possunt. Sed consuetudo invalescit per actus privatarum personarum. Ergo consuetudo non potest obtinere vim legis per quam lex removeatur.

Objection 3

Further, the making of laws belongs to public persons whose business it is to govern the community. But custom arises through acts of private persons. Therefore, custom cannot obtain the force of law so as to abolish a law.

REPLY 3

Ad tertium dicendum quod multitudo in qua consuetudo introducitur duplicis conditionis esse potest. Si enim sit libera multitudo, quae possit sibi legem facere, plus est consensus totius multitudinis ad aliquid observandum, quod consuetudo manifestat, quam auctoritas principis, qui non habet potestatem condendi legem nisi inquantum gerit personam multitudinis: unde, licet singulae personae non possint condere legem, tamen totus populus condere legem potest. Si vero multitudo non habeat liberam potestatem condendi sibi legem, vel legem a superiori potestate positam removendi, tamen ipsa consuetudo in tali multitudine praevalens obtinet vim legis, inquantum per eos toleratur ad quos pertinet multitudini legem imponere: ex hoc enim ipso videntur approbare quod consuetudo introduxit.

Reply 3

The community in which a custom is introduced may be of either one of two conditions. For, if it is a free community, able to make its own laws, then the consensus of the whole community towards some observance which has become customary is stronger than the authority of the sovereign who does not have power to make laws, except insofar as he represents the people. Hence, although individual persons cannot make laws, yet the whole people can. But, if the community does not have the free power to make its own laws or to abolish laws laid down by a higher authority, nonetheless a prevailing custom in such a community can obtain the force of law, if it is tolerated by those to whom it belongs to make laws for that community; for, by that very fact, they seem to approve what the custom introduced.

Comment

The first part of this Reply is based directly on the doctrine of popular sovereignty described in *q. 90, a. 3.*

ON THE CONTRARY

Sed contra est quod Augustinus dicit in epistola ad Casulanum (*Casulan,* xxxvi), *Mos populi Dei et instituta majorum pro lege sunt tenenda. Et sicut praevaricatores legum divinarum, ita et contemptores consuetudinum ecclesiasticarum coercendi sunt.*

On the Contrary

St. Augustine, in a letter to Casulan (*Casulan,* xxxvi) says: "The custom of God's people and the institutions of our ancestors are to be accepted as laws. And those who contemn the customs of the Church should be corrected as are those who disobey divine laws."

CORPUS

Dicendum quod omnis lex proficiscitur a ratione et voluntate legislatoris: lex quidem divina et naturalis a rationabili Dei voluntate; lex autem humana a voluntate hominis ratione regulata. Sicut autem ratio et voluntas hominis manifestantur verbo in rebus agendis, ita etiam manifestantur facto: hoc enim unusquisque eligere videtur ut bonum quod opere implet.

Manifestum est autem quod verbo humano potest et mutari lex, et etiam exponi, inquantum manifestat interiorem motum et conceptum rationis humanae. Unde etiam et per actus maxime multiplicatos, qui consuetudinem efficiunt, mutari potest lex, et exponi, et etiam aliquid causari quod legis virtutem obtineat, inquantum scilicet per exteriores actus multiplicatos interior voluntatis motus et rationis conceptus efficacissime declarantur. Cum enim aliqud multoties fit, videtur ex deliberato rationis judicio provenire.

Et secundum hoc consuetudo et habet vim legis, et legem abolet, et est legum interpretatrix.

Corpus

Every law comes from the reason and will of the legislator. The Divine Law and the Natural Law proceed from the reasonable will of God, but human law comes from the will of man regulated by reason. However, just as the reason and will of man are manifested by speech, so they can also be made known by deeds, for a man seems to choose as a good that which he carries out in action.

However, it is clear that law can both be changed and also interpreted by human speech, inasmuch as it can manifest the internal movement and conception of human reason. Hence, also through the multiplication of actions law can both be changed and intepreted, and something can be caused that obtains the force of law, inasmuch as through the multiplication of exterior acts the interior movement of the will and the concepts of the reason are most effectively declared. For when something happens many times, it seems to proceed from a deliberate judgment of reason.

And, accordingly, custom can have the force of law, abolish law and also interpret it.

Comment

The basic philosophical doctrine applied in this *Corpus* is that explained in *q.* 90, *a.* 3, *c.* wherein St. Thomas asserts that the authority to make civil law resides, first of all, in the whole people.

Rulers, of whatever kind, have authority to make laws only insofar as they have received authority from the people. They are vicegerents who have the "care" of the community. St. Thomas therefore sees custom as arising from the reason and will of the people and therefore as being able to abolish laws, interpret laws, and obtain the force of law.

Positivists and others have trouble in accounting for customary law since they need an Austinian-like sovereign and sanctions for the existence of a law. [For example, see H. L. A. Hart's discussion, *The Concept of Law,* pp. 43–46.] St. Thomas has no such problem. His problem concerns the initial acts giving rise to custom and when it can be said to have the support of the "whole" people.

St. Thomas holds that only a justified initial act can legitimately give rise to a custom. The initial act is justified if it occurs in a case in which the law fails.

Law is a dictate of Practical Reason, that is, it is primarily an act of reason (*q.* 90, *a.* 1, *c.*) but Practical Reason always involves the will. The various expressions used in this *Corpus* confirm this view.

St. Thomas speaks of all law as coming from the reason and will of the lawgiver (*a ratione et voluntate legislatoris*) of the Natural and Divine Laws proceeding from the "reasonable will of God" (*a rationabli Dei voluntate*) and of human law as proceeding from "the will of man regulated by reason" (*a voluntate hominis ratione regulata*). The reason functions as providing the formal cause [internal reference] which regulates the action of the will. The will functions as an efficient cause moving the reason to its own act as a formal cause. This mutual interplay of reason and will exercising two different kinds of causality constitutes the Practical Reason as opposed to Speculative Reason. All this is in accord with St. Thomas's profound philosophical analysis of human acts [278–283], as opposed to the voluntarists who hold that law proceeds primarily from the will [313–331].

This Article is quite clear and is consistent with the previous Articles in the *Treatise*. There is only one real problem. In the Reply to Objection 3, St. Thomas cites a case in which a people is not free to make its own laws. I have not been able to identify such a people. St. Thomas does not refer to it in the *Corpus*. It appears inconsistent with St. Thomas's general doctrine on popular sovereignty.

ARTICLE 4
UTRUM RECTORES MULTITUDINIS POSSINT IN LEGIBUS HUMANIS DISPENSARE?
WHETHER THE RULERS OF THE COMMUNITY CAN DISPENSE FROM HUMAN LAW?

OBJECTION 1

Videtur quod rectores multitudinis non possint in legibus humanis dispensare. Lex enim statuta est pro communi utilitate, ut Isidorus dicit (*Etym.* v, 21). Sed commune bonum non debet intermitti pro privato commodo alicujus personae, quia, ut dicit Philosophus in I. *Ethic., bonum gentis divinius est quam bonum unius hominis.* Ergo videtur quod non debeat dispensari cum aliquo ut contra legem communem agat.

Objection 1

It seems that rulers of the community cannot dispense from human laws. For law is established for the "common benefit," as Isidore says (*Etym.* v, 21). But the Common Good should not be set aside for the convenience of an individual, because, as the Philosopher says (*Ethic.* i., 2), "The good of the nation is more godlike than the good of one man." Therefore, it seems that no one should be dispensed from acting in accordance with the common law.

REPLY 1

Ad primum ergo dicendum quod quando cum aliquo dispensatur ut legem communem non servet, non debet fieri in praejudicium boni communis, sed ea intentione ut ad bonum commune proficiat.

Reply 1

When anyone is dispensed so as not to follow the common law, this ought not be done to the prejudice of the Common Good but with the intention of promoting it.

OBJECTION 2

Praeterea, illis qui super alios constituuntur, praecipitur Deut. I, 17, *Ita parvum audietis ut magnum; nec accipietis cujusquam personam, quia Dei judicium est.* Sed concedere alicui quod communiter denegatur omnibus videtur esse acceptio personarum. Ergo hujusmodi dispensationes facere rectores multitudinis non possunt, cum hoc sit contra praeceptum legis divinae.

Objection 2

Those who are placed over others are commanded as follows (Deut. I, 17): "Hear both the little and the great and do not take account of any man's person for the judgment is God's," but to grant someone what is generally denied to others seems to be favoring a person. Therefore, the rulers of the community cannot make dispensations of this sort, because to do so is against a precept of the Divine Law.

Comment

The command is taken from Moses' instruction to his judges. Since this is part of the law revealed in the Old Testament, it is part of the Divine Law. [*q.* 91, *aa.* 4 and 5.] Moses' instruction to his judges closely parallels the oath of office taken by United States Federal Judges.

REPLY 2

Ad secundum dicendum quod non est acceptio personarum si non servantur aequalia in personis inaequalibus. Unde, quando conditio alicujus personae requirit rationabiliter ut in ea aliquid specialiter observetur, non est personarum acceptio, si ei aliqua specialis gratia fit.

Reply 2

It is not respect of persons if equality is not maintained among unequal persons. Hence, when the condition of some person reasonably requires that something special be done for him, it is not respect of persons if he be granted special favor.

OBJECTION 3

Praeterea, lex humana, si sit recta, oportet quod con-
sonet legi naturali et legi divinae: aliter enim non congrueret
religioni, nec conveniret disciplinae; quod requiritur ad legem, ut Isidorus dicit (*Etym*. v, 3). Sed in lege naturali et
divina nullus homo potest dispensare. Ergo nec etiam in lege
humana.

Objection 3

Further, human law, in order to be right, must agree with the
Natural Law and the Divine Law, otherwise it would not "foster
religion" nor "promote discipline" as Isidore says (*Etym*. v, 3). But
no man can dispense from the Natural Law or the Divine Law.
Therefore, neither can he dispense from human law.

Comment
For Isidore's requirements for law, see *q*. 95, *a*. 3.

REPLY 3

Ad tertium dicendum quod lex naturalis, inquantum
continet praecepta communia, quae nunquam fallunt, dispensationem recipere non potest. In aliis vero praeceptis,
quae sunt quasi conclusiones praeceptorum communium,
quandoque per hominem dispensatur, puta quod mutuum
non reddatur proditori patriae, vel aliquid hujusmodi. Ad
legem autem divinam ita se habet quilibet homo sicut persona
privata ad legem publicam cui subjicitur. Unde sicut in lege
humana publica non potest dispensare nisi ille a quo lex
auctoritatem habet, vel is cui ipse commiserit, ita in praeceptis
juris divini, quae sunt a Deo, nullus potest dispensare nisi
Deus, vel is cui ipse specialiter committeret.

Reply 3

The Natural Law, insofar as it contains general precepts which
never fail, cannot admit of dispensation. But in other precepts, which
are, as it were, conclusions from the general precepts, sometimes a

man can make a dispensation, for example, that a loan be not returned to a traitor to his country, or something similar. However, every man stands to the Divine Law just as a private person does to the public law of which he is a subject. Hence, just as no one can dispense in human public law except the man from whom the law has its authority or his delegate, so also in the precepts of Divine Law, no one can dispense except God or him whom God has empowered to do so.

ON THE CONTRARY

Sed contra est quod dicit Apostolus, (I Cor., xi, 17), *Dispensatio mihi credita est.*

On the Contrary

The Apostle says (I Cor., xi, 17), "Dispensation is entrusted to me."

CORPUS

Dicendum quod dispensatio proprie importat commensurationem alicujus communis ad singula. Unde etiam gubernator familiae dicitur 'dispensator', inquantum unicuique de familia cum pondere et mensura distribuit et operationes et necessaria vitae. Sic igitur et in quacumque multitudine ex eo dicitur aliquis dispensare quia ordinat qualiter aliquod commune praeceptum sit a singulis adimplendum.

Contingit autem quandoque quod aliquod praeceptum quod est ad commodum multitudinis ut in pluribus non est conveniens huic personae vel in hoc casu, quia vel per hoc impediretur aliquid melius, vel etiam induceretur aliquod malum, sicut ex supra dictis (*q.* 96, *a.* 6) patet. Periculosum autem esset ut hoc judicio cujuslibet committeretur, nisi forte propter evidens et subitum periculum, ut supra dictum est (*ibid.*). Et ideo ille qui habet regere multitudinem habet potestatem dispensandi in lege humana quae suae auctoritati innititur, ut scilicet in personis vel in casibus in quibus lex deficit, licentiam tribuat ut praeceptum legis non servetur.

Si autem absque hac ratione pro sola voluntate licentiam tribuat, non erit fidelis in dispensatione, aut erit imprudens: infidelis quidem, si non habet intentionem ad bonum commune; imprudens autem, si rationem dispensandi ignoret; propter quod Dominus dicit, (Luke, xii, 42), *Quis, putas, est fidelis dispensator et prudens, quem constituit dominus super familiam suam?*

Corpus

Dispensation, properly speaking, denotes a measuring out of some common thing to individuals. Hence, the head of a family is also called a "dispenser" since he distributes to each member of the family, according to weight and measure, work and the necessities of life. So, in each community, someone is said to "dispense" because he determines how each member is to fulfill some common precept.

However, it sometimes happens that some precept that, in most cases, is for the benefit of the community is not useful for a particular person or in a particular case because it either hinders some greater good or even causes some evil, as is clear from what has been said above (*q. 96, a. 6*). However, it would be dangerous to leave this judgment to any individual, except perhaps in the case of a clear and sudden emergency, as was said above (*ibid.*). Consequently, he who governs a community has the power to dispense from a human law that rests on his authority, so that, when the application of a law to persons or cases fails, he can grant permission that the law be not observed. If, however, without such a reason and of his mere will, he grants dispensation, he will be an unfaithful and imprudent dispenser; unfaithful, if he does not act with a view to the Common Good, imprudent if he ignores the reason for dispensing. For this reason, the Lord said (Luke, xii, 42), "Who do you think, is the faithful and wise dispenser [Douay, "servant"] whom the master will place over his family?"

Comment

St. Thomas recognizes (in this Article as in *q. 91, a. 6*) that human (positive) laws promote the Common Good for the most part, but that there are cases wherein the application of the law would be detrimental. He also recognizes that the determination of these exceptions cannot be left to individual citizens (except in evident and sudden emergencies).

St. Thomas gives the right to make the determination to the lawgiver. He who makes the law can dispense from it. This is the interpretation of the dispensing power used in Canon Law. The Bishop can dispense from the positive laws he has made for his Diocese; the Pope can dispense from papal positive legislation.

In Anglo-American law, the courts make the determination in exceptional cases. Often, when the strict or literal application of a law would, in the opinion of the Court, lead to injustice, the Court will appeal to "Natural Justice."

The important and permanent point made by St. Thomas is that, when such cases do occur there should be a legal way of handling them.

It should be noted that the question here is not about unjust laws (see *q. 95, a. 5*) but about just laws for the Common Good which fail in individual cases as described in the *Corpus*.

ABOUT THE TRANSLATOR

R. J. Henle, S.J., received his doctorate in Philosophy and Classics at the University of Toronto. He is currently Professor Emeritus of Philosophy and Jurisprudence at St. Louis University. Fr. Henle has published hundreds of books, articles, and reviews. Noteworthy among them are his Latin Series, Marquette Aquinas Lecture, *Method in Metaphysics, St. Thomas and Platonism,* and *Theory of Knowledge.*